*A Companion to the Works of Adalbert Stifter*

*Studies in German Literature, Linguistics, and Culture*

# A Companion to the Works of Adalbert Stifter

Edited by Sean Ireton

Rochester, New York

Copyright © 2025 Editor and Contributors

*All Rights Reserved*. Except as permitted under current legislation, no part of this work may be photocopied, stored in a retrieval system, published, performed in public, adapted, broadcast, transmitted, recorded, or reproduced in any form or by any means, without the prior permission of the copyright owner.

First published 2025 by Camden House

Camden House is an imprint of Boydell & Brewer Inc.
668 Mt. Hope Avenue, Rochester, NY 14620, USA
and of Boydell & Brewer Limited
PO Box 9, Woodbridge, Suffolk IP12 3DF, UK
www.boydellandbrewer.com

Our Authorised Representative for product safety in the EU is
Easy Access System Europe - Mustamäe tee 50, 10621 Tallinn,
Estonia, gpsr.requests@easproject.com

ISBN-13: 978-1-64014-107-0

**Library of Congress Cataloging-in-Publication Data**
Names: Ireton, Sean Moore, editor.
Title: A companion to the works of Adalbert Stifter / edited by Sean
Ireton.
Description: Rochester : Camden House, 2025. | Series: Studies in
German literature, linguistics, and culture ; 249 | Includes
bibliographical references and index.
Identifiers: LCCN 2024040284 (print) | LCCN 2024040285 (ebook) |
ISBN 9781640141070 (hardback) | ISBN 9781805435662 (pdf) |
ISBN 9781805435679 (epub)
Subjects: LCSH: Stifter, Adalbert, 1805–1868—Criticism and
interpretation. | LCGFT: Literary criticism. | Essays.
Classification: LCC PT2525.Z5 C66 2025 (print) | LCC PT2525.Z5
(ebook) | DDC 833/.7—dc23/eng/20241214
LC record available at https://lccn.loc.gov/2024040284
LC ebook record available at https://lccn.loc.gov/2024040285

The publisher has no responsibility for the continued existence or accuracy of URLs for external or third-party internet websites referred to in this book, and does not guarantee that any content on such websites is, or will remain, accurate or appropriate.

To Jim Walker, "ein Bruder des Felsens" (Stifter, *Der Hochwald*)

# Contents

| | |
|---|---|
| Abbreviations of Frequently Cited Works | ix |

Introduction: Stifter's Life and Works      1
*Sean Ireton*

## Part I: Genre and Style

1    Stifter's Epic Style      37
*Tove Holmes*

2    Stifter and the Genre Conventions of Cultural Journalism      58
*Sean Franzel*

3    All Eyes on the Streets: Transformations of Public Work, Leisure, and Ritual in *Wien und die Wiener*      86
*Vance Byrd*

4    Stifter's Late Style      110
*Samuel Frederick*

## Part II: Texts and Contexts

5    The Birth of Realism out of the Spirit of Melodrama: Stifter's *Feldblumen*      137
*Erica Weitzman*

6    Backward Glances: Registers of the Past in Stifter's *Die Mappe meines Urgroßvaters*      162
*Jessica C. Resvick*

7    Lessons from Stifter's *Bunte Steine*      181
*Zachary Sng*

8    Absence and Omnipresence: On the Significance of Waste in Stifter's *Der Nachsommer*      200
*Lars Rosenbaum*

# Part III: Elements and Environments

9   Stifter's Stones        227
*Jason Groves*

10   Stifter's Glaciers        250
*Matthew H. Birkhold*

11   Cheerful Terror: Stifter and the Aesthetics of Atmosphere        273
*Alexander Robert Phillips*

12   Stifter's Bavarian-Bohemian Bioregionalism        294
*Sean Ireton*

Selected Bibliography        323

List of Contributors        337

Index        341

# Abbreviations of Frequently Cited Works

*HKG*  Stifter, Adalbert. *Werke und Briefe: Historisch-Kritische Gesamtausgabe*. Edited by Alfred Doppler, Wolfgang Frühwald, Hartmut Laufhütte, et al. Stuttgart: Kohlhammer, 1978–.

*IS*  Stifter, Adalbert. *Indian Summer*. Translated by Wendell Frye. 4th ed. New York: Peter Lang, 2009.

*MS*  Stifter, Adalbert. *Motley Stones*. Translated by Isabel Fargo Cole. New York: New York Review Books, 2021.

*PRA*  *Sämmtliche Werke*. Edited by August Sauer, Franz Hüller, Kamill Eben, Gustav Wilhelm, et al. 19 vols. Prague: Calve; Reichenberg: Kraus, 1901–40; Graz: Stiasny, 1958–60.

*VASILO*  *Vierteljahresschrift des Adalbert-Stifter-Instituts des Landes Oberösterreich*

# Introduction: Stifter's Life and Works

*Sean Ireton*

To say that Adalbert Stifter was born on October 23, 1805, and died on January 28, 1868, may be technically true, but as with so many aspects of his life and work, details of this sort are both murky and misleading. The *Ordnung*—whether ethical order or petty orderliness—that ruled his existence and dominate his oeuvre is often but a front concealing deeper unrest, including chronic melancholy, self-destructive passion, and existential despair. Thus, to rectify the ignominy of his premarital conception and restore some semblance of order to his very origins, Stifter often tweaked his professional résumés and autobiographical accounts by shifting his birth year to 1806. (His parents, Magdalena Friepes and Johann Stifter, were wedded on August 13, 1805, hence just over two months before his birth.) The circumstances surrounding his death were likewise disorderly, if not messy. Around 1:00 am during the night of January 25–26, 1868, Stifter slit his throat with a razorblade yet did not expire from this self-inflicted wound until two days later. This act of (attempted) suicide might be interpreted as the culmination of Stifter's tumultuous life as lived between the lines of his self-corrective fiction and well over a century's worth of largely reverent literary-historical scholarship. It is, at any rate, an eerie enactment of a lamentation expressed through his analogue Augustinus in the fourth version of *Die Mappe meines Urgroßvaters* (My Great-Grandfather's Notebook) which was written during the final years of his life and published posthumously in 1939. Here Stifter reminisces on his humiliating struggles as a private tutor in Vienna during the 1830s, summing up his impoverished "existence" (the German word *Existenz* can of course mean both subsistence and existence) with the fateful words: "Mir ist es schon lange bis zur Kehle" (*HKG* 6,2:31; I've had it up to my neck [literally: throat] for a long time now). The fundamental question thus remains: What are the continuities in Stifter's life and work that, beneath the veneer of a normative *ordo* that he continually strove to uphold, led him to slash his throat during one of his innumerable dark hours? What, in other words, is the precise connection between his (according to eyewitness accounts) blood-soaked bedsheets from January 1868 and the (to all appearances) purer pages and tidier tableaux of his vast literary production from 1840 onward? Though not a definitive answer to this complex question, the following insight by Thomas Mann offers an initial cue for further reflection: "Man hat oft den Gegensatz hervorgekehrt zwischen Stifters blutig-selbstmörderischem Ende und der edlen Sanftmut seines Dichtertums. Seltener ist beobachtet worden, daß hinter der stillen, innigen Genauigkeit gerade seiner Naturbetrachtung eine Neigung zum Exzessiven, Elementar-Katastrophalen, Pathologischen wirksam ist" (The contrast has often been stressed between Stifter's violent suicidal death and the noble gentleness of his writings. What critics have seldom noticed is that behind the tranquil, tender precision of his observation of nature there lurks a tendency to excess, a penchant for natural catastrophe and pathological elements).[1]

My introduction to this volume consists of three main parts. First, I will give a condensed biographical account of Stifter's personal and intellectual life. Although he tended to lead a staid bourgeois existence and remained, to the end of his days, more an inveterate provincialist than a refined cosmopolite, there is no lack of nuances to the traditional image of his personality and the conventional understanding of his literary activity. Following up on Thomas Mann, I will therefore probe such systemic "cracks" in both his life and work, as bookended by his ill-defined birth and the ill-executed death mentioned above. Following this diachronic approach, I will present a more synchronic, cross-examinational analysis of three keywords—and, by extension, chief concepts—that permeate Stifter's opus and shed interpretive light on its meaning. These words are: *Ordnung* (order), *Ding* (thing), and *sanft* (gentle). As any Stifter enthusiast knows, and any inquisitive reader will soon find out, these may well be the most frequently occurring words in his entire fiction—excepting of course standard articles, pronouns, conjunctions, and prepositions. Finally, I will present a formal overview of the volume, explaining its conceptual structure and commenting on its individual chapters.

## Biographical Sketch

While Günter Grass's mouthpiece Oskar Matzerath may well have "delivered" the most famous prenatal—and ensuing birthing—scene in Germanophone literature, Adalbert Stifter does not rank far behind in narrating, both in utero and as a neonatal newcomer to this world, the future trajectory of his petite bourgeois life. Though not as mischievous let alone malicious as "das kleine Oskarchen" in *Die Blechtrommel* (The Tin Drum, 1959), "der Stifter-Bertl," as he was nicknamed throughout

---

1 Thomas Mann, *Die Entstehung des Doktor Faustus: Roman eines Romans*, in *Gesammelte Werke in dreizehn Bänden*, vol. 11 (Frankfurt am Main: Fischer, 1990), 145–301, here 237; *The Story of a Novel: The Genesis of Doctor Faustus* (New York: Knopf, 1961), 139.

his childhood, did not exactly lack in destructive tendencies. Two examples of such peculiar parallels, yet also salient divergences, between Oskar and Bertl merit further explication. In an autobiographical and uncharacteristically rhapsodic fragment that Stifter composed toward the end of his life, he describes a kind of numinous connection to the "things" (*Dinge*) of the natural world. Indeed, his murky memories of birth seem to conflate the embrace of his fellow humans with the presence of forests, as if both were equally part of his primordial experience upon exiting the womb.[2] Furthermore, he alludes to a psychologically scarring incident from his youth, one that no doubt reinforced the sense of guilt that plagued him throughout his (Austrian Catholic) life. As his grandmother rebukes him in this instance: "Mit einem Knaben, der die Fenster zerschlagen hat, redet man nicht" (One doesn't talk to a boy who has broken the windows).[3] This impish act, which was later reworked in "Die Pechbrenner"/*Granit* (The Pitch-Burners/Granite, 1849/1853)[4]— whereby the first-person narrator merely soiled the floors of the house with pitch-coated feet rather than more ruinously shattered its windows— of course pales in comparison to Oskar's superhuman *Zersingen* (singing to bits) of glass objects throughout the city of Danzig, whether household crystal, church windows, or schoolteacher spectacles. Nonetheless, it serves as initial testimony of Stifter's sometimes more harmful than gentle propensities and, moreover, as a point of departure for what would

---

2    See Adalbert Stifter, "Mein Leben," in *Gesammelte Werke in vierzehn Bänden*, vol. 14, ed. Konrad Steffen (Basel and Stuttgart: Birkhäuser, 1972), 116–21, here 118. Also found in Kurt Gerhard Fischer, *Adalbert Stifters Leben und Werk in Briefen und Dokumenten* (Frankfurt am Main: Insel, 1962), 678–82, here 680.

3    Stifter, "Mein Leben," 119/681.

4    As a general practice throughout this volume, *both* publication dates will be provided with respect to those works by Stifter that were initially serialized in literary journals and subsequently released in book form. Later in the introduction, I will explain more thoroughly this greater philological problem of *Journalfassungen* versus *Buchfassungen*. It should also be noted that many journal issues appeared toward the end of a given calendar year but officially bore the imprint of the following annum. Such, for instance, is the case above with "Die Pechbrenner," which was already on the market in late 1848. On a more technical formatting note, Stifter's stories are sometimes italicized in scholarship, while other times they appear in quotes; there is no discernible standard in either Anglophone or Germanophone secondary literature. Thus, as a further general practice in this volume, the original journal versions will appear in quotes given that they were either serialized in installments or otherwise comprised part of a greater publishing organ. The revised and mostly expanded book versions, on the other hand, will be italicized even though they, too, were included in larger collections, namely the six-volume *Studien* (Studies, 1844–50) and the two-volume *Bunte Steine* (Motley Stones, 1853). Most of them, however, have since acquired the status of definitive, stand-alone works and today are often published individually.

4 ♦ Sean Ireton

become a lifelong leitmotif of (self-)destruction.[5] As one biographer has summed up these early picaresque years, here in key adjectival fashion: "Ein *sanfter* Musterknabe war er nicht" (He was not a *gentle* paragon of youth).[6]

## Adalbertus Stifter Bohemus Oberplanensis (1805–26)

Born in the southern Bohemian village of Oberplan (better known today by its Czech name Horní Planá) on October 23, 1805, Stifter was baptized as "Albert," after the given name of his godfather, Albert Pranghofer. Ultimately, however, he adopted the more popular regional variant of "Adalbert," an appellation that became solidified when he began his secondary schooling at the Benedictine monastery of Kremsmünster in November 1818. Here he was entered into the official academic register as "Adalbertus Stifter Bohemus Oberplanensis." These latter two terms shed important biographical light on this canonical Germanophone author of obscure geographic origins and humble socioeconomic beginnings. Oberplan was situated in an isolated pocket of the Austrian Empire, on the northeastern fringes of the Bohemian Forest, which remained a relatively primeval region by European standards. Though deforestation was beginning to take a heavy toll on the environment, early modern settlement and agriculture had gradually been transforming the landscape from an uninterrupted forested expanse to a vast patchwork of woodlands and farmlands. Several stories by Stifter reflect (on) this anthropogenic transformation, especially *Der Hochwald* (The Mountain Forest, 1841/1844), the book version of *Die Mappe meines Urgroßvaters* (1847), and *Der beschriebene Tännling* (The Inscribed Fir-Tree, 1846/1850). Oberplan or Horní Planá, which both literally translate as "high plain," thus derives its name from being a typical Central European *Rodungsgebiet* or "clearance area"; in this case, one that dates to the twelfth century, when migrating Slavs and Bavarians carved out a community atop a hillock in the thick of the Bohemian wilderness, as for instance narrated in Stifter's historical epic *Witiko* (1865–67). During the fourteenth century, the King of Bohemia (Charles IV) granted Oberplan official status as a *Marktflecken*, meaning that it could hold a regular market and thus engage in postfeudalistic commerce. Flax eventually emerged as the main local resource

---

5    Further oft-cited incidents of cruelty during Stifter's childhood include the following: He once impulsively stabbed a younger brother in the side with a knife, though did not exactly revel in the resulting flow of blood; He also once put the family cat into the kitchen oven (or, more likely, its main heating duct), but the shrieking animal was soon rescued by the adults in the room.

6    Peter A. Schoenborn, *Adalbert Stifter: Sein Leben und Werk*, 2nd ed. (Tübingen and Basel: Francke, 1999), 25. My emphases.

and, in the generations that immediately preceded Stifter, led to a lucrative domestic textile production. Indeed, Stifter's father Johann played a pivotal role in the shift from preindustrial weaving to precapitalist marketing by peddling homespun linen transregionally. This forward-thinking move proved fatal, for the traveling salesman was killed by the very vehicle that he employed to transport his wares: in November 1817, halfway between the Upper Austrian towns of Wels and Lambach, his loaded wagon tipped over and crushed him. This accident occurred exactly one year before his (half-orphaned) son Adalbert would be admitted to the nearby abbey of Kremsmünster.

Stifter's formative years at Kremsmünster between 1818 and 1826 signal a new chapter in his life. Nevertheless, one should not underestimate the familial and existential vacuum that the premature death of his father left behind. In purely financial-numerical terms, five young children and a widow lost their provider; on a deeper, emotional level, the twelve-year-old Stifter suffered such grief that he resolved to starve himself to death. Nevertheless, the older generation in the Oberplan household took over and promoted their grandson's development. His paternal grandparents Augustin and Ursula, for instance, assisted in homegrown matters, instilling in him a wealth of local knowledge—ranging from agricultural practices to folkloric traditions—that would later fuel his nostalgic imagination and shape his storytelling skills. Stifter's maternal grandfather, Franz Friepes, proved instrumental in promoting his formal education and securing him a spot at the elite gymnasium of Kremsmünster. The specially adapted admission process was also instrumental in this regard. Due to his provincial provenance, Stifter's primary-school education did not compare favorably to that of candidates from more cultured corners of the Empire, especially when it came to urbane subjects such as Latin. His entrance interview, however, could not have been more suited to his Bohemian backwoods background, as he was quizzed exclusively on the geography and ecology of his homeland—in other words, subject matter (mountains, forests, rivers, flora, and fauna) that he could prattle about endlessly. Stifter was thus given a kind of personalized bioregional-based exam rather than anything remotely resembling the standard classical model. As it turned out, his shrewd benefactor was a priest named Placidus Hall, who would play a crucial pedagogical and even paternalistic role during Stifter's next eight years at Kremsmünster. Later in life, Stifter referred to him as a "second father" and memorialized him in the transfigured Freiherr von Risach, who mentors the young protagonist Heinrich Drendorf in *Bildungsroman*-like fashion throughout all three volumes of *Der Nachsommer* (Indian Summer, 1857). Risach, moreover, can be said to embody Stifter's essential notion of *das sanfte Gesetz* or "the gentle law," which Pater Placidus may well have inspired, if only more in name than in concept.

Some further facts about Kremsmünster in this biographical context are in order. Established as a monastery in 777, its Benedictine monks opened a public gymnasium in 1549, one that had become scientific in orientation long before Stifter enrolled in 1818. As one of the most progressive or at least free-thinking of Catholic orders, the Benedictines were not averse to embracing the natural sciences, which were otherwise more of a Protestant pursuit. In the specific case of Kremsmünster, astronomy was the main field of inquiry such that an eight-story astronomical observatory, dubbed "der mathematische Turm" (the mathematical tower), was constructed between 1748 and 1758. During Stifter's era, this edifice also became a hub of geophysical and meteorological research; it even showcased a statue of Johannes Kepler (a Protestant) on one of its stairwell landings. Stifter, for his part, profited from his education at and, more generally, his relocation to Kremsmünster. Much of his literary work is informed by the earth and atmospheric sciences and he generally upheld a firm physico-theological worldview, as was inculcated in him during these foundational years in which the core curriculum revolved around religion, geography, history, natural history, mathematics, and (inevitably) Latin. Late in life, he even contemplated writing a novel about Kepler but abandoned this plan for reasons of ill health and due to other personal and professional complications. More broadly in terms of Stifter's geophysical horizons, Kremsmünster is located midway between the Bohemian Forest and the Upper Austrian Alps, the two principal settings of his fiction. He in fact first began to explore the Alps, or at least their foothills, during these gymnasium years, and his crowning opus *Der Nachsommer* can be read as a holistic homage to the natural and cultural landscape of Upper Austria—its landed estates, parklands, forests, waters, glaciers, and lofty crags. In the end, Kremsmünster functioned as a both liberating *and* controlling environment for Stifter. On the one hand, it offered an intellectual-ideological liberalism combined with a more literal sense of plein-air liberation; on the other, it demanded a psychological submission to sociopolitical order and a tacit acceptance of state control. These two (Austrian) tendencies are rooted in the history of Kremsmünster and would become the prime polarizing forces in Stifter's later life and work. Initially a bastion of Catholic education and scientific exploration, from its founding by Benedictine monks to its Enlightenment heyday during the reign of Emperor Joseph II, Kremsmünster became an institution subject to governmental influence if not surveillance under Franz II and his Habsburg successors. Under such rulership, excessively liberal curricular content was suppressed, including the works of Goethe, Schiller, and even certain writings by Kant. To be sure, Storm and Stress is inherently subversive stuff, but even Weimar classicism and Kantian libertarianism were omitted from the new agenda of k.-k.-Kremsmünster. Nonetheless, in Stifter's case one has the sense that the academic discipline and monastic-like order of this

## Vicissitudes in Vienna (1826–48)

In the fall of 1826, Stifter moved to Vienna to study law. As it would turn out, he lived in the Austrian capital for twenty-two consecutive years, longer than any other location during his lifetime. Nevertheless, almost none of his fictional narratives take place there, at least in their entirety, and even his coedited nonfictional collection of essays *Wien und die Wiener* (Vienna and the Viennese, 1841–44) features only twelve of his own contributions (plus a preface) out of fifty-four total chapters. Granted, as is often the case with modern authors and their so-called "transcendental homelessness" (Lukács), they write out of a deep sense of nostalgia and, so to speak, stick to the childhood milieu they know best, no matter where on the map they have since migrated. With respect to Stifter, this literary-biographical truism holds true insofar as he continually revisited, in a creative-authorial mode, the Bohemian Forest that he had outwardly long left behind. Nevertheless, this is only the partial—or at least initial— truth of the matter, for during his early years at the University of Vienna, he spent his summer vacations back in Bohemia. And there was an escalating romantic reason why.

During Stifter's repeated visits to his Bohemian homeland, he tended to avoid Oberplan, spending the bulk of his time in the nearby town of Friedberg (Czech: Frymburk) and the surrounding countryside. As a child, he had not ventured into the deeper interior and upper elevations of the Bohemian Forest, but he now began to do so, visiting such (later) narrative locales as the ruins of Castle Wittinghausen, the Plöckensteinsee (Lake Plöckenstein or Plešné jezero), and the Dreisesselberg (Three-Chair Mountain or Třístoličník)—not to mention numerous densely wooded points of interest in between. Back in Oberplan, he felt alienated in a home that was now dominated by a stepfather and augmented by a half-brother, for his mother had since remarried and propagated the already robust family line. It was, in sum, a crowded house, both physically and, even more so for Stifter, psychologically. Friedberg, on the other hand, promised new social and emotional outlets, including a budding love interest. Stifter's university roommates hailed from this slightly larger and more bourgeois Bohemian township, and they introduced him to its sociocultural nucleus, namely the Greipl household, the head of which (Matthias) was a wealthy commercial wholesaler—in contrast to Johann Stifter and his lower-rung status as a peregrine purveyor of linen. Matthias's daughter, Franziska (Fanny), soon became the focal point of Stifter's existence, to the detriment of his academic career. As he obsessed over Fanny, he began to flail in his studies and fail to make his rent payments, becoming a persona non grata among both professors and creditors. He also fell out of favor with the Greipls, who now definitively deemed him a marital mismatch for their daughter and prohibited any further contact with her. His studies soon fizzled out, yet he continued to lead a precarious economic existence as a private instructor. Though he engaged in a handful of attempts to secure teaching positions at diverse institutions in Vienna, Linz, Prague, and even the Forst-Lehranstalt Mariabrunn (one of the first forestry academies founded in Austria), none of these more wishful than practical solicitations met with success. All the while, Stifter persevered as best he could by tutoring in upper-class Viennese households; he even instructed Prince Metternich's son in physics and mathematics. Moreover, throughout the late 1830s, he tried his hand as a painter of both natural and urban landscapes, and in 1839 five of his works were exhibited at the prestigious Viennese Academy for Fine Arts. Despite this initial public recognition as a visual artist, Stifter would soon thereafter make his literary debut, and in fact breakthrough.

In the meantime, however, he was forced to make marital compromises based on his sunken social station. In November 1837 he married Amalie (also spelled Amalia) Mohaupt, an uneducated and not inexperienced confidante/paramour—that is, a kind of precursor to the fin-de-siècle *süßes Mädel*—who had found gainful employment as a capable cleaning lady, a talent that is not to be underestimated in Stifter's world of tidiness and orderliness. She was thus able to provide her still emotionally enervated husband (Fanny had recently married an upright government official) with a long-lasting stable, albeit somewhat stolid, domestic existence. Though she apparently never perused a single page that her husband wrote and generally remained indifferent to his literary occupation, she became the proverbial pillar in their relationship and Stifter grew unable to function without her in any other capacity than writing. Given that domesticity exercises a major motivic if not thematic presence in Stifter's oeuvre, one wonders to what extent Amalie played an influential role in this otherwise broader Biedermeier trend. According to numerous testimonials, the Stifter household in Vienna, and later in Linz, was spotlessly clean and meticulously ordered, not unlike the interiors—or, for that matter, exteriors—in much of Stifter's fiction. Yet this immaculate surface effect could also be interpreted as an aesthetic cover-up or perhaps compensation for a deeper, darker truth that must have torn at Stifter, given the degree to which it suffuses his work. For he and Amalie not only remained childless, but two attempts at raising foster children (in each case a familial niece) ended in failure, indeed tragedy. Whereas Josefine Stifter died of tuberculosis after less than two years living with her adoptive parents, Juliane Mohaupt spent a total of twelve years with the aging couple but ran away from home at least twice, the final time ending up drowned in the Danube. As it turned out, she had long been physically mistreated by her aunt, which only reinforces the strife that must have reigned in an ostensibly orderly domicile. Again, traces of such domestic turmoil can be discerned on a deconstructive level in several texts, but Stifter also paid more direct tribute to the free-spirited waif Juliane in tales such as *Kazensilber* (Cat-Silver, 1853) and *Der Waldbrunnen* (The Forest Well, 1866). In the end, however, he was plagued by the lack of marital offspring, even wracked by guilt for this seeming existential-procreational deficit. Much of the melancholy that infuses his work can, at any rate, be attributed to this brute fact, as for instance evidenced in two of his most despondent tales, both of which delve deep into the dilemma of child-lessness: *Der Hagestolz* (The Bachelor, 1845/1850) and *Der Waldgänger* (The Forest-Goer, 1847).

As hinted at above, Stifter's unforeseen fame as a writer began on the heels of his rising renown as a painter. In 1840, his story "Der Condor" (The Condor) appeared in the journal *Wiener Zeitschrift für Kunst, Literatur, Theater und Mode* (Viennese Magazine for Art, Literature, Theater, and Fashion) and became an immediate hit, catapulting him into the literary limelight. Stifter enjoyed both critical and popular success throughout most of the 1840s, though his detractors gradually increased as his plotlines became more plodding, his style more manneristic, and his narrative "universe" too parochial for contemporary tastes. Nevertheless, during these early creative years he was all the rage in Viennese circles, ascending to an elite cultural status that was inconceivable given his dismal academic performance and dire economic predicament just a decade earlier. More generally, though he had been crafting poems and composing the prose piece *Julius* during the 1830s, he failed to evince any proven artistic talent beyond that of a painter before the watershed year of 1840. By the end of the decade, however, he had published some two dozen *Erzählungen*, some of them short (less than thirty pages), most of them medium-length (between fifty to sixty pages), and a handful of them novella-like in scope (that is, over one hundred pages). Yet this steady output is only "half of the story." Quite literally.

Stifter engaged in an unprecedented practice of not only revisional writing but also revised publishing. That is, throughout the 1840s and early 1850s, he amended and often outright transformed his stories as they were originally serialized in literary magazines, reissuing most of them in the six-volume *Studien* (Studies, 1844–50) and two-volume *Bunte Steine* (Motley Stones, 1853) book editions. All totaled, nineteen of his tales exist in two separately published forms, dubbed the *Journalfassungen* (journal versions) and *Buchfassungen* (book versions). As Wolfgang Matz notes, this self-editing regimen is unique in literary history. Stifter not only republished his previously printed tales; he rewrote and, especially in the case of *Bunte Steine*, retitled and even reconceived them.[7] As a result, his artistic evolution becomes apparent not just within the broader spectrum of his oeuvre but, more narrowly, within the textual parameters of an individual tale and its respective redux. In the process, Stifter purged his original stories—which had been long circulated as autonomous literary creations in their own right—of any lingering romantic residue, whether Jean-Paulesque scurrilities and eccentricities; uncanny and preternatural elements reminiscent of Hoffmann and Tieck; or more diffuse moods of sentimentality and tones of pathos. The barely middle-aged Stifter thus made, within the span of a single decade, rash progression from passé romanticism to premature realism. As Matz observes in alternative literary-historical terms, Stifter's medial modus operandi during the 1840s is so extreme that it could be considered analogous to the elder Goethe and Schiller rewriting classicist versions of their early Storm-and-Stress sensations *Die Leiden des jungen Werther* (The Sufferings of Young Werther, 1774) and *Die Räuber* (The Robbers, 1781).[8] In less speculative fashion, Stifter himself provides direct testimony of this shift from romantic indulgence to classical restraint in *Feldblumen* (Wildflowers, 1840/1844), whereby the narrator's enthusiasm for "father" Jean Paul in the journal version is replaced by his veneration of "father" Goethe in the *Studien* edition. Thus, within the course of a mere four years and, more narrowly, within the context of the same basic work, Stifter takes a considerable literary-historical leap in terms of both inspiration and emulation. From his own genetic-artistic perspective, he sheds revealing light on this process of radical revisionism in a letter to his brother Anton, dated February 13, 1847. Here he explains, for instance,

> daß man doch zu solchen Almanacherzählungen sich nicht mehr die Mühe gibt, wie zu einem selbständigen Buche, indem eine Almanacherzählung eine bestellte ist, die ich jährlich machen muß, ob mir etwas einfällt oder nicht, während ein Buch meine eigene Aufgabe ist, die aus meinem Wesen herauswächst, und die ich mit Liebe hege und großziehe. (See *HKG* 1,9:29)

---

7    See Wolfgang Matz, *Adalbert Stifter, oder Diese fürchterliche Wendung der Dinge: Biographie* (Göttingen: Wallstein: 2016), 186–95. See also Schoenborn, *Adalbert Stifter: Sein Leben und Werk*, 256–74. Ironically, perhaps even deliberately, Matz emulated Stifter by reissuing this second edition of his original intellectual biography from 1995, adding only minimal material yet making numerous stylistic purges, most of which analogously attempt to eliminate emotive excesses and nonessential subjectivisms. See Wolfgang Matz, *Adalbert Stifter, oder Diese fürchterliche Wendung der Dinge: Biographie* (Munich: Hanser, 1995).

8    Matz, *Adalbert Stifter* (2016), 193.

[when it comes to writing such stories for almanacs, one simply doesn't put forth the same effort as with a standalone book; almanac stories are commissioned, and I have to comply on a yearly basis, regardless whether something comes to mind or not, whereas a book is my own endeavor, one that grows out of my very nature and that I cherish and nurture with love.]

Inevitably, this greater discussion of *Journalfassungen* versus *Buchfassungen* raises central questions concerning textual interpretation and scholarly reception. While modern readership tends to prioritize the book versions, which are logically more mature and masterful works of art, there is something to be said for the raw immediacy and naïve artistry of the journal publications, especially given the popular periodical culture of the time. Moreover, in the German academic world there has long been a kind of qualitative bias against subjective-romantic literature versus more objective-classicist literary modes, an attitude that not only applies to epochal romanticism versus classicism per se but also to more deeply rooted ahistorical mentalities and sensibilities. Whether this oft-drawn distinction remains a crude consequence of Goethe's famous dictum "Das Klassische nenne ich das Gesunde und das Romantische das Kranke" (I call the classic healthy, the romantic sickly)[9] or has some other authoritative attribution, the fundamental fact is that the publishing preference in Germany and Austria lies almost entirely with the *Buchfassungen*.[10] Similarly, in the English-speaking world, translations of Stifter seem to focus solely on the revised book versions and largely ignore, in their respective forewords or prefaces, the importance of the journal iterations. (See the selected bibliography at the end of this volume.) In the end, readers of Stifter need to be aware of this strange situation and its potential for interpretive relativization. While many of his "twin" tales are divergent enough, in both form and content, to merit two separate analyses, some underwent lesser degrees of alteration. The most extreme examples of each tendency are: *Die Mappe meines Urgroßvaters*, the book version of which is a thoroughly transformed and unrecognizable work;

---

9    See J. P. Eckermann, *Gespräche mit Goethe*, ed. Hellmuth Steger (Zurich: Stauffacher, 1969), 259; Johann Wolfgang Goethe, *Conversations with Eckermann (1823–1832)*, trans. John Oxenford (San Francisco, CA: North Point Press, 1984), 248. This famous remark by Goethe is from April 2, 1829. For a pithier variant ("Klassisch ist das Gesunde, romantisch das Kranke"), see Johann Wolfgang Goethe, *Maximen und Reflexionen*, in *Werke*, vol. 12 (Hamburg: Christian Wegner Verlag, 1960), 487 (no. 863).

10   A notable exception is the recent annotated paperback edition (totaling 1,640 pages) that contains *all* of Stifter's stories in their original journal or almanac form. See Adalbert Stifter, *Sämtliche Erzählungen nach den Erstdrucken*, ed. Wolfgang Matz (Munich: Deutscher Taschenbuch Verlag, 2005).

## 12 ♦ SEAN IRETON

and *Der Hochwald*, which experienced only a handful of minor stylistic adjustments. In between these two extremes, however, seventeen additional texts demand to be read twice, with differing results.[11]

### Late Summer in Linz (1848–68)

1848 was a pivotal year in Stifter's life and work, which is not surprising given its historical significance throughout the German lands, particularly in major centers of (imperial) government like Vienna. While the initial March revolts echoed his hopes for liberal reform (he was even voted to be an electoral delegate in the Frankfurt National Assembly), these were soon dashed by riotous violence and what he perceived as ruinous mob rule. In early May, he moved to the much smaller and calmer city of Linz, where his bourgeois liberalism ceded to petty bourgeois conservatism and his popularity as an author waned. In 1849, almost immediately upon his translocation, he accepted a salaried position as *Inspektor der oberösterreichischen Volksschulen* (Inspector of Primary Schools for Upper Austria), which, on the one hand, reflects his lifelong interest in pedagogy but, on the other, attests to the bureaucratic trajectory of his new-found life in Linz. Thus, on a similar note, in 1853 he was appointed regional conservator by the *k.k. Zenralkommission zur Erfoschung und Erhaltung der Kunst- und historischen Denkmale* (Imperial-Royal Central Commission for the Investigation and Preservation of Art and Historical Monuments). This title basically says it all with respect to Stifter's late-summerly respite in a cultural environment that is all about the maintenance of tradition and order. That is, much like the twilight years of Risach as narrated in *Der Nachsommer*, a novel that is significantly set during the post-1815 *Restauration* period that preceded the upheavals of 1848, Stifter's own restorative reprieve in the very same Austrian province will prove to be the concluding chapter of his languishing literary career and ever more stagnating existence.

In the wake of 1848, the fashionable journals that in large part contributed to Stifter's success began to fade from the publishing scene. In the end, this mass-marketing decline might be considered an auspicious development, as it allowed Stifter to try his hand at much longer narratives, meaning multi-volume novels that exceeded a thousand pages, at least in their original imprint. These are the previously mentioned *Der Nachsommer* and *Witiko*, both of which, however, bear, somewhat perversely, the generic subtitle "Erzählung." His most famous collection

---

11 For a representative analysis that does interpretive justice to both textual variants, see for instance Brigitte Prutti, "Zwischen Ansteckung und Auslöschung: Zur Seuchenerzählung bei Stifter—*Die Pechbrenner* versus *Granit*," *Oxford German Studies* 37, no. 1 (2008): 49–73.

of medium-length tales, *Bunte Steine*, was published in 1853, yet four out of the six stories appeared in journals issued before the events of 1848. Clearly, Stifter was floundering rather than flourishing as a critically acclaimed and publicly admired author, and this final phase of his production—which continued to be prolific—has since been received with varying degrees of enthusiasm. On a literary-technical level, his newly wrought minimalistic prose and tautological narrative logic alienated contemporary readers. In a broader cultural sense, he was becoming irrelevant; few seemed to care about a senescent scribe living in the past and harking back to long-gone national (Austrian) and regional (Bohemian) glory, particularly when such retrospective-revisionist narratives—namely *Der Nachsommer* and *Witiko*—required hundreds of pages of uneventful reading. Nevertheless, his final work, the semi-autobiographical *Aus dem bairischen Walde* (From the Bavarian Forest, 1868), which was written in November 1867 and published posthumously the following year, can be considered a late masterpiece—indeed, an impeccable piece of prose by any standard. Thomas Mann, for instance, considered this narration of a cataclysmic snowstorm both "unübertrefflich" (unsurpassable) and "unerreichbar gut" (unattainably good), using it as a model for the most famous chapter of *Der Zauberberg* (The Magic Mountain, 1924), which is simply and elementally titled "Schnee" (Snow).[12] One would be hard pressed to find higher praise for this terminal stage of Stifter's writing career.

This final, auto-fictional narrative harbors undeniable signs of Stifter's declining mental health. A more scrutinous biographical inquest into his last years shows that he suffered from numerous physical as well as psychological afflictions, including obesity, alcoholism, irritability, spells of dizziness, bouts with fever, and what we would today call "panic attacks." As mentioned above, two foster daughters had died within days of one another (in April 1859), thereby driving home an irreversible sense of childlessness and, increasingly, loneliness as he entered old age. In October 1867, he visited Oberplan for the final time, installing, together with his siblings, a memorial plaque for his mother in the town church. (She had passed away back in 1858). In late January of the following year, he sliced his throat with a razor, whereupon a doctor stitched up the wound and a priest administered the last rites. Two days later, during the early morning hours of January 28, 1868, he expired; the official cause of death was declared as hectic fever (*Zehrfieber*) resulting from chronic liver cirrhosis. On January 30, the Linz-based composer and organist Anton Bruckner conducted the choir that sang at his burial.

---

12   These remarks stem from a letter to Ernst Bertram, dated August 6, 1918. For this observation by Mann, I am indebted to Matz, *Adalbert Stifter* (2016), 359–60.

# The Gentle Order of Things

Even casual readers of Stifter will be struck by a certain cluster of words that recur throughout his texts, often to the point of excess. Such words, which tend to appear more than once in a single sentence or multiple times within a single paragraph, would ordinarily be deemed redundant, at least by literary stylistic norms. Ultimately, however, they function like leitmotifs, underscoring core concepts in Stifter's worldview. These keywords include *Ordnung* (order), *Ding(e)* (thing[s]), and *sanft* (gentle). In the following, I will comment on all three, offering select samples from tales published during the 1840s and early 1850s in both *Studien* and *Bunte Steine*, albeit also with unavoidable nods to *Der Nachsommer*. In the end, it will become apparent that, though they largely operate independently within a given context, they sometimes combine twofold or even threefold, thereby reinforcing Stifter's normative and ever more conservative view of reality, which might best be characterized as a "gentle order of things." And while it may seem outmoded to dwell on such overinterpreted if not cliché notions in Stifter's oeuvre, the thematic-motivic and ultimately dynamic combination of all three makes, in my view, for productive (and at times deconstructive) reading—both for seasoned scholars and interested newcomers.

### *Dinge*/Things

The word *Ding* may well be the most recurrent and polyvalent noun in Stifter's oeuvre. Put more negatively from a technical writing standpoint, it is perhaps the most overused and empty of words in his literary output. Nevertheless, he employs it with headstrong intention, seeming to care little for conventions of style or perceptions of superfluity. Notable uses or, depending on one's perspective, flagrant abuses of this key word abound in his tales. Compare, for instance, the following excerpts from the first few pages of *Granit* and consider especially the multivalence of the word *Ding*, or its plural form *Dinge*, as highlighted in all four examples:

> (1) Unter den *Dingen*, die ich von dem Steine aus sah, war öfter ein Mann von seltsamer Art. (One of the *things* I saw often from that stone was a man of a most peculiar sort.)

> (2) "Was hat denn dieser heillose eingefleischte Sohn heute für *Dinge* an sich?" ("What sort of no-good *things* has this unholy son of my flesh gotten up to this time?")

> (3) wo ich selber in den letzten Tagen eine große Menge dieser *Dinge* [Ruthen und Zweige] angesammelt hatte. (of which *things*

INTRODUCTION: STIFTER'S LIFE AND WORKS ◆ 15

[switches and branches] I had amassed a large collection in the past few days.)

(4) diese fürchterliche Wendung der *Dinge* (this appalling turn of *things*)

(*HKG* 2,2:24–27; *MS*, 12–14, translation slightly modified)

Here Stifter provides a summation of the various, indeed multifarious, "things" that set the story into motion: the local grease-man Andreas plays a prank on the child narrator by applying pitch to his bare feet, whereupon the latter soils the floors of his family home and the brush-wood he has collected as kindling is suddenly turned against him in the form of corporal punishment, administered by his outraged mother for the domestic disorder caused by his innocent antics. In the oft-overlooked introduction to *Bunte Steine*, as opposed to its far more analyzed preface, Stifter offers an even more condensed panoply of *Ding*-polyvalence, as evidenced in the first paragraph:

Als Knabe trug ich außer Ruthen Gesträuchen und Blüthen, die mich ergözten, auch noch andere *Dinge* nach Hause, die mich fast noch mehr freuten, weil sie nicht so schnell Farbe und Bestand ver-loren wie die Pflanzen, nemlich allerlei Steine und Erd*dinge*. Auf Feldern an Rainen auf Haiden und Hutweiden ja sogar auf Wiesen, auf denen doch nur das hohe Gras steht, liegen die manigfältigsten dieser *Dinge* herum. Da ich nun viel im Freien herum schweifen durfte, konnte ich es nicht fehlen, daß ich bald die Pläze entdeckte, auf denen die *Dinge* zu treffen waren, und daß ich die, welche ich fand, mit nach Hause nahm. (*HKG* 2,2:17; my emphasis)

[As a boy I took home twigs plants and flowers that caught my fancy, and other *things* too that pleased me almost better still because they did not lose their color and vitality as quickly as the plants did, namely all kinds of stones and *things* of the earth. On fields on marges on heaths and pastures and even on meadows where nothing grows but high grass these *things* lie about in profusion. As I was allowed to roam far and wide, I inevitably discovered the places to find these *things*, and took home what I found. (*MS*, 9; my emphasis)][13]

13   Note that this translation by Isabel Fargo Cole adheres to Stifter's original idiosyncratic punctuation, which may be perplexing to modern readers given the utter lack of serial commas.

16 ♦ Sean Ireton

Things, in sum, can be anything and everything for Stifter—they even include unspecified "Erddinge" or "things of the earth," whatever exactly these may be (beyond already specified "stones"). Throughout his writings, things stand for all kinds of natural as well as anthropogenic phenomena, whether flora and fauna, geological formations and meteorological fluctuations, felled forests and tilled fields, rustic homesteads and interior households, village affairs and social structures, human words and actions—indeed human beings themselves, as in the case of the wagon-greaser Andreas mentioned above. As *realia*, things (compare Old English *þing*, German *Ding*, Latin *res*) are what make up Stifter's fictional *reality*, and they consequently serve as the narrative basis for his unique and literalized brand of *realism*. According to a number of critics, Stifter's personal attitude toward things ranges from pious devotion to neurotic fetishization, while his more intellectual relation to them encompasses the realms of aesthetics, ethics, and even epistemology.[14] One might thus choose to align his thing-oriented realism with Bruno Latour's notion of "hybrid entities" or "quasi-objects," which blend the traditional boundaries of nature and culture to create a "parlement des choses" and new kind of *contrat social*, one that extends from the inanimate to the human.[15] Alternatively, one might hark back to Eichendorff, whose pithy poem "Wünschelrute" (Dowsing Twig, 1835) says even more about the infinite potential of "things" to articulate reality in all its plenitude: "Schläft ein Lied in allen Dingen / Die da träumen fort und fort, / Und die Welt hebt an zu singen, / Triffst du nur das Zauberwort" (A song sleeps in all things, / Which dream on and on, / And the world begins to sing, / If you only find the magic word).[16] Independent of these intertextual extremes, ranging from German romanticism to French postmodernism, a more internalized reading of Stifter's *Buchfassungen* and later unamended narratives reveals an ever more phenomenal and post-subjective world, one in which "things" dominate rather than merely perforate the narrative. Indeed, rather than endlessly debate the extent to which Stifter was a "realist" writer or otherwise adhered to the principles and practices

14  See for example: Thomas Macho, "Stifters Dinge," *Merkur: Deutsche Zeitschrift für europäisches Denken* 59 (2005): 735–41; Christian Begemann, "Ding und Fetisch: Überlegungen zu Stifters Dingen," in *Der Code der Leidenschaften: Fetischismus in den Künsten*, ed. Hartmut Böhme and Johannes Endres (Munich: Wilhelm Fink, 2010), 324–43; and Claudia Öhlschläger, "Ethik kleiner Dinge: Adalbert Stifter, Francis Ponge, W.G. Sebald," *Weimarer Beiträge* 62, no. 3 (2016): 325–45.

15  For this connection to Latour's *We Have Never Been Modern* (1991), see Macho, "Stifters Dinge," 738–39.

16  For this connection to Eichendorff's poem, see Begemann, "Ding und Fetisch," 335; and Macho, "Stifters Dinge," 735.

of 'realism,'[17] one might more productively think of him as a practitioner of "thing-ism." His narrative modus operandi lends itself, after all, to phenomenological approaches, more specifically as a kind of literary pre-enactment of Husserl's call for a "return to the things themselves,"[18] perhaps even of recent "thing theory" ranging from Heidegger to Bill Brown. As Stifter has for instance stated in self-effacing yet nonetheless revealing fashion: "Ich habe wirklich kein Verdienst an meinen Arbeiten, ich habe nichts gemacht, ich habe nur das Vorhandene ausgeplaudert" (I really deserve no merit for my works, I have done nothing, I have only blabbered forth that which is given).[19] One would be hard pressed to find a more hands-off definition of authorial representation or a more sincere submission to phenomenal reality.

### *Sanft*/Gentle

On this noninterventionist note, Stifter's notion of the gentle law (*das sanfte Gesetz*), or of gentleness (*Sanftheit*) in general, constitutes another key to unlocking his work and better understanding the ideas, as well as deeper ideology, embedded therein. Ever since its first formulation in the

---

17  For standard discussions of Stifter in the context of German Realism, see: Martin and Erika Swales, *Adalbert Stifter: A Critical Study* (Cambridge: Cambridge University Press, 1984), 218–33; and Robert Holub, "Adalbert Stifter's *Brigitta*, or the Lesson of Realism," in *A Companion to German Realism, 1848–1900*, ed. Todd Kontje (Rochester, NY: Camden House, 2002), 29–51. For a more recent and revisionist reckoning with so-called German Realism and Stifter's place therein, see Erica Weitzman, *At the Limit of the Obscene: German Realism and the Disgrace of Matter* (Evanston, IL: Northwestern University Press, 2021), esp. 24–48. On a more general note, it is unfortunate that Erich Auerbach's classic study on representational tendencies in literature is mainly restricted to his professional field of Romance philology and thus does not include Germanophone masters of mimesis such as Stifter, whom Auerbach admits to reading merely "for pleasure and relaxation." See Erich Auerbach, *Mimesis: The Representation of Reality in Western Literature*, trans. Willard R. Trask (Princeton, NJ: Princeton University Press, 2003), 571. Auerbach also includes Goethe and Gottfried Keller on his personal reading list of preferred authors that wrote in his native tongue.

18  For a classic phenomenological reading of Stifter's prose style and narrative techniques, see Wolfgang Preisendanz, "Die Erzählfunktion der Naturdarstellung bei Stifter," *Wirkendes Wort* 16 (1966): 407–18. Christian Begemann, for his part, argues that from the mid-1840s onward—specifically in the book version of *Die Narrenburg* (The Castle of Fools, 1844)—Stifter increasingly strives to keep his narrative ego in check and allow, in quasi-phenomenological fashion, the objects to present themselves of their own accord. See Christian Begemann, *Die Welt der Zeichen: Stifter-Lektüren* (Stuttgart: J. B. Metzler, 1995), 206–7.

19  Letter to Louise von Eichendorff from March 23, 1852. Cited in Fischer, *Adalbert Stifters Leben und Werk*, 280.

journal version of "Brigitta" from 1844 (see *HKG* 1,2:255), the gentle law has appeared in Stifter's writings only a handful of times as such in name, but its workings have been endlessly hinted at in the singular adjectival form of *sanft*, a word that can modify an apparent infinite number of "things." Indeed, if *Ding/Dinge* is the most frequently and idiosyncratically deployed noun in the Stifterian canon, *sanft* holds that distinction as an adjective. Stifter overuses it—along with its variations and compounds *Sanftheit* (gentleness), *sanftmütig* (meek), *Sanftmut* (meekness), and at times the verb *sänftigen* (to soothe, to mildly restrain)—in deliberate leitmotif-like fashion, thereby underscoring its omnipresence and more innate governance in everyday reality.[20] He even goes so far as to create characters that exemplify this ethos of restraint (compare especially the epithetical "sanftmütige Obrist" or "meek Colonel" in the *Mappe*) and to construct plot scenarios if not entire narratives that illustrate the inevitable sway of this natural-social-political ideal (compare especially *Brigitta* and *Der Nachsommer*). The former tale, in fact, forges a link between the presence of *things* and the effect of *gentleness* from its very opening lines: "Es gibt oft *Dinge* und Beziehungen in dem menschlichen Leben, die uns nicht sogleich klar sind, und deren Grund wir nicht in Schnelligkeit hervor zu ziehen vermögen. Sie wirken dann meistens mit einem gewissen schönen und *sanften* Reize des Geheimnisvollen auf unsere Seele" (*HKG* 1,5:411; There are often *things* and relationships in human life which are not at once clear to us and whose basis we are unable promptly to lay bare. These then affect our souls with a certain beautiful and *gentle* charm of the mysterious.)[21] Later in the text, the narrator draws a similar connection between things (by which he here means the diverse agricultural phenomena that he observes on the landed estates of his Hungarian host) and the prevailing mood of the natural-cultural environment in which he finds himself ever more enmeshed:

> Da ich einmal längere Zeit auf der Besitzung des Majors war, da ich die Theile derselben übersah, und verstehen lernte, da die *Dinge* vor mir wuchsen und ich an dem Gedeihen derselben Antheil nahm: hatte mich das gleichförmig *sanfte* Abfließen dieser Tage und Geschäfte so eingesponnen, daß ich mich wohl und ebenmäßig angeregt fühlte. (*HKG* 1,5:437–38; my emphasis)

20   Though he occasionally injects the synonymous or at least analogous adjective/adverb *sacht(e)* into his narratives, especially when describing natural landscapes (for example the "soft" or "gentle" undulations of hills and dales), *sanft* remains his "magic" word—in Eichendorff's sense of an all-encompassing, epiphanic *Zauberwort*.

21   Adalbert Stifter, *Brigitta, with Abdias, Limestone, and the Forest Path*, trans. Helen Watanabe-O'Kelly (London: Angel Books; Chester Springs, PA: Dufour Editions, 1990), 97. My emphasis; translation slightly modified.

# INTRODUCTION: STIFTER'S LIFE AND WORKS ♦ 19

[When I had been on the Major's estates for a longer period, when I had an overview of its parts and had learned to understand them, when *things* grew in front of me and I took an interest in their growth, the *gentle* succession of these days and occupations wrapped me round so that I felt myself well and evenly stimulated.][22]

Additional examples could easily serve to illustrate the same basic point that Stifter's perceived world of things is often inflected by a pervasive sense of gentle ordinance. Readers intrigued by this interconnectedness will find plenty such evidence in the textual tissue of his tales including the two novelistic tomes, *Der Nachsommer* and *Witiko*. Nevertheless, another text deserves mention, both because it tends to receive little scholarly scrutiny and, here more importantly, features one of the most peculiar imbrications of *Dinge* and *Sanftheit* in Stifter's entire oeuvre. The underappreciated tale *Zwei Schwestern* (Two Sisters) from the sixth and final volume of *Studien* (1850)—the original journal version was published as "Die Schwestern" (The Sisters) in 1846—invokes, for instance, a plethora of interconnective moments between natural-agricultural objects and mild meteorological-environmental conditions (see esp. *HKG* 1,6:261). Here within a single paragraph, Stifter enumerates the "manigfaltigen seltsamen Dinge[-]" (manifold curious things) that his first-person narrator, with an eye for picturesque detail, encounters during a sojourn in the Italian Alps. Interestingly, the enumeration of such items includes both that which the narrator sees laid out before him *and* that which he finds lacking in this harsh mountainous terrain, one that does not conform to traditional categories of European landscape aesthetics: "Die Maler haben eigentlich diese Dinge noch nicht gemalt; denn da war kein Baum, kein Gesträuchlein, kein Haus, keine Hütte, keine Wiese, kein Feld, sondern nur das sehr dürftige Gras und die Felsen"; (The painters have not yet painted these things; here there was no tree, no bush, no house, no cottage, no meadow, no field to be seen, but only crags and sparse growth). Stifter is well known for his inventories of nature, but here he oddly engages in an index of absence more than of presence. Just as odd is the sudden shift to something (read: some *thing*) that takes on increasing gentle qualities and subtleties:

In allen Stufen des matten Grün, Grau und Blau lag das fabelhafte Ding hinaus; schwermüthig dämmernde schwebende webende Tafeln von Farben stellten sich hin, und die Felsen rissen mattschimmernde Lichtzukungen hinein; und wo das Land blos lag, und etwa nur Sand und Gerölle hatte, drangen Flächen fahlen Glanzes oder sanft gebrochene Farbtöne vor.

22  Stifter, *Brigitta, with Abdias, Limestone, and the Forest Path*, 116. My emphasis; translation slightly modified.

[The marvelous thing extended in countless gradations of faint green, gray, and blue; soaring, interweaving slabs of color materialized, darkening in melancholy, pierced by faintly glimmering flickers of light from the jagged mountains; and where the landscape lay bare, covered only by sand and scree, there advanced stretches of pallid radiance or gently refracted tints of color.]

Two things are stylistically striking in this passage, and they are both perforce related. Stifter not only neglects to specify, from the outset, what this "marvelous thing" is. He furthermore seems to regard it as ineffable, for his language is uncharacteristically muddled, both in terms of metaphor and syntax. Of course, context dictates that he is describing the multihued early evening sky and the lingering, post-sunset radiance on the alpine landscape, which, in turn, appears to reciprocate with its own display of light effects. In sum, he is devoting perhaps more painterly than writerly attention to atmospheric conditions and geographic features. Either way, this artistic technique leads to two further evocations of "sanft," the first of which modifies the coloration of the southern heavens, the second the obscuration of the distant Lombardian flatlands. Stifter, in sum, capitalizes on the connection between his operative words *Ding(e)* and *sanft* such that they combine to present an expansive descriptive tableau, or what is here referred to as the "Größe des Bildes" (greatness/vastness of the picture).

On a less textual and more theoretical level, *das sanfte Gesetz* or "the gentle law" as elaborated in the preface to *Bunte Steine* remains Stifter's shorthand interpretation of the world. More specifically, it functions as a universal principle predicated on a correspondence between the equilibrium of nature and the moral status quo of humanity. As an interpretive mantra in discussions of Stifter, it has become famous and grown tedious, for along with the preface, in which it made its first programmatic appearance, it has been the subject of never-ending scholarly debate. While many scholars have tacitly accepted its fundamental premises, others have been less complacent and, so to speak, "gentle" in their criticisms. In the main, two such camps exist. Some critics maintain, intratextually, that Stifter's conception of the gentle law and broader argumentation as laid out in the preface are riddled with logical fallacies, pseudo-scientific claims, and ideological presuppositions.[23] Others object to his explanatory preamble

23   For a sampling of such studies, see in chronological order: Swales and Swales, *Adalbert* Stifter, 27–47; Eric Downing, "Common Ground: Conditions of Realism in Stifter's 'Vorrede,'" *Colloquia Germanica* 28 (1995): 35–53; Hans P. Gabriel, "Prescribing Reality: The Preface as a Device of Literary Realism in Auerbach, Keller, and Stifter," *Colloquia Germanica* 32 (1999): 325–44; Eric Downing, *Double Exposures: Repetition and Realism in Nineteenth-Century German Fiction* (Stanford, CA: Stanford University Press, 2000), 24–40; Hartmut

INTRODUCTION: STIFTER'S LIFE AND WORKS ♦ 21

as a suitable literary-theoretical vehicle, faulting it for its lack of coherent intertextual connections to the stories or for its deficiencies in trying to elucidate them in such proactive fashion.[24] Furthermore, many of the ideas and examples put forth in the preface are hardly unprecedented, as Stifter drew freely from the writings of Herder, Kant, Goethe, Schiller, and others, in effect piecing together a potpourri of eighteenth-century liberal humanism.[25] Nevertheless, in an introduction such as this, one should not sell short *any* idea of literary-historical impact or import.

Stifter's point of departure in the preface concerns the opposition between *groß* and *klein* or "great" and "small." Indeed, this paratext is at bottom an apologia in defense of the latter over the former, spurred in large part by Friedrich Hebbel's derisive poem from 1849 "Die alten Naturdichter und die neuen" (The Old and the New Nature Poets). Here Hebbel mocks Stifter and other eighteenth and nineteenth-century aesthetes for focusing on diminutive phenomena such as beetles and buttercups while ignoring more grandiose subjects such as humanity and the cosmos. Stifter's oft-cited response to this critique runs as follows:

> Weil wir aber schon einmal von dem Großen und Kleinen reden, so will ich meine Ansichten darlegen, die wahrscheinlich von denen vieler anderer Menschen abweichen. Das Wehen der Luft das Rieseln des Wassers das Wachsen der Getreide das Wogen des Meeres das

---

Laufhütte, "Das sanfte Gesetz und der Abgrund: Zu den Grundlagen der Stifterschen Dichtung 'aus dem Geiste der Naturwissenschaft,'" in *Stifter-Studien: Ein Festgeschenk für Wolfgang Frühwald zum 65. Geburtstag*, ed. Walter Hettche, Johannes John, and Sibylle von Steinsdorff (Tübingen: Niemeyer, 2000), 61–74; Sabina Becker and Katharina Grätz, "Einleitung: Ordnung, Raum, Ritual bei Adalbert Stifter " in *Ordnung—Raum—Ritual: Adalbert Stifters artifizieller Realismus*, ed. Sabina Becker and Katharina Grätz (Heidelberg: Universitätsverlag Winter, 2007), 7–16.

24  Eugen Thurnher, for instance, contends that the preface is more applicable to *Der Nachsommer* than to the stories contained in *Bunte Steine*, while Frederick Stopp suggests that the stories help illuminate the preface more than vice versa. See Eugen Thurnher, "Stifters *Sanftes Gesetz*," in *Unterscheidung und Bewahrung: Festschrift für Hermann Kunisch zum 60. Geburtstag, 27. Oktober 1961*, ed. Klaus Lazarowicz and Wolfgang Kron (Berlin: De Gruyter, 1961), 381–97; here 396; and Frederick Stopp, "Die Symbolik in Stifters 'Bunten Steinen'" *Deutsche Vierteljahresschrift für Literaturwissenschaft und Geistesgeschichte* 28 (1954): 165–93.

25  For detailed accounts of these connections, see Sepp Domandl, "Die philosophische Tradition von Adalbert Stifters 'Sanftem Gesetz,'" *VASILO* 21, nos. 3/4 (1972): 79–103; and Walter Hettche, "Kommentar," in *HKG* 2,3:80–120. Martin and Erika Swales more emphatically point to the influence of Herder, asserting that the preface "reads like a shorthand version" of his *Ideen zur Philosophie der Geschichte der Menschheit* (Ideas on the Philosophy of Human History, 1791). See Swales and Swales, *Adalbert Stifter*, 30–32.

Grünen der Erde das Glänzen des Himmels das Schimmern der Gestirne halte ich für groß: das prächtig einherziehende Gewitter, den Bliz, welcher Häuser spaltet, den Sturm, der die Brandung treibt, den feuerspeienden Berg, das Erdbeben, welches Länder verschüttet, halte ich nicht für größer als obige Erscheinungen, ja ich halte sie für kleiner, weil sie nur Wirkungen viel höherer Geseze sind. Sie kommen auf einzelnen Stellen vor, und sind die Ergebnisse einseitiger Ursachen… . Die Einzelheiten gehen vorüber, und ihre Wirkungen sind nach kurzem kaum noch erkennbar. (*HKG* 2,2:10)

[But so long as we are speaking of great and small things, I shall put forth my views, which are likely to differ from those of many people. The wafting of the air the trickling of the water the growing of the grain the surging of the sea the budding of the earth the shining of the sky the glimmering of the stars is what I deem great; the thunderstorm that looms in splendor, the lightning that cleaves houses, the storm that drives the breakers, the fire-spewing mountain, the earthquake that buries whole lands, these I do not deem greater than those first phenomena, indeed I deem them smaller, for they are the results of one-sided causes. … The particulars pass, and a short time later their effects are barely seen. (*MS*, 3–4; translation slightly modified)]

Here Stifter problematizes, by way of concrete examples, the categories of *groß* and *klein*, inverting their conventional significations and categorizations. His notion of the gentle law effectively reverses the traditional fascination with nature's so-called "sublime" manifestations and calls for a deeper appreciation of its quotidian processes. In alternative terms, it embraces intransience over ephemerality: meteorological disturbances and natural disasters are, after all, fleeting happenstances rather than enduring climatic or environmental conditions of permanency. Though Stifter is often credited, yet also sometimes criticized, for his insistence on the polarity of *groß* versus *klein*, whether in theory (the preface) or in practice (*Bunte Steine* and *Der Nachsommer*), he is hardly alone among scientific contemporaries in upholding this binary. His mentor and fellow Bohemian Andreas von Baumgartner, for instance, published an article in 1860 titled "Das Große und das Kleine in der Natur" (The Great and Small in Nature). And the famed Austrian meteorologist Karl Kreil operated with the same terminological toolkit in some of his publications, including his principal opus *Klimatologie von Böhmen* (Climatology of Bohemia) from 1865.[26] In sum, Stifter is hardly the fossilized fogey that

---

26  For more on this greater scientific context within Habsburg Austria, see Deborah R. Coen, *Climate in Motion: Science, Empire, and the Problem of Scale* (Chicago, IL: University of Chicago Press, 2018), esp. 153–57; and Agnes Hoffmann, "A Poetics of Scaling: Adalbert Stifter and the Measures of Nature around

he is often made out to be in present-day assessments of his allegedly regressive worldviews.

Beyond the parameters of the preface, Stifter integrates this regulative notion of gentle order into the narrative fabric and thematic framework of his texts, above all those (re)written, and to a significant extent (re)conceived, after the revolutions of 1848. In the specific case of *Bunte Steine*, five of the six tales were previously published in journals; only *Kazensilber* was expressly written for the book edition, which Stifter organized to be both symmetrical and petrological in scope. In other words, it comprises two volumes, each of which contains three stories bearing (newly minted) titles relying on geological and mineralogical nomenclature. Each of the stories further revolves around a decisive cataclysmic event, whether an epidemiological outbreak (the plague in *Granit*); an abrupt weather event (a thunderstorm in *Kalkstein* [Limestone], a snowstorm in *Bergkristall* [Rock Crystal], and a hailstorm in *Kazensilber*); a fateful domestic crisis (adultery and its consequences in *Turmalin* [Tourmaline]); or a violent military conflict (the Napoleonic invasions in *Bergmilch* [Rock Milk]). Yet these natural and human-induced occurrences ultimately remain more disruptive than destructive; that is, passing phenomena that do not upset the ostensible natural and ethical order of things. Indeed, the post-catastrophic restoration in each storyline is also to be understood as a *Restauration* in the historical-political sense of the term; that is, as a countermeasure to the turmoil that prevailed in the German lands during the first half of the nineteenth century, especially in the wake of March 1848. The bloodshed that resulted from these populist uprisings deeply unnerved Stifter and prompted him to reaffirm his humanistic-bourgeois views in subsequent writings, often by devising ever more prescriptive analogies between humanity and nature. Indeed, as mentioned earlier, such events prompted him to move from Vienna, one of the hotbeds of revolutionary violence, to Linz, the politically dormant hub of provincial Upper Austria. Whether this corrective endeavor proves more artistic or dogmatic ultimately remains for the reader to decide. To be sure, some tales navigate this literary-theoretical tightrope better than others. What cannot be denied is that Stifter's crowning achievement (at least in conception, though many would argue also in execution), *Der Nachsommer*, implements the mechanisms of the gentle law on all possible levels, whether the human-social, natural-ethical, or aesthetic-philosophical. Indeed, the placid prose and Apollonian ambience[27] of the novel exem-

---

1850," in *Before Photography: German Visual Culture in the Nineteenth Century*, ed. Kirsten Belgum, Vance Byrd, and John D. Benjamin (Berlin and Boston, MA: De Gruyter, 2021), 267–92; esp. 269–72.

27 Nietzsche famously praised *Der Nachsommer*, which he most likely read during the summer of 1878, as one of the few great works of German prose—along

24 ♦ SEAN IRETON

plifies the gentle law as much as its conversationist-restorationist content does, though deconstructive readings can easily see through such conflict-free conceit.

As I have suggested earlier in this introduction and will further indicate in the next section, Stifter's precept of gentle order is compromised by moments of passion and chaos, which is a fictional find that reflects his own factual psycho-biographical background. For now, I will merely point out that the word *sanft* has not only wholesome but also holistic implications. Though Stifter never alludes to this key etymological connection anywhere in his writings, the modern German *sanft* derives from Old Germanic *sampia-*, which in turn stems from an Indo-European root (*sem-*) that means "one" or "together in one." Other New High German words share this root, for example the preposition *samt* ("along/together with"), the adverb/prefix *zusammen* ("together"), and the verb *sammeln* ("to collect"), the last of which is both a hobbyistic-scientific activity that dominated Stifter's life and a motivic aspect that pervades his work. The crucial adjective *sanft* thus harbors, though perhaps buried in the historical residue of its linguistic origins, the ideas of unity and totality.[28] Stifter stresses this "togetherness" often enough throughout the preface, insisting that the spheres of human affairs and natural processes function as homeostatic systems in which every constituent part, no matter how small or seemingly insignificant, has its rightful place and intrinsic worth. According to Wolfgang Matz and Helmut Bachmaier, Stifter's gentle law espouses an ethics of coequality ("Gleichrangigkeit"), equilibrium ("Gleichgewicht"), and an inherent right ("Eigenrecht") that applies to the existence of all things ("allen Dingen").[29] In other words, Stifter can be viewed as a kind of proto-ecologist and perhaps even incipient environmental ethicist. This eco-egalitarian mentality, indeed implicit morality, is manifested in his fiction insofar as he tends to fashion language and construct narratives that allow for all entities to exist at the same basic rank, without (anthropocentric) privilege or prejudice. The key caveat here is

---

with Goethe's writings, Lichtenberg's aphorisms, Jung-Stilling's autobiography, and Keller's collection of tales *Die Leute von Seldwyla*. See Friedrich Nietzsche, *Menschliches, Allzumenschliches I und II*, vol. 2 of *Kritische Studienausgabe*, ed. Mazzino Montinari and Giorgio Colli (Munich: Deutscher Taschenbuch Verlag, 1999), 599. Lesser known is his remark, from a posthumously published fragment, that *Der Nachsommer* remains "das einzige deutsche Buch *nach* Goethe, das für mich Zauber hat" (the only German book *after* Goethe that I find magical). See Nietzsche, *Kritische Studienausgabe*, vol. 13, 634.

28  I expand here on a linguistic cue provided by Domandl, "Die philosophische Tradition von Adalbert Stifters 'Sanftem Gesetz,'" 99.

29  See Matz, *Adalbert Stifter* (2016), 273–80; and Helmut Bachmaier, "Nachwort," in Adalbert Stifter, *Bunte Steine: Erzählungen* (Stuttgart: Reclam, 1994), 363–91; here 368–69.

"tends to," for such is not always the case in his earlier texts, particularly the more subjective *Journalfassungen*. Nevertheless, from the mid-1840s onward, Stifter increasingly creates an overarching sense of pan-phenomenal order, one in which things gently abide.

## *Ordnung/*Order

Stifter's deployment of things and enforcement of the gentle law presuppose his superstructural notion of order. In other words, much of the above concerning the ubiquitous presence and motivic function of substantive *Dinge* and the adjectival *sanft* is subsumed under the umbrella concept of *Ordnung*. In the end, this regnant concept is but a doctrinaire construct, imposed upon an historically and politically fluctuating reality that Stifter was ill-prepared to accept. I have already pointed out many such inconsistencies and outright ruptures with respect to his personal life versus his remedial literary career. But his ultra-normative notion of *Ordnung* serves as the ultimate corrective to these fracases and failures, including his self-destructive proclivities and summative act of a nearly botched suicide. As is clear from biographical-based scholarship, or for that matter to any discerning readership, a kind of romantic-melancholic-demonic "dark side" lurks beneath the tranquil surface of Stifter's prose and behind the orderly facades of his domestic settings as well as more well-known nature descriptions. Indeed, this stifled force sometimes breaks through in furious fashion, not unlike the irruptive incidents that flare up in many of his tales. In the following, I will offer select examples of such isolated threats to the otherwise dominant sway of order found in his fiction.

In *Der Nachsommer*, Risach carefully cultivates an entire demesne of domestic tidiness and agronomic orderliness. His solution to the problem of insect infestation remains, however, the most elaborate of all his stewardship stratagems. Maximizing the inbuilt checks and balances of ecosystems, specifically the insectivore niche-function of birds, he has perfected a system of feeding and fostering a wide range of ornithological species. Despite such environmentally friendly solutions to ecological imbalances on his property, Risach does not hesitate to employ cruder anthropocentric tactics such as outright killing a particular species—the *Rotschwanz* or redstart—that preys on useful honeybees rather than on the caterpillars that harm his precious rosebushes. These "Rotschwänze" must therefore be dealt with, in Risach's not so gentle words, "ohne Gnade mit der Windbüchse zu tödten" (*HKG* 4,1:170; by killing them without mercy with the air rifle, *IS*, 100; translation slightly modified). This is but one example of anthropogenic violence, perpetrated no less by a character conceived as the very embodiment of the gentle law, that would seem to undercut Stifter's system of order—or at least slip through its flawed cracks.[30] In *Der Hochwald*, the veteran woodsman Gregor, another steward of nature (though not yet, at this early stage of Stifter's writing career, a true embodiment of the gentle law), commits two perplexing acts of destruction. Granted, the first is relatively harmless within the greater ecological scheme of things, but the language in the following scenario is curious and indeed incongruous. Here Gregor explains the unique structure of an aspen leaf only to then ravage the very exemplar that he extols:

> "Sehet nur, liebe Jungfrauen, wie schmal der Fuß ist, womit der Stiel am Holze, und das Blatt am Stiele steht, und wie zäh und drehbar dieser ist—sonst ist es ein sehr schönes Blatt."
>
> Bei diesen letzten Worten hatte er einen Zweig von einer der Espen gerissen und ihn Clarissa hingereicht. (*HKG* 1,4:247)

> ["Now observe, dear maidens, how slender the base is where the leafstalk attaches to the stem and the leaf to the stalk, and how durable and twistable the latter is—overall, what a beautiful leaf."
>
> With these last words he tore off a branch from one of the aspens and handed it to Clarissa.]

Similarly, in a later scene Gregor lashes out against nature after delivering a pantheistic discourse in its very honor. In this case he praises the "Geier" (buzzard) as an integral niche species against its common vilification as an opportunistic scavenger. Despite his homage, he impulsively offers to shoot a specimen circling above them so that his protegées Clarissa and Johanna can better admire its plumage. As it turns out, owing to intricate plot details that are not relevant here, a mysterious and inauspicious stranger ends up killing the bird, but more important is the basic fact that Gregor intends to take the life of a creature that he has just eulogized for its critical ecological function. And, moreover, he almost does so to gratify the trivial wants of humans. His dignified biocentrism thus swiftly cedes to exploitative anthropocentrism, and he becomes tacitly complicit in the decimation of diverse ornithological species that occurred during the mid-nineteenth century in Bohemia.[31]

---

30    For a more detailed discussion of Risach's regulative agronomic regime as both subjectively motivated and objectively destructive, see Begemann, *Die Welt der Zeichen*, 343–49. Also see Lars Rosenbaum's chapter in this volume, which partially relies on Begemann's argument.

31    Compare for instance the following statistics on alleged "harmful bird species" that were shot in the kingdom of Bohemia during the single year of 1857: 69 eagles, 202 owls, over 800 hawks, and more than 17,000 falcons, harriers, and vultures. See Helmuth Schrötter, "Adalbert Stifters ökologische Naturschau im Lichte der Nachhaltigkeit," in *Waldbilder: Beiträge zum interdisziplinären Kolloquium "Da ist Wald und Wald und Wald" (Adalbert Stifter), Göttingen, 19.*

Lest one think that these observations on species depredation are exaggerated or constitute mere narrative lapses, I briefly draw attention to one of the most shocking episodes in Stifter's entire oeuvre. His elaborate chronicle of a lavish hunting festival in *Der beschriebene Tännling* is replete with a chilling ruthlessness if not sadism as he narrates the systematic slaughter of several animal species, including deer, hares, badgers, foxes, martens, even a singular lynx and bear. As Wolfgang Matz has observed with respect to this scene: "Man ist versucht, darin den Ausbruch seiner eigenen latenten Gewaltsamkeit zu sehen, die er sein ganzes Leben über zu zügeln suchte" (One is tempted to see in it the outburst of his own latent brutality, which he sought to control his entire life).[32] On a more general note, Matz points to Stifter's regular bouts with ill health, both physical and mental, which likely put him on an inexorable path of suicidal despair. According to Matz, Stifter's "inner demons"[33] further included moodiness, wrathfulness, destructiveness, and even cruelty. His dogmatic embrace of order and authority must therefore, at least in part, be seen as a creative corrective to his choleric and manic temperament.

These destructive inclinations and quasi-deconstructive interpretations aside, Stifter's texts otherwise bask in serene order, both in terms of natural and cultural constancy. Again, I will cite some examples from his less scholarly scrutinized texts, including once more *Zwei Schwestern*, which, in its detailed depictions of environmentally specific and ecologically sound husbandry practices, resembles a shorter version of *Der Nachsommer* or a longer version of *Brigitta*. But first, a key sequence in *Der Hagestolz* serves as a summary statement of Stifterian order. Here the protagonist, an adolescent named Victor, is urged by his mother to pack up and organize his room before an impending journey to his reclusive uncle, who dwells deep in the Upper Austrian Alps: "gehe nun hinauf in deine Stube, und bringe alles in Ordnung" (*HKG* 1,6:27; go up to your room and put everything in order). After Victor dutifully obliges and arranges all sorts of domestic "Dinge" (see esp. *HKG* 1,6:30), his final day at home is spent further organizing, an activity in which his entire family presumably participates. As Stifter now writes in redundant yet revealing fashion: "man ordnete das schon Geordnete noch einmal" (*HKG* 1,6:40; things that had already been put in order were put in order again).[34] In more accurate terms, this statement is not so much rhetori-

---

*und 20. März 1999*, ed. Walter Hettche and Hubert Merkel (Munich: iudicium, 2000), 68–74; here 72.

32  Matz, *Adalbert Stifter* (1995), 242. The key second clause of this sentence is deleted in the revised edition from 2016.

33  Matz, *Adalbert Stifter* (1995), 11. These quoted words are also deleted in the second revised—and less subjectivized—edition from 2016.

34  For alternative, yet linguistically loose, translations of these citations, see "The Recluse," in Adalbert Stifter, *Limestone and Other Stories*, trans. David Luke

cally redundant as it is situationally tautological, for what is the point of rearranging what has just been arranged? This is but fastidiousness for fastidiousness's sake. In *Zwei Schwestern*, the maintenance of both household and agrarian order similarly remains a constant concern—indeed, incessant obsession—and the recurring words *Ordnung*, *ordnen*, and even *ordnungsgemäß* serve as verbal variations on the same basic rehashed theme: things must gently and orderly reside in their proper place. At one point in the text, all three of these critical Stifterian ingredients appear in a condensed, unified scene. The narrator, like his nameless counterpart in *Brigitta* and (the practically unnamed) Heinrich Drendorf in *Der Nachsommer*, is paying an extended visit to a landed estate, here in the northern Italian highlands rather than in the Hungarian grasslands or Upper Austrian lowlands. Worried about the whereabouts of his "Dinge" (read: belongings) after the furniture in one of his rooms has been rearranged, he is assured by the gardener that everything is "in Ordnung," whereupon he relievedly reclines among the "sanft[e]" cushions of his guestroom sofa (see *HKG* 1,6:301). This neatly narrated scenario perfectly sums up Stifter's unbending insistence on the gentle order of things.

## An Overview of this Volume

This volume is arranged according to three structural-perspectival principles, which intend to shed variegated light on Stifter's robust body of work. The first section serves as both a generic and stylistic survey of his oeuvre, showcasing his often-underestimated narrative breadth and depth, including his forays into nonfictional modes of authorship. The second section, in contrast, focuses on specific texts within broader thematic contexts, offering a more prismatic approach to reading and interpreting Stifter. The conceptual reasoning here is to allow a given work, whether an individual tale (*Erzählung*) of varying scales or a cohesive collection of interrelated stories such as *Bunte Steine*, to illumine tendencies and constancies in Stifter's fiction. The third and final section is ecocritical in emphasis, which, given the predominantly natural settings of his texts and his penchant for copious nature descriptions, has become a logical trend in Stifter scholarship. Such eco-ekphrasis occurs not only with respect to forests but also includes mountainous environments, more specifically the geological structures and glaciological features of the Upper Austrian Alps. In the end, this tripartite organization is not meant to be "overly orderly" in a hardcore Stifterian sense (as for instance adumbrated above) but rather strives for some semblance of heuristic symmetry in rendering justice to Stifter's prolific literary production over the course of a quarter century. Between these two authorial bookends, a wealth of

(New York: Harcourt, Brace & World, 1968), 149–276; here 165, 177.

narrative and discursive material lies ripe for scholarly interpretation and general readerly consumption, as this companion aims to demonstrate. Each of the three schematic sections outlined above is broken down into four chapters, which I summarize in the following.

In the opening chapter, "Stifter's Epic Style," Tove Holmes examines the ways in which Stifter's descriptive and repetitive prose—especially as evidenced in the near plotless *Der Nachsommer*—and his highly, if not purely, phenomena-based landscape paintings create an overwhelming sense of depth and space at the expense of character development and visual foreground. In the process, she argues that Stifter's unique "epic" literary style relativizes the importance of the human actors and establishes a different kind of narrative, one in which the natural world and the interrelations between things (see above: *Dinge*) become more salient. In the specific case of the—near nameless—Heinrich Drendorf, his maturation process is enframed by the greater environment within which he interacts. As a result, Stifter transforms—if not undermines—the genre expectations of the *Bildungsroman*, which, in his hands, presents more a panoptic textual landscape than it does a linear teleological trajectory.

In "Stifter and the Genre Conventions of Cultural Journalism," Sean Franzel grapples with the literary-historical and reception-theoretical tension between periodical serialization and the emerging standard of single-author book-format publication. Whereas the former genre is inherently occasional and inevitably ephemeral, the latter promotes textual intransience and the classicized conceit of aesthetic completion. Stifter of course embraced both worlds, as most of his stories first appeared in popular cultural journals and were then transformed into more "enduring" and "consummate" works, whether in the six-volume *Studien* or two-volume *Bunte Steine* collections. In the end, Stifter can be read—somewhat against the grain of traditional scholarship, which tends to focus on aspects of spatialization and detemporalization in his texts—as an "emphatic writer of time" insofar as he problematizes notions of transience and permanence in certain writings, including select essays that he contributed to *Wien und die Wiener* and miscellanea that appeared in the posthumously published *Vermischte Schriften* (Miscellaneous Writings, 1870).

As mentioned earlier, Stifter lived longer in Vienna than in either Bohemia or Linz. Vance Byrd's chapter, "All Eyes on the Streets: Transformations of Public Work, Leisure, and Ritual in *Wien und die Wiener*," details the extent to which Stifter became invested in seemingly all aspects and levels of Viennese life and culture. The voluminous collection of essays, sketches, dialect poetry, and local-color dialogues that comprise this multi-author, multi-perspectival, and ultimately multimedial project, whose full title reads *Wien und die Wiener in Bildern aus dem Leben* (Vienna and the Viennese in Sketches from Life), attests to Stifter's oft-overlooked collaborative skills and—not surprisingly given his provincial background—ambivalent cosmopolitan existence. Though he remained a staunch moralist with respect to what he, deep down, perceived as urban ills, this unique opus that he co-created depicts a precursive panoply of modern sociohistorical developments ranging from urbanization to industrialization to secularization. As Byrd's rich analysis shows, Stifter may well have felt out of his element while residing in the largest German-speaking city that existed at the time, but it was not for lack of trying—specifically, trying to do narrative justice to the infinite facets of a national metropolis and its myriad inhabitants.

While *Wien und die Wiener* constitutes a unique work within the Stifterian canon in terms of both genre and style, his late fiction from the 1860s has been viewed as downright bizarre, indeed aberrant. It both vexed his contemporary readers and has long since perplexed scholars. In the concluding chapter of this section, "Stifter's Late Style," Samuel Frederick scrutinizes this peculiar plain prose and analyzes its naked narrative logic. In an oddly anachronistic sense, tales such as *Der Kuß von Sentze* (The Kiss of Sentze, 1866), *Der fromme Spruch* (The Pious Saying, 1869), and *Witiko* revel in a kind of neutral or zero-degree writing nearly a century before Barthes, Beckett, and the postwar "antinovel" movement of the *nouveau roman*. As Frederick maintains, these late texts by Stifter are anemic in terms of narrative necessity and plot-driven momentum; indeed, they often devolve into empty tautologies and manneristic superficialities. Yet herein lies the deeper and perhaps unresolvable tension in this final phase of his work: Stifter strives to find some measure of certitude in the continuity of history but rejects the contingency that it ultimately reveals.

In "The Birth of Realism out of the Spirit of Melodrama: Stifter's *Feldblumen*," Erica Weitzman follows up on the trajectory of the previous section yet applies categories of genre and style to a specific text, offering a wealth of literary-historical context in the process. As Weitzman argues, despite Stifter's reputation for producing works associated with boredom, precision, and stasis rather than with the heightened affects and grand gestures of melodrama, his early epistolary novella *Feldblumen* contains stock elements taken straight out of the melodramatic playbook. Weitzman examines, in detail, how Stifter borrows from this generic repertoire yet refashions it to fit his own burgeoning artistic-realistic agenda. *Feldblumen* is thus not merely a realistic melodrama (or melodrama shifting into a realist mode) but a melodrama *of* realism, in which potentially fatal errors of perception are ultimately resolved and the requisite "virtue-vindicated" plot becomes no less than the virtue of adequate representation itself.

*Die Mappe meines Urgroßvaters* remains Stifter's most enduring work, at least insofar as it preoccupied him both at the beginning and again toward the end of his writing career. Its first iteration appeared serially in

1841–42 while its third and fourth lingered in an unfinished state during the mid-1860s. In between these separate stages, the *Studien* version from 1847 stands as one of Stifter's most magisterial works. As Jessica C. Resvick contends in her chapter, "Backward Glances: Registers of the Past in Stifter's *Die Mappe meines Urgroßvaters*," the multi-phase *Mappe* project serves as a monument to Stifter's poetics. Its heightened degree of retrospectivity and self-reflexivity—as evinced in the processes of reminiscing, writing, and editing that inform both the structure and storyline of the text itself—allows for a more recuperative engagement with the past and its inexorable ephemerality. Here, through the multiple and indeed multi-perspectival narratives collected within the portfolio-like *Mappe*, the past can better be registered and reflected upon, albeit never fully arrested. As the Obrist gazes back into his personal past, striving to keep his wife alive at least in memory, he reenacts Orpheus's original "backward glance" in the underworld but of course cannot retroactively arrest her fatal fall. He can, however, retrospectively come to terms with it and thereby regain some modicum of *Sanftmut* or placidity.

In "Lessons from Stifter's *Bunte Steine*," Zachary Sng expands the textual focus to include several different stories (plus the preface) from this 1853 assemblage of motley metaphorical stones. More broadly, Sng contextualizes these within Stifter's longstanding interest in pedagogy, an interest that gradually became a professional calling as he evolved from an oft-disgruntled private tutor in Vienna to an engaged school inspector in Upper Austria. All the while, however, he remained committed to education, publishing essays on pedagogical reform and even coediting a voluminous middle-school primer containing some two hundred humanistic texts (mainly in the form of excerpts) from antiquity to the contemporary age. Analogously, *Bunte Steine*, whose stories feature children either as main characters or as motivating forces behind the action, conveys its own pedagogical program, one that involves instructive attention with respect to small or insignificant things and their place within the operations of the gentle law. But what exactly does *Bunte Steine* have to teach us? Sng's pursuit of this question leads to a nuanced reading of the sundry texts and their rich pedagogical contexts.

Lars Rosenbaum's chapter "Absence and Omnipresence: On the Significance of Waste in Stifter's *Der Nachsommer*" affords revealing glimpses into the diverse forms of detritus that remain hidden within the narrative of the novel but, paradoxically, play an integral role in its serenely narrated world. In other words, though grime and refuse of all kinds (for example, dirty laundry, domestic clutter, garden and kitchen waste, workshop wood shavings, and attic junk) are constantly being cleaned up or otherwise removed from sight, the operative orderliness of the Rosenhaus is predicated precisely on such remnants and scraps, most of which are reused or repurposed in a variety of ways. Unlike modern

*Wegwerfgesellschaften* (throwaway societies), Risach's estate functions as a *Wiederverwertungswirtschaft* (recycling economy), for it maximizes on-site renewable resources and thereby engages in sustainable economic-ecological practices. Rosenbaum's chapter thus perfectly pivots to the next section of the volume, which examines elemental and environmental facets of Stifter's work, ranging from rocks and minerals to snow and ice, from material and aesthetic atmospheres to physical and cultural bioregions.

The lapidary title of Jason Groves's chapter, "Stifter's Stones," is general enough to accomplish several important tasks in view of the pervasive geological and petrological discourse found in stories by Stifter. Beyond obvious examples such as *Bunte Steine* (especially the first two tales *Granit* and *Kalkstein*) and *Der Nachsommer*, the novella *Abdias* (1843/1847) narrates an array of erosional forces and anthropogenic debris that symbolically underscore the deformative *dis*array imperiling the sociopolitical order of mid-century Austria, at least as perceived by Stifter and his culturally conservative (gentile) kin. *Abdias*, in other words, reflects the intense public debate surrounding Jewish emancipation and assimilation, and it does so through a rich yet furtive motivic deployment of tropes involving stoniness and sandiness as well as dinginess and shabbiness. As Groves pointedly suggests, Stifter's *gentle* law does not seem to apply to the Jewish community and might therefore, at least here in this outlying tale of abrasion, better be characterized as a *gentile* law to better mark its cultural specificity.

Stifter's interest in glaciology paralleled yet paled in comparison to his fascination with geology. In the end, this discrepancy is only natural given that the former was still a fresh field of inquiry whereas the latter was fast becoming an established science. The Austrian geographer Friedrich Simony was a key figure in the emerging exploration of glaciers, both in terms of scientific theory and alpine practice. Indeed, he and Stifter became close friends (*Duzfreunde*), even though they only met a couple of times in person. (Their common Bohemian heritage and unbridled nature enthusiasm surely played a role in this instant affinity.) As Matthew H. Birkhold demonstrates in his chapter, "Stifter's Glaciers," their intellectual bond concerning all things geological and glaciological became textually cemented in *Bergkristall* and *Der Nachsommer*. And even though Stifter never once set foot on a glacier, in fact only managed to view them from afar (read: from below tree line), he nevertheless embraced the mimetic challenge of narrating them with immediacy, borrowing from and expanding on Simony's accounts of his glacial excursions in the Austrian Alps.

Stifter, however, not only narrates stones and glaciers; he also invokes elemental atmospheres in a host of fictional and nonfictional texts. In his chapter, "Cheerful Terror: Stifter and the Aesthetics of Atmosphere,"

Alexander Robert Phillips probes the reciprocal relation between the scientific consciousness and aesthetic experience of varied atmospheric conditions, including extreme weather events (*Die Mappe, Kalkstein, Kazensilber*) tropospheric aeronautics (*Der Condor*), and cosmic phenomena such as solar eclipses ("Die Sonnenfinsternis am 8. Juli 1842" [The Eclipse of the Sun in 1842]). As Phillips argues and already insinuates in the main title of his chapter, atmosphere for Stifter signifies not only stability and order but is also a thing of terror. A "bright" or "cheerful" (both adjectives are conveyed by the German word *heiter*) day can rapidly take a meteorologically terrible if not humanly terrifying turn. In the end, Stifter's scientifically informed atmospheric aesthetics bring together art, ethics, and their correlation to non-human systems in ways that critically reflect important shifts in eco-aesthetic discourse during the nineteenth century.

In the final chapter of this eco-oriented section, "Stifter's Bavarian-Bohemian Bioregionalism," I make a case for Stifter as a bioregional writer. In alternative terms, I examine his profound place-based writing through the lens of North American bioregional theory and aesthetics. My chapter culminates in a close reading of *Der beschriebene Tännling*, whereby I probe its potential as a paradigmatic example of literary bioregionalism. Given its acute narrative prioritization of place over people, its thematic representation of environmental fragility and recovery, and its descriptive absorption in the biota of the Bohemian Forest, this underexamined story by Stifter may well be his masterpiece in terms of delivering a "bioregional poetics"—long before such environmental-literary categories were even on the horizon of terminological possibility.

# Part I

# Genre and Style

# 1: Stifter's Epic Style

*Tove Holmes*

ADALBERT STIFTER'S monumental novel *Der Nachsommer* (Indian Summer, 1857), which spans three volumes in the critical edition, bears the subtitle "Eine Erzählung"—a story. While this diminutive genre designation can be understood as a vestige from a drawn-out process of composition, it leaves open the question of genre and draws attention to the form of the text. In response to criticism the novel received, Stifter moreover claimed that readers had the wrong genre expectations, commenting in a letter to his publisher Gustav Heckenast that whoever "eine Heiratsgeschichte liest und hiebei rückwärts eine veraltete Liebesgeschichte erfärt, der weiß sich mit dem Buche ganz und gar nicht zu helfen" ([whoever] reads a wedding tale and, in so doing, retroactively experiences an old love story, is missing the entire point of the book).[1] This begs the question: What comes to the fore if the marriage plot fades into the background, and how might the formal qualities of the text itself draw readerly attention to what is really at stake? Based on an examination of the stylistic decisions and genre characteristics of *Der Nachsommer*, and with a consideration of Stifter's landscape painting, I will examine the ways in which both artistic media use formal techniques of creating depth and space rather than guiding the focus toward the protagonists and foreground. In the process, I argue that Stifter's novelistic style relativizes the importance of the human actors, disrupting expectations of the figure-ground relationship and creating a new kind of narrative in which the surrounding environment and the connections between things come more clearly into view.

Stifter composed *Der Nachsommer* over the course of nearly ten years, during which time a novella with the title *Der alte Hofmeister* grew into the burgeoning novel that is typically considered a prime nineteenth-century representative of the *Bildungsroman* genre. In letters to his publisher regarding revisions he undertook during this lengthy writing

---

1    Letter to Heckenast from November 2, 1858, in *HKG* 4,4:166. Translations are my own unless otherwise noted. For an overview of Stifter's contemporary reception, see: Moriz Enzinger, ed., *Adalbert Stifter im Urteil seiner Zeit* (Vienna: Böhlau, 1968).

process, Stifter repeatedly expresses the intention to cleanse his text, to create the "Einfachheit der Antike" (simplicity of antiquity).[2] Similarly, in his Preface to *Bunte Steine* he characterizes the literature he aspires to create as "epic": "Wenn wir die Menschheit in der Geschichte wie einen ruhigen Silberstrom einem großen ewigen Ziele entgegen gehen sehen, so empfinden wir das Erhabene, das vorzugsweise Epische" (*HKG* 2,2:15; When we see mankind move through history like a serene silver river toward a great eternal goal, we sense the Sublime and particularly the Epic, *MS*, 7). Critics have correspondingly characterized his writing as "ontological" or frozen for all time;[3] or as an enactment of the moral law.[4] In line with critical expectations surrounding the *Bildungsroman*, stylistic decisions undertaken in Stifter's revision process are understood as being in the interest of "Mässigung und Reinigung des Ichs" (moderation and purification of the subject).[5] Readers recognize a moral implication to the protagonist's mastery of his emotional life, and at the same time, an "epic objectivity" is thought to emerge from consciousness.[6] The priority of objectivity over subjectivity aligns with novel theory of the time, and Stifter's efforts to achieve objectivity have been variously located in his attempts at abstraction of particulars in order to achieve a "sensible whole" (*sinnvolles Ganzes*).[7] It has also been associated with the "Unbestimmtheit" or vagueness that comes about as a function of the first-person narrator, which, according to Margret Walter-Schneider, constitutes the "Quelle des Eindrucks von Großartigkeit" (source of the impression of grandeur).[8] Christian Begemann describes the style of the

2    Letter to Heckenast from March 22, 1857, in *PRA* 19:15.

3    Joseph Peter Stern, "Adalbert Stifters ontologischer Stil," in *Adalbert Stifter: Studien und Interpretation, Gedenkschrift zum 100. Todestage*, ed. Lothar Stiehm (Heidelberg: Lothar Stiehm Verlag, 1968), 103–20.

4    Martin and Erika Swales, *Adalbert Stifter: A Critical Study* (London: Cambridge University Press, 1984), 157.

5    Davide Giuriato, "Manier und Stil," in *Stifter-Handbuch: Leben—Werk—Wirkung*, ed. Christian Begemann and Davide Giuriato (Stuttgart: J. B. Metzler, 2017), 217–21; here 218.

6    For a more in-depth overview of the older secondary discussion surrounding Stifter's style and the ways it has been understood as "epic," see Paul Böckmann, "Die epische Objektivität in Stifters Erzählung *Die Mappe meines Urgroßvaters*," in *Stoffe, Formen, Strukturen: Studien zur deutschen Literatur: Hans Heinrich Borcherdt zum 75. Geburtstag*, ed. Albert Fuchs and Helmut Motekat (Munich: Max Hueber Verlag, 1962), 396–423; here 399. Regarding the tension between subjectivity and objectivity of the epic in Stifter, in which "the subjectivism refuses to be banished" despite "an explicit, almost didactic will toward [its] transcendence," see Swales and Swales, *Adalbert Stifter*, 25.

7    Giuriato, "Manier und Stil," 219.

8    Margret Walter-Schneider "Das Unzulängliche ist das Angemessene: Über die Erzählerfigur in Stifters *Nachsommer*," *Jahrbuch der Deutschen Schillergesellschaft* 34 (1990): 317–42; here 335.

late novels as a "textuelle[s] Verfahren der Auslöschung des subjektiv Besonderen" (textual process of erasing the subjectively particular)[9] and, in his view, especially forms of repetition in *Der Nachsommer* lend objective truth value to subjective statements.[10] The revisions also show an effort to eliminate jumps in time as well as the awareness of the temporal distance between the narrated events and the narrative presence.[11] More generally regarding stylistic developments of his late period, which began during the composition of the *Nachsommer,* deconstruction-oriented critical literature has tended to emphasize how Stifter's style brings the text itself to the fore: language tries to get beyond the medium to objects themselves but ends up putting the medium on display, attenuating its claim to realism.[12] Here I will take a different angle by examining the ways in which the novel's thematic focus on mediating conditions are reflected in formal techniques of rendering certain things visible while blending out the foreground. While deemphasizing the foreground, or the figure in a figure-ground relationship, would appear to subvert the genre designation of the *Bildungsroman* since it draws some attention away from human actors, it can perhaps be understood as a reorientation of the priority of *Bildung* to include more than the singular human trajectory.[13]

In his classic study *Die Theorie des Romans* (The Theory of the Novel, 1916), Georg Lukács characterizes the epic as giving the extensive totality of life, which is embodied in the hero. Its modern descendent, the

9 Christian Begemann, *Die Welt der Zeichen: Stifter-Lektüren* (Stuttgart: J. B. Metzler, 1995), 327.

10 For an overview of the critical discussion about the effects of repetition in Stifter's style, see Cornelia Zumbusch, "Der Nachsommer," in *Stifter-Handbuch*, 98–108; here 104.

11 Walter Hettche, "Die Dokumentation der Handschriften zu Stifters *Nachsommer* und ihr textanalytisches Potential," in *Stifter und Stifterforschung im 21. Jahrhundert: Biographie—Wissenschaft—Poetik*, ed. Johann Lachinger and Hartmut Laufhütte (Tübingen: Max Niemeyer Verlag, 2007), 235–59. Stifter rejected the subtitle suggested by his publisher, "Eine Erzählung aus unseren Zeiten" (A Narrative of our Time), due to the temporal specificity that detracted from its sense of epic permanence.

12 Begemann, *Die Welt der Zeichen*, 204, 225, and passim; Albrecht Koschorke, "Das buchstabierte Panorama: Zu einer Passage in Stifters Erzählung 'Granit,'" *VASILO* 38, nos. 1/2 (1989): 3–13; Joseph Vogl, "Der Text als Schleier: Zu Stifters *Der Nachsommer,*" *Jahrbuch der Deutschen Schillergesellschaft* 37 (1993): 298–312.

13 Elsewhere I have argued for the educational project of the *Nachsommer* to be constituted in a sustained visual schooling, and that most of what we learn about the protagonist comes indirectly, via his increasing visual sensitivity. See: Tove Holmes, "'...was ich in diesem Hause geworden bin': Stifter's Visual Curriculum," *Zeitschrift für deutsche Philologie* 129, no. 4 (2010): 559–78.

novel, must create its own totality since this is no longer directly given.[14] According to Mikhail Bakhtin, the epic concerns itself with an absolute and valorized past at an unbreachable distance to the present—even from the standpoint of the epic narrator—and with a collective tradition rather than the individual personal experience, which becomes the object of the novel.[15] The novel, and especially the *Bildungsroman* since its inception with Goethe's *Wilhelm Meisters Lehrjahre* (Wilhelm Meister's Apprenticeship, 1795–96), has been understood as having an anthropological focus.[16] It is a genre that embodies Aristotle's mimetic priority of people in action.[17] However, there have been important attempts at reconceptualizing the possibility of long-form narratives such as the epic and novel to accommodate more-than-human perspectives on time and space. In *Modern Epic*, Franco Moretti suggests that a different style is required, a weaker grammar than human consciousness is necessary to accommodate both the individual and the encyclopedic aspects of the long narrative form. For Moretti, identity construction is not historical or temporal, but geographical, and in the novel's quest to restore lost transcendence digression becomes its primary mode and the main purpose of epic action.[18] In her classic study *Darwin's Plots*, Gillian Beer examines how the shifting scientific paradigm challenged nineteenth-century narratives to incorporate larger time structures and resist tidy narrative teleology.[19] Wei Chee Dimock, for her part, argues for the value of epic for what she calls its cellular nature, a modular structure which can combine repeated small formulaic elements to create ever new thematic clusters and accommodate vast spans of time.[20] Current trends in ecocriticism, which itself arose as a pushback against deconstruction, examine how

---

14   Georg Lukács, *Die Theorie des Romans: Ein geschichtsphilosophischer Versuch über die Formen der großen Epik* (Munich: Deutscher Taschenbuch Verlag), 1994.

15   Mikhail Bakhtin, *The Dialogic Imagination,* ed. Michael Holquist, trans. Caryl Emerson and Michael Holquist (Austin: University of Texas Press, 1990), 13.

16   Arne Höcker, Franziska Schweiger, and Lauren Shizuko Stone, "Material Worlds—Novelistic Matters of the Nineteenth Century," *Colloquia Germanica* 47, no. 3 (2014): 183–87; here 183.

17   Aristotle, *Poetics*, trans. James Hutton (New York and London: W. W. Norton, 1982), 50.

18   Franco Moretti, *Modern Epic: The World System from Goethe to García Márquez,* trans. Quintin Hoare (New York: Verso, 1996), esp. 1–7.

19   Gillian Beer, *Darwin's Plots: Evolutionary Narrative in Darwin, George Eliot, and Nineteenth-Century Fiction,* (London: ARK Paperbacks, 1983).

20   Wai Chee Dimock, "Low Epic," *Critical Inquiry* 39, no. 3 (2013): 614–31; see also Tobias Boes, "Reading the Book of the World: Epic Representation in the Age of Our Geophysical Agency," *Novel: A Forum on Fiction* 49, no. 1 (2016): 95–114; here 107.

genre prefigures the binary of centrism versus relationality. Regarding the epic, Ursula Heise for instance writes:

> Epic … in which the fate of the entire known world is usually at stake, has made a comeback as a way of establishing a planetary scope in storytelling, though only in combination with sometimes radically modernist narrative strategies. … In their search for modes of representation that might accommodate ecological dynamisms, disequilibria, and disjunctions along with ecosystems' imbrications in heterogeneous human cultures and politics, combine allegory with modernist and postmodernist experimental modes that resist any direct summing up of parts into wholes or any simple foregrounding of connectedness at the expense of disjunction and heterogeneity.[21]

These reconceptualizations of the epic mode do not assume that the "extensive totality" of life can be accommodated under a singular narrative arc or within the scale of human time and thus seek formal strategies that extend beyond these.

One notorious characteristic of Stifter's style often disparaged by critics is his abundant use of description, a tendency which comes into its own in *Der Nachsommer* and other late works. In a scathing review, Stifter's contemporary Friedrich Hebbel recalls Lessing's prescribed economy of descriptive detail in his 1766 treatise *Laokoon*: "Anfangs schüchtern und durch die Erinnerung an Lessings Laokoon in der behäbigen Entfaltung seiner aufs Breite und Breiteste Beschreibungsnatur vielleicht noch ein wenig gestört, machte er [Stifter] bald die Erfahrung, daß dieser einst so gefärliche Laokoon in unseren Tagen niemand mehr schadet" (At first shy and perhaps a bit disturbed by the recollection of Lessing's Laocoon in the stately development of his exhaustive and wide-ranging descriptive nature, he soon learned that this once so dangerous Laocoon no longer harms anyone these days).[22] Elsewhere Hebbel complains of Stifter's "ausartende[r] Genre" (degenerating genre), and of an "Aufdröseln der Form" (unraveling of form) and a "Zerbröckeln und Zerkrümeln der Materie" (splintering and crumbling of matter).[23] These claims of formlessness, splintering, and lack of coherence are reminiscent of the more general critiques of the descriptive mode extending back to *Laokoon* and earlier. Hebbel's use of the term "genre" implies misplaced priority of

---

21  Ursula Heise, *Sense of Place, Sense of Planet: The Environmental Imagination of the Global* (New York: Oxford University Press, 2008), 64.

22  Friedrich Hebbel, "Der Nachsommer" in *Werke*, vol. 3, ed. Gerhard Fricke, Werner Keller, and Karl Pörnbacher (Munich: Hanser, 1965), 682–83; here 682.

23  Friedrich Hebbel, "Das Komma im Frack," in *Werke*, vol. 3, 684–87; here 687.

small, static, and relatively meaningless vignettes rather than the actions of the protagonist, which constitute the overall mythos or plot.[24] As a result, the supposedly unimportant or marginal begins to grow and blossom: "Da fängt das 'Nebenbei' überall an zu florieren" (At this point the incidental starts to flourish everywhere).[25] Lukács singles out this missing hierarchy of importance in descriptive literature as being particularly egregious: "das Erzählen gliedert, die Beschreibung nivelliert" (narration structures, description flattens).[26] And while our focus is diverted away from the actions of the characters, they themselves become increasingly passive, spectators like us to the images being described. Regarding a scene in Flaubert's *Madame Bovary*, Lukács writes:

> Die Gestalten sind ... hier ausschließlich Zuschauer. Damit werden sie für den Leser gleichartige und gleichwertige Bestandteile der nur vom Standpunkt der Milieuschilderung wichtigen Geschehnisse, die Flaubert beschreibt. Sie werden Farbenflecke in einem Bild. Und das Bild geht über das bloß Zuständliche, über das Genrehafte nur insofern hinaus, als es zum ironischen Symbol der Philisterhaftigkeit überhaupt erhöht wird. Das Bild erlangt eine Bedeutung, die nicht aus dem inneren menschlichen Gewicht der erzählten Ereignisse folgt, ja die zu diesen fast überhaupt keine Beziehung hat, sondern durch Mittel der formalen Stilisierung künstlich erzeugt wird.[27]

> [The characters ... are nothing but observers of this setting. To the reader they seem undifferentiated, additional elements of the environment Flaubert is describing. They become dabs of colour in a painting which rises above a lifeless level only insofar as it is elevated to an ironic symbol of philistinism. The painting assumes an importance which does not arise out of the subjective importance of the events, to which it is scarcely related, but from the artifice in the formal stylization.][28]

As descriptions gain autonomy from the human struggles of the protagonists and the temporal arc of narrative and plot, the protagonists have less agency than the scenes they are placed in. The setting itself becomes

---

24   Cf. Aristotle, *Poetics*, 50.

25   Hebbel, "Das Komma im Frack," 685.

26   Georg Lukács, "Erzählen oder Beschreiben?" in *Begriffsbestimmung des literarischen Realismus*, ed. Richard Brinkmann (Darmstadt: Wissenschaftliche Buchgesellschaft, 1969), 33–85; here 53. Translated as Georg Lukács, "Narrate or Describe?," in *Writer and Critic, and Other Essays*, trans. and ed. Arthur Kahn (New York: Grosset and Dunlap, 1971), 110–48; here 127. Translation altered.

27   Lukács, "Erzählen oder Beschreiben?" 39.

28   Lukács, "Narrate or Describe?" 115.

animated, imbued with importance not through the events themselves but through formal and stylistic qualities of the text, as foreground and background are reversed. As Hegel asserts in this vein, in order for the individual to maintain significance after the age of heroes, the actors must become spectators, near-lifeless onlookers to the unfolding scene.[29] Description has been traditionally associated with visuality, not least by Lessing, who aligned it with painting and other "arts of space."[30] In this sense, the text takes on qualities of a landscape scene, and Hebbel's accused "genre" can be understood as painted scenes of "das Nebenbei," the marginal or otherwise unremarkable which becomes newly important or visible in the first place due to these stylistic choices. Given his priority of class struggle, it is understandable that Lukács would object to the formal blending-out of human actors. However, I suggest that an environmental-visual poetics can be derived precisely through this stylistic change of focus.

*Der Nachsommer* is narrated in the first person by a protagonist who, we learn after about eight hundred pages, is named Heinrich Drendorf.[31] We never get a description of him and only learn about his character and development obliquely based on what he sees and describes. The novel's plot consists of his oscillations between three different domiciles as well as some mountain abodes where he explores geological and glaciological formations or *Gebilde*. His more formalized and nearly two-year-long *Bildungsreise* or educational journey, when it finally occurs toward the very end of the novel, is comical in its breathless brevity, a scant paragraph compared to the hundreds of pages that precede it.[32] According to Samuel Frederick, Stifter narrates spatial coordinates rather than temporal sequences, moving toward a "post-narrative" literary form in which digressions erode smooth narrative arcs.[33] Building on this observation,

29   See Moretti, *Modern Epic*, 11–16.

30   Gotthold Ephraim Lessing, "Laokoon oder über die Grenzen der Malerei und Poesie," in *Werke und Briefe, Werke 1766–1769*, ed. Wilfried Barner, Klaus Bohnen, Gunter E. Grimm, et al., vol. 5/2 (Frankfurt am Main: Deutscher Klassiker Verlag, 1990), 116–23.

31   The name Heinrich Drendorf appears on *HKG* 4,3:243, that is, 820 pages into the 859 total over the three volumes.

32   As Sean Ireton notes, the upshot of this seemingly superficial journey is that the protagonist returns with a tan: "alles ... fand mich sehr gebräunt" (*HKG* 4,3:256; everyone ... found me quite tanned," *IS*, 463). See Sean Ireton, "Geology, Mountaineering, and Self-Formation in Adalbert Stifter's Der Nachsommer," in *Heights of Reflection: Mountains in the German Imagination from the Middle Ages to the Twenty-First Century*, ed. Sean Ireton and Caroline Schaumann (Rochester, NY: Camden House, 2012), 193–209; here 204.

33   Samuel Frederick, *Narratives Unsettled: Digression in Robert Walser, Thomas Bernhard, and Adalbert Stifter* (Evanston, IL: Northwestern University

Tobias Boes sees in Stifter's descriptions of Heinrich's repeated wanderings to the same places in accordance with the changing seasons the establishment of spatial density, of the irreducible specificity of these particular environments.[34] From the standpoint of novelistic style, I would add that Heinrich's habitual activities and repeated observations are not only apparent over the course of the novel but are built into its various formulations themselves. For instance: "Als ich einmal das offene Land kennen gelernt, und Fichten und Tannen auf den Bergen stehen gesehen hatte, thaten mir jederzeit die Bretter leid, aus denen etwas in unserem Hause verfertigt wurde, weil sie einmal solche Fichten und Tannen gewesen waren" (*HKG* 4,1:29; When I got to know the open countryside and had seen proud stands of spruce and fir on the mountains, I was sorry about the boards from which things were being made in our house, since at one time they too had been such spruce and firs, *IS*, 20–21, translation altered). The temporal specificity of "einmal," the visual impression of spruce and fir trees once gained, is eclipsed in importance by the central clause containing the repeated experience with woodwork in Heinrich's childhood home. The repetition of "einmal" toward the end of the sentence also serves to undermine the association of this word with a singular incidence, as it here refers to a general state in the past. As Cornelia Zumbusch observes, these kinds of stylistic priorities that place activities within a temporal and spatial frame rather than focus on singular narrative actions came about in the process of Stifter's revisions. She compares a line from *Der alte Hofmeister* with its equivalent in the so-called "Linzer Handschrift," an early draft of *Der Nachsommer* composed in Stifter's own late-summerly Upper Austrian domicile. *Der alte Hofmeister* leads much more directly toward an object of narrative: "Ich kam einmal auf einer meiner vielen Gebirgswanderungen zu einem kleinen schneeweissen Männchen" (Once, on one of my many mountain hikes, I came across a little snow-white man).[35] Even though there is mention of temporal cyclicality (upon one of my many mountain hikes), our attention is drawn to the singularity of this particular instance and focuses on the activity of the characters rather than on their surroundings. The sentence also contains a narrative direction or suspense, which is eliminated in the revisions. In the later version we read: "Ich hatte es mir seit einer Reihe von Jahren zu einer lieben Gewohnheit gemacht, in der schönen Jahreszeit die Gebirge unseres freundlichen Oberlandes zu besuchen" (For a number of years I had made it a fond habit of visiting the mountains of our

---

Press, 2012), 143 and passim.

34   Boes, "Reading the Book of the World," 111–12.
35   *HKG* 4,5:9; Zumbusch, "Der Nachsommer," 99.

friendly highland during the fine season).[36] The subject, verb, and object of this sentence are separated by interjections that establish seasonal rhythms and weather patterns. The temporal and spatial context in which the human subject exists are the main event and focus of the sentence. Even the change of title between the two works (*Der alte Hofmeister* versus *Der Nachsommer*) reflects a fundamental shift from human actors to meteorological conditions.[37]

Along with establishing surrounding context and eliminating narrative suspense through repetition, ritualized actions, and cyclical patterns, the style of *Der Nachsommer* remains as literal and concrete as possible by dispensing with metaphors or figures of speech. Instead, two literal objects are often put into relation with each other, such as the "Gegensatz[ ] des Wassers und der Berge" (*HKG* 4,2:28; contrast of water and mountains, *IS*, 190), in an evident effort to establish relationships and connections rather than perceive things in isolation. The priority of relationality and juxtaposition in form and theme can be seen in the following passage, which seeks to understand the formation of the earth's crust by way of an analogy to frost designs on windowpanes:

> Wenn das Wasser in unendlich kleinen Tröpfchen, die kaum durch ein Vergrößerungsglas ersichtlich sind, aus dem Dunste der Luft sich auf die Tafeln unserer Fenster absetzt, und die Kälte dazu kömmt, die nöthig ist, so entsteht die Decke von Fäden Sternen Wedeln Palmen und Blumen, die wir gefrorene Fenster heißen. Alle diese Dinge stellen sich zu einem Ganzen zusammen, und die Strahlen die Thäler die Rücken die Knoten des Eises sind durch ein Vergrößerungsglas angesehen bewunderungswürdig. Eben so stellt sich von sehr hohen Bergen aus gesehen die niedriger liegende Gestaltung der Erde dar. Sie muß aus einem erstarrenden Stoffe entstanden sein, und streckt ihre Fächer und Palmen in großartigem Maßstabe aus. Der Berg selber, auf dem ich stehe, ist der weiße helle und sehr glänzende Punkt, den wir in der Mitte der zarten Gewebe unserer gefrorenen Fenster sehen. Die Palmenränder der gefrorenen Fenstertafeln werden durch Abbröcklung wegen des Luftzuges oder durch Schmelzung wegen der Wärme lückenhaft und unterbrochen. An den Gebirgszügen geschehen Zerstörungen durch Verwitterung in Folge des Einflusses des Wassers der Luft der Wärme und der Kälte. Nur braucht die Zerstörung der Eisnadeln an den Fenstern kürzere Zeit als der Nadeln der Gebirge. (*HKG* 4,1:43)

---

36  *HKG* 4,5:20. Striking here as well is the affective register (e.g., "lieb[e] Gewohnheit," "freundliches Oberland") underlining that the surrounding context and habitual actions are not separate from emerging subjectivity.

37  Cf. Boes, "Reading the Book of the World," 111.

[When moisture in the form of tiny droplets that can be scarcely seen even with a magnifying glass comes onto our window panes from the vapor in the air, and the necessary cold temperature also sets in, then the whole sheet of lines stars fans palms and blossoms that we call frosted windows is created. All these things come together as a whole, and the rays valleys ridges and knots of ice are wondrous to behold when examined through a magnifying glass. In a like manner you can see the configurations of the Earth at the lesser altitudes from the peaks of very high mountains. The Earth must have originated from a hardening substance and expanded its parts to a tremendous magnitude. The mountain itself on which I was standing is the brilliantly gleaming white point which we can see in the tender web of our frosted window. The edges of the palm leaf design on our frosted window are broken or incomplete because of disintegration due to a draft of air or melting due to heat. Damage and changes to the mountains' configurations occur through weathering, i.e. the influence of water air heat and cold. The only difference is that the destruction of the ice needles on the windows takes a shorter period of time than the destruction of the needles on the mountains. (*IS*, 28, translation altered)]

The terms are seemingly exchanged: "Fächer und Palmen" describe the progressive formations of the landscape, and "die Strahlen die Thäler die Rücken die Knoten" describe the view of the frosted windowpanes through a magnifying glass, suggesting a kind of comparability between them even while the narrator takes care to point out the different time scales at play. The narrator's standpoint (on a mountain) is described as if it were the central node of the ice crystal patterns on the glass, thus technically in the middle of things but diminished in scale to the point of human uninhabitability. This interweaving of images and the interpolation of his perspective into an impossible scale draws attention to the disproportion on the other side—of human existence compared to the formations of the earth—and contributes to the sense of relative unimportance of his own person in relation to the things he is describing. At the same time, the analogy to the rime makes the movements of the earth across millennia more relatable to the human eye. It also temporalizes the frost image on its micro-scale in a way that would likely not otherwise be evident. The repetition of terms across spatial and temporal scales, along with the list of elements, characteristically not separated by commas, create a kind of semantic mesh or web that echoes the "Gewebe" on the thematic level, a network of forces rather than discrete and singular elements.

In another passage of landscape description, we see elements put into relation to one another, along with repeated words, digressions, and here also a form of animation in which, grammatically, the landscape elements move and act on their own under the observing gaze:

Jedermann kennt die Vorberge, mit welchem das Hochgebirge gleichsam wie mit einem Übergange gegen das flachere Land ausläuft. Mit Laub- oder Nadelwald bedeckt ziehen sie in angenehmer Färbung dahin, lassen hie und da das blaue Haupt eines Hochberges über sich sehen, sind hie und da von einer leuchtenden Wiese unterbrochen, führen alle Wässer, die das Gebirge liefert, und die gegen das Land hinaus gehen, zwischen sich, zeigen manches Gebäude und manches Kirchlein, und strecken sich nach allen Richtungen, in denen das Gebirge sich abniedert, gegen die bebauteren und bewohnteren Theile hinaus. (*HKG* 4,1:45)

[Everyone is familiar with the foothills that extend out from the Alps toward the more open country, as if they were a transitional phase. Covered by deciduous or coniferous forests, they extend amidst the most pleasing colors; here and there a bluish mountain peak can be seen towering in the background; occasionally, they are interspersed by a shining meadow; between their slopes they gather all the waters sent out by the mountains and bring them to the more open country; a number of buildings and chapels are in evidence, and the hills extend in several directions and get progressively lower as they near the developed and inhabited regions. (*IS*, 30)]

Despite the fact that "everyone is familiar with the foothills," these are again described in detail, a form of implicit repetition adding to the literal repeated formulations "hie und da," "manches," "gegen das Land." This is anything but a static, momentary image, even while one might not expect landscape elements to be movable.[38] Everything in this scene is in transition, going from one place to another and in all directions. Strikingly, the formulations imply that these things move of their own accord due to the active verbs "dahinziehen," "auslaufen," "zeigen," "führen," "sehen lassen," and reflexive verbs such as "sich strecken" and "sich abniedern." The overall impression is mesmerizing and somewhat disorienting due to this unexpected motion and action, something akin to Lukács's animated setting from a passive observer position. Even if everyone already knows these hills, their constant state of motion and transition warrants repeatedly returning to look at them.

Beyond simply recording "what is there," descriptive notations in *Der Nachsommer* serve to locate the observer in space as well as create spatial relationships between the different elements in the described scenes. Incidentally, this priority of depth and relationships is also echoed in Stifter's critique of the new medium of photography:

---

38  For more on the dynamization of description in Stifter, see Elisabeth Strowick, "Poetological-Technical Operations: Representation of Motion in Adalbert Stifter," *Configurations* 18, no. 3 (2010): 273–89.

Im Ganzen bin ich den Photographieen Feind, sie müssen außer Verhältniß sein, weil jede Sammellinse nur treue Bilder gibt, wenn der Gegenstand nicht in der Raumtiefe, sondern in einer Ebene ist, die parallel der Linsenbreite ist, und weil jeder Mensch in dem Augenblicke, als er von der Linse gefangen wird, starr sein muß, also nicht der ist, der er ist, woher meistens der Mangel an Leben in den Photographieen rührt.[39]

[On the whole I am no fan of photographs, they will always be out of proportion because every converging lens only gives true images if the object is not in the depth of space, but in a plane that is parallel to the width of the lens, and because every person at the moment when he is caught by the lens must be rigid, he's not who he is, which is usually where the lack of life in the photographs comes from.]

The foreground figure appears frozen and lifeless, undifferentiated against a flat background. The images are "außer Verhältniß," unable to represent the relations between things in space that is the object of Stifter's novelistic style. As the formulation also implies, the way in which something or someone is represented makes them become what they are—"nicht der ist, der er ist"—a suggestive idea when it comes to the importance of style and form in creating the object of narration, and particularly in the case of a narrative of subject formation. Stifter's formulation here regarding photography echoes the critiques of literary description itself: that the subjects appear frozen, and the space and time of the narrative becomes unstructured. This priority of locating objects within a surrounding context is reflected on the thematic level of *Der Nachsommer*, namely in the protagonist's efforts to learn how to see depth: "Die Gebirge standen im Reize und im Ganzen vor mir, wie ich sie früher nie gesehen hatte. Sie waren meinen Forschungen stets Theile gewesen. Sie waren jezt Bilder so wie früher blos Gegenstände. In die Bilder konnte man sich versenken, weil sie eine Tiefe hatten, die Gegenstände lagen stets ausgebreitet zur Betrachtung da" (*HKG* 4,2:34; The mountains stood before me with a glory and completeness as I had never seen in them before. They had always simply been part of my research. Now they were images, just as before they had been merely objects. You could lose yourself in the images because they had depth; the objects were just lying there for examination, *IS*, 193). Rather than focusing on the familiar mountains, the narrator is now able to see compositions involving these but featuring the space surrounding the objects. The interstitial space functions as the medium that brings them together into a constellation rather than having each element appear equidistant and discrete. He notices that seeing space

39   Letter to Gustav Heckenast from July 20, 1857, in *PRA* 19:35.

is easier under meteorological conditions that partially inhibit the gaze, likely because this makes the mediating circumstances themselves more apparent. He is also able to create these situations through his paintings: "Auf diese Weise [durch Canadabalsam, TH] dürfte es zu erreichen sein, daß die Darstellung von Körpern gelänge, die in einem Mittel und in einer Umgebung von anderen Körpern schwimmen" (*HKG* 4,2:38; In this way [through Canadian balsam, TH] it might be possible to reach the point of successfully depicting bodies immersed in some medium and in an environment of other bodies, *IS*, 195). Rather than each distinct body, the "Umgebung" or proximity of other bodies within a surrounding medium is the object of representation. The formal techniques of juxtaposing large and small scales, near and far objects, seen throughout the novel can be understood as creating an immersive context for objects to "swim" in, which is also the goal of Heinrich's painting practice.

The protagonist's ability to see landscape elements in relation to each other and ordered according to aesthetic principles is contrasted with the scientific partialization with which he is said to have regarded the natural world earlier on in the novel. Placing elements in relation to each other, whether on the stylistic or thematic level, can be seen as an attempt to create a kind of totality in the sense of Alexander von Humboldt, who serves as model for Stifter's Heinrich and whose scientific projects depended on the kind of relational thinking Heinrich learns via aesthetics.[40] Even while working within the modern scientific paradigm, which increasingly regarded objects of study as discrete and unrelated, Humboldt sought to regain the image of "das Ganze," his magnum opus *Kosmos* attempting to unite everything again into an aesthetic whole. Hannes Etzelstorfer paraphrases Humboldt's conviction: "dass die Aesthetik die Aufgabe habe, dem voranschreitenden Zerfall einer ganzheitlichen Natursicht ein das Wissen bewahrendes, in sich stimmiges Weltbild gegenüberzustellen" (that aesthetics has the task of confronting a progressively disintegrating holistic view of nature with a knowledge-preserving, coherent worldview).[41] Humboldt's holism based on aesthetics, expressed in what he called "Naturgemälde" or verbal nature paintings, appears nostalgic against the increasingly quantified nineteenth-century scientific norms of statistics and compounding data sets, yet his relational thinking formed the basis of new ideas and integrated fields of study including ecology

---

40 See Kurt-H. Weber, *Die literarische Landschaft: Die Geschichte ihrer Entdeckung von der Antike bis zur Gegenwart* (Berlin and New York: De Gruyter, 2010), 330–36.

41 Hannes Etzlstorfer, "'Die Wolken, ihre Bildungen [...] waren mir wunderbare Erscheinungen'" ("Nachsommer"): Bemerkungen zu Adalbert Stifters Motivrepertoire als Landschaftsmaler," in *Sanfte Sensationen: Stifter 2005, Beiträge zum 200. Geburtstag Adalbert Stifters*, ed. Johann Lachinger, et al. (Linz: StifterHaus, 2005), 61–74; here 68–69.

and climate science. Bringing Humboldt's holism back to matters of style in Stifter, according to Heinz Drügh, Humboldt disciplined himself to avoid including too much narration in his accounts, which he regarded mainly as entertainment against the scientific value of description, a priority which Drügh recognizes in *Der Nachsommer* as well.[42] The epic totality that is missing from the modern novel is evoked in Stifter's text by the mediating elements and the relations between things.[43] Moreover, seeing things in relation to each other renders those things different: "Durch Luft Licht Dünste Wolken durch nahe stehende andere Körper gewinnen die Gegenstände ein anderes Aussehen" (*HKG* 4,2:38; The objects gained a different appearance through air, light, haze, clouds, through other bodies close to them, *IS*, 195). By implication, the protagonist himself exists within this depth of space that his developing sensibilities increasingly flesh out, and he himself is changed through this experience, though this *Bildungsprozess* is only an indirect implication of the stylistic and thematic priorities, the "animated setting." The fact that he is not included in the visible field, as part of the composition, disrupts the figure-ground relationship by placing most of the attention on an increasingly nuanced backdrop.[44]

I will now turn to Stifter's own practice of landscape painting, which he pursued throughout his life and which he considered to be the initial locus of his artistic talent. As he writes in 1836: "Als Schriftsteller bin ich nur Dilettant und wer weiß, ob ich es auf diesem Felde weiter bringen würde, aber als Maler werde ich etwas erreichen" (As a writer I am only a dilettante and who knows whether I would make any progress in this field, but as a painter I will achieve something).[45] The critical reception largely disagrees on this point, but based on the relatively

---

42   Drügh discusses in detail Humboldt's influence along with the discursive and formal relevance of geography for description in *Der Nachsommer*. See Heinz Drügh, *Ästhetik der Beschreibung: Poetische und kulturelle Energie deskriptiver Texte (1700–2000)* (Tübingen: Francke, 2006), 280–97; esp. 284–85.

43   Moretti contends that the modern epic emerges out of a discontent or insufficiency with the scientific outlook of the nineteenth-century novel. See Moretti, *Modern Epic*, esp. 35–55.

44   There is a well-established connection between landscape and subjectivity, which might suggest that these landscapes themselves could be understood as a representation of the protagonist. However, as Kurt-H. Weber contends, landscapes in *Der Nachsommer* are not just a reflection of human ideals or stand as the 'symbol of the soul' that they represented in Romanticism, given their empirical focus (*Die literarische Landschaft*, 334). I see the relationship between Heinrich and the landscapes he describes and paints as related, but indirectly, as a reflection of a subjectivity re-constituted through his visual attention.

45   Cited in Fritz Novotny, *Adalbert Stifter als Maler* (Vienna and Munich: Schroll, 1979), 13.

small oeuvre that survived his own destructive self-critique, he is credited with achieving the highest level of the craft within the Biedermeier style, and also being ahead of his time in a few respects.[46] One feature of his landscape paintings that links them to the realist period more broadly and appears innovative in its own right is the absence of symbolic, metaphysical, or metaphorical content.[47] What is also often missing is a focus on the foreground, a priority that I suggest links his painting practice to his novelistic style in *Der Nachsommer*. Fritz Novotny, in his definitive study and catalogue of Stifter's paintings, comments that it is precisely this aspect—"Durchbildung des Vordergrundes ... der 'Prüfstein eines Landschaftsmalers'" (development of the foreground ... the "touchstone of a landscape painter")—that often looks clumsy in Stifter's works, if it is present at all.[48] His painter's notebook, which he kept between 1854 and 1867 and which contains meticulous notations of his works in progress including the amount of time spent on each one, often evinces the establishment of the background and atmosphere but mentions that the foreground is still missing: "Himmel fertig ... Vorder/Mittelgrund nur skizziert"; "Bis auf den Vordergrund gezeichnet. Die Luft gemalt" (sky finished ... foreground/middle ground only sketched in; Everything except the foreground drawn in. Painted the air).[49] Here again we see the attention paid to depth, atmosphere, and context, whereas the foreground is blended out entirely or added only as an afterthought. Novotny also discusses Heinrich's painting in *Der Nachsommer*, his difficulty painting landscapes "weil es sich hier darum handelte, ein Räumliches, das sich nicht in gegebenen Abmessungen und mit seinen Naturfarben, sondern gleichsam als die Seele eines Ganzen darstellte, zu erfassen" (because here it was a question of grasping a spatial element that did not present itself in given increments and with its local colors, but, as it were, as the soul of an entirety).[50] The composition of the whole, rather than anything that would stick out of this and become evident as a discrete entity, is the priority. What Stifter "achieves" (*erreichen*) is thus perhaps a sense of composition and style in which dynamism is created precisely in the movement between the elements and the dispersion of the focus into the broader surroundings.

Stifter's notebooks disproportionately make mention of painting the "air" of his larger landscape compositions in relation to the other

---

46   This is especially true of his sketches. See "Stifter als Maler und Zeichner," *Stifter-Handbuch* 221–30, here 221.

47   Weber, *Die literarische Landschaft*, 334.

48   Novotny, *Adalbert Stifter als Maler*, 9.

49   Cited in Novotny, *Adalbert Stifter als Maler*, 16. Novotny discusses similar instances on 5, 7–9, and passim.

50   Novotny, *Adalbert Stifter als Maler*, 18.

elements, thereby suggesting that this encompassing medium constitutes the primary aesthetic focus. In the case of his cloud studies, the air and sky are quite literally (i.e., titularly) the main event. Here there is no real protagonist to speak of, but activity, temporality, and dynamism, nonetheless. The constant changeability without a coherent subject or clear direction of the activity means that these images resist the logic of representation in which a previously existing subject is re-presented aesthetically.[51] The *Bildung* or formation is everything, even while the substance itself is fleeting and nonmaterial, making this an image primarily consisting of movement as it extends through time and space. Foreground and background continually trade places as the blue of the sky is set off by the mass of cloud forms. With reference to Goethe's own series of cloud studies, Joseph Vogl observes that such meteorological formations are not objects per se but rather a becoming, a perceptual event on the border of imperceptibility.[52] It is moreover a semiotic event that draws on all the powers of language to describe, one that is resistant to representational logic as it never remains "itself" and is fundamentally unrepeatable.[53]

In *Der Nachsommer*, Heinrich also describes clouds, for instance: "Die Wolken, ihre Bildung ihr Anhängen an die Bergwände ihr Suchen der Bergspitzen so wie die Verhältnisse des Nebels und seine Neigung zu den Bergen waren mir wunderbare Erscheinungen" (*HKG* 4,1:39; Another wondrous phenomenon were the clouds: their formations, their clinging to the mountain walls and seeking the peaks; likewise, I admired the fog and its affinity to the mountains, *IS*, 26). The nominalizations "Anhängen" and "Suchen" solidify movements into protagonists, phases of activity which morph into each other due, not least, to Stifter's typical lack of commas. Here again we see the importance of relationships or "Verhältnisse" of the clouds and mists to the mountain slopes rather than either natural phenomenon in isolation. The subject inserts himself into the end of the sentence as somewhat of an afterthought, and only to grammatically anchor the perceptual coming-into-being of the meteorological spectacle.

The focus on clouds and atmospheric conditions is evident in *Westungarische Landschaft* (Western Hungarian Landscape, fig. 1.2). Here the foreground is indeed populated by a group of diminutive human figures, arguably serving as *repoussoir*, as well as a cluster of

51 See Etzlstorfer, "'Die Wolken, ihre Bildungen [...] waren mir wunderbare Erscheinungen,'" 69; According to Novotny, Stifter produced hundreds of cloud studies, only a few of which have survived, 11. Novotny moreover emphasizes the historical novelty of cloud studies in the nineteenth century, 10. This increase is coeval with their discovery as a scientific object. See Joseph Vogl, "Wolkenbotschaft," in *Wolken*, ed. Lorenz Engell, Bernhard Siegert, and Joseph Vogl (Weimar: Verlag der Bauhaus Universität, 2005), 69–79; here 70.

52 Vogl, "Wolkenbotschaft," 72.

53 Vogl, "Wolkenbotschaft," 72–74.

Figure 1.1. Adalbert Stifter, *Wolkenstudie* (Cloud Study), circa 1840. Oil on paper, 21.5 x 32 cm, Galerie Belvedere, Vienna. https://commons.wikimedia.org/wiki/File:Adalbert Stifter - Wolkenstudie - 5900 - Österreichische Galerie Belvedere.jpg.

Figure 1.2. Adalbert Stifter, *Westungarische Landschaft* (Western Hungarian Landscape), 1841. Oil on canvas, 36 x 44.5 cm. http://www.zeno.org/Kunstwerke/B/Stifter,+Adalbert%3A+Westungarische+Landschaft.

towering tree stumps. The dark mass of seemingly dead wood in the foreground is relatively undefined and colorless compared to the scene it is placed in. It shares the focus with the visual dynamism and expanse of space behind it and serves as a reference point, primarily allowing access into the space beyond, even while it occupies a good portion of the foreground. Here one might recognize something akin to Caspar David Friedrich's "Rückenfiguren" or back-turned figures, which do not confront the viewer with their subjectivity but rather act as the viewer's identificatory passage beyond them and deeper into the image.[54] Similarly, as with Heinrich in *Der Nachsommer*, we are not supposed to pause over the image of Heinrich (which indeed we never get) but rather see past him to what he is looking at. Other formal aspects invite the eye to become absorbed deeper into the image as well: The vertical trajectory of the topped tree is echoed by the verticality of the cloud mass, and after the eye initially perceives this analogy it ultimately settles on the much more nuanced and animated cloud formations in the background. The literal and figurative atmosphere, the moisture in the surrounding air and the timbre of the storm that is possibly approaching, set off against the more solid forms of objects in the landscape, constitutes the subject of the paintings as visual event, even while these multitudinous phenomena are not really "there," per se.

In another example, this one taken from Stifter's series of cityscapes (*Blick auf Wiener Vorstadthäuser* [View of Viennese Suburban Houses], fig. 1.3) a jumble of houses and trees occupy the fore- and midground, the overall effect of which does not allow the eye to rest on any singular element of the *Gesamtbild* or complete picture. The forms of houses and shrubs are largely painted in dead palette without much value differentiation. The sky, which takes up a full half of the painting, is similarly undifferentiated, fading from yellow to blue with only a few suggestions of clouds in the upper left corner. Even though there is no discernible object in this upper half of the painting, the moisture in the air which facilitates the color transition still grabs the attention more than anything else in the composition. The foreground is occupied by a dark mass of bushy trees, a half-painted-in wall, and the open door of a shed, none of which are particularly worked through in paint or captivating to eye. It would be difficult to identify a primary point of interest or main protagonist. Here it is clearly the relationship between the midground and background, rather than either one in isolation, that makes up the interest of the painting.

One of Stifter's most experimental works from his later period is called *Die Bewegung* (Movement), which exists in two different compositions and media, one in oil on canvas (I, 1858–62) and the other in pen and ink (II,

---

54   For more on Friedrich's back-turned figures, see Richard Wollheim, *Painting as an Art* (Princeton, NJ: Princeton University Press, 1987), 166–68.

Figure 1.3. Adalbert Stifter, *Blick auf Wiener Vorstadthäuser* (View of Viennese Suburban Houses), 1839. Oil on panel, 33.7 x 41 cm, Galerie Belvedere, Vienna. Public Domain at Wikimedia: https://commons.wikimedia.org/wiki/File:Adalbert_Stifter_-_Blick_auf_Wiener_Vorstadthäuser_(1839).jpg.

1858). *Die Bewegung I* (fig. 1.4) features what appears to be a large rock at relatively close range in the middle of a stream. Pebbles and sand are visible in the stream bed, and reflections of light dance off the surface of the water, finding their medial correspondence as a glaze on the surface of the canvas, which contrasts with the matte rock formations. The rock itself, which takes up a good portion of the center of the painting, is relatively undifferentiated, with a few shadowy areas contrasting slightly with the base color and indicating undulations in the rock surface. The sunlight is apparently coming at an angle from the top right of the composition, and behind the rock, as the latter mainly lies in shadow while casting its own shadow on the water in the bottom-left foreground. Even though the stone occupies so much of the composition, given its lack of definition and lighting it is difficult to focus on this area, and the eye seeks out the surrounding light and water instead. The titular movement can be understood as the motion of the surrounding water as it glides past the rock. Like in the "Gegensatz[ ] des Wassers und der Berge"(*HKG* 4,2:28; contrast of water

Figure 1.4. Adalbert Stifter, *Die Bewegung I* (Movement I), 1858–62. Oil on canvas, 24 x 32.4 cm. http://www.zeno.org/Kunstwerke/B/Stifter,+Adalbert: +Die+Bewegung+[1].

and mountains, *IS*, 190), the dynamism and interest exists in the relationship between two elements rather than in either one separately. This effect is mirrored in the movement of the viewer's eyes as these seek a place of rest but are continually rebuffed from the dark mass in the center. The time implicit in the idea of movement is also reflected in the spans of time Stifter worked on the composition, as meticulously recorded in his painter's notebook.[55] While the objects themselves appear static and dead, the goal here is evidently to capture things that are not immediately visible except within a set of relationships.

According to Lukács, novelistic totality as opposed to the epic is "built upon the notion of an irreconcilable gap between human subjectivity and the natural world."[56] On the other hand, Theodor Adorno characterizes epic discourse as precisely the tension between the unchanging material and the impulse of narrative to locate the singular: "das Eindeutige und Feste [trifft] mit dem Vieldeutigen und Verfließenden zusammen[ ], um davon gerade sich zu scheiden (what is solid and unequivocal comes together with what is ambiguous and flowing, in order to immediately part

---

55  For more on Stifter's notebook, see Novotny, *Adalbert Stifter als Maler*, 16.
56  Cited in Boes, "Reading the Book of the World," 107.

from it again).[57] The invariance of myth hits up against the telos of narrative, which is to differentiate according to conceptual logic. In Stifter's *Nachsommer*, perhaps, we can see an attempt through stylistic means to uphold this tension, to subvert the singular into the material context, and to some extent the human subject into his surroundings, precisely through juxtaposition. In Stifter's highly geo-descriptive picturesque novel, as in his analogous landscape paintings, context and relationships are the focus rather than the narrative teleology. In this way, we might recognize a kind of anti-epic in the sense of Lukács and Bakhtin, which foreground the subject and plot trajectory. Instead, we find something more akin to Lukács' animated setting or Hebbel's burgeoning periphery, although in this case descriptions can also facilitate connections, movement, and dynamism between things. The focus in the surroundings creates the depth of space and time in which the habitual actions take place, itself a kind of epic cosmos and one in which a wider variety of things gain importance. This shift is achieved through a variety of stylistic techniques in the text: the priority of description and repetition rather than narrative suspense; the leveling of discourse and story chronologies; the elimination of the subjunctive, the fantastical, and figures of speech, in order to render language as concrete as possible. In both novel and paintings, we moreover see an emptying out of the foreground where one might expect the protagonist to be found, and instead the establishment of contrast or juxtaposition between elements that disallows either to be contemplated separately, rendering evident the scale between things and bringing larger timeframes into perspective. The protagonist's development is reflected off the framing environment that these stylistic priorities bring into view: flora and fauna, geological formations, even tectonic shifts in the earth's crust. Genre expectations are transformed in the process, whereby the *Bildungsroman* itself becomes more like a textual landscape.

57 Theodor W. Adorno, "Über epische Naivität," in *Noten zur Literatur*, vol. 11 of *Gesammelte Schriften*, ed. Rolf Tiedemann, 7th ed. (Frankfurt am Main: Suhrkamp, 2020), 34–40, here 34. English translation: Theodor W. Adorno, "On Epic Naiveté," in *Notes to Literature*, ed. Rolf Tiedemann, trans. Shierry Weber Nicholson (New York: Columbia University Press, 2019), 48–52, here 48. Adorno also comments on the impulse of nineteenth-century authors to make descriptive language as concrete as possible, which he sees as being related to their aspirations in the visual arts: "Die Genauigkeit des beschreibenden Wortes sucht die Unwahrheit aller Rede zu kompensieren. Der Drang Homers, einen Schild wie eine Landschaft zu beschreiben … dieser Drang ist der gleiche, der … Goethe, Stifter und Keller immer wieder dazu trieb, zu zeichnen und zu malen anstatt su schreiben" (37; The precision of descriptive language seeks to compensate for the falseness of all discourse. The impulse that drives Homer to describe a shield as though it were a landscape … that is the same impulse that repeatedly drove Goethe, Stifter, and Keller … to draw and paint instead of writing, 50).

# 2: Stifter and the Genre Conventions of Cultural Journalism

*Sean Franzel*

STIFTER'S BODY OF work is a typical, yet particularly interesting case of how nineteenth-century authors straddled the publication contexts of multi-author journals, anthologies, and annuals and of single-author books and collected works editions.[1] As is the case with nearly all authors in the mid-nineteenth century, the vast majority of Stifter's writings were first published in cultural journals and anthologies. At the same time, he aspired to have his single-author collections elevate him above the status of a mere writer for journals. His notorious obsession with reworking his texts—polishing and filing them down (*ausfeilen*), as he put it—is unique in literary history.[2] Stifter's affirmative vision of what Johannes John calls "the utopia of the finished text" is undeniable, something that has led scholars to apply classicizing conceptions of completion and monumentality to Stifter's mature work, with ideals of perfection (*Vollendung*) informing the critical works editions published not long after his death. These editions sought to profile him as a "classic" German-language author, an aspiration arguably supported by Stifter's stated affinity to Goethe later in life.[3] The first critical edition of Stifter's works (Prague-Reichenberg, 1901–79), is based in the editorial principle of presenting readers with the final authorized version of specific writings (what Goethe deemed the *Ausgabe letzter Hand*), and sought to "unify works in seamless

---

1    On the distinction between journal-based literature and book-length single author publications, see Nicola Kaminski and Jens Ruchatz, *Journalliteratur—ein Avertissement* (Das Pfennig-Magazin zur Journalliteratur 1) (Hanover: Wehrhahn, 2017).

2    See Wolfgang Matz, *Adalbert Stifter, oder Diese fürchterliche Wendung der Dinge: Biographie* (Göttingen: Wallstein: 2016), 187.

3    See Johannes John, "Die Utopie des 'fertigen' Textes," *Stifter-Jahrbuch* 20 (2006): 99–115. On Stifter's self-proclaimed kinship with Goethe, see Alfred Doppler, "Stifter im Kontext der Biedermeiernovelle," in *Adalbert Stifter: Dichter und Maler, Denkmalpfleger und Schulmann: Neue Zugänge zu seinem Werk*, ed. Hartmut Laufhütte and Karl Mösender (Tübingen: Niemeyer, 1996), 207–19; here 207.

completeness [*lückenlose Vollständigkeit*]."[4] Such an editorial undertaking devalues journal versions as incomplete, as pre- or *Ur*-versions in comparison to their "final" book versions, akin to Goethe's *Ur-Faust*.[5] In effect, the late nineteenth- and mid-twentieth-century curation of Stifter's oeuvre tasked itself with extracting his writings from the chaotic sea of ephemeral print and securing their final, stable form—to the extent that such an undertaking was even possible.

Nevertheless, Stifter's work as an author and editor clearly bears the traces of the broadly popular cultural journals and anthologies in which he published, and he was quite proactive in adapting their genre and format conventions across his entire career.[6] The cultural journals (*Kulturzeitschriften*) of the period featured a mixture of historical and popular-scientific observation, literary entertainment, fashion reporting, and travel correspondence that provided the groundwork for the so-called *Bildungspresse* of the later nineteenth century.[7] Leading belletristic journals of this sort included the *Morgenblatt für gebildete Stände* (Morning Pages for the Educated Classes, 1807–65), the *Zeitung für die elegante Welt* (Paper for the Elegant World, 1801–59), and the *Wiener Zeitschrift für Kunst, Literatur, Theater und Mode* (Viennese Journal for Art, Literature, Theater, and Fashion, 1817–49). Stifter published in this last journal multiple times, and its title encapsulated the thematic range of mid-century cultural periodicals.[8] Later, so-called *Familienzeitschriften* would become popular in the second half of the century, for instance *Die Gartenlaube*

4    Jens Stüben, "Stifter-Editionen," in *Editionen zu deutschsprachigen Autoren als Spiegel der Editionsgeschichte*, ed. Botho Plachta (Tübingen: Niemeyer, 2005), 403–31; here 404.

5    Stüben, "Stifter-Editionen," 408.

6    For earlier scholarship on Stifter's activities as an author for journals, see Friedrich Sengle, *Biedermeierzeit: Deutsche Literatur im Spannungsfeld zwischen Restauration und Revolution 1815–1848*, 3 vols. (Stuttgart: J.B. Metzler, 1972); and Doppler, "Stifter im Kontext der Biedermeiernovelle." On Stifter's adept navigation of multiple publication venues, see Gustav Frank, "Publikationssituation und -organe," in *Stifter-Handbuch: Leben—Werk—Wirkung*, ed. Christian Begemann and Davide Giuriato (Stuttgart: J.B. Metzler, 2017), 357–62; here 357.

7    On the term and definition of *Kulturzeitschrift*, see Alphons Silbermann, "Die Kulturzeitschrift als Literatur," *Internationales Archiv für Sozialgeschichte der deutschen Literatur* 10 (1985): 94–112. On later nineteenth-century periodical literature, see Gerhart von Graevenitz, "Memoria und Realismus: Erzählende Literatur in der deutschen 'Bildungspresse' des 19.Jahrhunderts," in *Memoria: Vergessen und Erinnern*, ed. Anselm Haverkamp and Renate Lachmann (Munich: Wilhelm Fink, 1993), 282–304; here 286–87.

8    On the journal and Stifter's contributions to it, see Nicola Kaminski, *Flüchtiges fixieren? Ephemeres edieren? Die Sonnenfinsternis am 8.Juli 1842 in der "Wiener Zeitschrift für Kunst, Literatur, Theater und Mode" und in der Stifter-Philologie* (Das Pfennig-Magazin zur Journalliteratur 9) (Hanover: Wehrhahn, 2023).

(The Garden Bower, 1854–1944) and *Die Gartenlaube für Österreich* (The Garden Bower for Austria, 1866–69); Stifter published in the latter and I will return to some of these articles at the end of this chapter. The four-page journals of the earlier half of the century such as the *Morgenblatt* or the *Wiener Zeitschrift* presented readers with a heterogeneous mixture of shorter texts that often foregrounded visual metaphors as part of their genre conceits: "sketches," "tableaus," "portraits," "physiognomies," and more. These journals also presented readers with a range of different kinds of texts, illustrations, and advertisements, training them to be consumers of various kinds of print, including emerging forms of print luxury. These journals called upon readers to negotiate the interconnected spheres of commerce, politics, theater, the literary market, fashion, and more: to "translate" between different realms and spaces of experience, as Birgit Tautz puts it.[9] At the same time, they established patterns of continuity through serialized articles that revisited recurring events or places, especially cities, which commonly served as extended metaphors for the present day as well as for temporal and historical disjunction, such as the clash of the "old" and the "new."[10]

Stifter integrates the conventions and formats of cultural journalism into his broader literary production in several key ways. His multi-author, multi-installment illustrated anthology *Wien und die Wiener, in Bildern aus dem Leben* (Vienna and the Viennese, in Pictures from Life, 1841–44) takes up the principle of dynamic, moving images so common in the journals, pocketbooks, and almanacs of the period. Louis-Sébastien Mercier (1740–1814) pioneered the genre of the urban tableau, which was continued in France and throughout Europe with influential projects such as *Les Français peints par eux-mêmes* (The French as Depicted by Themselves, 1840–42), a collection that included contributions from influential writers and artists such as Balzac and Daumier. *Wien und die Wiener* is just one set of "pictures" of Vienna among many, and just one alongside a glut of similar works published in London, Paris, Berlin, Rome, Leipzig, etc. The first of several anthology projects that Stifter undertook, it was distributed in fifteen double installments between 1841–1844 and contained thirty engraved plates of figures featured in the articles. The pace of publication—bimonthly, or roughly six times a year—lent the project a regularized periodicity akin to a cultural journal or literary almanac, and readers might well have collected the installments and bound

---

9    See Birgit Tautz, *Translating the World: Toward a New History of German Literature Around 1800* (State College, PA: Pennsylvania State University Press, 2018).

10    See Bernhard Fischer, "Paris, London und anderswo: Zur Welterfahrung in Hermann Hauffs *Morgenblatt* der 1830er Jahre," *Jahrbuch der Deutschen Schillergesellschaft* 51 (2007): 329–73; here 330.

them together as a whole, as with other periodicals of enough stature to warrant preservation.[11] The entirety was reprinted in book form in 1844, at which time editions with hand-colored images became available. Stifter authored twelve of the fifty-five articles, and he later reworked one important piece for a journal and planned to republish more. *Wien und die Wiener* must play a central role in any reckoning of Stifter as a writer for cultural journals, as indeed evidenced by the recent historical-critical edition (see *HKG* 9,1), which reprints the anthology in its entirety, rather than winnowing out the pieces written by the only author still recognizable to non-specialists.[12]

The theme of collecting heterogenous materials is central in Stifter's work, as multiple scholars have noted, and it is a theme that links his work to the publication formats of serialized print.[13] Stifter's work with anthologies continued with his six-volume story collections *Studien* (Studies), which came out in quasi-serialized three-year intervals in 1844, 1847, and 1850. Along with his influential 1853 collection *Bunte Steine* (Motley Stones), Stifter also co-edited a literary anthology for Austrian

11 See Frank, "Publikationssituation und -organe," 359.

12 The recent Brandenburg edition of Kleist's works engages in a similar practice with respect to the *Berliner Abendblätter* (1810–11), as the editors chose to reprint the journal's entire run rather than merely reproduce the pieces authored by Kleist himself. For an approach that attempts to do justice to such multiple authorship, see Vance Byrd "Beautiful Form? *Vienna and the Viennese* and Stifter's Urban Sketches," *Croqués par eux-mêmes: La societé à l'épreuve du panoramique,* ed. Nathalie Preiss and Valerie Stiénon. Special issue of *Interférences littéraires/ Literarire interferenties* 8 (2012): 155–69.

13 A variety of scholars have examined how Stifter's writings are informed by logics of collecting. This includes Sabine Schneider's exploration of non-teleological narrative practices based in models of aggregation and incomplete or partial collection, Samuel Frederick's exploration of dialectics of collecting and dispersal, Katharina Grätz's and Kathrin Maurer's work on Stifter and historicism, and Nicolas Pethes's study of Stifter's use of archival operations that collect related textual genres. See Sabine Schneider, "Vergessene Dinge: Plunder und Trödel in der Erzählliteratur des Realismus," in *Die Dinge und die Zeichen: Dimensionen des Realistischen in der Erzählliteratur des 19. Jahrhunderts,* ed. Sabine Schneider and Barbara Hunfeld (Würzburg: Königshausen & Neumann, 2008), 157–74, here 170; Samuel Frederick, *The Redemption of Things: Collecting and Dispersal in German Realism and Modernism* (Ithaca, NY: Cornell University Press, 2022); Katharina Grätz, *Musealer Historismus: Die Gegenwart des Vergangenen bei Stifter, Keller und Raabe* (Heidelberg: Universitätsverlag Winter, 2006); Kathrin Maurer, "Adalbert Stifter's Poetics of Collecting: Representing the Past against the Grand Narrative of Academic Historicism," *Modern Austrian Literature* 40, no. 1 (2007): 1–17; and Nicolas Pethes, *Literarische Fall-Archive: Zur Epistomologie und Ästhetik seriellen Erzählens am Beispiel von Stifters Mappe* (Berlin: Alpheus Verlag, 2015).

schools under the descriptive yet laborious title: *Lesebuch zur Förderung humaner Bildung in Realschulen und in andern zu weiterer Bildung vorbereitenden Mittelschulen* (Reader for the Advancement of Humanist Education in Junior High-Schools and in Other Continuing Educational Preparatory Middle Schools, 1854).[14] *Bunte Steine* adopted common practices of yearly almanacs and pocketbooks, coming out in fall of 1852 in coordination with the market for Christmas and New Year's presents in the form of literary anthologies, and is even subtitled "Ein Festgeschenk" (A holiday gift). Both *Studien* and *Bunte Steine* gather reworked pieces first published in journals, and are prime examples of the practices of collecting, compiling, and juxtaposing that are key to Stifter's activities as an editor of his own and others' work.[15] Each of these projects invokes modes of gathering heterogenous material, including mineral collection in *Bunte Steine* and scientific data collection and painterly studies alike in the *Studien*, and each furthermore suggests the possibility for a potentially ceaseless ongoing collection. As Stifter would write in the introduction to *Bunte Steine*: "Weil es unermeßlich viele Steine gibt, so kann ich gar nicht voraus sagen, wie groß diese Sammlung werden wird" (*HKG* 2,2:19; As more stones exist than can be counted, I cannot say in advance how long this collection shall be, *MS*, 10).

In his early writings but also at times in his later work, Stifter often adapts the narrative persona of a fool (*Narr*). This narrative conceit has clear connections to the realm of satirical cultural journals, some of which personified their journal through various mischievous observer figures, for instance the "tattler," "spectator," "devil in Paris," participants in carnival, and more. The foolish narrator position has roots in the German literary tradition; Jean Paul's satirical play with modes of "foolish," journal-based authorship in particular was a significant influence on Stifter's early work.[16] Along with adapting Jean Paul's humorous, ostentatiously

---

14   On the periodicity of the *Studien*, see Frank, "Publikationssituation und -organe," 360–61. On the school anthology project, see Cornelia Blasberg, *Erschriebene Tradition: Adalbert Stifter oder das Erzählen im Zeichen verlorener Geschichten* (Freiburg: Rombach, 1998), 114–77. On the anthology format, see Nora Ramtke and Seán Williams, "Approaching the German Anthology, 1700–1850," *German Life and Letters* 70, no. 1 (2017): 1–21.

15   See Jessica Resvick, "The Author as Editor: The Aesthetics of Recension in Adalbert Stifter's *Die Mappe meines Urgroßvaters*," in *Market Strategies and German Literature in the Long Nineteenth Century*, ed. Vance Byrd and Ervin Malakaj (Berlin and Boston, MA: De Gruyter, 2020), 147–68. On compilation as authorial mode more generally, see Petra McGillen, *The Fontane Workshop: Manufacturing Realism in the Industrial Age of Print* (New York: Bloomsbury, 2019).

16   On Jean Paul and the question of journal authorship, see Sean Franzel, *Writing Time: Studies in Serial Literature 1780–1850* (Ithaca, NY and London: Cornell University Press, 2023).

"foolish" tone, Stifter's writings from the 1840s engage with notions of periodical literature's occasionality, ephemerality, and often diminutive stature.[17]

Finally, Stifter's engagement with the genre and format conditions of cultural journalism also facilitated his exploration of writing about different temporalities and the passing of time, with which the realm of serial print was and is commonly associated. The trope of the city as heterochronic space had of course been a commonplace of literary entertainment for decades and one that lay at the heart of *Wien und die Wiener*, which juxtaposes various frames of time, ranging from a day, a night, a moment, a season, even seconds or minutes, with the time of "world history" and the "history of the human race." These plural modes of time correspond to specific generic and affective registers: as the editors state, some of the anthology's images will be "serious," others "cheerful."[18] Stifter's understanding of time and his vision thereof in *Wien und die Wiener* in particular have been evaluated as paradoxical or contradictory due to the anthology's many perspectival shifts, whereby time appears at one moment cyclical, at another progressive and linear, at one moment leading to inextricable death, at the next to regenerative life.[19] Rather than resolving these contradictions, I would propose that the anthology's serial format enables a contrapuntal approach to time that corresponds to the temporalities of cultural journalism.

Suggesting that Stifter is an emphatic writer of time is, however, something of a provocation, for his work has long been interpreted as being preoccupied mainly with detemporalized spatial representation, not least because of the prominent role of vision therein. As Catriona MacLeod notes, his writings (and paintings) are characterized by the

---

17   On Stifter's journalistic engagement with the present day through the lens of economics, see Maximilian Bergerngruen, "'*Ueber unsere gegenwärtige Lage*': Stifters literarische Interventionen gegen die ökonomische 'Gegenwart' (Journalistisches, *Mappe, Nachsommer*)," in *Aktualität: Zur Geschichte literarischer Gegenwartsbezüge vom 17. bis zum 21. Jahrhundert*, ed. Stefan Geyer and Johannes F. Lehmann (Hanover: Wehrhahn, 2018), 271–96.

18   See Adalbert Stifter, "Aussicht und Betrachtungen von der Spitze des St. Stephansthurmes," in *Wien und die Wiener* (Pesth: Heckenast, 1844), xxi. I have opted to cite from the original anthology publication throughout this essay and refer to it as *WuW*; this version is reproduced in *HKG* 9,1.

19   On the disjointed view of history in *Wien und die Wiener*, see Matz, *Adalbert Stifter*, 143–44. See also Christian Begemann, *Die Welt der Zeichen: Stifter-Lektüren* (Stuttgart: J. B. Metzler, 1995), 82; and Gerhard Plumpe, "Zyklik als Anschauungsform historischer Zeit: In Hinblick auf Adalbert Stifter," in *Bewegung und Stillstand in Metaphern und Mythen: Fallstudien zum Verhältnis von elementarem Wissen und Literatur im 19. Jahrhundert*, ed. Jürgen Link and Wulf Wülfing (Stuttgart: Klett-Cotta, 1984), 201–25.

"constant tension between the depiction of mobility and fixity"; Eva Geulen, for her part, describes this tension in terms of the semantics of the still life (*nature morte*) and its paradoxical association with both life and death.[20] In much of the scholarship, his work is associated with the spatialization and deceleration of time to the point of immobility, that is to say with a form of stasis that breaks with or mitigates the temporal (and political) experience of modernity.[21] The association of his work with fixity, stasis, and boredom goes back to Friedrich Hebbel's well-known accusation that Stifter focuses too much on spatial description and not enough on the unfolding of narrative action, that his literary work is, in effect, too painterly.[22] Following Hebbel, Georg Lukács suggests that Stifter atomizes literature into stand-alone moments, into a "series of static images" (*Reihe von Zustandsbildern*) that merely "follow" rather than develop "out of" each other, "single images that in an artistic sense hang next to each other as unconnected as the images in a museum."[23] Lukács's critique is based in an ideal of unified narrative form and developmental coherence (*Zusammenhang*) that he finds lacking in Stifter, an ideal that undergirds the notion of the complete, "classical" work. Such an ideal applies, at best, peripherally to *Wien und die Wiener*, but it is ironic that Lukács's formulations aptly describe the anthology's very format. A key part of reconsidering Stifter's engagement with serial forms of cultural journalism involves rethinking the temporal ramifications of his writings. To this end, this chapter explores several programmatic elements in *Wien und die Wiener* that address temporal patterns manifested by serialized images, as well as a piece published much later in his life. It is in ostensibly small and minor works that one can find reflections on time and literary legacy that help better situate Stifter's work at the intersection of multi-author journals and single-author, book-length, supposedly "complete" works.

20  Catriona MacLeod, *Fugitive Objects: Sculpture and Literature in the German Nineteenth Century* (Evanston, IL: Northwestern University Press, 2014), 112; Eva Geulen, "Depicting Description: Lukács and Stifter," *The Germanic Review: Literature, Culture, Theory* 73, no. 3 (1998): 267–79.

21  See Sabina Becker and Katharina Grätz, "Einleitung: Ordnung, Raum, Ritual bei Adalbert Stifter," in *Ordnung, Raum, Ritual: Adalbert Stifters artifizieller Realismus*, ed. Sabina Becker and Katharina Grätz (Heidelberg: Universitätsverlag Winter, 2007), 7–16; here 12–14.

22  See Friedrich Hebbel, "Das Komma im Frack," in *Werke*, vol. 3, ed. Gerhard Fricke, Werner Keller, and Karl Pörnbacher (Munich: Hanser, 1965), 684–87.

23  See Georg Lukács, "Erzählen oder Beschreiben?," in *Probleme des Realismus I: Essays über Realismus* (Neuwied and Berlin: Luchterhand, 1971), 197–242; here 220.

## Viewing and Reviewing "Fleeting Images"

In the preface to *Wien und die Wiener,* Stifter and his co-editor Franz Stelzhamer promise "images" or "pictures" of ever-changing life, a *tableau mouvant* of a city in flux: "Es ist Zweck und Ziel dieser Blätter, nicht etwa eine Statistik Wiens zu bringen, sondern in ernsten und heitern Bildern, wie in einem Kaleidoskop Scenen dieser Hauptstadt vorüber zu führen, ... so dass sich dem Leser nach und nach ein Bild des Lebens und Treibens dieser Residenz zusammen male" (*WuW,* unpaginated preface; It is the purpose and aim of these pages not to offer a statistical study of Vienna, but rather to let serious and cheerful pictures pass by, as in a kaleidoscope ... so that the reader gradually paints together an image of the life and activity of this capital city). The format of this multi-author anthology is based in readers juxtaposing literary images and illustrations cumulatively, with new material coming out gradually. The literary and artistic categories of the image are decidedly multivalent and flexible, and interchangeable genre distinctions delineating miscellaneous short pieces run rampant in the journal landscape of the period: images, letters, sketches, studies, memoirs, physiognomies, daguerreotypes, dreams, travel images can all refer to more or less the same type of small form.[24] Such texts are also often qualified in temporal terms, with the common designation "flüchtige Bilder" (fleeting images) linking method of composition (a quick sketch), topic (scenes from daily life), publicational medium (in periodicals), and the public's need for more, that is, serial continuation. The size and length of such pieces are subject to alteration, with authors and editors able to dilate "images" out or compress and contract them as needed and as requested by readers. The temporal index of such images and their connection both to the fleeting present and to different historical moments lead to the coinage of the *Zeitbild,* or image of time.[25] This temporal index is also enhanced by the common association of such images and the periodical more generally with new visual media such as the panorama, stereoscope, telescope, and, later, lithography and the daguerreotype.[26]

24 Sengle, *Biedermeierzeit,* vol. 2: *Die Formenwelt,* 788. Thomas Althaus speaks of the "rhizomatically proliferating composition of travel images (*Reisebilder*)"; see Thomas Althaus, "Bildrhetorik," in *Darstellungsoptik: Bild-Erfassung und Bilderfülle in der Prosa des 19. Jahrhunderts,* ed. Thomas Althaus (Bielefeld: Aisthesis, 2018), 9–35; here 31.

25 See Dirk Göttsche, "'Zeitbilder' zwischen Kleiner Prosa und Zeitroman: Zur Modellierung zeitgeschichtlichen Erzählens im 19. Jahrhundert," in Althaus, *Darstellungsoptik,* 247–65.

26 See Vance Byrd, *A Pedagogy of Observation: Nineteenth-Century Panoramas, German Literature, and Reading Culture* (Lewisburg, PA: Bucknell University Press, 2017); and Patricia Mainardi, *Another World: Nineteenth Century Illustrated Print Culture* (New Haven, CT: Yale University Press, 2017).

The flexible genre of the time-specific image facilitates experiments with both empirical description and subjective modes of narrative, it accommodates multiple narrative voices and enables fluid pathways between fiction and factual or journalistic observation, and it is a natural extension of the periodical format.[27] This is a time when mass-market periodicals such as *Die Gartenlaube* begin their steady rise, not least because of the growing ease of reproducing images.[28] As stated in *Die Gartenlaube*, the journal's aim is to present readers with a "composite total image" (*zusammengesetzte[s] Gesamtbild*), a metaphorical operation based in viewing multiple images and evocative of Stifter and Stelzhamer's notion of "painting together" (*zusammen malen*).[29] Such composite viewing is a media-based operation that relies on a steady stream of new images, or what Thomas Althaus calls "a visual aesthetics of cyclical-serial production."[30] Various scholars have theorized these interrelated genre and format conventions. In the context of the work of Adolph Menzel and Theodor Fontane, Gerhart von Graevenitz describes the structure of "double images" (*Doppelbilder*) in which ensembles of images bring different visual principles or visual worlds into resonance and place the old alongside the new.[31] Graevenitz shows how Fontane incorporated the visual realm of illustrated periodicals, museums, and world exhibitions into the literary imaginary, multiplying temporal frameworks as much through fraught juxtaposition as any kind of neat synthesis.[32] Relatedly, Nicola Kaminski and Volker Mergenthaler

27 As Martina Lauster puts it: "flexibility and potential infinity of composition is the hallmark of sketch collections, comparable to the form of the journal and ... at odds with the closed form of the volume edition." Martina Lauster, *Sketches of the Nineteenth Century: European Journalism and its Physiologies, 1830–50* (New York: Palgrave MacMillan, 2007), 30–31.

28 See Willi Wolfgang Barthold, *Der literarische Realismus und die illustrierten Printmedien: Literatur im Kontext der Massenmedien und visuellen Kultur des 19. Jahrhunderts* (Bielefeld: transcript, 2021).

29 *Die Gartenlaube* 9 (1853): 91. Glossing this statement, Graevenitz describes the publication program of the illustrated family press as consisting in creating a "simultaneous image (*Simultanbild*) out of images of the most distant and the closest [things]." Gerhart von Graevenitz, "Wissen und Sehen: Anthropologie und Perspektivismus in der Zeitschriftenpresse des 19.Jahrhunderts und in realistischen Texten: Zu Stifters *Bunten Steinen* und Kellers *Sinngedicht*," in *Wissen in Literatur im 19.Jahrhundert*, ed. Lutz Danneberg and Friedrich Vollhardt (Tübingen: Niemeyer, 2002), 147–89; here 152.

30 Althaus, "Bildrhetorik," 31.

31 Gerhart von Graevenitz, *Theodor Fontane: Ängstliche Moderne; Über das Imaginäre* (Konstanz: Konstanz University Press, 2014).

32 For Graevenitz, the temporal awareness of the epoch is a "grotesque chronotope" consisting of multiple co-existing images of historical time. Graevenitz, *Theodor Fontane*, 703.

have examined literary applications of the art-historical genre convention of the *Gegenstück* or *Gegenbild* (companion or counter-piece or image), including by Stifter, who uses both terms in his writings. As Mergenthaler puts it in the case of the early story *Der Condor*, Stifter presents readers with "a series (*Reihung*) of four linguistically generated images that join together as if in a cabinet exhibit."[33] As Kaminski and Mergenthaler have shown, periodicals shift the notion of *Gegenstück* beyond a dualistic logic of paired images toward more open-ended forms of textual and visual proximity and sequence. *Doppelbild* and *Gegenstück* are terms that mark coexistence, but they also imply open-ended sequence and the promise that more images will come.

As in many European contexts, the genre of city-based "images of life" became especially popular in the first half of the century in Vienna, and there were numerous predecessors to and competitors with Stifter's project, including Willibald Alexis's *Wiener Bilder* (Viennese Images, 1833), Adolph Glassbrenner's *Bilder und Träume aus Wien* (Images and Dreams from Vienna, 1836), Francis Milton Trollope's *Vienna and the Austrians* (1838), Heinrich Adami's *Alt- und Neu-Wien* (Old and New Vienna, 1841), and Franz Gräffner's *Kleine Wiener Memoiren* (Small Viennese Memoirs, 1844).[34] These anthologies have predecessors in the earlier seventeenth- and eighteenth-century urban calendars of fools (*Narren-Kalender*), which mirrored a given city's foibles back to itself. Nineteenth-century anthologies often appeared in unfixed, irregular installments (or "zwangslosen Heften"), allowing for open-ended continuation, and they thus have a symbiotic relationship with periodicals of varying periodicities. Just one node in a composite and ever-growing network of multiple "images" of European metropoles, Stifter's multi-author anthology pursues various ways of framing its depiction of the city. As he and Stelzhamer state: "Wenn der Kritiker sagt, daß doch Werth und Gehalt dieser Aufsätze so sehr verschieden sei, so antworten wir ihm: der Leser ist selber nicht anders" (*WuW*, unpaginated preface; If the critic says that the value and contents of these articles are so disparate, we will reply: the reader himself is no different). Texts, illustrations, readers, and writers are as jumbled as the city and its inhabitants, as the anthology presents readers with a variety of different scenes, from public parks and markets to the postal system and shop advertisements, from the goings-on of carnival

33  See Nicola Kaminski and Volker Mergenthaler, *Zuschauer im Eckfenster 1821/22 oder Selbstreflexion der Journalliteratur im Journal(text)* (Hanover: Wehrhahn, 2015); and Volker Mergenthaler, "'Stücke,' 'Bilder' und 'Daguerrotype': Stifters 'Condor' und die Künste," in Althaus, *Darstellungsoptik*, 183–200; here 190.

34  See Kai Kauffmann, *"Es ist nur ein Wien!" Stadtbeschreibungen von Wien 1700–1873: Geschichte eines literarischen Genres der Wiener Publizistik* (Vienna: Böhlau, 1994), 351–428.

to winter salon scenes and summer excursions to the outskirts of the city. The collection toggles between scenes of individual figures and larger collective events and accounts by multiple authors of figures from the "lowest and highest classes" including shop employees, ragpickers, students, cooks, servant girls, carriage drivers, and more. The frontispiece for the 1844 book version (see Figure 3.1 in the next chapter) helps to visualize some of the anthology's heterogeneity by presenting an ornamental ensemble that folds individual images of social types on display in the anthology into the visual conceit of a fireworks show, as the images seem to explode both all at once and one after the other. The process of examining individual images in greater detail necessitates sequential viewing— looking at one after the other or jumping around—thereby also evoking aspects of the kaleidoscope and panorama.

The frontispiece for the serial installments of the early anthology publication likewise suggests techniques of previewing and reviewing. Again, *Wien und die Wiener* was published in double installments, and this image (see Figure 2.1) by Carl Mahlknecht, the illustrator of *Wien und die Wiener*, would have accompanied each double set, with minor updates to content and numeration at the bottom quarter of the page. In the middle, a fool (*Narr*) shows an image to viewers, recalling earlier satirical depictions of Viennese life allegorized by a fool holding up a mirror to the populace (a so-called "Narren-Spiegel"). This scene also clearly suggests a photographic image of the city, with the camera box labeled "Daguer" right next to him, thus presenting readers with a clash of competing representational regimes: satirical, allegorical city literature and theater on the one hand; and modern, proto-realistic photography on the other. The masks above the window conjure up tragic and comedic theater and reinforce a "physiognomic" approach to the representation of different faces: Is the figure in dark clothing the fool's melancholic twin, a real chimney sweep (*Rauchfangkehrer*), or just dressed up as one for carnival?[35] By manifesting contrasting temporal and aesthetic registers, namely theatricalized allegory and realism, this clash partakes of the logic of the *Doppelbild* described by Graevenitz. In turn, the "daguerreotype" comes up repeatedly in *Wien und die Wiener*, which, as a genre distinction, operates similarly to the sketch or "flüchtiges Bild" and can also connote accuracy in depicting "individual types or portraits and mark[ing] social standing."[36] In the context of this frontispiece, the fool figure presents different social types with satirical images of themselves. The image

---

35  In an anthology article on Viennese carnival there is mention of a "Rauchfangkehrerball" as part of the social entertainments of the season. See C. F. Langer, "Wiener Carnevals-Freuden," in *Wien und die Wiener*, 383–99; here 391.

36  See Byrd, *A Pedagogy of Observation*, 146.

Figure 2.1. Frontispiece of the original serialized version of *Wien und die Wiener*.

also engages with Stifter's adoption of a "foolish" narrative position as a marker of his own distinctive authorial voice in the anthology.

Scenes of viewing and reviewing organize Stifter's first piece for the anthology titled "Aussicht und Betrachtungen von der Spitze des St. Stephansthurmes" (View and Observations from the Top of St. Stephan's Tower), which presents an account of the panoramic view from Vienna's most iconic church spire over the course of a single morning. However, rather than jumping right into this promised prospect, the piece begins with two and a half pages of preliminary remarks that take the reader through a series of different views. Rather than starting atop the tower, the piece begins with a more notional picture of the living city:

So entrollen wir denn vorerst vor dem geneigten Leser dieser Blätter die ungeheuere Tafel, auf der dies Häusermeer hinauswogt, ein Leben in sich tragend, so bunt und heiter, daß man wähnt, es diene nur dem Augenblicke und der Stunde, und die Göttin die hier herrscht, sei die Freude—und sie ist es auch—denn der Mensch, die Tausende, die hier strömen, arbeiten, sorgen, sich vergnügen, und in Hast und bewundernswertem Geschicke die Frucht jeder Minute zu brechen wissen—sie ahnen es nicht, dass sie Lettern sind, heitere schöne Letern, womit die Muse das furchtbare Drama der Weltgeschichte schreibt. (*WuW*, v)

[So, for the time being, let us first roll out before the well-meaning reader of these pages the giant tableau upon which this ocean of houses billows out, carrying a life in itself, so colorful and cheerful, that one would think that it only serves the moment and the hour, and that the goddess reigning here is that of joy—and she does indeed—for the individual, the thousands who stream by, work, are concerned, seek pleasure, and hastily and with admirable skill know how to make the most of every minute—they do not realize that they are letters, cheerful beautiful letters with which the muse writes out the frightful drama of world history.]

The dynamic, multidirectional movement conjured up by this initial preview is presented as a two-dimensional image ("Tafel") (a "Tableaux" [*sic*] as Stifter puts it in a letter), and this first view is a preview of sorts.[37] The repetition of "vor" ("vorerst vor") plays on the spatial and the temporal meanings of the word, namely "before," "prior to" and "in front of."[38] Spanning from the individual to the masses, people structure their activities according to a variety of frames of time. The vision of differently paced yet somehow organized movements is modified by the metaphor of these figures as letters on a page or tablet that Clio, the muse of history, is in the process of writing out. Though the city's inhabitants follow little more than their own individual needs and desires, from the right perspective, their momentary concerns take on world-historical status. This "cheerful" image of the muse of history writing out people as letters on the page of history serves as a metaphor for the organization of heterogeneous phenomena into a single narrative. This is a key media effect of the anthology, where the flow of the text simulates a set of moving images by placing them into sequential order but also allowing for various possible modes of reorganized reviewing.

---

37  See Byrd, *A Pedagogy of Observation*, 139.

38  In a related context, Elisabeth Strowick shows how Stifter registers perception's dependence on pre-knowledge. Elisabeth Strowick, *Gespenster des Realismus: Zur literarischen Wahrnehmung von Wirklichkeit* (Munich: Wilhelm Fink, 2019), 67.

Stifter then invites the reader to review this initial world-historical preview, to enjoy a second viewing, inwardly ("im Geiste"), as preparation for the proper view from atop the tower:

> Nun lieber Leser, schaue dir noch einmal im Geiste dieses bewegte Leben an, und es wird dir bedeutungsvoller scheinen, als vordem, und dann, wenn du dein Herz vorbereitete hast zu Erhabenheit und Scherz, zur Freude, wie zur Vertrübnis—dann folge mir, dass wir unsere Augen schweben lassen über dieser Riesenscheibe, die da wogt und wallt und kocht und sprüht, und sich ewig rührt in allen ihren Theilen. ( *WuW*, vi)

> [Now, dear reader, observe inwardly once more this moving life, and it will seem more meaningful to you than before, and then, when you have prepared your heart for sublimity and humor, for joy and somberness—then follow me, so that we can let our eyes hover over this giant disc that billows and flutters and cooks and sprays and moves eternally in all of its parts.]

This passage again invokes the multidirectional mixture of emotions on offer with these views, before previewing the activity of climbing up the tower, promising that the narrator and reader will allow "[their] eyes" to hover over the "giant disc" that is the city. This promised shift in perspective transitions from the viewing of a hypothetical two-dimensional plate or picture ( *Tafel*) perpendicular to the ground to the viewing of the city as a two dimensional "disc," one that appears to spread out over and parallel to the ground from the height of the tower. Once more we are dealing with different views of the city from shifting vantage points.[39] And yet once more Stifter defers the tower view, postponing it until the next morning: "dann morgen früh mit Tagesanbruch geh mit mir, ich führe dich bis zur Spize deiner geliebten Pappel empor, und zeige dir von dort herab die Zauberei dieser Welt" ( *WuW*, vii; then tomorrow, at daybreak, come with me, I will take you to the top of your beloved poplar, and will show you from there the magic of this world). As an extended framing device, these first two and a half pages of the piece model the encounter with multiple images, and, more specifically, with plural views of the city, the anthology's central topic. These pages set in motion a process of continued views and create anticipation for the ones to come.

The remainder of this piece unfolds across a half day, as the narrator finally takes a friendly reader up the tower, peppering the synoptic overview of the city's past, present, and future with personal apostrophes and directives. The piece maps the changing appearance (and atmosphere

---

39  See Elisabeth Strowick, "Poetological-Technical Operations: Representation of Motion in Adalbert Stifter," *Configurations* 18, no. 3 (2010): 273–89; here 275–76.

conditions) of the awakening city as the sun falls on ever more of it, and as the viewers move around the tower, telescopes in hand. The first section of this view begins in a register familiar from seventeenth- and eighteenth-century allegorical accounts of Vienna, casting buildings as symbolic manifestations of positive and negative forces in society.[40] The viewers survey the city's boundaries and suburbs, its fortifications, the train depot, markets, the public art gallery in the Belvedere castle and more, as the narrator describes established institutions as well as more disruptive forces such as train travel and unfettered commercialism. These ruminations cycle through multiple temporal frames, from the moment and the single day to the century, the "epoch," and world history, and they map multiple temporal processes, including both the erosion and preservation of the old, both constant change and historical repetition.

We reach a turning point, however, with the gesture to abandon the allegorical, world-historical register and turn the viewer's gaze to "the history of a single day": "Aber lasse selbst Weltgeschichte Weltgeschichte sein, und denke und male dir nur recht deutlich die Geschichte eines einzigen Tages, einer einzigen Nacht, wie sie hier etwa sein mag" ( *WuW*, xviii; But let world history be world history, and think and paint quite clearly for yourself the history of a single day, a single night as it might occur here). Though the unfolding of a single day remains the organizing principle, the view turns to individual figures and daily life, as the narrator offers a multiplicity of genre scenes in miniature. Lovers, mother and child, a solitary person mulling suicide, evening entertainments, businessmen counting their day's earnings, and more are lightly sketched in little more than a sentence or phrase, separated (as we saw in previous chapters) by dashes, a convention from periodical publication used to break up distinct units of information or news.[41] (See Figure 2.2.) On the one hand, these sketches, offered in what Sengle calls a "Sekundenstil" (style of the second), present a general sense of heterogeneity.[42] In effect, this sketch-like style sets in motion the transformation of people into letters promised above. But as the reader of subsequent articles will find out, these snapshots are themselves also abbreviated versions of subsequent articles, previews of material to come. Subsequent articles expand upon a variety of topics: workers across various professions, pleasure seekers, melancholy dreamers, the masses enjoying popular spectacles, and more.

---

40   See Kauffmann, *"Es ist nur ein Wien!,"* 396.

41   On dashes facilitating jumps from one image to another ("Bild-Sprünge"), see Joseph Vogl, "Der Gedankenstrich bei Stifter," in *Die Poesie der Zeichensetzung: Studien zur Stilistik der Interpunktion*, ed. Alexander Nebrig and Carlos Spoerhase (Berlin: Peter Lang, 2012), 275–94; here 280. See also Strowick, *Gespenster des Realismus*, 71.

42   Sengle, *Biedermeierzeit*, vol. 2, 73.

—— XVIII ——

Laß sie, es ist so die Art des menschlichen Geschlechtes! Mancher nun von denen, auf die ich oben deutete, mag wohl noch zur Zeit, als wir heraufstiegen, bei der Lampe gesessen und der Formel nachgesonnen haben, und als da unten das Leben, für dessen Wohl er sorgt, erwachte, löschte er die Lampe aus, und suchte kurzen Schlummer — oder auch Er suchte ihn nicht, sondern wandelt jetzt unter den Wachenden, wie einer aus ihnen, und läßt sich von seinen Untergebenen berichten, was sie meinen und was noth thut. Ist dir dieses Treiben noch nichtig? wächst dir nicht eine furchtbare ernste Bedeutung aus dem Gewirre dieses Häusermeers empor? Ein Stück, und manchmal schon bedeutende Stücke der Weltgeschichte wurden hier geprägt, und werden noch geprägt werden.

Aber lasse selbst Weltgeschichte Weltgeschichte sein, und denke und male dir nur recht deutlich die Geschichte eines einzigen Tages, einer einzigen Nacht, wie sie hier etwa sein mag. Es ist kein Glück auf dieser Erde, es sei so intensiv und innig, daß es nur eben noch ein Menschenherz ertragen kann: heute Nacht war es in diesen Mauern. Der verzagende Jüngling — es waren zwei Lippen, so unerreichbar, wie die Sterne des Orion — heute streiften sie zum erstenmale über die seinen, und da saß er auf seiner Stube, und hielt sich mit beiden Händen die Augen zu. daß ers festhalte, ja daß ers nur begreife, das Glück, und daß es ihm beim Licht des Tages nicht entschwinde. — Das Kind entschlief im Arme einer neuen, fast fabelhaft schönen Puppe. — Eine Jungfrau lag vor dem Bilde der Gebenedeiten, und flehte, daß jeder Tag so schön sei, wie heute; denn sie war mit dem Längstgeliebten eingesegnet worden. — Einer hat das große Loos gezogen — Einer in den Armen der schönsten Frau gezittert — Tausend Lippen mögen sich gefüßt, tausend Arme in einander geschlungen haben. — Dem Dichter erschien in der trunkenen Sommernacht sein Ideal zum erstenmal sichtbarlich, und der Astronom zählte die Sterne. — Eine Mutter besuchte mit der Lampe nach Mitternacht ihre rosenrothen, schlummernden Engel, — Geizhälse zählten das Geld — Träume zuckten durch tausend Herzen — Wüstlinge feierten eine Orgie — der Spieler trug das ganze Vermögen von zwei andern nach Hause — und was da ruhte im sorgenfreien Schlummer, über das wurde feenhaft der goldgestickte Traumteppich gewoben, daß sie sanken und schwebten in einem Meere der Wunder. Aber auch, es gibt keinen Jammer und kein Unglück, es sei mir gräulich immer: heute war es auch in dieser Stadt. — Der Tod ging in hundert Häuser, und zerdrückte überall ein Herz. — Ein blasser Mann lud eine Pistole, im Zimmer neben ihm schläft sein Weib und Kind, morgen ist Kassenuntersuchung, und dann Festung, wenn er nicht früher — — — er wischt die Stirne, es ist ihm fast märchenhaft ferne, wie er auch einmal unten gegangen, wie eben die Nachtwandelnden, und

Figure 2.2. A dash-strewn page from the original
serialized version of *Wien und die Wiener*.

Seen in this light, these greatly abbreviated snapshots can serve as narrative chunks that can seed further writing by being expanded upon and dilated out.[43] This passage also shows how a single tableau-like article can function as a repository for multiple images, each with a temporal

43 These represent examples of scaling effects that Agnes Hoffmann has recently explored in fruitful ways in Stifter's work more generally. See Agnes Hoffmann, "A Poetics of Scaling: Adalbert Stifter and the Measures of Nature around 1850," in *Before Photography: German Visual Culture in the Nineteenth*

and affective footprint, mimicking the format of the cultural journal as a whole. The piece ends as the church bell rings at midday, as narrator and viewer descend to the city streets and readers are offered a gesture of conclusion: "Nimm die Menschen und Bilder, wie sie kommen. Jetzt ein kleines unbedeutendes Wesen, jetzt ein tiefer Mann voll Bedeutung; jetzt Scherz, jetzt Ernst, jetzt ein Einzelbild, jetzt Gruppen und Massen—und all dies zusammen malet dir dann zuletzt Geist und Bedeutung dieser Stadt" (*WuW*, xxi; Take the people and images as they come. Now a small meaningless being, now a deep man full of meaning; now humor, now seriousness, now a single image, now groups and masses—finally, paint all of this together into the spirit and meaning of this city). Though the text marks a kind of ending, this "finally" (*zuletzt*) is provisional at best, not least because of this piece's clear introductory function. With the different "nows" that follow rapidly one after the other, the observer is implored to continue to observe the city, with subsequent days (and subsequent articles) presenting ongoing possible histories.

## "Foolish" Collections

Like "Aussichten und Betrachtungen," Stifter's anthology piece "Wiener Wetter" (Viennese Weather) programmatically reflects on the anthology's format. Readers with even passing familiarity with Stifter know how important weather is in his writings, and scholars have extensively explored the status of both regular and irregular weather events in his work.[44] Recording atmospheric conditions plays a key role in Stifter's work in the 1840s for various journals and anthologies, including his 1842 article on the solar eclipse, as well as in his first published story, *Der Condor* (1840), which involves a balloon flight to collect data. In turn, weather is a topic intimately intertwined with various forms of serial print. Since the early days of print, weather patterns and seasonal norms were central topics of calendars and almanacs, and such print organs served as

---

*Century*, ed. Kirsten Belgum, Vance Byrd, and John D. Benjamin (Berlin and Boston, MA: De Gruyter, 2021), 267–92.

44   See Michael Gamper, "'Luft Licht Dünste Wolken': Wahrnehmung und Darstellung der Atmosphäre bei Adalbert Stifter," in *Flüchtigkeit der Moderne: Eigenzeiten des Ephemeren im langen 19. Jahrhundert*, ed. Dirk Oschmann, Michael Bied, and Sean Franzel (Hanover: Wehrhahn, 2017), 135–56. On Stifter's engagement with environmental and atmospheric issues, see also Sean Ireton, "Adalbert Stifter and the Gentle Anthropocene," in *Readings in the Anthropocene: The Environmental Humanities, German Studies, and Beyond*, ed. Sabine Wilke and Japhet Johnstone (New York: Bloomsbury, 2017), 195–221; and Timothy Attanucci, "The 'Gentle Law' of Large Numbers: Stifter's Urban Meterology," *Monatshefte* 112, no. 1 (2020): 1–19.

important sites where natural and media-based periodicities intersect.[45] At the same time, though, the topic of weather reveals certain limits to print's predictive power.[46] The early and mid-nineteenth century witness the proliferation of use-oriented, predictive weather almanacs, which are often spoofed by belletristic collections such as *Wien und die Wiener* for their unfounded claims, something that "Wiener Wetter" picks up on through its engagement with competing literary and scientific modes of recording weather events.[47]

The narrator persona of the piece is clearly identifiable as Stifter's creation for the anthology, self-identifying as a playful yet melancholy fool: "Ich war eigentlich seit meinen Studien her ein Grübler, obwohl zu Zeiten ein lustiger Vogel und Schalk, vorzugsweisen beschäftigte ich mich mit Sammlungen von Käfern und Altertümern, an Wettersammeln dachte ich nicht, ich meinte auch, es gäbe kein solches Ding, obwohl ich auch schon damals an gewissen Wettern meine Freude hatte" ( *WuW*, 336; Actually, I had long been a brooder ever since my studies, though at times a silly bird and fool, and I primarily occupied myself with collections of beetles and antiquities. Collecting weather didn't cross my mind; I also thought such a thing did not exist, although even then I took great pleasure in certain kinds of weather). Likening an interest in typologizing weather and its effects on people to collecting antiques from the secondhand market, or Tandelmarkt (the topic of another programmatic anthology piece), the narrator introduces the neologism "Wettersammeln" (weather collecting). What does it mean exactly, to "collect" weather: how does one preserve meteorological events so as to keep them somehow present or integrated into the lifeworld of people, whether in a predictive capacity or as a memory of significant historic weather events? Is collecting weather similar to representing it as part of a landscape painting, freezing dynamic weather events on the canvas and turning something only diffusely objective into an object through the artistic process?[48] Collecting weather implies medial transposition into writing or image (one might also recall Stifter's later story *Nachkommenschaften* [Decendants], whose central figure is a landscape painter who obsessively—foolishly— paints the same moor under different times of the day and weather conditions). Collecting thus deals both

45  See Achim Landwehr, *Geburt der Gegenwart: Eine Geschichte der Zeit im 17. Jahrhundert* (Frankfurt am Main: Fischer, 2014).

46  As John Durham Peters puts it: "It would be fruitless to publish local weather reports in eighteenth-century newsletters that took weeks to circulate. Only weather oddities and wonders had legs." John Durham Peters, *The Marvelous Clouds: Towards a Philosophy of Elemental Media* (Chicago, IL: University of Chicago Press, 2015), 249.

47  See Katharine Anderson, *Predicting the Weather: Victorians and the Science of Meteorology* (Chicago, IL: University of Chicago Press, 2005), 41–82.

48  On weather as quasi-object, see Gamper, "'Luft Licht Dünste Wolken.'"

with unique events and the relationships that arise between them by being placed into patterns of proximity and succession.

Stifter was well informed about the still nascent science of meteorology and was friends with one of its practitioners, the Viennese scientist Andreas Baumgartner.[49] He is not averse to making thinly veiled references to acquaintances in his works by rearranging letters in their names, so it is possible the narrator's scientist friend named "Grimbucker" is a playful citation of Baumgartner. It is this Grimbucker figure who encourages the narrator to become involved in municipal meteorology, proposing that, because he likes the rarities and "fantasy objects" (*Fantasiestücke*) of the Tandelmarkt, he must be taken with the "Meteorsammlungen und Wetterkatalogen … und all den sonderbaren Wirkungen auf das physiologische und sociale Leben, die solche Wetterräritäten hervorbringen" (*WuW*, 337; the meteor collections and weather catalogues … and all the unusual effects that these kinds of weather rarities have upon the physiological and social life). The neologism "meteor collection" could suggest both a collection of meteorites or just a synonym for "Wettersammlung."[50] In conjunction with "weather catalogues," though, the term also calls to mind serial publications that track the movements of the heavenly bodies from year to year, which at the time are still called "Ephemerides."[51] This characterization of collecting information about "weather rarities" evokes the early modern fascination with the curious as well as more modern forms of statistical and scientific data.

The narrator tells of becoming involved with municipal meteorologists and of his visits to the city's various observation stations. He takes over the association's "philosophische Section, d.h. für die, welche Schlüße ziehen muß" (*WuW*, 337; philosophical section, that is to say for the one who is responsible for drawing conclusions), but he is quickly removed from office after suggesting that "man soll auch solche Beobachter creiren, welche die Scherz- und Schimpfszenen sammeln, die bei schnellem Wetterwechsel und argem Wüthen desselben in einer so volkreichen Stadt notwendig vorfallen müßten" (*WuW*, 337; one should also create those kinds of observers who collect scenes of jokes and scoldings that would necessarily have to happen in such a populous city with quick changes in the weather and the anger that follows). The

49   See Michael Gamper, "Meteorologie/Wetter," in Begemann and Giuriato, *Stifter-Handbuch*, 253–57; and Kathrin Maurer, "Adalbert Stifter's Poetics of Clouds and Nineteenth-Century Meteorology," *Oxford German Studies* 45, no. 4 (2016): 421–33.

50   Although the proper term would be "Meteoritensammlung"—metorites are a lot easier to collect than meteors!

51   See Peter Gendolla, "Auf 50 Meter genau: Die neuen Ephemeriden," in *Ephemeres: Mediale Innovationen 1900/2000*, ed. Ralf Schnell and Georg Stanitzek (Bielefeld: transcript, 2005), 217–35; here 219–22.

meterological association does not take kindly to this suggestion, fearing that such "annals" would turn it into the laughingstock of the scientific community. In response, then, rather than presenting his collected observations of "die gesellige, die anthropologische, die närrische [Seite]" (the sociable, the anthropological, the foolish side) of Viennese weather in any official organ, the narrator opts to publish them in *Wien und die Wiener*: "und da ich in dieser Hinsicht eine ganze Menge von Daten zusammengebracht habe, die in keinem unserer Kataloge Platz greifen dürfen, so nehme ich die Gelegenheit dieser Blätter wahr, dem Publikum einige derselben darzulegen, da ich vermuthe, daß es daran mehr Freude haben dürfte, als an den dicken wissenschaftlichen Katalogen, obwohl sie Herr Grimbucker in rotes Leder einbinden ließ (*WuW*, 338; And because I have brought together a large amount of data in this regard that cannot occupy any place in our catalogues, I now take the occasion of these pages to present some of this data to the public, for I would guess that it would take more pleasure in this than in the thick scientific catalogues, although Herr Grimbucker has had them bound in thick red leather). These remarks continue to riff on ephemeral, periodical publication, aligning humorous sketches with "occasional," fleeting pages rather than with any monumental permanence secured by thick leather binding. Stifter thus links science and entertainment to distinctly alternative publication formats. Additionally, the piece highlights the interrelated periodicities of print and weather (ab)normalities. The narrator leaves it open which is of more lasting value, the work of dry weather "catalogues" or playful literary "images."

Opening "the sack of my observations," the narrator then follows a similar pattern to the introductory "View," starting with an overarching allegorical approach before "painting" "more piquant" individual "scenes of specific weather outbreaks" (see *WuW*, 342). Calling descriptions of the four seasons in Vienna the "most awful commonplace," the narrator nonetheless half-heartedly begins with a loosely allegorical discussion of the seasons in Vienna, mentioning locations and activities discussed in other anthology pieces as they regularly occur across the calendar year, including student life, manual laborers, excursions into the countryside and more, again establishing connections to descriptions of these sorts of things in other articles. However, the narrator interrupts this physiognomy of the seasons rather abruptly to turn to so-called "rhapsodischen Wetterscenen und ihren Wirkungen" (*WuW*, 344; rhapsodic weather scenes and their effects). Implying discontinuity, the term rhapsodic derives from epic poets stitching pieces of text together, with the sketches that follow again mimicking miscellaneous formats of cultural journalism (indeed, it was common to associate short, disjunctive style with French periodicals[52]). Like the "history of a single day" in "Aussichten und Betrachtungen," this closing section jumps from weather scene to scene rather than tracking cyclical, seasonal patterns. In effect, we have another instance of Stifter writing time through a series of heterogenous sketches rather than via the linear time of the seasons of or of a unified narrative. The text takes on the appearance of an archival collection of multiple related sorts of texts (a "Sack meiner Beobachtungen" [*WuW*, 342; sack of my observations]).[53]

The narrator deliberately begins with "more entertaining weather," namely bad weather, addressing the effects of heavy rainstorms and lingering with a particularly extreme rain- and ice storm (*WuW*, 347). Sketching "das Portrait eines Tages, den ich selbst in Wien erlebte" (*WuW*, 347; the portrait of a day that I personally experienced in Vienna), the narrator describes an ice storm where a sudden drop in temperature causes the rain to freeze. This is an important precursor to the ice storm episode in the *Studien*-version of the *Mappe meines Urgroßvaters,* which likewise presents an account of the ice from a first-person narrator. In contrast to the seriousness of the *Mappe*, though, where the storm is narrated by a doctor who braves the storm to visit ailing patients, here, the narrator is forced out of his house solely by the desire to witness extraordinary, at times hilarious city scenes: "Welche verrückte Gestalten man in solchen Tagen sieht, welche Gesichterschneider, welche zerknüllte Hüte und zerfetzte Regenschirme, kann nur der ermessen, den seine Pflicht an solchen Tagen zu Beobachtungen antreibt" (*WuW*, 349; Only the person who is propelled by duty to make these observations can measure the kinds of crazy figures and faces one sees on such days, the crumpled hats and mangled umbrellas). The narrator then turns to unusual windstorms (noting one of the biggest recorded storms of this kind, on July 19, 1828), then to fog. The effects of thick November fogs "haben wir theils oben schon angedeutet, theils gedenken wir es in einem anderen Artikel dieses Werkes, unter dem Titel 'Salonleben' näher auszuführen" (*WuW*, 350; was already mentioned in part above, and will in part be expanded upon in a different article of this work with the title "Salon Life"). As in the "View" article, Stifter presents readers with an "image" and with the promise that it will be fleshed out in more detail in serial continuations. This is a logic of presenting brief sketches that could be expanded upon, in which case these scenes' temporal frame would be extended. Some are slowed down, while others are sped up by being treated cursorily.

---

52  Theodor Mundt aligns the laconic, rhapsodic style of many Vormärz authors with the French. Theodor Mundt, *Die Kunst der deutschen Prosa* (Berlin: Veit und Comp, 1837), 114–15.

53  Nicolas Pethes has shown how this archival quality is a feature of Stifter's writings more generally; see Pethes, *Literarische Fall-Archive.*

Looking ahead to Stifter's subsequent body of work, this piece also lays the groundwork for a life-long obsession with writing about and painting atmospheric events. Treating this repository of weather scenes as a sketchbook for future projects gives additional meaning to the notion of "collecting weather," where the use-value of such a collection is primarily for literary or painterly reworking. Here we catch a glimpse of a writer recording observations that can be translated into future writing.

Here, too, we might return one final time to the fool figure from the frontispiece (Figure 2.1): is he not himself the weather collector? At first glance, he seems to hold a daguerreotype reproduction of the scene that the people (and we ourselves) are looking at, but could the passing of time not have introduced subtle changes in the cloud cover, lighting, humidity, etc. so that the scene depicted in the image and the current view become increasingly different? Or, could it be that the image represents the same view, but on a different day, a different year? As weather patterns change, the day unfolds and the sun moves through the sky, the view changes and a gap opens up between the present and the earlier moment of producing the daguerreotype. On this line of thought, capturing a snapshot of time via the daguerreotype occurs under the sign of seriality, for it promises that more images will invariably follow. This promise is made by the weather on the one hand, and by the information at the bottom of the page: the current double installment is the fifteenth and sixteenth of twenty-four to thirty total. The images to come can fill the gap between the image and the city as it currently looks.

## "What is Time?" Stifter's Literary Legacies

I have argued that the "Aussicht und Betrachtungen" and "Wiener Wetter" articles both exhibit key features of Stifter's engagement with journal- and anthology-based literature. The anthology juxtaposes these articles as plural counter- or "double" images that accumulate meaning through proximity to other pieces. These texts likewise deposit various smaller anecdotes and "rhapsodic" sketches that subsequent writings might take up, expand upon, dilate or contract, priming such images for future rediscovery. These pieces' serial structure creates the drive for continued viewing, for moving on to the next text or image, for proceeding to the next moment in time or returning to previous ones. It likewise stands out that both of these texts come into view as ongoing or incomplete, that they program into reader experience the expectation for more images, more textual materials, more observations, rather than rounding out into a self-contained work. In closing, I would like to turn to the posthumous 1870 *Vermischte Schriften* (Miscellaneous Writings) anthology as a site that negotiates Stifter's literary legacy and its involvement with different patterns of continuation and completion. Stifter continues to write for journals up until his death, with most of his important late stories from the 1860s being published in various periodicals; he even returns to the conceit of the foolish narrator in *Nachkommenschaften* (Descendants, 1864), a text that explores the "foolish" serial proliferation of images.[54] The two-volume *Vermischte Schriften* reprint various essays and occasional pieces by Stifter on art, drama, education, painting, architecture and more first published in journals, and are edited by Johannes Aprent, Stifter's one-time collaborator.[55] These collected writings appear under the sign of a literary legacy based on future reencounter; however, the terms of such reencounter are ambivalent, for some of these texts are presented as foreign in their pastness and subject to decay rather than being prone for reactualization.

The *Vermischte Schriften* are a place for negotiating the status of these journal pieces vis-à-vis more full-fledged works and, as such, mark something of the beginning of the posthumous philological curation of Stifter's *oeuvre*. The first volume opens with the final version of Stifter's novel *Die Mappe meines Urgroßvaters* (My Great-Grandfather's Notebook). There Aprent presents the *Mappe* as "Bruchstücke aus dem unvollendet gebliebenen Werke" (fragments from the work that remained incompete). The *Mappe* stands in contrast to the occasional pieces surrounding it, which Aprent calls occasional "descriptive" or "reflective" essays.[56] On this account, the *Mappe* would have taken on the status of a proper work had Stifter been able to complete it, and is written under the sign of the "utopia of the finished text" (John) serving as an example of Stifter's propensity for reworking stories by expanding the size and scope of journal versions, sometimes to lengths perceived by contemporary and later readers alike as excessive.[57] Indeed, this text would go on to become a work ripe for work-genetic scholarship and an important locus for subsequent critical editions to test out their techniques of securing given texts'

---

54   See Elisabeth Strowick, "'Nachkommenschaften': Stifter's Series," in *Truth in Serial Form: Serial Formats and the Form of the Series, 1850–1930*, ed. Malika Maskarinec (Berlin and Boston, MA: De Gruyter, 2023), 83–114.

55   See Walter Hettche and Johannes Johns, "Editionsgeschichte," in Begemann and Giuriato, *Stifter-Handbuch*, 365–68, here 365.

56   Johannes Aprent, "Vorwort," in Adalbert Stifter, *Vermischte Schriften*, vol. 1 (Pesth: Heckenast, 1870), n.p.

57   John, "Die Utopie des 'fertigen' Textes," 105. On Stifter's propensity for expanding journal versions, see Matz, *Adalbert Stifter*, 186–95. On later editorial efforts to trim what was perceived to be excessive description from his writings, see Samuel Frederick, *Narratives Unsettled: Digression in Robert Walser, Thomas Bernhard, and Adalbert Stifter* (Evanston, IL: Northwestern University Press, 2012), 129–70.

"final" versions.[58] Deeming the *Mappe* a fragmentary work highlights the tension between finished works and more occasional, journal-based writings, yet, at the same time, the format of the *Vermischte Schriften* bundles them together, prompting readers to constellate early and late work in various ways. The dates of publication of some of the essays are noted, as are the journals in which they were first published. As Aprent notes, such essays help to fill in a broader picture of Stifter's life: "Sie gehen neben den größeren Arbeiten des Dichters einher oder füllen die Zeiten zwischen denselben aus, und geben so in ihrer Gesammtheit den Eindruck eines in vielseitiger Thätigkeit sich erfüllenden Lebens" (They accompany the poet's larger works or they fill in the times between them, and thus in their totality give the impression of a life fulfilled by multi-faceted activity).[59] On this account, the totality (*Gesammtheit*) of these pieces is different from the totality of a single work, for it serves to help readers better understand the course of the author's life rather than gain a vision of aesthetic form as manifested in individual works.

But my interest in the *Vermischte Schriften* is not primarily guided by the utopian horizon of the completed work. Instead, I would ask us to consider a different piece from the *Vermischte Schriften* that comes down rather differently on intersecting questions of serial form and temporal awareness than both the *Mappe* and the pieces from *Wien und die Wiener* collected there. Stifter wrote several short essays for the illustrated family weekly *Die Gartenlaube für Österreich* (1866–69), founded by Leopold von Sacher-Masoch, which are included in volume two of the *Vermischte Schriften*, with their publication year and location indicated. These pieces reflect the pedagogical values of the family journal; one ruminates on the garden bower as a routinized site of serial relaxation and edification, and two more address the celebration of Christmas and New Year's Eve. These pieces are instances of a common, even ubiquitous genre convention of cultural journals, they are written in a tone accessible to the mixed family audience, and they play on Stifter's reputation as a pedagogue.[60] The piece "Der Sylvesterabend" (New Year's Eve) appears in the journal's final issue of the year in 1866 and begins with reported speech discussing the holiday:

> "Der Sylvesterabend ist da," sagen die Leute, "ein Jahr ist in einigen Stunden aus, und ein neues beginnt."

58    For recent reconsiderations of Stifter's attempts to rework this piece, see Barbara N. Nagel, "Versioning Violence: On Gender, Genetics, and Jealousy in Adalbert Stifter's Mappe," *Zeitschrift für deutsche Philologie* 139 (2020): 287–307; and Resvick, "The Author as Editor."

59    Aprent, "Vorwort," n.p.

60    Indeed, the *Bunte Steine* anthology was first conceived of as a collection of stories for and about children; see Sabine Schneider, "Epochenzugehörigkeit und Werkentwicklung," in Begemann and Giuriato, *Stifter-Handbuch*, 196–205.

"Es ist ein wichtiger Zeitabschnitt," sagen die andern, "er hat das, er hat jenes gebracht, was wird der neue bringen?"

Und wie viele fragen: "Was ist die Zeit?" [61]

["New Year's Eve is here," people say, "a year is up in a few hours and a new one begins."

"It is an important period of time," the others say, "it's brought the one thing and the other, what will the new one bring."

And, as many ask, "what is time?"]

These anonymous statements evoke the tone, if not the content, of year's end reflections, but this reported speech might just as well serve as a kind of personalization of the ubiquitous ways that journals and newspapers mark the end of the year—the one journal has a poem about time, the other speculates predictively, the other offers more general ruminations on time, etc. Turning from what other people/papers have to say, Stifter shifts to a first-person perspective: "Und ich, wenn wir von etwas so Ungeheuerem reden, von einem Abschnitte der Zeit, frage: 'Was ist die Zeit?' 'Und kann mann sie abschneiden und zerschneiden?' (When I speak of something so enormous as a period of time, I ask: "what is time?" "And can one cut it up and cut it apart?").[62] As we have already seen, the question of segmenting and scaling frames of time is central to Stifter's poetics. He then goes into an extended reflection on time as perhaps the most unknowable part of life: "Sie ist das Geheimniß der ganzen Schöpfung, wir sind in sie eingehüllt, kein Pulsschlag, kein Blick der Augen, kein Zucken einer Fiber ist außer ihr, wir kommen nicht aus ihr heraus, und wissen nicht, was sie ist" (It is the secret of all of creation, we are enveloped in it, no heartbeat, no gaze of the eyes, no twitch of a fever takes place outside of it, we cannot step out of it, and do not know what it is).[63]

Readers are taken through an extended reflection on time, on different ways it can be perceived and measured, its relationship to space, and more. These ruminations fit well with the popular pedagogy of the journal and are evocative of Augustine's famous reflections on time in the *Confessions*. Stifter wraps up this section by returning to the conceit of reported speech, giving the floor to a kind of no-nonsense common man:

"Nun," wird einer sagen, "wozu die müssigen Fragen, wozu das müssige Gerede, das man nicht einmal überall versteht, und dem gar niemals eine Lösung wird, und sehr wahrscheinlich auch gar nicht noth thut? Wozu das?"

---

61  "Der Sylvesterabend," in *Vermischte Schriften*, vol. 2, 310.
62  "Der Sylvesterabend," 310.
63  "Der Sylvesterabend," 310.

Der Mann hat Recht, ich werde die Lösungen dieser Fragen nie finden, und thue die Fragen doch immer wieder, und schreibe sie hier gar in einer Sylvesterabendrede auf, und werde sie wieder thun, und mit mir werden sie diejenigen thun, die ähnliche Wege wandeln, und alle diejenigen müssen uns verzeihen, denen nicht, wenn sie vor dem Bilde von Sais säßen, die Finger zuckten, den Schleier wenigstens zum Theile zu lüften.[64]

["Wait a moment," someone will say, "what's the point of these idle questions, what's the point of this idle talk that people don't even understand in the first place and that there isn't even a solution for and probably isn't even necessary in the first place? What's the point?"

The man is right, I will never find the solutions to these questions, and yet I ask these questions time and again, and even write them down here in a New Year's Eve speech, and will ask these questions again, and people will ask them with me who travel down similar paths, and the others will have to forgive us, all the people who, when sitting in front of the image of Sais, don't feel the twitch in their fingers to at least partially raise the veil.]

Ruminating about time is idle (*müssig*)—this claim bears a similarity to certain scenes in Stifter's early writings where the narrator reports on what others think about him; though this piece here is not outright humorous in tone, "idle" (*müssig*) and "foolish" (*närrisch*) are not far apart in the moral compass of the provincial *Bildungsbürger*. This passage is also structured through repetition, with the first-person narrator underlining the repetitive quality of his reflections. Again we have reference to a process of repeated, ongoing observation, a process of past, present, and future temporal reflection, as well as reference to concomitant processes pursued by others who likewise engage in such processes. Even if these undertakings are "idle" they are collective, evoking a sense of a subset of journal readers as well as more diffuse processes of observation. His emphasis on continuing these reflections marks a particular dedication to temporal observation as well as to understanding time by breaking it up into different segments.

It is at this point that the essay pivots to perhaps more familiar territory, or at least to what naïve readers might have expected: "Ich kehre zu dem bürgerlichen Sylvesterabende zurück" (I return to the populace's celebration of New Year's Eve). The article proceeds to sketch how people spend the end of the year, whether by gathering with one's family, meeting in the local Gasthaus, whether with young people carrying on, or lonely people passing a night without company. This impressionistic surveying of different figures and social types is reminiscent of the anthology tableaus of the "Aussicht und Betrachtungen" or "Wiener Salonleben."

64  "Der Sylvesterabend," 315–16.

The middle-class (*bürgerlich*), domestic family setting is rather predictable in the context of the *Gartenlaube* journal, Biedermeier rather than urban chic. The piece ends by addressing customs of holiday gift giving and well wishing (again, something with which Stifter is quite familiar, with his *Bunte Steine* being marketed as a *Festgeschenk*). In this reflection on the passage of time, Stifter closes with the performative gesture of marking the occasion through writing:

> Und ehe ich die Feder niederlege, schreibe ich noch auf das Blatt: Ein freudenreiches neues Jahr für alle, welche diese Zeilen lesen, und für alle, welche sie nicht lesen, und daß der Himmel füge, daß das Gute, das manchen zu Theil ist, daure, und daß der tiefe Schmerz, der in manches Herz gekommen ist, sich mildere. [65]

> [And before I put down the quill, I write on the sheet: a joyous new year for all who read these lines, and for all who do not read it, and may heaven provide that the good that befalls certain people persist and that the deep pain that has come in certain hearts be softened.]

This rather stock gesture of well-wishing once more draws attention to the process of writing. Even if we do not know what time is, it can still be marked, observed, and perceived. Stifter's somewhat curious extension of directing his new year's wish to people who do not read his lines might well be read as an oblique gesture toward future reception, with the arrival of the wishes with certain audiences at some future moment occurring via circuitous and indirect pathways. Similar to the passage above, Stifter opens up a space for repetition and reencounter, here via the reference to the lack of reception in the present and to forms of reception that remain outside the control of the author. This is a more impassive sense of literary legacy, open to the possible reception of minor works rather than insistent about the enduring greatness of larger ones. Furthermore, this is a gesture of marking time and a style of authorship in line with journal literature. Stifter demonstratively dons the mantle of "Austrian writer," but one who writes and reflects on recurring topics such as the new year's address that are a staple of the popular press.

Ulrike Vedder has described how Stifter's writing envisions various scenes of successful and failed transfer and inheritance, as well as scenes of transmitting writing "beyond intention, transmissions that manifest positive effects, but in a different mode" that eschews direct and intentional transfer, and this scene seems like a perfect example of just such a mode.[66] Throughout this chapter I have suggested ways in which we

---

65  "Der Sylvesterabend," 320.

66  "Eine Schreibeweise jenseits der Intention, Übertragungen, die positive Effekte zeitigen, aber in einem anderen Modus." Ulrike Vedder, "Erbschaft und

might think of this mode as one that emerges from and reflects upon journal literature and its serial logics. Stifter sends his wishes off into the world and off out onto the sea of print, uncertain where or when they will arrive. Taken together with the essay's reflections on time, this closing remark is very much in the same orbit as the observations on the city, its inhabitants, and its weather in the two pieces considered above, namely as a mode of depersonalized observation that lends itself to repetition and continuation and that does not depend upon—indeed, that resists—any kind of finality or completion. It is striking that, even in this late and altogether minor piece, Stifter so readily and comfortably inhabits a mode of journal-based writing. Even if it is foolish to write about time, such folly is hard to resist and calls out for more: more imitators, more writing, more images, more attempts to lift the veil and perceive time in its smallest and largest segments.

---

Gabe, Schriften und Plunder: Stifters testamentarische Schreibweise," in *History, Text, Value: Essays on Adalbert Stifter*, ed. Michael Minden, Martin Swales, and Godela Weiss-Sussex (London: University of London Press, 2003), 22–34; here 31.

# 3: All Eyes on the Streets: Transformations of Public Work, Leisure, and Ritual in *Wien und die Wiener*

*Vance Byrd*

ADALBERT STIFTER REMINDED readers in "Wiener Salonscenen" (Viennese Salon Scenes), the final installment of *Wien und die Wiener in Bildern aus dem Leben* (Vienna and the Viennese in Sketches from Life, 1841–44), that his roots were in rural Upper Bohemia: "Ich glaube dem Leser schon gesagt zu haben, daß ich so glücklich war, meine Kindheit nicht in den Mauern der großen Stadt verlebt zu haben" (*HKG* 9,1:444; I believe I have already told the reader that I was so fortunate not to have spent my childhood behind the walls of the big city). He explained that writing about the city was not that much different from writing about life in the countryside: "es ist hier, wie überall: die Einseitigkeit gebiert den Ekel, und die Vielseitigkeit die Harmonie" (*HKG* 9,1:439; it is here as it is everywhere: one-sidedness breeds disgust, and diversity [breeds] harmony). Stifter thought that it could be boring at a Viennese salon, and that there could be plenty of "Koth, Steine und Morast" (*HKG* 9,1:439; filth, stones, and morass) in an Alpine landscape). Despite his claims to the contrary, the opinion persists that he was more interested in rural than in urban life and that it would be a mistake to claim otherwise. This observation was cemented long ago for a variety of reasons: autobiographical remarks found in his letters and fiction; a narrative focus on nature; a publication history and scholarship privileging realist fiction over administrative correspondence and cultural criticism; an emphasis on single rather than collective authorship; and little scholarly consideration for mid-nineteenth-century city life and leisure.

In this chapter, I will show that *Wien und die Wiener*, Stifter's most extensive publication addressing the transformation of urban life, public trades, and faith around 1840,[1] captures in word and image sketches in

---

1    While I will cite from *Wien und die Wiener in Bildern aus dem Leben* based on the now standard *Historisch-Kritische Gesamtausgabe*, the *HKG* volumes of

which much was new in old Vienna. I will trace how he and the other contributors crafted vivid sketches of the city with what Stifter calls "Hauptstadttaugen" (*HKG* 9,1:248; eyes of the metropolis). To do so, they adopted a rich variety of generic conventions—frontispiece, illustrated and non-illustrated prose essays, dialect poetry, the remediation of musical scores, retrospective narration, dramatic and humor-filled dialogues, multiple points of view—to fictionalize the social geographies and topographies that were changing before their very eyes. In my examination of *Wien und die Wiener*, I will point out that their collective assessment of work and leisure in Vienna is on the whole a rather moralistic and conservative project. Their moralizing inquiry into gender relations, consumer and leisure cultures, public trades, and religious practice ultimately are nostalgic attempts at keeping the old way of doing things present in the minds of readers. Through their participation in broader European debates on modern life, I conclude that we as readers do not gain a truthful picture of how things were in Vienna at the time. Instead, we see writers whose craft and purpose were in the process of transformation and who did not shy away from telling readers how things, ethically, *ought* to be.

## Literature and the Transformation of Viennese Public Life

Written in collaboration with at least seven other authors, the fifty-five essays in *Wien und die Wiener* were part of a longer tradition of sketches of urban life circulating widely in the graphic arts, photography, songs, travel literature, feuilleton, and in material culture since at least the seventeenth century in Europe.[2] By the first decades of the nineteenth cen-

---

Stifter's letters remain difficult to access, even in Germany. Like most scholars, I therefore rely on *Adalbert Stifters Sämmtliche Werke*, ed. Gustav Wilhelm (Prague: J. G. Calve, 1916), which I will cite parenthetically using the abbreviation *SW*, volume number, and page number. Whenever known, I name the author of a given essay or letter unless I am making a generalization about the entire collection. All translations are my own.

2    Jeremy D. Popkin, *Panorama of Paris: Selections from "Tableau de Paris"* (University Park, PA: Penn State University Press, 1999); Martina Lauster, *Sketches of the Nineteenth Century: European Journalism and its Physiologies, 1830–50* (Basingstoke: Palgrave Macmillan, 2007); Wolfgang Kos, "Einleitung," in *Wiener Typen: Klischees und Wirklichkeit*, ed. Wolfgang Kos (Vienna: Wien Museum and Brandstätter, 2013), 14–23; here 14–15; Jens Wietschorke, "Urbane Volkstypen: Zur Folklorisierung der Stadt im 19. und frühen 20. Jahrhundert," *Zeitschrift für Volkskunde* 110, no. 2 (2014): 215–42; here 220; Christiane Schwab, "Sketches of manners, esquisses des moeurs: Die journalistische Gesellschaftsskizze (1830–1860) als ethnographisches Wissensformat," *Zeitschrift für Volkskunde* 112, no. 1 (2016): 37–56.

tury, fiction and nonfiction on Vienna proliferated, including titles by Johann Pezzl, Wolfgang Menzel, Willibald Alexis, Franz Pietznigg, Adolf Glassbrenner, Francis Trollope, Braun von Braunthal, Heinrich Adami, and Matthias Koch.[3] These publications on contemporary city life registered, according to the historian Brian Ladd, the "radical reorganization of communities, of industry and labor, of family life, and of technology."[4] Ladd attributed many of these changes to the nineteenth-century project of cleaning up the streets and emptying them of messy social life and commerce.[5] The result of this shift were sanitary improvements, increased traffic circulation, class segregation, the separation of trades, and the disappearance of other types of public work. Permanent stores and market halls replaced hawkers and temporary booths and stalls for the public sale of goods; and the enclosure of street commerce led to storefronts and the rise of window shopping. These transformations, in Ladd's opinion, created a noteworthy sense of nostalgia for what had been lost.[6]

Stifter had been living in Vienna for fifteen years when he took over editorial responsibilities for *Wien und die Wiener*. He and the other contributors sensed that changes were afoot in the seat of the Habsburg Empire. These writers and illustrators addressed the destruction of old buildings and squares, the development of steamships and railways, and new forms of social interaction in public space. They worried, too, about the spread of secularism and how it tested Christian faith. In coming to terms, literarily, with a period of rapid transformations, the contributors portrayed characters who remained steadfastly dedicated to the common good. The expansion of public institutions was central to the Vienna

---

3 Stifter assured his publisher that the collection would be better than the others on the market, including Adami's *Alt- und Neu-Wien* (1841–42) (*SW* 17,1:99), for which Stifter's own contributor Franz Stelzhamer also wrote essays (*SW* 17,1:81–82). The crowded market for books on Vienna between 1825 and 1845 is addressed in the critical review of *Wien und die Wiener* published in *Österreichische Blätter für Literatur und Kunst* 11, no. 80 (July 5, 1845): 217. This situation was examined in publications on nineteenth-century journalism in German. See for instance Wilmont Haacke, "Deutschlands erste Feuilleton-Anthologie: Adalbert Stifters 'Wien und die Wiener' aus dem Jahre 1844," *Zeitungswissenschaft. Monatsschrift für internationale Zeitungsforschung* 19, no. 9/10 (1944): 236–52; here 237. See also Wilmont Haacke, "Stifter als Meister der kleinen Form," *VASILO* 10 (1961): 119–31.

4 Brian Ladd, *The Streets of Europe: The Sights, Sounds, and Smells That Shaped Its Great Cities* (Chicago, IL: University of Chicago Press, 2020), 8.

5 Ladd, *The Streets of Europe*, 9–11.

6 Ladd, *The Streets of Europe*, 70–71. One contemporary reviewer characterized *Wien und die Wiener* as "ein herrliches Genrebild mit elegischem Grundton" (a wonderful genre picture with an elegiac undertone) in *Österreichische Blätter für Literatur und Kunst* 11, no. 80 (July 5, 1845): 619.

presented in the collection. The contributors thus inventoried new welfare institutions, such as specialized hospitals for the poor, schools, orphanages, institutes for the deaf and blind, veterans homes, banks, and insurance agencies. Rulers, nobles, merchants, police officials, and ordinary people were depicted providing care and protection for the poor and destitute in the Empire.

Indeed, Stifter and the other writers maintained that not so much had changed when one looked more closely around Vienna and into the hearts of the Viennese. They asserted that the latter were mindful of their place within a longer history of the natural environment and the Habsburg Empire. The city maintained its verdant appearance and the Viennese upheld their moral character: they displayed benevolence and warmth. More importantly, their relation to the monarchy had not changed at all: "Ihr Bollwerk ist die Liebe, und ihre Laufgräben sind die Adern des österreichischen Volks voll warmen, deutschen Blutes" (*HKG* 9,1:160; Their bulwark is love, and their trenches are the veins of the Austrian people full of warm, German blood). By taking in this comprehensive picture of Viennese public life and trades around 1840, those new to the city were supposed to feel like they had been there before, while those who already knew the city should feel nostalgic and perhaps even patriotic when they read *Wien und die Wiener* in newspaper installments or later as an illustrated book.[7]

## How to Picture Vienna

The sketches in *Wien und die Wiener* are an exercise in control over the impermanence of the visible world.[8] The aesthetic practice and poetic conventions established for sketches conjure up images of artists and writers surveying life unfolding right before their eyes. In their effort to depict everyday lifestyles in contemporary Vienna, the contributors and editor of the collection tried to find the most accurate and appropriate language possible. Knowledgeable of a broader European tradition of travel accounts, physiognomies, and humorous caricatures, they turned

7    For more on nostalgia, Habsburg history, and the permanence of nature, see Vance Byrd, "The Politics of Commemoration in *Wien und die Wiener* (1841–44)," *Journal of Austrian Studies* 47, no. 1 (2014): 1–20.

8    Ian Hacking, "Making Up People," in *Reconstructing Individualism: Autonomy, Individuality, and the Self in Western Thought*, ed. Thomas C. Heller, Morton Sonsa, and David E. Wellbery (Stanford, CA: Stanford University Press, 1986), 222–37; here 226; Schwab, "Sketches of manners, esquisses des moeurs," 44–45; Jens Wietschorke, "Die Stadt als Tableau," in *Wiener Typen: Klischees und Wirklichkeit*, ed. Wolfgang Kos (Vienna: Wien Museum and Brandstätter, 2013), 26–31; here 27.

to a variety of rhetorical strategies and textual conventions for describing the complexity of Viennese society around 1840. In fact, the publication inventoried numerous ways of comprehending the sight of city life. The metaphorical language of "tableaux, a glass pane, a body of water, a stroboscope, a panorama, a lorgnette, daguerreotypes, geometrical figures, and geological objects,"[9] as well as genre painting, the outline ("Umriss"), and comparisons to forests and trees are all used to describe the sight of Vienna and its environs. In the end, this media inventory underlined that there was no single way to capture the essence of this unique city.[10]

Matthias Bauer has argued that intermedial references in *Wien und die Wiener*—likening visual encounters in the city to stroboscopes, panoramas, or photography—were strategies for understanding urban experience and that this tendency was hardly exceptional.[11] I agree with Bauer's claim that some scholars have relied on anachronistic comparisons to late-nineteenth-century and twentieth-century optical devices and mass media, such as film, in an attempt to convey how Stifter's narratives functioned and to make claims about the modernity of these works. Both Bauer and I, by contrast, have examined media environments contemporaneous with Stifter's fiction.[12] For instance, in his preface to the collection Stifter uses the kaleidoscope as a metaphor for viewing city life. Here he suggests that the impressions captured in the essays appear to be like fragmented pieces of colored glass rotating arbitrarily and reflecting light, just as they do inside a kaleidoscope's cylindrical tube. Yet Stifter does not refer to this toy to convey a random or chaotic image. On the contrary, as David Brewster (1781–1868) had argued in his treatise on the development of this optical instrument, the kaleidoscope elevated simple forms "into one perfect whole."[13] Stifter thus informs readers that they will encounter lighthearted and serious scenes, both good and mediocre

9    Byrd, "Politics of Commemoration," 6.

10    For a recent broad assessment of inventorying, see Sean Franzel, Ilinca Iurescu, and Petra McGillen, "Media Inventories of the Nineteenth Century: A Report from Two Workshops," *Goethe Yearbook* 28 (2021): 285–96.

11    Matthias Bauer, "Stadtbild und Stadttext: Zur Wechselwirkung von Intermedialität und Urbanität bei Adalbert Stifter und anderen," in *Zwischen Gattungsdisziplin und Gesamtkunstwerk: Literarische Intermedialität 1815–1848*, ed. Stefan Keppler-Tasaki and Wolf Gerhard Schmidt (Berlin: De Gruyter, 2015), 143–72; here 143.

12    Bauer, "Stadtbild und Stadttext," 147; Vance Byrd, "The Photographic Sketch and Panoramic Observation," in *A Pedagogy of Observation: Nineteenth-Century Panoramas, German Literature, and Reading Culture* (Lewisburg, PA: Bucknell University Press, 2017), 133–69.

13    David Brewster, *A Treatise on the Kaleidoscope* (Edinburgh: Archibald Constable & Co., 1819), 17.

literature, throughout the pages of *Wien und die Wiener*. He emphasizes that all of the essays—despite their differences in tone and quality—should be read together and against each other so that the true essence of Vienna could be revealed through the imagination (see *HKG* 9,1:n.p.). These stories were thus meant to surprise and delight as their images appeared juxtaposed fleetingly and charmingly, like in a kaleidoscope.

Margaret Cohen's writing on panoramic literature provides a useful framework for understanding this dynamic kaleidoscopic picture of conflict and aesthetic transformation as reflected in the depictions of city life and public work in *Wien und die Wiener*. Cohen argues that new ways of scientifically studying and representing "referentially verifiable space" emerged in literature and art during the July Monarchy (1830–48). She characterizes this shift in France in terms of its "close attention to external, above all visible, material details (objects, clothes, physical appearance, food, gestures, weather, speech)" which all conveyed "the sensuous materiality of contemporary Parisian reality."[14] Cohen defines the character of this realist art and literature in two main ways. She proposes that textual heterogenericity conveyed how writers, illustrators, and editors during this period brought together short and formally varied stories appearing in feuilleton collections and anthologies.[15] As a result, the content of these heterogeneric works typically presented a social heteroglossia: a broad spectrum of different text types within one publication helped express different ways of living. To put it another way, the visual and verbal representations that these authors created served to capture the experience of people observing urban life from a variety of social backgrounds and at various locations in a modern metropolis.[16]

The contributors presented a multitude of voices from above and below, speaking to their audience from religious processions, parks, restaurants, flea markets, salons, and, above all, from the streets. One gains a sense of heterogeneric virtuosity and social heteroglossia when the characters in *Wien und die Wiener* speak for themselves in dialogues (see, for instance, *HKG* 9,1:27–28, 35–39, 44–48, 306–7, 310), which are often written in strong Viennese dialect (see *HKG* 9,1:65–67, 86, 303–4). Sometimes the sketches include song, which is reproduced with a musical score and lyrics on the page (see *HKG* 9,1:20–21). Furthermore, this individuality is apparent when we consider the voices writing for the collection. Stifter wrote the preface and twelve of these essays, and authors

---

14  Margaret Cohen, "Panoramic Literature and the Invention of Everyday Genres," in *Cinema and the Invention of Modern Life*, ed. Leo Charney and Vanessa R. Schwartz (Berkeley: University of California Press, 1995), 227–52; here 231.

15  Cohen, "Panoramic Literature," 231–32.

16  Cohen, "Panoramic Literature," 243.

92 ♦ Vance Byrd

of Austrian popular literature completed the other forty-three contributions in a variety of styles. While their essays easily outnumbered his own, Stifter's impression on the collection as an editor is significant and included writing the introductory frame, rejecting weak essays, stepping in when contributors did not turn in their work on time, polishing prose, dealing with censors, as well as extended negotiations with his publisher and friend Gustav Heckenast. Stifter thus lent the publication his own signature, even though it was a product of constitutive generic diversity and multiple authorship. The complex interplay of textual heterogenericity and social heteroglossia is central to the editorial and authorial presentation of *Wien und die Wiener* in both word and image. In terms of visual language, each of the thirty installments included an illustration prepared by Wilhelm Böhm and etched by Carl Mahlknecht, artists who collaborated on the frontispieces as well. This visual material—the frontispiece and illustrations—indexed the varieties of public life that were undergoing radical transformation in European cities such as Vienna.

The frontispiece for *Wien und die Wiener* from the year 1844, for example, adopts the visual layout and summary function reserved for nineteenth-century installment literature. One might think here of the light-blue wrappers covering the monthly installments of Charles Dickens's *Oliver Twist*. The frontispiece frames the collection as a series of episodes depicting the Viennese as a people overwhelmingly engaged in public trades and outdoor leisure pursuits (see Figure 3.1). These twelve sketched vignettes seem to be taken from the shadowy crowd of anonymous figures located in the lower portion of the illustration. Engraved images of a female ragpicker, a woman and children listening to an organ grinder's music, people on promenades, a laundrywoman, a shoemaker's apprentice, coach drivers and horses, a male bone picker, a milkmaid, and a woman carrying a pitcher and basket all speak to us in visual language before we even begin to read the volume's essays. We see destitute men and women doing the dirty work of collecting public refuse. Other women appear laboring under heavy loads, their faces marked by expressions of suffering. A woman driving a horse and loaded cart with an air of confidence especially stands out. Here on the frontispiece, such women at work may be out-of-doors and unaccompanied in public but women at leisure always appear in the company of men or children.

How do we reconcile these contrasting messages about the role of women in Viennese society and their presence in the public sphere? Fancy dresses, cloaks, and top hats in several vignettes on the frontispiece suggest that leisure can be a stratified affair and takes place beyond the city center, as indicated by faintly sketched trees and structures far in the background. We might ask whether the image layout represents a hierarchy: Does the frontispiece suggest that male sociability and leisure reign supreme in the collection? In any case, these vignettes encircle the title

Figure 3.1. The frontispiece for the 1844 book edition of *Wien und die Wiener*. Wien Museum Inv.-Nr. 97544/1, CC0. (https://sammlung.wienmuseum.at/objekt/524530/).

and publication date, and the floral cornucopia's ornamental details near the top and the dynamic verticality of fireworks exploding around the figures suggest both abundance and the ephemeral fizzling out of such vibrant displays; these ways of life are appearing and disappearing before our eyes. The dynamism of these pictures is also suggested by the faint outlines sequentially representing the horse's head in motion; the speed of the horse-drawn carriage's rolling wheels will be confirmed inside the collection. The layout and images of the frontispiece are thus an example of the appropriation of generic conventions for installment literature to represent city life from a variety of social positions and locations. It is heterogeneric and elaborates the social heteroglossia of Vienna. As a material text, the frontispiece functions visually as a partial table of contents previewing aspects of Viennese work and leisure that the subsequent individual essays in *Wien und die Wiener* will then depict.

Like the colorful fragments brought together yet held apart at the end of the kaleidoscope's tube, the chapter and page format of the publication presents potential social tensions and conflicts inherent to nineteenth-century city life. Yet the textual materiality and permanence of the bound volume make the serially fragmented newspaper issues into a whole. Inside the 1844 book edition, the frontispiece figures, such as the Female Ragpicker (see Figure 3.2), reappear in richer detail and illustrate the essays. This form of repetition is accompanied by proliferation: here one finds more visual sketches of Viennese life than represented on the frontispiece. Here, too, life on or near the street predominates. The illustrators prepared thirty images of people standing at the thresholds of their respective establishments or entirely in the out-of-doors, selling clothes, chopped wood, groceries, fruit, goat's milk, dumplings, and junk; others beg for money to those leaning out windows inside their homes onto the street level. The book edition forms a bond that permits the regularity of encountering these illustrated types and locations time and again on the verso.[17] This image placement establishes a spatiotemporal order for reading the collection in which the poor who pick trash and bones as well as the affluent couples on promenades or traveling by horse-drawn coach are kept apart by the irregular page intervals separating each essay and title. Yet almost all of these illustrated figures depicted outside in public are united by a common visual strategy. The use of negative or blank space foregrounds the visible features of their bodily form, clothing, and of the objects that surround them. These characters may be kept apart based on their social class, but they will all be given the same level of

---

17 The illustration "Die Pudelschererin" (The Poodle Shearer) for Sylvester Wagner's sketch "Der Vogelmarkt" (The Bird Market) is the exception to the regularity of image placement in *Wien und die Wiener* (see *HKG* 9,1:415). It appears halfway through the story.

Figure 3.2. Colored illustration of "The Female Ragpicker" from the 1844 book edition of *Wien und die Wiener*. Wien Museum Inv.-Nr. 97544/4, CC0. (https://sammlung.wienmuseum.at/objekt/524546/).

narrative attention such that we will gain a close-up view of their lives. It is noteworthy that the negative space in Böhm's drawings drastically decontextualizes these social portraits and makes invisible most signs of city life. The stories of these solitary figures are elaborated in the pages that follow these illustrations.

## Telling Stories about Everyday Life in Vienna

The frontispiece, illustrations, and essay titles in *Wien und die Wiener* identify a location or a typical character who might be encountered out in public or within private spaces. In the essays themselves, the narrator's direct address to the reader focalizes and foregrounds the fiction of personal experience and direct observation about Viennese life. Yet there is no single way of starting a story about everyday life in Vienna. Heterogenericity, a fluid mixture of narrative approaches that capture the essence of public life, remains a consistent feature within the collection. Many stories begin with general observations and then shift to a narrower sketch of a particular social type or location. Others start in medias res followed by multiple instances of retrospective narration about an episode in Habsburg history or about an excursion to a specific site. And some contributors use a meandering spatial trajectory, often recessional and chronological from the city center to the countryside, plotted by a series of descriptive vignettes, in their respective efforts to characterize a Viennese type, activity, or location. These vignettes do not tell a coherent, fully developed story about a single character, the precise nature of public work, or location announced by the title. Instead, they provide sophisticated and varied glimpses into Viennese life—rich descriptions of work, leisure, and interactions with other characters—outlining the social distinctions and hierarchies *within* a given Viennese class or trade.

A fiction of repeated direct observation is central to the conclusions reached in these sketches. In "Das Stubenmächen" (The Chambermaid), we encounter a female type caught up in her world of books and beautiful fantasies. Under the guidance of the anonymous author's narrator, we observe her preoccupations and follow her across diverse locations. She reads, drinks coffee, and on occasion goes to the theater. This brief sketch leads us to imagine that the chambermaid's everyday leisure life unfolds in precisely such a detailed manner. The narrator has spotted a "type." As he reflects on this essentializing process of repeated direct observation: "Wer zwei oder drei Stubenmädchen gesehen, hat *alle* gesehen, so sehr sind sie ähnlich" (*HKG* 9,1:10; Whoever has seen two or three maids has seen them *all*, they are so alike). In "Leben und Haushalt dreier Wienerstudenten" (Life and Household of Three Viennese Students), to name another example, Stifter's narrator explains that he directs our attention on these students not because they are exceptional. Instead, they communicate something more general about others like them, that is "die ganze Gattung" (*HKG* 9,1:197; the entire type).

Such reading of physiognomies or social types extends to colonial and imperial references in the collection. Numerous essays comment on European conflicts with the Ottoman Empire, and the classification of ordinary objects falls under this shadow as well. The description of tobacco pipes in Anton Ritter von Perger's "Der Pfeifentod" (The Pipe Death) serves as an inventory of physiognomies on which national character is based. The writer's descriptive attention to these exotic sculptural objects originating from inside and outside of Europe, such as those thought to be Turkish, Chinese, Persian, Mexican, or used by indigenous tribes from North America, suggests how the activity of collecting and the sociability of smoking salons in Vienna formed the basis for clichés about entire peoples touched by imperial regimes and further calls attention to how the Viennese themselves were connected to colonial and racist thought. Here and elsewhere in *Wien und die Wiener*, the collection of *types* thus contributes to the proliferation and circulation of *stereotypes*.

We do not need to read carefully to conclude that many of these generalizations—gross simplifications, moral judgments, a bourgeois masculine perspective, imperialism—shape the pictures of modern life developed in *Wien und die Wiener*. The narrator declares in "Der Ladendiener des Modehändlers" (The Fashion Retailer's Clerk) that sketches are written "mit daguerreotypischer Genauigkeit" (*HKG* 9,1:9; with Daguerreotypic accuracy), a statement that underscores this tie to referential reality. In the collection's first social portrait, we are told that the male clerk is representative of his profession and social type or "Typus" (*HKG* 9,1:3). The detailed description of his interactions with others is essential for the construction of this character. The narrator creates a physiognomy based on his outward appearance, gestures, language use, workplace, and preferred leisure hangouts, which all ultimately confirm his vanity. He is a dapper fellow, we are told. He dresses elegantly, sports a manicured beard, smells of cologne, and smokes a cigar. He promenades, sips coffee at garden cafés, and rides horses. He attends balls in the evening and dances the waltz, albeit in a grotesque manner. When at work in the shop, this dandy alternatingly directs his gaze at the wares and then into the eyes of his female customers. His blinks, wrinkled forehead, raised eyebrows, and deft two-fingered handling of items are all part of the perfect yet affected way he controls his body and seeks to manipulate his clientele. The narrator informs us that one of the female customers wants to own something unique that the other ladies will envy. To make this purchase, she must face the male clerk's twofold manipulation. She is ashamed because the interaction has the air of an unwanted romantic advance, and it threatens to ruin her household budget. She knows that his hard sell and her vanity

("Eitelkeit") will jeopardize her marriage, but she ultimately falls for his flirtatious pitch (see *HKG* 9,1:2). Right from the outset of *Wien und die Wiener*, this sketch presents readers with an ambivalent message about women going out unaccompanied in public and an extended caricature of a salesclerk, who is depicted as an effeminate womanizer. The short sketch's attention to the visible—clothing, gestures, speech, and its concluding second-order reference to the illustration—and the series of social scenes help deliver a moralistic and foreboding message about male and female vanity in everyday Viennese consumer and leisure culture. His profession may not be on the verge of disappearance, but the story's critical edge lies in its subtle warning about leisure and commerce in the new Vienna.

The use of mixed generic conventions serves to convey the collection's moralizing message about life in public. While the beginning and middle sections of "Der Ladendiener" include snippets of casual conversation between the clerk and shopper mainly in present tense, "Der Musik-Enthusiast" (The Music Enthusiast) draws upon distinct strategies for narrating speech and creating a social type. After the anonymous author's introduction and below the caesura, the narration transports us to a past scene at an opera house. The gestures and dress of an audience member named Herr Purzl make him stand out, and the reproduction of his conversation at performances makes us question his reasons for being out in public. The writer draws attention to Purzl's behavior by using expanded spacing, punctuation, and parenthetical descriptions of his emotions, which draw upon textual conventions common to reading dramas and stage directions. One learns that the Music Enthusiast attends concerts regularly but knows little about music: "er glüht heute für das Classische, ihn entzückt morgen das Triviale, ihm ist Mozart und Donizetti identisch, und eine Beethovenische Symphonie macht denselben Eindruck auf, [*sic*] ihn als eine Parthie Variationen von Herz" (*HKG* 9,1:39; Today he burns for classical music. Tomorrow he is enchanted by the trivial. Mozart and Donizetti are identical to him, and a Beethoven symphony makes the same impression on him as a round of variations by [the composer Henri] Herz). He lacks discernment, and his reactions to performance are not in accord with public decorum. A recitative makes him break out in tears and "die darauf folgende Arie erschüttert ihn dermaßen, daß er den Pfeiler umarmend, in ein so unbändiges Stöhnen ausbricht, daß einige Umstehende in naiver Besorgtheit sich mit der gutmüthigen Frage an ihn wenden, ob er unwohl sei" (*HKG* 9,1:37; he is so shaken by the aria that follows that he lets out such an uncontrollable moan that some bystanders, out of naive concern, ask him kindly if he is unwell). Furthermore, his impromptu lectures on opera leave little room for Ulrike, the young woman sitting next to him in the box, to tell him and her father what she thinks about the performance. The descriptions of effusive and bad behavior suggest that the narrator has repeatedly studied Herr Purzl and the uncultured men like him who attend the opera. Humor and moral instruction outweigh referentiality or a journalistic purpose. It is notable that the essay conveys little information about the rich musical traditions in Vienna around 1840 or in the past. To find that kind of account, one would need to read Stifter's competitors, Francis Trollope, Heinrich Adami, and Matthias Koch, for instance.[18]

Such observations about characters indoors and from the upper levels of society in *Wien und die Wiener* contrast markedly with reflections on the working population. Several sketches of social types capture a moment when much of the work people did out on the streets was starting to disappear.[19] Drawing upon generic conventions of popular literature, the authors use colloquialisms and local dialect to convey a setting's atmosphere. These rhetorical strategies communicate where a given character stands in Viennese society. The strong lungs of Sylvester Wagner's female ragpicker project out onto the streets the melody "Hada'lumpweib," a vocalization which announces her work collecting rags around the city (see Figure 3.2). We know that since the end of the fourteenth century, actual rag-and-bone men and women collected scraps of fabric for making laid paper. In this vein, Wagner's character expresses—in dialect while traversing the city—ambivalence about new technologies of paper manufactured with wood pulp ("Bamrinden und so Zeug") rather than cotton and linen fiber. She attributes this recent development to the rapid expansion of literacy ("bei der jezigen Zeit, wo Alls schreiben kann, und wers no nöt kann, es in vier und zwanzig Stunden auf americanische Art lernt" [in this day and age, when everyone can write and whoever can't learns it the American way in twenty-four hours]) and the need for public advertisements to be posted "in allen Gassenöken" (*HKG* 9,1:67; on all the street corners), which suggests that more and more paper is needed for providing the Viennese with ephemeral material for reading in public.

The authors in *Wien und die Wiener* generally show little concern about the difficulty and precarity of public work. Such dirty and unhealthy labor was relegated to the bottom tier of the hierarchy of the papermaking workforce. These workers died young due to the noxious particulates contained in the rags and scraps of paper they had to handle

---

18  See Francis Trollope, *Vienna and the Austrians* (London: Richard Bentley, 1837), vol. 2, 100–7; "Italienische Oper," in *Alt- und Neu-Wien: Beiträge zur Beförderung lokaler Interessen für Zeit, Leben, Kunst und Sitten*, ed. Heinrich Adami (Vienna: Anton Mausberger, 1841), vol. 3, 18–25; Matthias Koch, *Wien und die Wiener: Historisch entwickelt und im Verhältnisse zur Gegenwart geschildert* (Karlsruhe: C. Macklot, 1842), 372–75.

19  Compare Ladd, *The Streets of Europe*; and Kos, "Einleitung," 16.

daily.[20] Moreover, ordinances to clean up the streets and the introduction of municipal trash collection led to the disappearance of the ragpicker.[21] In view of the above, the female ragpicker's informed complaint speaks directly to readers holding ephemeral newsprint in their hands; it reminds them where this paper actually comes from. And the ragpicker's song ultimately articulates the decline of her public role.

A second essay about paper and public work, Friedrich Reiberstorffer's "Der Zettelausträger" (The Poster Man), is a companion essay to Wagner's female ragpicker. This character pastes announcements on public walls so that this ephemeral material catches the eye of passersby. This activity requires knowledge of busy locations across Vienna and the ability to secure a prime spot for hanging up the posters before the competition beats one to it. Reiberstorffer's narrator notes that the poster man's appearance and worksites attest to his social status and its boundaries. Some deliver and post public announcements while wearing a tattered jacket made of rags or "ausgenähnten Lappen" (*HKG* 9,1:97). Others, more elegantly dressed, gain access to interior spaces, such as coffeeshops, beer halls, and private bourgeois interiors. Not out and about on public streets, these refined and literate individuals are, in Reiberstorffer's opinion, central to Viennese review culture. They do more than post and remove advertisements for theater. The writer explains that these men have a sense of what good literature and performance are all about, and their public work helps shape bourgeois taste (see *HKG* 9,1:99). Like the female ragpicker, however, this public work has a questionable future. Wooden boards on which theater announcements in standardized formats appear for days and weeks at a time pose new competition for their public role. This development, "ein Erzeugniß der Industrie und des Verschönerungsgeistes" (*HKG* 9,1:99–100; a product of industry and the spirit of beautification), operates at a slower temporality and proves less accurate, the narrator observes, but it is nonetheless a threat to the poster man's trade and transforms the public articulation of cultural criticism.

To be sure, the writers in *Wien und die Wiener* declared that there were limits to direct observation. We do not encounter a narrator like in Edgar Allan Poe's "The Man of the Crowd" (1840), who observes "with minute interest the innumerable varieties of figure, dress, air, gait, visage, and expressions of countenance" from the comfort of a coffee house,[22] yet who

---

20   Rudi Palla, "Fetzn, Bana, Ålt's Eisen," in Kos, *Wiener Typen*,170–173; here 170.

21   Ladd, *The Streets of Europe* 165.

22   Edgar Allan Poe, "The Man of the Crowd," in *Collected Works of Edgar Allan Poe: Tales and Sketches 1831–1842*, ed. Thomas Ollive Mabbott (Cambridge, MA: The Belknap Press of Harvard University Press, 1978), 505–18; here 507.

nonetheless leaves his window seat to follow a sixty-five or seventy-year-old man through the dark and rainy streets, obsessed because he could not grasp this one individual, even when he stood face-to-face with him.[23] In "Wiener Salonscenen," by contrast, Stifter's narrator, recently relocated to Vienna from the countryside, relates the first time he encountered the city's salon culture. In his humorous account, the country bumpkin saw salons everywhere. He went to get his hair cut at a salon, bought bread at a business called a salon, encountered salons for aesthetic and philosophical debates, ones in which dramatic roles were performed, art was copied, even ones where people smoked, played piano, and where tea was served (see *HKG* 9,1:440–41). Despite having the sense that salons were proliferating as far as the eye could see and beyond the bounds of useful characterization, he soon fixed his attention on an elegant house with large windows in which actual salons were held. He was not alone. Stifter and "die gaffende Menschenmenge" (*HKG* 9,1:444; the gaping crowd) tried in vain to catch a glimpse of the activity inside. When they attempted to peer through the windows, light from the heavens reflected back at them like diamonds. At best, they caught fleeting glimpses of shadowy figures moving behind heavy drapery on the nighttime occasions when a salon was taking place. Rather than directly witnessing the events transpiring inside, Stifter's narrator takes note of the watchful eyes of the police on horseback and on foot who maintained order outside on the Viennese streets (see *HKG* 9,1:444). The failed attempts of the crowd to peek into the private lives of the elites and the pervasiveness of state surveillance in Vienna underscores the limits of vision. The contributor's resort to opacity and refracted light demonstrate how they cautiously navigated the political terrain and the ephemerality of city life.

## Above and Below Vienna: Religion with City Eyes

I have painted a picture of Stifter and his collaborators attempting to capture the visible signs of everyday public life in *Wien und die Wiener*, and I have noted that many of their observations about work and leisure were moralizing and conservative in tone. In the final section of this chapter, I will examine how the collection fictionalized changes in Viennese religious practices as well. Christiane Schwab contends that city literature during this period was secular in nature.[24] Schwab argues that Early Modern, Enlightenment, and the immediate early nineteenth-century forerunners of Stifter's publication created figures who stood for universal moral values rather than more real-life individuals based on their

23   Poe, "The Man of the Crowd," 515.
24   Schwab, "Sketches of manners, esquisses des moeurs," 48.

circumstances in society.[25] Stifter's mid-century collection, by contrast, does some of both: it makes Christian religious claims about the Habsburg monarchy and social order while, at the same time, presenting a strikingly modern conception of Viennese public religious life. I agree with Daniel DiMassa's position that unreflective practices of Christian religion oftentimes seem to mean more than true piety in Stifter's realist literature and that this variance is part of the writer's larger "epistemological critique of religious faith."[26] In the following, I propose that Stifter's questions about Christian religious life cannot be separated from his critique of Viennese commercial life.

As we have seen, Stifter and the contributors experimented in a number of ways with the narrative representation of city life and public trades. Many essays in *Wien und die Wiener* open with a commanding overview establishing how the location and the people treated therein could best be situated. The frontispiece of 1844 is one such establishing snapshot, which notably does not include any visual references to Christian religious life. Stifter's introduction to the collection, "Aussicht und Betrachtungen von der Spitze des St. Stephansthurmes (Als Einleitung)" (Views and Observations from the Top of St. Stephen's Tower [As an Introduction]), however, is centered on an edifice expressly designed for public worship. In this text, Stifter's narrator situates us in the actual referential space as he approaches the city, with the reader, and climbs a church tower to take in a prospect of Vienna. The narrator's elevated perspective and his repeated trips to gain a view from this outlook help him outline the political and natural details on the horizon as well as the underlying forces governing the city and the existence of its inhabitants. He sees the connectedness of the monarchy and all its subjects, as well as their united effort for the common good. Using a corporeal metaphor reminiscent of Thomas Hobbes's *Leviathan* (1651/1668), Stifter suggests that the citizens of Vienna do not recognize they are central to the state's vitality: "sie fühlen es nicht, daß hier der Herzschlag einer großen Monarchie ist, die im Rathe der Völker sitzt, und das Geschick des Erdballes bestimmen hilft, und daß von diesem Herzschlage die Frische und Gesundheit der andern Gliedern abhängt" (*HKG* 9,1:n.p.; they do not feel that here is the heartbeat of a great monarchy, which sits on the council of nations and helps determine the fate of the globe, and that the vigor and health

---

25   Schwab, "Sketches of manners, esquisses des moeurs," 47.

26   Daniel DiMassa, "Stifter, Schleiermacher, and the Vision of a Higher Realism," *Colloquia Germanica: Internationale Zeitschrift für Germanistik* 54, no. 2 (2022): 393–409; here 396. DiMassa aligns Stifter's realism and thought on religion more closely with Goethe, Schleiermacher, and early nineteenth-century Spinozians. See his article for an excellent assessment of research trends on Stifter and religion.

of the other members depends upon this heartbeat). The monarchy's life-blood ("der einfach rothe Balsam") circulates throughout the body, and their individual efforts contribute to the maintenance of the entire body politic. The Viennese do not grasp their place in history when they are going about their everyday lives. It furthermore suggests that Christian imagery and expressions of faith will not be the focus of this narration about the seat of the Catholic Church in Viennese life.

This is not the first time the narrator has seen the city from such an elevated secular perspective. He tells the reader in the introduction to follow his guidance and return for a second more meaningful view of the city ("es wird dir bedeutungsvoller scheinen, als vordem," *HKG* 9,1:vi). The visual perspective shifts from the cathedral tower to pedestrian life on the outskirts of the city. From this removed perspective, the traveler regards the cathedral and the prior narrative position from a distance. Here, Stifter's narrator turns to nature and then commerce to describe the approach to Vienna. This second time the journey to and ascent of the cathedral tower is compared to climbing "jene schlanke zarte luftige Pappel" (*HKG* 9,1:vi; that slender delicate airy poplar tree), which is designated as the center of city life. This stable point of reference is visible from a great distance and guides us back into the city. Yet as the traveler continues toward Vienna, he encounters the pathways of infrastructure and circulation of natural resources and goods, commercial exchanges from the outskirts and into the city—subject matter that is addressed elsewhere in the collection, as well.

Sylvester Wagner's "Die Kohlbauern" (Coal Diggers), for example, describes the rural, deeply religious, and righteous people who transport coal wood from outlying forests and mountainous areas to the city center to be sold at the coal market. Once in Vienna, they sell their wood to "sachverständnige Feuerarbeiter oder Greißler" (*HKG* 9,1:102; expert people who work with fire and grocers). Wagner contrasts the traditional work of these good individuals trying to get by with those who enter the city for considerable financial gain. The point made in this essay about public work and natural resources is reinforced in the illustration to Wagner's "Der Greißler" (The Grocer) (see *HKG* 9,1:68). Here, the image of a stack of wood suggests that the Coal Digger's goods have been brought to market; the stack of newspaper reminds us of the Female Ragpicker's complaints (see Figure 3.3). Both details underscore a reading practice in which we connect essays across the collection. However, we should not let this picture of Christians from the countryside and participating in commercial life lead us too far astray from the introduction's message. Here, the closer we are to this poplar tree, the more it disappears from sight, and the soundscape of nature is replaced by the deafening roar of the city: "immer dicht, und immer lärmender" (*HKG* 9,1:vi; always dense, and ever noisier). Following the poplar tree into the secular city in

Figure 3.3. The colored illustration from the 1844 edition of *Wien und die Wiener* shows the grocer selling firewood delivered by the coal diggers and a stack of newspapers and books. Wien Museum Inv.-Nr. 97544/5, CC0. (https://sammlung.wienmuseum.at/objekt/524547/).

the introduction gives us an initial indication of the complicated critiques of commerce and industry found throughout *Wien und die Wiener*.

This critique can be perceived below St. Stephan's Cathedral, too. Stifter's "Gang durch die Katakomben" (Tour through the Catacombs) is a blistering critique of modern life in Vienna. The structure of the essay is circular: a here-and-now overview of modern life shifts to an inward retrospective journey into the depths beneath the Cathedral before the narrator emerges on the street level again. The introductory section inventories developments we might associate with modernity. He complains that the teeming, unenlightened masses are detached from intellectual pursuits; textual proliferation and circulation have led to narrower opinions and weakened thought. As Stifter's narrator further notes, the mass production of books has resulted in the creation of imagined worlds that are isolated and meaningless when compared with actual life. (Here, we recall the Female Ragpicker's reflections once again.) Modern life is invested in "das sogenannte Praktische" (so-called practical things), which finds expression as "das material-nützliche, oft sogar nur sinnlich-wollüstige" (*HKG* 9,1:50; materially useful, often only sensuously delightful). Furthermore, people are no longer interested in the greater good and have increasingly turned from Christianity. These investments mean that humans build railroads and factories; churches are no longer appreciated and the new ones that are built look like tenements. Capitalism is the new religion. One manifestation of this modernized way of life is that the passersby hardly take note of St. Stephan's Cathedral, an observation that is repeated in his essay "Die Charwoche in Wien" (Holy Week in Vienna). These comments are an important complement to "Aussicht und Betrachtungen von der Spitze des St. Stephansthurmes," in which Stifter claims that the secularized spire permits the identification of political borders and commercial networks and functions as the organizing force for Viennese and Habsburg life. In the essay on the catacombs, the narrator quips that we prioritize knowing the factual height of the cathedral over its deeper spiritual meaning (see *HKG* 9,1:50). We could conclude that there is little good to be taken from modern life as it is structured around St. Stephan's Cathedral at present. Faith is lost as a consequence of commercial progress.

In "Gang durch die Katakomben," like other essays in the collection, Stifter removes us spatially and temporally from being in the middle of things on the bustling church square and transports us into a retrospective mode in which we travel with the narrator to Vienna, as if it were our first time in the city. This spatiotemporal recessional move facilitates a critical assessment of what remains of how things once were. On the way to Vienna yet another time, the narrator visualizes a sea of houses, but the focus remains on the street-level around St. Stephan's Cathedral rather than the tower's heights, which is the perspective taken in Stifter's "Aussicht und Betrachtungen." Rather than a panoramic political and commercial view of the city, we take in the area radiating from the base of the cathedral. Streets and public life were being reorganized in the nineteenth-century city, and *Wien und die Wiener* explores how places for eternal rest were also in flux. The centrally located graveyard was no longer there because it had been removed "aus sehr nützlichen Sanitätsrücksichten" (*HKG* 9,1:51; due to very useful sanitary considerations). Traditionally, the dead were buried in churchyards, that is in immediate proximity to a church; now they are interred under its grounds to make space for less hallowed ventures. Instead of the "Garten der Todten" (garden of the dead), Stifter explains that one will find houses, stores with bright window displays, and horse-drawn coaches. These signs of population growth, industry, commerce, and class-segregated, speedy transportation have pushed out of sight the markers, crosses, and monuments that once stood on the sacred graveyard in public space (see *HKG* 9,1:51). More than telling us what we no longer see, Stifter invites us to imagine how the land has been leveled off, exposing the bones of those promised eternal peace. The cycle of disinterment and reinterment that modern life accelerated did not affect all equally; it, too, was a hierarchal affair. Those of lowest social station will be continuously disturbed; those with a bit more standing will be buried more permanently inside the cathedral; and yet others will find their final resting place underneath it, in the catacombs.

After laying out how the horizontal plane of the graveyard became even more stratified once it was rearranged underground, Stifter's narrator takes us to this subterranean realm. Rather than peace and darkness, the narrator conveys heightened emotions and a multisensory experience when entering this Viennese location, which recalls the din from the collection's introduction. He has entered the catacombs on more than one occasion but needs a guide so that he will not get lost or bewildered as he passes beneath this threshold of life and death. The catacombs suggest an ancient space where persecuted early Christians observed their faith, yet in Vienna, like in Paris, the catacombs are eerily modern due to the anonymity of those resting there. The continuous dislocations, disturbances, and distortions of skeletal remains have leveled any social distinctions. The spectacular display and rearrangement of human bones triggers emotions ranging from curiosity to shame. The tour of the catacombs reminds readers that all traces of human deeds and fame will one day disappear. Stifter underscores this fact by describing how "ein Blatt Geschichte" (a page of history) would be reduced to a single line of text over the centuries "bis auch endlich *diese* verschwindet" (*HKG* 9,1:60; until *this* too finally disappears). We lose our bearings and want to hold on to our place in history, but the visit to the catacombs reminds us that this is an impossibility. Within this liminal space, the resonant modernity sounding in a cacophony from above—the cathedral organ, choir singers, bells, the rolling wheels of carriages—is inseparable from the visual spectacle below.

This visual and acoustic confrontation of the new and the old is central to Stifter's pessimistic and secular concerns about the present and oblivion. The visitor is shocked back into the reality of city life upon leaving the catacombs. On this rainy November day, as the cathedral reaches skyward, he beholds how the evening lights illuminate the expensive clothes of passersby, the carriages, and the sound of people enjoying life (see *HKG* 9,1:62). Christian religion has no place in this modern burial ground nor above ground on the square.

St. Stephan's Cathedral is also the main setting of "Die Charwoche in Wien," an essay that examines secularization and industrialization in public life even more directly. Here, Stifter's narrator complains that there are few public signs of Catholicism in Vienna. He insists that his deep faith never left him, even after he moved to the city. To illustrate this claim, the narrator reflects on situations in which his faith was tested by secularization during Holy Week. These pictures from Vienna reproduce his reflections on social and communal practices. Despite his opening declaration of a religious upbringing, the narrator leaves no space for liturgical readings of the Passion on Palm Sunday and does not explain his personal experience of faith either then or on other occasions in Vienna. Instead, the essay provides lengthy exposition on largely secularized Catholic rituals, public spectacle, and commercial life that define who the Viennese are and who he himself had become since he moved to the city. Stifter's essay begins with the observation that Holy Week in Vienna shattered his childhood memories of the observance. As a child from rural Bohemia, he recalls that Holy Week was a period in which stores were closed and everyone participated fully in "die tiefe, die stille Feier" (*HKG* 9,1:248; the deep, silent festivity) and were not interested in worshipping things that were not for sale. He stayed at home at first rather than witness how the festivities became ever more secularized, "um sie nicht profaniren zu sehen" (*HKG* 9,1:248; in order not to see them be treated with disrespect). He had not yet learned how to set apart what was meaningful from the insignificant troubling aspects of the observance.

Once Stifter's narrator lived longer in Vienna, he began to see Holy Week differently, namely with the aforementioned "Hauptstadtaugen." Transformed, he confides that he no longer regards city life with as much prejudice. The retrospective narration of the observances in the continuation of the essay illuminates the mass experience of Christian faith and commerce and suggests that the essence of Viennese life is tied to this conflictual relation. As for the main stage for these observances, the narrator asserts that churches and graveyards were no different from other secular spaces for the Viennese, as they provided an occasion for communal experience. The residents performed the Holy Week rituals without reflecting on their true Christian meaning: "daß man endlich von einer Kirche zur andern, von einem Grabe zum andern ging, blos um die hier übliche Gewohnheit des

Gräberbesuchens mitzumachen" (*HKG* 9,1:248; that one went from one church to the other, from one grave to the next, just to go along with the customary habit of visiting graves). When the Viennese gathered at churches to carry out this part of the rituals or when they took part in a nearby procession, social distinctions were leveled.[27] For instance, those who walked and those who were driven in horse-drawn coaches disappeared when the Viennese population went out on foot, united in these Christian practices. He continues that the processions and prayers taking place out in public and inside the church brought people of the highest and lowest social ranks together, and some tried to dress up fancier than they ordinarily would for their station in life. He notes that the splendor of their robes kept them separate. Nonetheless, the Viennese were interested in the crowd, which Stifter's narrator reiterates elsewhere in the essay; they participated in the processions because they wanted to partake of the modern experiences of spectacle and crowds. For example, Holy Week was an occasion for people from the country and city to come together. The villagers effectively brought the forest into the cathedral on Palm Sunday insofar as they had harvested spruce and fir branches as well as carved and adorned them for the observance. Stifter's narrator then takes us into the church on Holy Monday, which was decorated in black mourning clothes, and the crowds were in the process of praying. Indeed, Holy Week is "die einzige Zeit des Jahres, wo die Kirchengänger vor der übrigen Volksmenge auffallend werden" (*HKG* 9,1:251; the only time of the year when churchgoers stand out from the rest of the crowd). The police and military were present to control the crowds, but, unlike a few years later in 1848, there were no violent uprisings. The Viennese, rather, came together to celebrate in peace.

At the beginning of the essay, Stifter's narrator suggests that industry and commerce played a minor role in Holy Week festivities in the countryside. For his depiction of city practices during this exceptional period, the narrator highlights the sensory experience of this conflict. On the one hand, the religious processions and crowded Catholic midnight mass are solemn spectacles amplified by the "Gewalt der Töne" (*HKG* 9,1:252; power of the sounds) produced by the choirs and church bells). On the other, the blinding daylight and the clamor of industry, "das dumpf herintönende Brausen und Arbeiten des Tages" (*HKG* 9,1:250; the muffled roaring sound and daily work), triggers a melancholic response when his

---

27 These details recall the anonymous essay "Allerseelentag" (All Souls' Day), which depicts Viennese residents visiting, cleaning, and adorning gravestones that are gradually disappearing from sight, like their loved ones (see *HKG* 9,1:107). These practices of remembrance unite the Viennese living and dead, regardless of social standing: "für dies Einemal schon *auf* der Erde so ohn Unterschied gleich, wie sie es erst *unter* der Erde, aber für immer st he sollen" (*HKG* 9,1:108; [that they live] for this one time already *on* earth without distinction, as they ought to be only *under* the earth, but forever).

narrator passes over the cathedral's threshold. He remarks that the towering visual presence of the cathedral caused him to reflect that he was in an architectural space his ancestors had built. Here, Stifter posits that his industrious and pious Viennese contemporaries share a bond with those who marshalled considerable labor to build this architecture for reasons of faith many years ago. These remarks about historical consciousness of aesthetics and politics appear, however, without any overt reflection on the continuities of Christian faith and practice.

While the loss of historical consciousness is a recurrent theme in *Wien und die Wiener*, the final paragraph of "Die Charwoche in Wien" returns to the issue of industry's cacophony. Here, Stifter's narrator notes that stores are not open on Easter Sunday. It is for this reason that the crowds rush from the Saturday church services to buy "Lebens- und Luxusgegenstände" (*HKG* 9,1:253; everyday items and luxury goods) for the following day. In the city, these provisions and unnecessary luxuries were meant to enhance the communal celebrations and splendor on Sunday, but they betray the secularization of the holiday as well. We have hints but no scenes of what Easter Sunday in Vienna was like. The essay ends on Holy Saturday without any reflection on Christian sacrifice and resurrection, nor on social practice, but these sketches contrasting commerce and public religious display are as close as we can get to depictions of Christian faith in *Wien und die Wiener*.[28]

*Wien und die Wiener* captures scenes depicting how emergent industrial capitalism was reshaping everyday work, leisure, and ritual in Vienna around 1840. These scenes presented a Vienna with "city eyes," which the writers wanted readers to imagine even if the city never quite existed in such fashion. In the foregoing pages, I have presented how inventorying complex facets of public life via a variety of writerly approaches was important for taking stock of old and new ways of urban existence. Even though we think of Stifter as the author of *Wien und die Wiener*, no single writer could achieve that or capture the essence of Vienna. Its anthology form and the fact that the essays not written by Stifter were removed in book editions invite selective engagement with the collection. We end up reading only the essays published under Stifter's name. However, I have demonstrated that centering and de-centering Stifter helps us discover the work's overall generic sophistication, moral tone, and political message. Ironically, Stifter's canonical position as an author of realist stories set in nature and cultural landscapes makes us better appreciate this "city literature" produced by him and his contributors. Their take on a rapidly changing Vienna paves the way for later pessimistic critiques of modern life, urban alienation, and the loss of faith and tradition.

---

28  For a discussion of Christianity and the limits of observation in Stifter's *Bunte Steine*, see DiMassa, "Vision of a Higher Realism."

# 4: Stifter's Late Style

*Samuel Frederick*

IN THE DECADE between the publication of *Der Nachsommer* (Indian Summer) in November 1857 and his death in January 1868, Stifter produced a body of work whose idiosyncratic style and peculiar narrative mode set it apart from his previous writing. In these texts, a starker and more austere form dominated by a highly artificial language of staid rhythms and methodical regularity contributes to a strikingly desolate and often plodding prose marked by ritual and repetition. The tendency toward recursive narration along with the stubborn rearticulation of speech acts, gestures, and superfluous actions result in stories that are empty of conventional content but at the same time full—of narrative excursiveness, of attention to minutiae and mannerism, of language in and of itself. The linguistic excess of these works contrasts sharply with their scarcity of action and significant occurrences, making the reading experience trying, even for admirers of Stifter's famously eventless style. Indeed, for this reason, the late work has until recently often been sidelined, if not simply ignored, by critics and readers alike.[1]

Two qualifications need to be made to this description of the late Stifter at the outset, however. First, this body of late work is not monolithic. Stifter produced a lot of material in his last decade, including the published stories "Zwei Witwen" (Two Widows, 1861), "Nachkommenschaften" (Descendants, 1864), "Der Waldbrunnen" (The Forest Fountain, 1866), "Der Kuß von Sentze" (The Kiss of Sentze, 1866), and two stories prepared by him for publication, though not published until after his death: "Aus dem bairischen Walde" (From the Bavarian Forest, first published 1868) and "Der fromme Spruch" (The Pious Saying, an altered version of which first appeared in 1869).[2] He also

---

1    "The late Stifter hardly had an audience anyway." Albrecht Koschorke, "Bewahren und Überschreiben: Zu Adalbert Stifters Roman *Witiko*," in *Vergessene Texte*, ed. Aleida Assmann and Michael C. Frank (Konstanz: Universitätsverlag Konstanz, 2004), 139–57. Interest in Stifter's late work has grown significantly in the past couple of decades.

2    Johannes Aprent, editor of the 1869 volume of Stifter's *Erzählungen* in which the story first appeared, tried to tone down many of the very features so

spent a good portion of this period laboring over two longer works: the novel *Witiko* (which appeared in three volumes in 1865–67) and a new book version of *Die Mappe meines Urgroßvaters* (My Great-Grandfather's Notebook; of which there are two different manuscripts, both fragmentary). Although some of these texts share resemblances, not all conform to the increasingly rigid and iterative mode that distinguishes in particular "Der Kuß von Sentze," "Der fromme Spruch," and *Witiko* (all three written primarily in the second half of his final decade), the latter two of which will be the focus of this chapter. The second qualification is that the distinctiveness of Stifter's late style is not in fact unprecedented. In the works from the 1860s we find the same idiosyncratic tendencies that characterize his early and, especially, middle period, including the persistent use of parataxis, the refusal to convey characters' inner lives with much complexity, and the insistence on emptying his stories of the tensions and conflicts that propel a plot forward. The difference is one of degree and frequency. The palpable stylistic shift that marks some of these late works, then, is less a departure from his established literary peculiarities than it is an intensification of them.[3] And yet, especially in the two works central to my inquiry, this intensification drastically alters the text's readability and narrativity in ways that demand renewed critical evaluation.

In the analysis that follows, I look at some of the distinguishing features of this late prose in an effort to identify more precisely its narrative

---

distinctive of this late phase of Stifter's writing. His edits reflect the same displeasure expressed by Leo Tepe, editor of *Die Katholische Welt*, to which Stifter first sent the story for publication in 1867. Tepe, who found the story "too boring," conveyed his criticisms in a rejection letter to Stifter: "The story is unnatural: stiff people like this do not exist, all of their conversations are vapid, interchangeable; everyday things are presented with endless pomposity; the plot is practically non-existent; the style is forced and full of repetitions; it's hard to believe the author is serious and sometimes one is inclined to take the whole thing as a caricature of aristocratic families." Quoted in the apparatus to Adalbert Stifter, *Sämtliche Erzählungen nach den Erstdrucken*, ed. Wolfgang Matz (Munich: Deutscher Taschenbuch Verlag, 2005), 1633. The version that Stifter had prepared and sent out for publication would not appear until 1960; the original manuscript version was published for the first time two years later in 1962. All translations of primary and secondary literature are mine.

3    Similar observations can be found among some of the scholars of the late period, most of whom agree that making a sharp divide between the middle and late work is untenable. See Albrecht Koschorke and Andreas Ammer, "Der Text ohne Bedeutung oder die Erstarrung der Angst: Zu Stifters letzter Erzählung *Der fromme Spruch*," *Deutsche Vierteljahresschrift für Literaturwissenschaft und Geistesgeschichte* 61, no. 4 (1987), 677–719; here 679–80; Helena Ragg-Kirkby, *Adalbert Stifter's Late Prose: The Mania for Moderation* (Rochester, NY: Camden House, 2000), 95; and Wolfgang Matz, *Gewalt des Gewordenen: Zu Adalbert Stifter* (Graz: Literaturverlag Droschl, 2005), 67–68.

logic. On the one hand, *Witiko* and "Der fromme Spruch," in particular (though these descriptions would equally apply to "Der Kuß von Sentze"), read like perverse manifestations of the chronicle, consisting of little more than an inventory of occurrences and speech acts bereft of explanation and embellishment. Weak in narrative necessity and momentum, these "Erzählungen" (stories)—as Stifter insisted on calling even the thousand-plus-page *Witiko*—also fail to convey historical meaning, which depends on movement and change. Yet it is this meaning, rooted in an idealized past, that is so important to Stifter, and which the relentless repetitions and formal mannerisms of his style are meant to maintain and secure. Herein lies the constitutive tension of the late work. Stifter desperately desires to anchor certitude and value in the continuity and purposefulness of history, but he at the same time rejects the change and contingency that such history entails.[4] This rejection manifests itself both thematically (in the emptiness of story content) and stylistically (in the recursiveness and artificiality of language), with pronounced effects on the overall form of these narratives. For although Stifter methodically establishes an ordered continuum of action in each of these works, he systematically excludes the causal connections that would grant this sequence the shape of a story. The exhaustive uniformity and repetitiveness of his style reinforce the monotony of this narrative structure, flatlining story dynamics and thereby undermining the purposefulness of action—a purposefulness essential to the history ostensibly being not just conveyed but also, somehow, maintained. Ultimately, the history Stifter wants to hold on to in these late stories can only be properly preserved by transforming it into the static space of an idyll, changeless and entirely free of conflict. As such, the idyll attests to the certainty of what was in order to provide security for the order and meaningfulness of what is to come.[5]

In "Der Kuß von Sentze," "Der fromme Spruch," and *Witiko* Stifter locates this conception of idyllic, unchanging, yet somehow still unfolding history in the legitimacy and succession of the family.[6] Indeed, this

---

4    Compare Stifter's claim in a letter to Gustav Heckenast from June 8, 1861, that history itself, not individuals, should be at the center of the historical novel: "in historical novels history is the primary concern [*die Hauptsache*] and the individual people are of minor importance [*die Nebensache*]." Quoted in Hans Joachim Piechotta, *Aleatorische Ordnung: Untersuchungen zu extremen literarischen Positionen in den Erzählungen und dem Roman "Witiko" von Adalbert Stifter* (Giessen: Wilhelm Schmidt Verlag, 1981), 73.

5    On Stifter's exclusion of history as "development" and his preference for "a static, spatial, unchanging reality," see Eric Downing, *Double Exposures: Repetition and Realism in Nineteenth-Century German Fiction* (Stanford, CA: Stanford University Press, 2000), 33.

6    In *Witiko*, the family is extended to the tribe and thus to a larger notion of political order and legitimacy. Alfred Doppler writes of *Witiko* that it aims to

divinely sanctioned community, governed by the logic of the sequence, is both grounded in history and transcends it. The family serves as a testimony to the continued upholding of order, law, and regularity over time that also guarantees its significance "beyond" time—as "eternal."[7] Here perpetuation coincides with preservation. However, the development usually necessary for that perpetuation (viz. the growth and flourishing of the family line) becomes subordinated to the principle of hereditary conservation—and in this subordination it is effectively neutralized. Succession consequently operates on the thematic and stylistic levels of these works as a principle of movement that remains untouched by contingency, conflict, or change. In these late stories one thing always follows another in predictable regularity; things just keep on going, even though they never really arrive anywhere. Such is the form of narrative driven by the impulse to preserve. At the chapter's end I will link this impulse to the logic of collecting, a key undertaking in Stifter's life and works that helps elucidate the constitutive tension of this late prose, the way in which its means seem to militate against its ends, the way in which its attempts to hold on to what was important in the past threatens to render that past meaningless not only in the present but also *as* part of the chain of historical development itself. Seen in this way, the lateness of Stifter's narrative mode of the 1860s might best be characterized as a lament that method and goal are irreconcilable.

# I.

Let us begin by examining some of the formal and rhetorical idiosyncrasies of this late work. An initial example that cuts to the core of this strange style is the paratactic proliferation of the conjunction "und" (and)

---

show the path "that leads from a family history (*Familiengeschichte*) to a universal history, and that presents the universal history as the story of a family (*Familiengeschichte*)." Alfred Doppler, "'Der Organismus ist gegliedert, und es fehlt nur die Texturung': Stifters poetische Verfahrensweise im *Witiko*," *VASILO* 29, nos. ½ (1980): 5–33; here 8. Cornelia Blasberg connects "the narrative motif of a hero's legitimization through his ancestry" to the novel's own attempt to legitimize itself (in her reading, through its provenance in the *Nibelungenlied*). See Cornelia Blasberg, *Erschriebene Tradition: Adalbert Stifter oder das Erzählen im Zeichen verlorener Geschichten* (Freiburg im Breisgau: Rombach, 1998), 289. The legitimacy and continuity of the family is a theme in many of Stifter's works, though it is particularly pronounced in the late period (see especially "Zwei Witwen" and "Nachkommenschaften," though also, of course, *Die Mappe meines Urgroßvaters*).

7    See Wolfgang Matz on Stifter's "reduction of human society to its smallest unity, the family ... as the basic, original unit of the human species and for this reason as eternal and without history." Matz, *Gewalt des Gewordenen*, 37.

## 114 ♦ SAMUEL FREDERICK

in the following sentence, also its own paragraph, from the second book of *Witiko*:

> Und Witiko wurde mit den Seinigen in der Nacht in der Burg gepflegt, und schlief innerhalb der Mauern derselben, und die gewählten Männer wurden in den Häusern des Burgfleckens gepflegt und beherbergt, und die anderen Männer und die Frauen, die mit dem Zuge gekommen waren, schliefen auf Decken in dem Lager, und Feuer brannten überall, und die Wachen waren rings um das Lager, und wurden abgelöst, wie es Witiko eingerichtet hatte. (*HKG* 5,2:310)

> [And Witiko was given hospitality with his own men at night in the castle, and slept within its walls, and the chosen men were given hospitality and shelter in the houses of the castle village, and the other men and women, who had come with the cavalcade, slept on blankets in the camp, and fires were blazing everywhere, and the guards were all around the camp, and were relieved, just as Witiko had ordered.]

The novel abounds in similar passages of extended parataxis, in which a series of simple actions are strung together by means of the repetition of a coordinating conjunction, typically "und" and "dann" (then).[8] This stilted and, in Stifter's usage, stubborn technique pervades both the heterodiegetic narration (as here) and the intradiegetic, quoted discourse of characters. Indeed, its prominence and persistence can be measured by the degree to which it infects the speech of the novel's characters, whose directly quoted discourse can rarely be distinguished from that of the narrator, as, for example, in Regimbert's long oration in the middle of book II (*HKG* 5,2:183–94). The prevalence of "und" even carries over into dialogue, where this repeated conjunction ceases to function strictly paratactically, instead assuming the form of anaphora, as in this exchange between Witiko and Bertha, in which the reiterated word at the start of each exclamation lends the back and forth a mechanical ceremoniousness:

> "Ach, was ihr für schöne Haare habt!" sagte das Mädchen.
> "Und was du für rothe Wangen hast," erwiderte er.
> "Und wie blau eure Augen sind," sagte sie.
> "Und wie braun und groß die deinen," antwortete er.
> "Und wie ihr freundlich sprecht," sagte sie.
> "Und wie du lieblich bist," antwortete er. (*HKG* 5,1:35)

---

8 The series, especially as it functions in *Witiko*, is discussed at length in Piechotta, *Aleatorische Ordnung*.

[ "Oh, what beautiful hair you have!" said the girl.
"And what red cheeks you have," he responded.
"And how blue your eyes are," she said.
"And how big and brown yours," he answered.
"And how kindly you speak," she said.
"And how lovely you are," he answered.]

Here anaphora binds erotic impulses to the forces of regularity and restraint, which are elsewhere exerted in the novel's paratactic performance of order and congruity.[9] Both forms of repetition—parataxis and anaphora—contribute to the text's overall imitation of the chronicle, an iterative mode of unembellished narration with emphasis on the sequence of events without much concern for their causes. This mode dominates even when narration slows down to convey simple speech acts, as in this exchange between the titular hero and his future wife. Ultimately, because the temporality of mere succession asserts itself over causality throughout most of *Witiko*, the novel's pace never actually quickens, even in scenes of excitation and agitation such as, most notably (and prominently), those describing battles. Narration consequently becomes an act of inventorying, its progression determined less by an outcome or goal than by the logic of concatenation. The resulting text loses both mimetic impact and narrative momentum, its words drawing attention to themselves, its repetitions producing a machine-like monotony.[10]

The impulse to list a series of actions instead of developing them finds its complement in a somewhat more conventional device, one appropriate in *Witiko*'s battle narratives: the epic catalogue. The stylistic idiosyncrasies of Stifter's late period find fertile ground in such inventories of warriors and weapons:

9    Ragg-Kirkby points to this passage as "surely one of the most typically fairytale-like passages of the whole novel" that in its evocation of the dialogue from "Little Red Riding Hood," in particular, comes off as "implicitly threatening." Ragg-Kirkby, *Adalbert Stifter's Late Prose*, 86. Dominik Finkelde rightly points to this passage's connection to the collection. He writes that it consists of a "grammatically enacted collection of attributes." See Dominik Finkelde, "Tautologien der Ordnung: Zu einer Poetologie des Sammelns bei Adalbert Stifter," *The German Quarterly* 80, no. 1 (2007): 1–19; here 14.

10    In his discussion of the repetitions in *Witiko*, which he finds on various levels (semantic, syntactic, structural, narrative), Dietrich Naumann draws attention to the sentence Huldrik speaks to Witiko, "Ihr seid gekommen, weil es so ist" (You have come, because it is so; *HKG* 5,2:287), as paradigmatic for how contingency and cause are canceled out in the necessity of logic and the sequence. See Dietrich Naumann, "Semantisches Rauschen: Wiederholungen in Adalbert Stifters Roman 'Witiko,'" in *Dasselbe noch einmal: Die Ästhetik der Wiederholung*, ed. Carola Hilmes and Dietrich Mathy (Opladen and Wiesbaden: Westdeutscher Verlag, 1998), 82–108; here 100.

116 ♦ SAMUEL FREDERICK

Da war Christ Severin der Wollweber mit einem Ahornschafte dem Packe der Nahrungsmittel und einem Sacke für die Beute, Stephan der Wagenbauer mit Schwert und Spieß dem Packe der Nahrungsmittel und dem Sacke für die Beute, David der Zimmerer mit Schwert und Streitaxt dem Packe der Nahrungsmittel und dem Sacke für die Beute, eben so Paul Joachim mit einem Spieße, Jakob mit Spieß und Schwert, Tom Johannes der Fiedler mit einem Spieße und einem großen Sacke für die Beute, ingleichen Maz Albrecht mit einem Ahornschafte, dann Peter Laurenz der Schmied mit einer Eisenstange und einer eisernen Wurfkeule, dann Urban, Zacharias, Lambert, und Wolfgang mit Ahornschäften, Gregor Veit mit Schwert und Spieß, dann viele von den jungen Leuten, und Knechte, die entbehrt werden konnten. (*HKG* 5,1:246–47)

[There was Christ Severin the wool weaver with an oak shaft a pack of provisions and a sack for the booty, Stephan the wagon builder with sword and spear a pack of provisions and a sack for the booty, David the carpenter with sword and battle axe a pack of provisions and a sack for the booty, as well as Paul Joachim with a shaft, Jakob with spear and sword, Tom Johannes the fiddler with a spear and a big sack for the booty, likewise Maz Albrecht with an oak shaft, then Peter Laurenz the smithy with an iron pike and an iron war cudgel, then Urban, Zacharias, Lambert, and Wolfgang with iron shafts, Gregor Veit with sword and spear, then many of the young people, and vassals, who could be spared from work.][11]

As rhetorical device, the epic catalogue performs repetition not in the recapitulation of the same but in the steady enumeration of the singular and distinct.[12] In this list, for instance, no name or epithet occurs more than once. What lends this catalogue of particulars its uniformity and constancy is the paratactic regularity with which these warriors and their trades are registered. Thus, although the sentence compiles a series of unique names, its form conveys a changeless sequence whose end effect is sameness. Stifter intensifies this formal repetition by adding to his catalogue of names what each man carries with him, even if these objects are no different than what the next man in the list is carrying. Consequently, a "Sacke für die Beute" appears four times in the sentence. The first three

11   I have retained in this translation another feature of Stifter's prose that I will only mention in this aside: the omission of commas in serial lists of nature and things. In this inventory, the comma only separates people, but not the things they carry. This idiosyncrasy makes for even more difficult reading, to be sure, but is representative of Stifter's list-making style.

12   A similar form, more closely related to the chronicle than the epic, is the genealogy. On the importance of the genealogical structure for Stifter's work, see Blasberg, *Erschriebene Tradition*, 27–80.

times it comes immediately before "dem Packe der Nahrungsmittel," so that the whole phrase "dem Sacke für die Beute und dem Packe der Nahrungsmittel" is repeated nearly word for word following the first three consecutive names on the list. Furthermore, Stifter inventories each "Spieß," "Schwert," and "Ahornschafte" separately, not shying away from indexing the first of these weapons upwards of five times in the same sentence.

This obsessive itemization stands out more starkly when, near the end of the list, Stifter quickly dispenses the names of four men, each denied a family name and epithet, and indicates that they all have "Ahornschäften." Has Stifter here become aware of how tiresome his repetitions can become? Does the flow of exact enumeration require the ebb of contractive concision? Similar gestures of ebb or exhaustion appear throughout the novel as a stand-in for the etcetera, some indication that the list could go on, but will not. For example, when the duke asks a group of warriors if they know Witiko, their identical answer is conveyed verbatim for each of the first four men, then a fifth time to take care of the rest:

> "Wir kennen ihn," sprach Bolemil.
> "Wir kennen ihn," sprach Lubomir.
> "Wir kennen ihn," sprach Otto.
> "Wir kennen ihn," sprach Zdik.
> "Wir kennen ihn," sprachen viele. (*HKG* 5,2:119)

> ["We know him," spoke Bolemil.
> "We know him," spoke Ludomir.
> "We know him," spoke Otto.
> "We know him," spoke Zdik.
> "We know him," spoke many.]

Are only the first four men named here because they are key players in the negotiations that follow, or is four the point at which such repetition runs its course? Why stop at four? Identical spoken phrases are provided five consecutive times later in the novel (*HKG* 5,2:316–17), suggesting that Stifter will relate the exact same statement unflaggingly if each person needs to be named. But, of course, it is possible to name each speaker without repeating the identical spoken declaration (e.g., "'We know him,' spoke Bolemil, Lubomir, Otto, and Zdik, one after the other"). Stifter typically refuses this kind of contraction, his methodical and meticulous repetitions evoking the real-time articulations of these men.[13] We cannot

13  Koschorke notes that Stifter refuses contraction even on the minute level of the preposition and article, so that in the hundreds of times we read of something occurring "in the forest," it is never "im Wald" but always "in dem Wald." For

118 ♦ SAMUEL FREDERICK

simply be told that each said the same thing; we need to experience that recursive attestation.[14]

That attestation points to the underlying logic of these lists, which conforms to that of ritualized discourse. The catalogue is not just for inventorying; it is also a key element in the litany and in ceremonial language.[15] Such formalized discourse is performative and supplicatory, typically not narrative. The story does not move forward with any directedness in these moments of ritualized speech; but neither does it provide descriptive detail. Stifter achieves a different kind of narrative suspension with this extreme mode of repetition than what readers of his middle work may be familiar with, where, though we may find ritualized speech patterns at work, they have to vie with the more dominant mode of description. Indeed, as narration in the late prose tends more and more toward the catalogue, in which actions are compiled and chronicled, as well as toward the ritual invocation, governed by formal repetition, Stifter's style becomes increasingly austere, leaving little room for the kind of lengthy descriptive passages for which his earlier work is known. The quotations from *Witiko* above, for instance, largely avoid descriptive details. And yet Stifter's penchant for paying attention to minutiae does not disappear entirely in these last works. Through a narrative technique already implemented in the middle period, particularly in *Der Nachsommer*, Stifter transfers his ekphrastic impulses and its attendant dilatory tactics from the representation of static scenes or landscapes to the presentation of dynamic action.[16] The result is not that single actions are described in any detail, using, as might be expected, an abundance of adverbial phrases. Rather, Stifter breaks down actions into multiple, simpler

---

Koschorke this insistence points to Stifter's refusal in this novel to leave anything out, to forget even a few letters. See Koschorke, "Bewahren und Überschreiben," 145.

14   For a different reading of Stifter's repetitions with a focus on three late stories I do not discuss in this chapter—viz. "Aus dem bairischen Walde," "Nachkommenschaften," and "Der Waldbrunnen"—as well as in his paintings and an autobiographical fragment, see Martina Wedekind, *Wiederholen—Beharren—Auslöschen: Zur Prosa Adalbert Stifters* (Heidelberg: Universitätsverlag Winter, 2005), 141–203.

15   The most wide-ranging and thorough discussion of ritual in Stifter can be found in Alice Bolterauer, *Ritual und Ritualität bei Adalbert Stifter* (Vienna: Verlag Edition Praesens, 2005). See also the collection of essays in Sabina Becker and Katharina Grätz, ed., *Ordnung—Raum—Ritual: Adalbert Stifters artifizieller Realismus* (Heidelberg: Universitätsverlag Winter, 2007); and Martin Swales, "Litanei und Leerstelle: Zur Modernität Adalbert Stifters," *VASILO* 36 (1987): 71–82.

16   For a detailed discussion of the problematic status of description in Stifter, and how what readers and editors found tedious in his works does not always correspond to conventional descriptiveness but rather to the narration of superfluous action, see Samuel Frederick, *Narratives Unsettled: Digression in Robert Walser, Thomas Bernhard, and Adalbert Stifter* (Evanston, IL: Northwestern University Press, 2012), 143–52.

acts, which, no matter how trivial, he narrates with little embellishment and in an iterative fashion. With the paratactic form as its engine, the resulting text indexes the incidental operations involved in the most mundane of activities. The following paragraph from "Der fromme Spruch" demonstrates this mode well:

> Sie trat von ihrer Stufe herab, und ging zu einem schwarzen Holzgetäfel, das sich an einer Stelle der Zimmerwand zeigte. Sie sperrte mit dem Schlüsselchen, das sie an ihrem Bande trug, das Getäfel auf, und man sah in das Innere eines Kästchens, in welchem ganze Reihen von Schlüsseln hingen. Sie nahm einen, schloß das Kästchen wieder zu, und gab den Schlüssel in die Hand Adams. Dann ging sie gegen die Tür. Die Anderen, auch die Kammerfrau, gingen hinter ihr her. Adam öffnete die Tür, und sie schritt hinaus. Sie ging an der Spitze ihres Geleites den hohen Schloßgang entlang, und blieb vor einer der großen Eichentüren, wie sie alle in dem großen Stockwerke des Schlosses Biberau gleich waren, stehen. Adam sperrte die Tür auf. Die Tante wendete sich um, trat vor Gerlint, und machte ihr ein Kreuz auf die Stirne.[17]

> [She stepped down and went to a black wooden panel that could be seen at one spot on the room's walls. With the little key she kept on her ribbon she unlocked the panel, and the inside of a little cabinet could be seen in which whole rows of keys hung. She took one, closed the cabinet, and gave the key to Adam in his hand. Then she went to the door. The others, including the lady-in-waiting, followed behind her. Adam opened the door, and she stepped outside. Leading her escort, she went along the heigh-ceilinged castle hall and stopped in front of one of the huge oak doors, which were all the same on this huge floor of the Biberau castle. Adam unlocked the door. The aunt turned around, stepped in front of Gerlint, and made the sign of the cross on her forehead.]

The actions detailed here belong to the subset of the simple activity "the aunt shows Gerlint her chambers," a subset that, because it consists of largely superfluous smaller acts that do not add anything to the main activity, would normally be elided. In this case, moreover, the main activity is itself already superfluous to the story, having been announced in the dialogue of the previous paragraph, which ends with the aunt telling her niece: "Ich versage mir es nicht, dir selber deine Stube zu zeigen" (I will

---

17   Stifter, *Sämtliche Erzählungen nach den Erstdrucken*, 1462. Subsequent references to this story are to the version reproduced in this edition (which, contrary to the title, is the first handwritten manuscript version) and will hereafter appear parenthetically in the body of the text.

not deny myself showing you your room myself). Stifter's choice to narrate the smaller steps involved in this act is—even beyond this repetition—quite peculiar. For one, the aunt does not exactly, as she says, show Gerlint the suite of rooms herself ("selber"), since she is accompanied by her servants, one of whom in fact carries out the activities of opening the doors which lead to these rooms and then also unlocking the door to the suite. The aunt passively looks on and then blesses the activity carried out by others. The central activity she undertakes (unlocking the panel to access the key needed to unlock the suite) serves as a surrogate act once removed from the actual act of unlocking and opening. In this way it shares elements of the ritual.[18] Furthermore, and fittingly, the aunt's announcement comes in a double negative declaration: she will *not deny* herself this activity. Of course, she does, in part, and the meticulous narration that follows seems less like an indulgence in the activity the aunt claims not to deny herself than a perverse prolongation that defers this very activity (itself not fully enacted by her). The apparent drive to account for minutiae thus misses its mark here. Not only do the actions catalogued not fully correspond to the activity announced; they undermine that activity's centrality and importance as part of the narrative. In this case, then, the detailed inventorying of action does not intensify but rather diffuses the narrative as the locus of directed and purposeful activity.

In *Der Nachsommer*, as diffuse a narrative as any, the detailed representation of actions that seems to matter little to the story in fact contributes to the novel's obsession with space, the mapping out of interior and exterior zones and their relation to one another. At first glance, the series of simple actions catalogued in the above quoted and related paragraphs from "Der fromme Spruch" appears aimed at establishing similar spatial relations. The aunt *steps down, approaches, opens, closes, goes, leaves, walks along, halts*, and *turns about*—all movements that trace out the interior spaces of the home. But what precise points of spatial orientation do these actions actually provide? The black panel is located at "one spot" on the wall—where exactly, we are not told. The aunt leaves by way of a door, but we do not know which one or where it is. The door in front of which she halts is "one of the large oak doors." Which one? It does not matter. They all look alike anyway, as the narrator remarks. The paragraph, then, consists of a series of superfluous actions that fill the space between dialogue and which *describe* what that dialogue already announced: the presentation of living quarters to a guest. I am not done with this passage yet—we will return, at the end of this chapter, to the stubborn way in which acts of *Schließen* (locking, closing, sealing) circulate here and throughout the novella—but it is worth considering how its concatenation of empty actions functions not

---

18   Bolterauer reads the entry into the room, specifically, as a ritual of initiation. See Bolterauer, *Ritual und Ritualität*, 269.

to map out any clearly defined spaces but rather to sound out the emptiness of these spaces, transforming meaningful, dynamic activity into hollow gestures, which, ossified, make up the skeletal structure of the text from which Stifter has stripped all ornamentation.

It is precisely such actions reduced to superfluous static images that Georg Lukács famously criticized in Stifter's work.[19] In this late story, as in *Witiko* and "Der Kuß von Sentze," we find an unusual number of extreme examples of this narrative mode in which action—not description—contributes to the text's peculiar rhythm and repetitiveness. Consider this paragraph from the second book of *Witiko*, which comes in between longer passages of dialogue:

> Nach diesen Worten ging Witiko von dem Knechte in den Stall. Er sah, daß die Pferde gut eingestellt und mit Decken versorgt worden waren. Er sagte Raimund noch genauer, was er thun solle, streichelte sein graues Pferd, und ging dann fort. Er ging über den Hof, und suchte den Saal, in welchem er einst von Heinrich empfangen worden war, und in welchem man das Mittagsmahl eingenommen hatte. Er kam in den Saal. Der Saal war gerade so wie damals, er hatte die Tische, die Waffen, und an einem Fensterpfeiler hing auf einem Nagel ein Kopfgoldreifchen mit kleinen Öffnungen. Es war aber niemand in dem Saale. Witiko ging durch eine Thür in ein weiteres Gemach. Auch dieses war leer. Als er in demselben stand, hörte er Tritte kommen, und Heinrich ging herein. Er führte Witiko durch ein zweites Gemach, das gleichfalls leer war, in ein drittes, in welchem Wiulfhilt saß. Sie stand von dem Stickrahmen auf, und ging Witiko entgegen. (*HKG* 5,2:141–42)

> [After these words Witiko went from the servant into the stables. He saw that the horses were well cared for and provided with blankets. He told Raimund more precisely what he should do, patted his grey horse, and then left. He crossed the courtyard and sought the great hall in which he had previously been welcomed by Heinrich and in which they had had their midday meal. He entered the great hall. The great hall was exactly as it was then. There were tables, weapons, and on one window pier hung a little golden corolla with small perforations. But nobody was in the great hall. Witiko went through a door into another chamber. This too was empty. As he was standing there he heard steps coming, and Heinrich entered. He escorted Witiko through a second chamber that was similarly empty into a third chamber in which Wiulfhilt was seated. She stood up from her embroidery and came toward Witiko.]

---

19 Georg Lukács, "Erzählen oder Beschreiben?" in *Probleme des Realismus I: Essays über Realismus* (Neuwied and Berlin: Luchterhand, 1971), 197–242; here 230.

Stifter's late style depends on this concatenation of empty actions, which here unfold in actual empty spaces. All the stylistic techniques detailed above—the displacement of description onto action, the stripping away of ornamental detail, the impulse to catalogue events, the use of repetitions and paratactic syntax to de-emphasize causality—are at work in this paragraph. The resulting narrative consequently lacks many of the conventional features of realist fiction. We have no narrator to provide explanation, no access to our main character's motivating thoughts, and no details that might establish a clearer mimetic or even symbolic picture of the scene. In the absence of psychological development and in the absence of motivated actions, the narrative is bereft of tension and any forward-directed movement.[20] But the result here is not that one thing simply follows another, without necessity; rather, the narrative impetus is directed backwards, towards a re-enactment of what has already happened. Witiko circles back from the stables to the castle, returning to the hall in which he was greeted during his previous visit. Everything, we are told, is "exactly as it was then"—with one difference: the people are missing. Witiko then wanders through a series of empty rooms before he finds those whom he had hoped to meet in the first hall. The entire action of this paragraph consists of the knight's attempt to return to the same state as before, to re-establish equilibrium, the state of sameness toward which all features of Stifter's late prose seem directed.[21] Repetition, then, is not just stylistic but also built into the narrative structure itself.[22] It prevents any kind of actual narrative development. Despite chronological time apparently taking its course, and even, as part of the historical material, struggles among the various tribes ostensibly shifting the balance of power, the novel seems never to arrive anywhere.[23] Its placidity remains constant.

20  "The late Stifter is remote from every psychology …. There is hardly any other character in a novel who is so far removed from every emotional stirring, from every personal development, than the young Witiko." Matz, *Gewalt des Gewordenen*, 76.

21  Despite this tendency to deflate tension and move toward stasis, the narrative does not conform to the model proposed by Peter Brooks, in which tensions are built up in order to find their "correct end," their "discharge," in "quiescence." Such tensions are not allowed to be built up in the first place in Stifter's late work. See Peter Brooks, *Reading for the Plot: Design and Intention in Narrative* (Cambridge, MA: Harvard University Press, 1984), 101–9.

22  This repetition of the same becomes almost absurd in "Der fromme Spruch," in which the siblings carry the same names as the cousins: Gerlint and Dietwin. As we will see, this doubling has important thematic consequences for the story's conception of familial preservation.

23  As Koschorke puts it, when things start to get exciting or tense, Stifter "removes the tempo." He also accurately notes that, "at the beginning everything

## II.

A number of scholars have drawn attention to these and related stylistic features of Stifter's late work, reading them in the context of the writer's obsessions with order, ritual, restraint, and restoration. The first of these—order—is the governing principle under which the other three operate. As Wolfgang Matz concisely puts it, "everything in Stifter's work is forcefully directed at order."[24] What precisely this order encompasses (the familial, the social, the political, the aesthetic, and more) and how it is conceived (as unity, as regularity, as disciplinarity, as divinely sanctioned law) have been variously—and at times irreconcilably—articulated in the literature.[25] Order is such an enduring category in Stifter scholarship because it applies equally to all periods of his literary productivity as well as to aspects of his personal life.[26] The picture that emerges is of a writer fixated on assuring the proper place of what makes up the world (including people and things) as a guarantee of meaning, stability, and certainty. Hence his concern with collections, with scientific observation, with the family structure and its legitimacy, and finally with the state as an instrument of social organization. The backdrop to this obsession with order is a world in which, because of rapid modernization and revolutions, the old certainties can no longer be taken for granted. In many ways *Der Nachsommer* is Stifter's consummate attempt to create an alternate world in which these guarantees are not threatened. In the late work, the idyll strived for in that novel metastasizes and begins to assert itself not just in the represented world but in the very language with which this world is represented. The compulsion for order in the late Stifter is as much a feature of the style as it is of the content of his work.

---

is already the way it should be at the end." Koschorke, "Bewahren und Überschreiben," 143, 154.

24   Matz, *Gewalt des Gewordenen*, 40.

25   For an overview of the (rather vast) literature on order in Stifter, see Werner Michler, "Ordnung(en)," in *Stifter-Handbuch: Leben—Werk—Wirkung*, ed. Christian Begemann and Davide Giuriato (Stuttgart: J. B. Metzler, 2017), 286–89.

26   Stifter was an obsessive list maker. Starting in 1854, he began keeping a "painter's diary," in which he fastidiously kept track of the details of his painting activity (precise date; time work begun, ended; subject matter; etc.). On this *Tagebuch über Malerarbeiten*, including a reproduction of a page from 1859, see Wedekind, *Wiederholen—Beharren—Auslöschen*, 143–64. See also the discussion of a journal Stifter kept in which he charted his health in great detail, noting physical and psychological symptoms, food intake, stool cycles, and more, in Jessica Resvick, "The Author as Editor: The Aesthetics of Recension in Adalbert Stifter's *Die Mappe meines Urgroßvaters*," in *Market Strategies and German Literature in the Long Nineteenth* Century, ed. Vance Byrd and Ervin Malakaj (Berlin and Boston, MA: De Gruyter, 2020), 147–70; here 163–66. Resvick includes reproductions from this diary on 163–64.

The highly formalized language Stifter mobilizes carries out this drive for order rhetorically, with iterative compulsiveness, and in doing so takes on the characteristics of the ritual, as already noted. Not surprisingly, ritualistic acts are central to both "Der fromme Spruch" and "Der Kuß von Sentze," and appear frequently in *Witiko*. In these works, order has spread from content to form and now returns to content with renewed fastidiousness. This repetitive and incantatory language of ritual, however, is not primarily representational. We saw earlier how Stifter's style tends toward the inventory or the catalogue, a mere list of persons, things, or events. The inventory of course does not so much represent a set of things as ascertain their existence in the world. Ritualized language takes this impulse to a cosmic level. It attempts to establish transcendent meaning, to make certain that this world's meaning is assured by the existence of another. In his discussion of Stifter's litaneutic mode, Martin Swales distinguishes the litany, which aims to bestow meaning or, as he puts it, "ontological certainty," onto the world, from the mere list, which simply registers the existence of things. Swales rightly notes that it is not so easy to differentiate the two in Stifter.[27] To register the things of the world (by compiling scientific data, by creating genealogies, by inventorying a collection) is also to appeal to their lasting importance on the cosmic scale, as the indices of the divine.

And this is precisely the problem. Stifter's ritualistic, repetitive language is only an *appeal*, not any confirmation or assurance. If the stylistic methods described above contribute to a fundamental drive for order, "to establish a meaningful unity of life," as Matz expresses the goal of both *Der Nachsommer* and *Witiko*, to what degree do these means undermine the ends? Matz distinguishes the late Stifter's narrative mode from that of *Der Nachsommer* by drawing attention to the artificiality of the late style. This more radical prose, replete with parataxis and litaneutic inventories, strives by means of these techniques of regimentation and uniformity to make whole what has lost meaning and place in the world. The "astonishing meticulousness" of these lists aims at accounting for every little thing, every particular that might otherwise be forgotten, and to rescue it in the order assured by the logic of succession.[28] One thing reliably follows the other. The result, however, militates against the very unity sought by this method, since the logic of sequentiality soon becomes tedious and meaningless, drawing attention to the same minute particulars that Stifter apparently wants to integrate into a meaningful whole. No such whole is assured, and in its "sterility" and "distance from reality," we are left with

---

27  Swales, "Litanei und Leerstelle," 76–77.

28  Quoted text from Swales, "Litanei und Leerstelle," 80. Matz, *Gewalt des Gewordenen*, 72, expresses best the idea of the rescue of lost, "scattered" meaning in chronology; Finkelde, "Tautologie der Ordnung," 13, echoes him.

little more than language itself, which, as Matz suggests, ceases to provide access to any world, calcifying instead into an opaque, impenetrable thing.[29]

This sterile, thingly language accomplishes the opposite of what Stifter ostensibly desires: it erodes the meaning of the text. Some scholars, most notably Albrecht Koschorke and Helena Ragg-Kirkby, identify the extreme manifestations of this style—its repetitiveness, its extended minimalism, its ritualistic antimimeticism—as distinctly proto-modernist.[30] Koschorke and Andreas Ammer find in "Der fromme Spruch" a tendency toward reduction that, combined with the attempt to create "order without resistance," ends in a performance of meaninglessness. With the "referentiality of words" brought to "zero," the text asserts its own existence alone, its "materiality as words." Ultimately, Koschorke and Ammer argue, the language of the late Stifter produces only "nullities and a sound that in its semantic indifference is synonymous with white noise."[31] Similarly, Ragg-Kirkby sees in Stifter's late prose an example of "twentieth-century Absurdism before the twentieth century," which in its excesses becomes the carrier of "a magnificently dystopian vision." *Witiko*, she writes, "is one enormous word-litany … a mirage of substance which simultaneously reveals its essential nothingness, indeed Nothingness as an absolute."[32] At times, these scholars seem to be projecting too much of their own modernist sensibilities onto the text, such as when Ragg-Kirkby describes the language of *Witiko* as "danc[ing] around the abyss, uttering one prolonged, silent scream." Stifter's style, she proclaims, is "perhaps too radical to be fully appreciated even today."[33] Although these descriptions may overstate the case, they help to conceptualize how Stifter's mania for order emerges out of—and thus necessarily also points back to—a world that is anything but stable, secure, and controllable. The frightening flipside of the compulsion for order as manifest in the texts' "excess

---

29  Matz, *Gewalt des Gewordenen*, 73. Koschorke and Ammer write: "Ritual is the form of the suspension of time in temporal representation." Koschorke and Ammer, "Text ohne Bedeutung," 706.

30  Martin Swales likewise remarks on Stifter's stylistic similarity to a number of modernist authors and post-war Austrian writers, including Gert Friedrich Jonke and Thomas Bernhard, and to authors of the Theater of the Absurd such as Beckett and Ionesco. See Swales, "Litanei und Leerstelle," 74–75, 76, 77, and 80. A number of Koschorke's and Ragg-Kirby's ideas are anticipated, with different emphases, in Piechotta, *Aleatorische Ordnung*.

31  Koschorke and Ammer, "Text ohne Bedeutung," 704, 711, 718.

32  Ragg-Kirkby, *Adalbert Stifter's Late Prose*, 74, 94, 106.

33  Ragg-Kirkby, *Adalbert Stifter's Late Prose*, 109. Ragg-Kirkby's language also comes across more as a one-dimensional parody of modernist angst that does not at all account for the subtleties and complexities of, say, Samuel Beckett (one of her examples). Next to Beckett, Stifter is utterly humorless.

of securely controlled repetitions" is the experience of loss.[34] The desperate attempt to exclude everything that might disrupt this order (from seemingly innocuous expressions of emotion to hints of more threatening chaos or insanity) is, by virtue of this desperation, never fully successful. Stifter's ritualistic and repetitive prose ends up exposing itself as artificial, revealing the order sought for (along with its divine guarantor) to be little more than a wish-image, his story worlds a mere fictional construct.

This construct, so critical to Stifter's method and aims, can best be understood in relation to one of his other obsessions, collecting. In the frantic attempt to hold on to the certainties increasingly eluding his grasp, Stifter classifies and organizes the world "into controllable, static categories."[35] The impulse for order can best be achieved in the artificial construct of the text itself, which doubles as a collection, the site where a series of related things are fixed and preserved. Stifter's tendency toward repetition and inventorying in the late work expresses a similar desire to establish and ascertain an assemblage of people, places, actions, and objects, all reduced to immobilized things in a static display. This analogy explains many of the more peculiar formal features of the late prose, in particular its tendency to line things up in paratactic sequences.[36] What Koschorke calls Stifter's "gesture to collect, conserve, archive" aims to preserve by freezing time, removing persons and objects from their natural, causal relations and placing them in an artificial series constituted by relations of contiguity.[37] Such preservation, however, necessarily denies them one of their key characteristics, namely change. Just as to preserve an object in the collection it must be made a thing, displaced from its sphere of meaningfulness and also petrified as artifact of a history long gone, so too are the elements in Stifter's late narratives removed from the contexts in which they would have meaning and fixed in an unchanging,

---

34    Ragg-Kirkby, *Adalbert Stifter's Late Prose*, 68.

35    Ragg-Kirkby, *Adalbert Stifter's Late Prose*, 49.

36    See Blasberg's description of *Witiko*: "The dynamic of collecting and repetition in the novel corresponds to Stifter's paratactic serial style." She also draws attention to the actual model of collecting involved in the composition of this novel, which aligns the author Stifter with the historian and his last novel with the anthology, in particular the volume he edited with Johannes Aprent (*Lesebuch zur Förderung humaner Bildung* [Reader for the Advancement of Humanist Education, 1854]). Blasberg, *Erschriebene Tradition*, 285, 284; on the *Lesebuch*, see 103–77.

37    Koschorke, "Bewahren und Überschreiben," 145, 149. An excellent discussion of collecting in Stifter can be found in Finkelde, "Tautologien der Ordnung." Finkelde points out that Stifter himself figures his writing in *Witiko* as a process of "finding," an activity resembling that of the collector (letter to Heckenast from January 1861, quoted by Finkelde, 3; discussed in relation to *Witiko*, 13–15). The resulting work reveals "the inner convergence between collecting as a motif and Stifter's language, which has the character of procedural minutes" (13).

highly constructed space in which they cease to function as we expect from a story, instead serving as reminders of the distance separating them from the realm of narrative necessity.

If Stifter is to preserve the Biedermeier values and traditions that are threatened by the social and political developments of the revolutionary and post-revolutionary years—what Matz calls his "stubborn clinging at all costs to what has been handed down [*am Überkommenen*]"—he must banish the movement of history itself from his carefully constructed story worlds.[38] But it is precisely history that he also aims to preserve, especially in *Witiko*, a novel that affirms the political legitimacy of the Austrian Empire's forebears. *Witiko* painstakingly safeguards the memory of this historical period in its effort "to put everything in its place, to leave out nothing, to forget nothing," as Koschorke puts it.[39] And yet this process of preservation leads to the neutralization of historical change; it empties out all that marks an action or event as meaningful and necessary. As in the collection, that which is ostensibly preserved is also thereby destroyed, or at the least stripped of its defining features.[40]

The reason Stifter's late stories and *Witiko* come across as so utterly alien and abstract lies precisely in the self-sabotage inflicted by this relentless, indeed perverse, desire to preserve, which ends up sealing off what should be the dynamic elements of the story in an artificial assemblage that has little relation to the real world.[41] In the collection that is the text, these story elements are immobilized. They may be pristinely presented, but they lack any affective intensity or narrative interest. And yet Stifter insists he has written "Erzählungen" (stories). To take him at his word requires asking what kind of temporality undergirds these works. It is not so much that *nothing happens* in them as that *things keep happening*, but without any real change or movement toward a goal. Stifter's style assures that moment follows moment without much incidence, that actions or occurrences lack necessity and purposefulness. Wolfgang Matz convincingly argues that in *Witiko* (where plenty of things actually happen) Stifter

---

38  Matz, *Gewalt des Gewordenen*, 41. Matz describes Stifter's fundamental fear as one of "historical movement as such" (37). See also, Downing, *Double Exposures*, 33, on Stifter's attempted "exclusion of temporality, of history ... from natural reality."

39  Koschorke, "Bewahren und Überschreiben," 145. Korschorke goes on to argue in this essay that Stifter ends up doing the opposite in his mania for re-writing, which ends up erasing the traces of things he wants to preserve. My argument takes a different angle on this same phenomenon.

40  On the paradoxical logic of collecting, see Samuel Frederick, *The Redemption of Things: Collecting and Dispersal in German Realism and Modernism* (Ithaca, NY and London: Cornell University Press, 2021), 31–65.

41  As Koschorke and Ammer note, the result ends up leaving us "no more coherent images of reality." Koschorke and Ammer, "Text ohne Bedeutung," 703.

develops the static, utopian, changeless idyll into a central feature of history itself, thereby revealing "the historical process as a constantly spinning stasis."[42] There is no room for anything new to happen here because everything of any consequence has already happened. The point of the story—the *Erzählung*—is to make certain that everything must happen *in this particular way*, and that even the most incidental actions are part of the pre-programmed machinery of history.

Ultimately, the only reason Stifter needs to ascertain this truth—so desperately, so insistently—is because it is, indeed, *not at all* certain.[43] Hence the motivation to preserve in the first place; hence the impulse of the manic collector; hence also the emotionless registration of trivial things and actions. To line things up with paratactic compulsion in the text is no different than lining things up in the glass display case of the collection. In both cases, these things have been lifted out of history in the very gesture of attesting to it. Elevated to the status of the always-already-happened, pure and unmoving, history is suspended in time and space, preserved in and as a rhetorical construct lacking any real content. Thus, we are left with movement without any change, an aimless wandering through the same spaces and an empty miming of meaningful or already completed actions.

# III.

This description should remind us of Witiko's ambling through empty castle halls or aunt Gerlint's ritualized movements on the way to her niece's chamber. Let us therefore return to the latter of these, the image of the aunt, her collection of keys kept safe in the wall-cabinet, and the various acts of *Schließen* that feed into and emerge from this motif throughout "Der fromme Spruch." Tropes of closing, locking, binding, joining, and sealing appear at regular intervals in the story. In the absence of any major occurrences, the regular opening of doors, gates, cabinets, boxes, gifts (themselves in receptacles that contain further receptacles), small containers, travel chests, and more, seems to comprise the story's primary activity. So much appears to depend on the keys that grant access to the spaces in and behind the locked doors, cabinets, and boxes, though it remains unclear who or what is supposed to be kept at bay by these barriers and locks. We read about how Gerlint keeps a key attached to a ribbon on her at all times. This key, however, only opens the wall cabinet,

---

42 Matz, *Gewalt des Gewordenen*, 38–39.

43 On this point Ragg-Kirkby is most convincing. Repetition in Stifter, she writes, is "disturbing rather than reassuring." It has "the effect of drawing attention to the anxiety from which it apparently tries to detract, rather than to the surety it purports to maintain." Ragg-Kirkby, *Stifter's Late Prose*, 65, 67.

a protected space in which she keeps all of her "andern Schlüssel" (other keys, 1451). These other keys abound throughout the story, though its inventory is not limited to them. For instance, a key is needed to open the "Palisanderkästchen" (little rosewood box) that Dietwin gives to his sister. Stifter plainly but methodically narrates not just the opening of the box but also the turning of the key in the lock of this little box: "Gerlint drehte den Schlüssel im Schlosse des Kästchens" (Gerlint turned the key in the lock of the box, 1456). We learn that the garden has areas that can only be accessed by opening a gate. Stifter makes clear that a key is needed for this act, too: "Dietwin öffnete mit einem Schlüssel die Tür des Gitters" (Dietwin opened the door of the gate with a key, 1488). This attention to the keys (*Schlüssel*) and their respective locks (*Schlösser*) bleeds into a broader semantic field, so that we see its traces in the repeated reminder that the setting of the story is Gerlint's "Schloss" (castle) and that young Gerlint had endured a time of "Abge*schloss*enheit" (seclusion) at her boarding school (1468; emphasis added).

Importantly, the only moments of decision in the whole story are also marked by variations of the same root word. The first appears when brother and sister "resolve" (beschließen, 1500) to leave the country; the second when young Gerlint affirms her decision to marry young Dietwin:

> "Und so bist du zu diesem Bündnisse entschlossen?" fragte die Tante.
> "Ich bin dazu entschlossen," antwortete Gerlint. (1511)

> ["And you are determined [*entschlossen*] to enter into this union?" the aunt asked.
> "I am determined [*entschlossen*]," Gerlint answered.]

When a few lines later we read, "Die Tante schloß sie in die Arme" (The aunt embraced her; literally, "closed her in her arms"), the motif seems to have come full circle. The embrace as expression of familial bond also recalls the titular "saying" of the story, "Die Ehen werden in dem Himmel geschlossen" (Marriages are made in heaven), whose image of covenantally "making," "binding," or "sealing" a union carries multiple registers of the same root word *schließ-/schloß-* with it:

> "Der Himmel *schließt* ja die Ehen," sprach der Oheim.
> "Er *schließt* sie, wenn eine rechte zu *schließen*, und wenn überhaupt eine zu *schließen* ist," antwortete die Tante.
> "Vielleicht *schließt* er mehrere," sagte der Oheim, "da bist ja du in dem *Schlosse*, dann Gerlint, Auguste, die Kammermädchen, Agathe. Nur für Judith hat er die Ehe schon *geschlossen*."
> ...

130 ♦ SAMUEL FREDERICK

"So *schließen* wir die Verhandlung über diesen Gegenstand," sprach die Tante.

"*Schließen* wir sie," erwiderte der Oheim, "da ja doch nichts zu verhandeln ist."

Sie *schlossen*, weil wirklich nichts da war, das verhandelt werden konnte. (1486–87; emphasis added)

["But it is heaven that makes (*schließt*) marriages," the uncle said.

"It makes (*schließt*) them, when there is a right one to make (*schließen*), and when there is at all one to make (*schließen*)," answered the aunt.

"Maybe it will make (*schließt*) more of them," said the uncle, "after all, you are in the castle (*Schlosse*), then Gerlint, Auguste, the chamber maids, Agathe. Only for Judith did it make (*geschlossen*) a marriage."

…

"Let us thus end (*schließen*) our negotiations on this matter," said the aunt.

"Let us end (*schließen*) them," responded the uncle, "since there really is nothing to negotiate."

They stopped (*schlossen*), because there was actually nothing that could be negotiated.]

Here, in Dietwin's initial recapitulation of the story's "saying," *Schließen* denotes not just the "making" or "binding" of a union but the "ratification" or "finalization" of a contract.[44] The nuptial agreement is "sealed" in heaven, divinely sanctioned, and this stamp of approval grants legitimacy to the union. But as the continued conversation makes clear, this "finalizing" is also a "termination" of sorts. In fact, this conversation echoes an earlier one between the siblings, in which the word for such termination is more explicit: "der arme Dietwin von der Weiden, der ältere, für den der Himmel keinen *Schluß* gefunden hat" (1480, emphasis added; poor Dietwin von der Weiden, the elder, for whom heaven did not find binding closure [*Schluß*]). Ultimately, that the marriage is "sealed" in heaven means that the culminating event of the story is already determined. Only what already was is; and what is to be ordains what was. There is no room for anything new.[45] Everything is and will always be repetition. What is providentially assured is "sealed," and whatever might disturb this placidly repeating sequence of events must be "closed out."

---

44   The idiom predates Stifter and likely comes from Matthew 16:19: "And I will give unto thee the keys of the kingdom of heaven: and whatsoever thou shalt bind on earth shall be bound in heaven." Importantly, it is "keys" that do the celestial binding.

45   Koschorke and Ammer, "Text ohne Bedeutung," 700.

Chief among those wayward tendencies is sexual desire. Thus, the act of "sealing" the union of the younger generation closes off specifically erotic possibilities, including the incestuous ones imagined by brother and sister, in which the niece is attracted to her uncle and the nephew to his aunt. These potential bonds within the family must be thwarted, the illicit desires diverted. Furthermore, they must not be spoken, which is why the conversation between the siblings in the passage just quoted, as in the earlier ones broaching this subject, is "cut off."[46] Here the act of *Schließen* evokes the various other images of containers and barriers in the story to suggest that the siblings Gerlint and Dietwin fear but at the same time desire these incestuous relations. On the one hand it is hard not to see an erotic charge to the attentive narration of keys turning in their locks.[47] But on the other hand, these and related images evoke something less explicitly sexual: the shutting out, closing in, and sealing off a space where the family unit can be properly preserved. This preservation nonetheless still requires sexual reproduction, and in the story this act is assured in an incestuous bond of sorts, even if it is a more acceptable one (the cousins are adopted, but nonetheless blood relatives, being the children of Gerlint and Dietwin's other siblings). The whole plot—insofar as there is one—culminates in the union of young Gerlint and Dietwin, leading to the realization of what aunt Gerlint calls "dem Glücke der Familie, die so geschlossen fortgeht" (1497; the fortune of the family that, enclosed and complete in this way, keeps going). Here "geschlossen" means "forming a cohesive unity," which both implies and denotes the exclusion of others, bringing back in the image of "closing out" or "locking away." Only tightly "sealed off" from the outside, replicating itself from within (the identical names of the aunt/niece and the uncle/nephew only drive this point home), can the truly fortunate family "keep going."

This perpetuation of the family under the auspices of preservation comprises the entire action—and regulating moral law—of "Der fromme Spruch" and "Der Kuß von Sentze" (as well as, though less directly, *Witiko*), where it also expresses and enacts the narrative principle of Stifter's late work: the story "keeps going," but only by virtue of the repetition of the same.[48] This principle conforms to the logic of collecting,

46   On the expressivity of silence in this story, see Korschorke and Ammer, "Text ohne Bedeutung," 677–78. Matz sums up: "What is spoken in 'Der fromme Spruch' is what is inconsequential, and it is Stifter's great art to narrate this inconsequentiality in order to make what remains unspoken visible." Matz, *Gewalt des Gewordenen*, 72.

47   Koschorke and Ammer proceed from the "fact" that "at the center of the story is the unspoken incestuous desire of the siblings." Koschorke and Ammer, "Text ohne Bedeutung," 686.

48   On the preservation of the family in "Der Kuß von Sentze," see Frederick, *The Redemption of Things*, 69–100.

which in turn is governed by the forces of succession and *Schließen*, the perpetuation of a series of the same and the safekeeping of this series by means of enclosure. Stifter's radically austere and iterative style is a direct consequence of mobilizing these conflicting forces—one unbounded and seeking to move forward, the other bounded and seeking stasis—for the same end. If the perpetuation both of the family and of the story ensure a fundamental connection to the idealized past, then to keep things the way they were and were always meant to be, as Stifter desires, is to seal off and lock away, to suspend both family and story, thereby threatening that connection.[49] In his late work, Stifter insists on having it both ways. He preserves what matters most to him—the family, its story, and its history—in a manner that allows for its perpetuation only as an accretion of the same, as a repetition of what already was. The stylistic and narrative manifestations of this repetition, as we have seen, cancel out causality and stymie story dynamics, effectively cutting his characters off from the living, changing world.

The model for this combined preservation and perpetuation is not just the collection, but, specifically, the naturalia collection, different forms of which preoccupied Stifter in both his life and work.[50] The collecting of plants and animals poses an especially vexing problem, for in order for the living specimen to be preserved it has to be immobilized, its life effectively taken from it: the plant is flattened and dried, the animal stuffed or pinned.[51] This paradox complicates the very undertaking, pitting means against ends. A similarly conflicted process describes Stifter's late narratives, which can only secure meaning by means that at the same time threaten that meaning, which tell of people and events only by fixing them in time, maintaining sameness in the face of the contingencies of historical change. It thus hardly matters to Stifter's project of historical preservation that "Der fromme Spruch" is set in the near-present day (a detail that the first editor removed before printing it), because it tells of people who act according to rules and rituals that pay no heed to the

---

49   I am echoing Witiko's mother's words about him: "daß Witiko so ist, wie er gewesen ist, und er wird auch in der Zukunft so sein" (that Witiko is the way he was, and in the future will also be). To which his aunt replies, "Witiko kann ja nicht anders sein als er ist" (*HKG* 5,3:93; Witiko cannot really be other than as he is).

50   In "Der Kuß von Sentze" the activity of collecting assumes a key role in the story. On moss collecting in this novella, see Frederick, *The Redemption of Things*, 89–100.

51   The exception to this kind of collecting of animals and plants might be found in the zoo and garden, respectively. Risach's uncaged animals and flourishing gardens in *Der Nachsommer* thus represent an altogether different vision of collecting naturalia.

changes of the modern world and indeed seek to maintain the old one as if it had never disappeared in the first place.[52]

The strict, austere, and ordered language of Stifter's late style is, ultimately, violent, as is the act of collecting with which it shares a conflicted logic. Stifter addresses this problem at the core of his narrative project—the fact that by "sealing" or "locking" in the elements of the world he most wishes to preserve he is also thereby taking the life out of them—in equally conflicting ways. On the one hand, he tries to evade the problem by treating his lifeless characters as somehow untouched by earthly concerns. For in removing any and all contingencies from his stories Stifter also removes the contingency of death itself.[53] And yet, because Stifter can only preserve by sacrificing the thing he wants to save, because he can only hold on to these characters (and the ideals for which they stand) by taking the life out of them, these texts end up conveying a deep sense of sorrow. In the end, then, what Stifter preserves is not tradition or history or family or even meaning writ large, but rather the loss of these very certainties.

This consequence of his late style, palpable in the tension between means and ends, as I have laid them out in this chapter, can also be felt in the profound melancholy that colors nearly all the interactions between his characters.[54] It is almost as if they, too, recognize—as Stifter must have—that there is no place for them in the actual world anymore. Only in the artificial spaces of the text does their existence make any sense. Indeed, only here does their discourse join that of Stifter's narrators to fill up the desolate spaces that he has left behind. Emptied of all conventional realist content, these late texts become sealed-off echo chambers in which Stifter's late style—at once mournful and methodical, monotonous and manic—reverberates.

---

52   Stifter's attempt to preserve tradition in the face of a tradition that has lost its meaning applies equally to *Witiko*. As Wolfgang Matz notes, Stifter's Middle Ages are only a "Biedermeier projection." But he clings to this past nonetheless, "conjuring up the tradition that he himself only preserves as an empty shell …." Matz, *Gewalt des Gewordenen*, 44.

53   The moss collected in "Der Kuß von Sentze," for instance, offers a way out of the bind, since it can be resuscitated after being desiccated, flattened, and filed away in the collection. See Frederick, *The Redemption of Things*, 94, 98–100.

54   A less generous or sympathetic reading might call the mood that colors all character interactions in these works "indifference." In the absence of any access to these characters' inner lives the reader is left to read the claims they make to having emotions (and there are such claims) next to the inability to express these emotions in any complex or believable way as an indication either of having no real emotions at all (their claims being mere simulation or dissimulation) or—as I read them—of the profound inability to make their inner lives meaningful for themselves and others, a radical disconnect that points to despondency, if not despair.

# Part II

# Texts and Contexts

# 5: The Birth of Realism out of the Spirit of Melodrama: Stifter's *Feldblumen*

*Erica Weitzman*

"MELODRAMA" IS NOT a word usually associated with Adalbert Stifter. The author whose third chapter of his most famous novel infamously turns on the question of whether or not it will rain, the author who devotes pages upon pages of text to detailed descriptions of gardening techniques or parquetry or snowdrifts, the author who seems himself to have lived a life of domestic tedium and bureaucratic obligation, broken up only by the pleasure of his copious meals, is not exactly known for his flamboyant emotionality or action-packed plots.[1] While Stifter's peers admired his eye for detail and patient attunement to nature, they also criticized what they saw as a certain pedantic fastidiousness and a neglect of genuine human concerns in favor of a timeless, God's-eye view of the world.[2] In the age of the bourgeois tragedy and the social novel, Stifter, so ran the general consensus, was an outlier. At worst, his writings were deemed ploddingly reactionary and insipid; at best, they were seen as the work of a talented if limited miniaturist: masterly, at times even lovely— but dull.

In the intervening years, of course, the fortunes of the author whom his contemporary Friedrich Hebbel notoriously dubbed "de[r] Mann der ewigen Studien" (the man of eternal studies)[3] have changed. The radical stasis of many of Stifter's texts, which caused him to be a source of frustration and mockery in his own time, have made him newly interesting for a modernist or postmodernist tradition suspicious of both

---

1    On Stifter's eating habits and day-to-day life, see e.g. Wolfgang Matz, *Adalbert Stifter, oder Diese fürchterliche Wendung der Dinge: Biographie* (Göttingen: Wallstein: 2016), esp. 281–86.

2    See e.g. Julian Schmidt, *Geschichte der deutschen Literatur seit Lessing's Tod*, vol. 3 (Leipzig: Herbig, 1858), 377: "Stifter vergißt, daß Gott nicht das Publicum des Dichters bildet" (Stifter forgets that God is not the author's intended audience).

3    Friedrich Hebbel, "Das Komma im Frack," in *Werke*, vol. 3, ed. Gerhard Fricke, Werner Keller, and Karl Pörnbacher, (Munich: Hanser, 1965), 684–87; here 686.

conventional plot and psychological depth and eager to find precedents for cooler, less classically characterological forms of narrative literature. Meanwhile, more recent critics have discovered in Stifter a prescient witness to the preeminence of things, an idiosyncratic, but for that reason all the more perceptive, chronicler of the objective reality of a natural world independent of and indifferent to the lives of its human inhabitants.[4] Stifter's monomaniacally detailed nature descriptions, once considered to be mere Biedermeier kitsch, are now read as pitiless portrayals of the phenomenal world, of the uncanny processes of physical becoming and appearing rather than a static replica of the way things are and always have been. In short, in the past few decades, Stifter has become an all but obligatory touchstone for readers interested in questions of phenomenology, thing studies, ecocriticism, posthumanism, material culture, and the history of science, not to mention poststructuralist approaches to language, epistemology, semiotics, visual culture, and representation. For suspense, spectacle, passion, and high drama, however, Stifter is still—to put it mildly—hardly anyone's first point of reference.

This prevailing idea of the antidramatic, indeed staid nature of Stifter's work is one that is promoted, not least, by Stifter himself. In his artistic manifesto of a sort, the preface to his short story collection *Bunte Steine* (Motley Stones), Stifter lays out the case against sensational representation that secured his reputation amongst his peers as a meticulous but slightly tedious painter of idylls and still lifes. For Stifter, arguing counterintuitively, the sublime spectacles and violent emotions favored by the authors of Young Germany and the *Sturm und Drang* are in fact not noteworthy events, but merely "einseitige" (one-sided) effects of the same laws of nature that also govern such phenomena as "Das Wehen der Luft das Rieseln des Wassers das Wachsen der Getreide das Wogen des Meeres das Grünen der Erde das Glänzen des Himmels das Schimmern der Gestirne" (*HKG* 2,2:10; the wafting of the air the trickling of water the growing of grain the surging of the sea the budding of the earth the shining of the sky the glimmering of the stars, *MS* 3)—things which, in their very universality and *un*remarkableness, are for Stifter what is truly worthy of attention. For Stifter's paradoxically empiricist update of German idealism, the task of art is to describe the usual, not the extraordinary; the normal, not the eccentric; the rule, not the deviation from it.

---

4    One of the first critics to take this approach is Hannah Arendt, who inverts the erstwhile criticism of Stifter's descriptive pedantry to praise the fact that "he describes the slow, steady, and blessed process of the growth of a human being as it lives and blossoms and dies together with the trees and flowers of which it takes care during its lifetime." Hannah Arendt, "Great Friend of Reality: Adalbert Stifter," in *Reflections on Literature and Culture*, ed. Susannah Young-ah Gottlieb (Stanford, CA: Stanford University Press, 2007), 110–14; here 111.

The dramatic sublime and the high tragic-melodramatic favored by the star authors of the day are for Stifter but temporary swerves from what actually matters, the regular occurrences of both nature and human existence that shape life far more meaningfully than their showy but momentary aberrations. Honesty in art requires a resistance to being seduced by that which is most sensational or strange. A literature that would portray the truth of the world must portray that world in the truth of its fundamental stability.

And yet, not only is it the case that the sensational and the strange are clearly *not* excluded from Stifter's writings, as many critics have observed;[5] the standard and the everyday are also themselves staged in a way that belies Stifter's stated goal of harmonious normalcy and puts his work in the ambit of the melodramatic indeed. What Thomas Mann famously called Stifter's "Neigung zum Exzessiven" (penchant for excess)[6] is evident in practically all of Stifter's texts, where the at times precious emphasis on purity and order does not hide the latent threat of their undoing. But Stifter's "penchant for excess" appears not only in the appearance of those conspicuously anomalous elements such as storms, plagues, miracles, madmen, etc. that populate his stories, nor even in his quixotic endeavor to claim these elements for the aggressive normalcy of "the gentle law" itself.[7] It appears also and especially in Stifter's inordi-

---

5    On Stifter's ostensible "poetics of the normal" as in fact "the literary revelation of what hides and maintains itself in the margins, deviations, and exceptions," see Paul Fleming, *Exemplarity and Mediocrity: The Art of the Average from Bourgeois Tragedy to Realism* (Stanford, CA: Stanford University Press; 2009), esp. 139–62; here 162; also Eric Downing, *Double Exposures: Repetition and Realism in Nineteenth-Century German Fiction* (Stanford, CA: Stanford University Press, 2000), esp. 30–31.

6    Specifically: "hinter der stillen, innigen Genauigkeit gerade seiner Naturbetrachtung [ist] eine Neigung zum Exzessiven, Elementar-Katastrophalen, Pathologischen wirksam" (precisely behind the quiet, earnest exactitude of his treatment of nature runs a penchant for excess, for the elemental-catastrophic, for the pathological). Thomas Mann, *Die Entstehung des Doktor Faustus: Roman eines Romans*, in *Gesammelte Werke in dreizehn Bänden*, vol. 11 (Frankfurt am Main: Fischer, 1990), 145–301; here 237; Thomas Mann, *The Story of a Novel: The Genesis of Doctor Faustus* (New York: Knopf, 1961), 139, translation significantly modified. See also Walter Benjamin's remarks on the oscillation in Stifter between the detail and the extreme. Walter Benjamin, "Stifter," in *Gesammelte Schriften*, vol. 2.2, ed. Rolf Tiedemann and Hermann Schweppenhäuser (Frankfurt am Main: Suhrkamp, 1977), 607–10, esp. 609; Walter Benjamin, "Stifter," in *Selected Writings*, vol. 1: *1913–1926*, ed. Marcus Bullock and Michael W. Jennings (Cambridge, MA: Harvard University Press, 1996), 111–13; esp. 112.

7    See Fleming, *Exemplarity and Mediocrity*, 160–61; also Helena Ragg-Kirkby, *Adalbert Stifter's Late Prose: The Mania for Moderation* (Rochester, NY: Camden House, 2000).

nate efforts to transform every facet of his writing, and indeed every detail of the world, into the sign of a consummate meaningfulness that the well-nigh tyrannical universality of "the gentle law" anyway already implies.

In what follows here, I will explore the origins of this effort towards consummate meaningfulness and its relevance for melodrama through a reading of Stifter's early epistolary novella *Feldblumen* (Wildflowers).[8] First, I will show how Stifter's work rests on a generic foundation of melodrama, including such classically melodramatic features as secret identities, hidden benefactors, and eleventh hour resolutions, and extending to such sensationalistic and seemingly un-Stifterian phenomena as long-lost identical twins, brutal highway murders, and mysterious travelers from exotic lands. However, as I will also show, these stereotypically melodramatic elements in *Feldblumen*—which, as in most of Stifter's other works, are largely leached of their dramatic force—are in the end only proxies for what is truly melodramatic in Stifter's novella, namely the striving for a more unmediated, intense, or pure form of expression that is no less a feature of the melodramatic mode than the mustachio-twirling villain and the dark and stormy night. What Franziska Schößler has called the "Schönheits- und Mäßigungsprogramm" (beauty and moderation program)[9] of *Feldblumen*'s worldview is thus in fact merely the conclusion to the passionate drama of signification and representation that the novella also performs: a drama that is melodramatic not just in its incidentals, but in its premises, insofar as it is the drama of melodramatic contingency (and its overcoming) itself. Ultimately, as I will argue, what *Feldblumen* stages is the melodrama of Stifter's attempted exit from melodrama, the sensational eradication of melodrama's epistemological turmoil as the paradoxical prerequisite of a narrative realism in which nothing is ever again supposed to happen.

## I: Coups de théâtre

Melodrama, like realism or like the novel itself, is an ill-defined genre. Literally meaning "music play," the word was coined in the eighteenth

---

8    Like many of Stifter's tales, *Feldblumen* exists in two versions, the so-called *Buchfassung* of 1844 and the earlier 1840/41 *Journalfassung*. The difference between the two versions is primarily stylistic, entailing minor changes in word choice and orthography, though it also includes some more substantial alterations, above all the streamlining or cutting of particularly digressive or whimsical-romantic passages. Unless otherwise indicated, all quotations here are from the *Buchfassung*.

9    Franziska Schößler, "Feldblumen," in *Stifter-Handbuch: Leben—Werk—Wirkung*, ed. Christian Begemann and Davide Guiriato (Stuttgart: J. B. Metzler, 2017), 19–23; here 20.

century to describe a certain form of light opera or musical pantomime fashionable at the time in Italy and France. In the German-speaking world, the term was imported through Jean-Jacques Rousseau's 1762/70 *Pygmalion*, designated by Rousseau as a "mélo-drame" in order to distinguish it from the bel canto style of Italian high opera.[10] However, it did not take long for the word to free itself from its usage as a simple genre designation and take on the expanded meaning it continues to have today: as a largely pejorative term for an art of hyperbolic sentimentality, Manichean dramatic conflicts, and schematic resolutions, usually intended for a popular or less refined audience. Melodrama, in this sense of the term, is a "debased or failed tragedy":[11] the sublime suffering and fearsome anagnorises of classical drama cheapened into vulgar histrionics for the sensation-seeking masses. Its typical coding as a low, feminine, or queer genre, which makes up part of its interest for contemporary critics, also corresponds to its earlier dismissal as a potentially less respectable, and certainly less serious form of literature and performance. Even the irony and camp toward which melodrama tends on its outer edges is not enough to save it from the whiff of disreputableness and unintentional self-parody that inevitably accompanies it. Melodrama substitutes spectacle for awe, hysteria for pathos, mood swings for meaning: a simultaneously chintzy and exalted form of art that mirrors the pretentions of its presumably unsophisticated audience in the very innocence of its extravagance.[12]

In his influential study on "the melodramatic imagination," the literary scholar Peter Brooks accordingly defines melodrama as "the mode of excess."[13] For Brooks, melodrama is characterized above all by the exaggeratedness and, at the same time, the perpetual inadequacy of its representations. Melodrama's fevered plots and overwrought rhetoric mean it is forced to perpetually up the ante, to turn up the dial ever higher in the

---

10   See Peter Ihring, "Melodramatisch," in *Ästhetische Grundbegriffe: Historisches Wörterbuch in sieben Banden*, ed. Karlheinz Barck, et al., vol. 4: *Medien–Populär* (Stuttgart: J. B. Metzler, 2002), 59–72, esp. 62–63; also Christine Gledhill, "The Melodramatic Field: An Investigation," in *Home Is Where the Heart Is: Studies in Melodrama and the Woman's Film*, ed. Christine Gledhill (London: British Film Institute, 1987), 5–39, esp. 19.

11   Gledhill, "The Melodramatic Field," 5. It should be noted that this is not Gledhill's own judgment, but merely her restatement of the common view.

12   On the literary-historical origins of modern melodrama (particularly the sentimental novel and the bourgeois tragedy) and melodrama's correspondingly ambivalent ideological position, see Thomas Elsaesser, "Tales of Sound and Fury: Observations on the Family Melodrama," in *Home Is Where the Heart Is*, ed. Gledhill, 43–69, esp. 45–46.

13   Peter Brooks, *The Melodramatic Imagination: Balzac, Henry James, Melodrama, and the Mode of Excess* (New Haven, CT: Yale University Press, 1995).

effort to achieve sublimity through sheer force of wanting. But such over-the-topness, Brooks goes on to argue, is not a bug but a feature: "for the action played out on the [melodramatic] stage is ever implicitly an emblem of the cosmic ethical drama, which by reflection illuminates life here below, makes it exciting, raises its stakes."[14] In other words, insofar as melodrama is built on the premise that the domestic and the everyday can *also* be the site of existential struggle, that lives no different from the lives of those sitting in the theater can also be caught up in the eternal moral battle, disproportion is the founding gesture of the genre. The consequence of this heightened everydayness is a representational mode in which every signifier is exaggerated, overemphasized, redoubled in the unspoken suspicion that the signifier alone, attached to such lowly material, will not be enough. Hence melodrama's tendency to declamation and stock gestures—a "theater of 'shapes' rather than 'substance'"[15]—in which signs are presented so to speak less for their own sakes than as emblems for the ineffable pathos they are meant to express.[16] Wanting to say something greater than its own content can bear, melodrama says the saying. The excessiveness of melodrama corresponds to the loftiness of its denotative ambitions: "The literal drama is unremittingly overburdened by a weight of mysterious and grandiose reference beyond itself."[17]

To a cultivated citizen of Austria-Hungary in the early nineteenth century such as the young Adalbert Stifter, the concept of melodrama would hardly have been unknown. Besides the influences from France and Italy, the Czech-Austrian composer Georg (Jiří) Benda is usually credited with the development of the genre in the German-speaking world (as a variant of *Singspiel* combining extravagant emotionality with the

14  Brooks, *The Melodramatic Imagination*, 54.

15  Brooks, *The Melodramatic Imagination*, 104. Brooks' phrase is specifically in reference to Victor Hugo's romantic dramas, but is no less applicable to melodrama in general.

16  One might think here of Walter Benjamin's comments on the allegorical "bombast" of baroque theater: "Diese Dichtung war in der Tat unfähig, den derart ins bedeutende Schriftbild gebannten Tiefsinn im beseelten Laut zu entbinden. ... Niemals ist unbeschwingter gedichtet worden. ... Seine Schrift verklärt sich im Laute nicht; vielmehr bleibt dessen Welt ganz selbstgenugsam [*sic*] auf die Entfaltung ihrer eigenen Wucht bedacht." Walter Benjamin, *Ursprung des deutschen Trauerspiels* (Frankfurt am Main: Suhrkamp, 1963), 226; "This poetry was in fact incapable of releasing in inspired song the profound meaning which was here confined to the verbal image. ... Never has poetry been less winged. ... Its writing does not achieve transcendence by being voiced; rather does the world of written language remain self-sufficient and intent on the display of its own substance." Walter Benjamin, *The Origin of German Tragic Drama*, trans. John Osborne (London: Verso, 1998), 200–1.

17  Brooks, *The Melodramatic Imagination*, 105.

alternation of music and spoken text), influencing later composers of no less stature than Mozart, Beethoven, and Schubert. The new genre was of course not without its critics: while some saw it as a way to rescue opera from empty virtuosity, others faulted its repetitive structure and the frequent absurdity of its plot elements, as well as its failure to take advantage of music's actual nonverbal emotional power.[18] Melodrama, according to this view, is neither fish nor fowl, at once a trivialization of serious theater and a corruption of music's abstract expressivity through the admixture of declamation and spectacle. Such a view is one that Stifter explicitly voices in *Feldblumen*, where he has his mouthpiece and alter ego, the young painter Albrecht, repudiate the trivial amusements of musical theater in favor of the moral clarity of instrumental music: specifically, Beethoven's *Pastoral Symphony*, which Albrecht overhears from a side room at the party where he will, just thereafter, make his future beloved's acquaintance. Bathed in the room's milky light, the notes of the German composer's program music evoke in Albrecht a corresponding concert of emotions, leading him to exclaim, in the letter he writes to his interlocutor, Titus, "Wie ist diese Musik rein und sittlich gegen den leichtfertigen Jubel unserer meisten Opern! Auf unbefleckten weißen Taubenschwingen zieht sie siegreich in die Seele" (*HKG* 1,4:77; How pure and moral this music is in contrast to the frivolous merriment of most of our operas! On spotless white dove's wings it moves victoriously into the soul).

To be sure, Albrecht's comment is basically merely articulating a certain romantic commonplace about the superiority of interiority and sincerity in art over the entertaining and the merely virtuosic.[19] And yet Albrecht's preference for a "pure and moral" music, albeit ostensibly directed at popular and hybrid—read: melodramatic—forms of art, also betrays a certain predilection for the melodramatic mode that his comment would, on first sight, seem to reject. For what the text/music alternation of melodrama proper points to—and, *a fortiori*, the operatic tonality of melodrama in general—is an attempt, however clumsy, to finally overcome the limits of the sayable, to transcend through the greater emotional register of melody both the discursive and the beautiful and leap as it were directly into the sublime.[20] Thus, even leaving aside the irony that Albrecht's remark occurs in the context of what is literally

18  See Austin Glatthorn, "The Legacy of 'Ariadne' and the Melodramatic Sublime," *Music & Letters* 100, no. 2 (2019): 233–70, esp. 243–52.

19  See Norbert Miller, "Stifter und die Musik," in *Stifter-Handbuch*, ed. Begemann and Guiriato, 236–40, esp. 238.

20  See Glatthorn, "The Legacy of 'Ariadne' and the Melodramatic Sublime," esp. 241–42. On Stifter's not infrequent use of music scenes to punctuate his own literary works, see Theophil Antonicek, "Musik in den Erzählungen Adalbert Stifters," *Jahrbuch des Adalbert-Stifter-Instituts des Landes Oberösterreich* 19 (2012): 21–36.

144 ♦ Erica Weitzman

the overture to his own operatic intrigue, Albrecht's praise of the "white dove's wings" of Beethoven's pure music is already a wish for a more immediate expressive order: a *melodramatic* order in which representation achieves the level of the non-representable, in which image, meaning, reception, and affect all "move victoriously into the soul" in one single upwards flight.[21]

*Feldblumen* is not one of Stifter's better read works. The basic plot is simple: a budding painter and poet makes the acquaintance of a vaguely mysterious group of cultivated aristocrats, falls in love with a young woman of their circle, finds his love requited, and after a small contretemps finally gets the girl, the money, and a ready-made coterie eager to encourage and support his art. In this sense, *Feldblumen* can be read as a fairly standard *Künstlerroman*, in which a young artist, initially unsure of himself and his talents, eventually finds his place in the world and— at once financially, professionally, and erotically—comes into his own. However, as in most of Stifter's works, the devil (or the drama) is in the details. Though in many ways a precursor to Stifter's later texts (in particular, *Der Nachsommer* and *Nachkommenschaften*), the novella is an odd hybrid, combining its epistolary coming-of-age story with a largely tensionless marriage plot, dilettantish meditations on art and beauty, metafictional japes à la Jean Paul, flourishes of benign intrigue, and a lurid backstory that clashes tonally with the often saccharine geniality of the novella itself. Meanwhile, the coincidences and correspondences that propel *Feldblumen*'s plot at times approach the laughable. At the opening of the novella, Stifter's narrator, a self-described lover of beauty, is obsessed with a certain attractive young woman he keeps seeing around the city: most recently, walking into St. Anne's Church with an older woman whom Albrecht takes to be her mother, and later, on a day trip to a local nature spot, accompanied by the older woman and a younger veiled figure. The classical beauty of this woman, whom he calls "mein Modell" (*HKG* 1,4:47; my model), leaves him indifferent to all others—until, that is, he glimpses the face of a different beautiful woman in Vienna's Paradiesgarten, as she turns around to look at Albrecht in response to a leading remark. Soon thereafter, Albrecht learns from his friend and fellow painter Lothar that the second woman is one Princess Fodor, a married Russian noblewoman who has coincidentally just sat for Lothar for

---

21   One sign of *Feldblumen*'s melodramatics is its use of the vocative to convey ineffable or overpowering emotion, e.g. (in the two pages narrating Albrecht's climactic declaration of love): "O Angela, o Braut, o Gattin!" "O Titus!" and "O, ich Thor! ich Thor!" (*HKG* 1,4:129–30; O Angela, o bride, o wife! / O Titus! / O, what a fool am I! What a fool!). On "the recourse to inarticulate cry and gesture" as the marker of "a kind of fault or gap in the code, the space that marks its inadequacies to convey a full freight of emotional meaning," see Brooks, *The Melodramatic Imagination*, 67.

her portrait, and who, as Lothar relates, is as cold on the inside as she is handsome on the outside. A few weeks later, at a party at the home of his new friend Aston, a wealthy (and stereotypically eccentric) Englishman, Albrecht is introduced to a young woman named Angela, whose arrival Aston's circle has been anticipating for months. This Angela turns out to be not only gifted with taste and learning (imparted to her, it is reported, by a mysterious "tutor"), but also the veritable doppelganger of the woman from the Paradiesgarten, whose image Albrecht has meanwhile been keeping on him in the form of a borrowed miniature of Lothar's life-sized painting. Albrecht immediately falls in love with Angela, all the while remaining in the dark about her origins, her identity, and her relation both to the Russian princess and to his present company (including a certain "nabob" that the wily Aston keeps mentioning will any day now arrive on the scene). The next two months are spent by Albrecht in the constant company of Angela, keeping up a sort of impromptu book club with her and Aston's two daughters in a state of chaste infatuation. One day, however, as Albrecht stops by Aston's house to say his goodbyes before leaving for a painting tour in the mountains, Angela reveals that she and Aston's family are planning to decamp for good to France in two weeks' time. Taken aback by the news, Albrecht declares his love to Angela there on the spot, in the selfsame music room of Aston's house where they had first met only weeks before. Angela confesses her love in return, telling Albrecht to leave and come back to Aston's at precisely four that afternoon to announce their betrothal. Later that day, walking through the park in a dazed happiness, Albrecht spies a couple by a fountain. Just as he is at the point of turning away, he realizes that the woman is Angela herself, arm in arm with another man. Crushed, Albrecht packs up and departs for his mountain tour, leaving only a curt note of goodbye for Aston. In the mountains, Albrecht runs into a mysterious man that he has seen occasionally around the city without ever being introduced. This time, however, Albrecht talks to him and, finding him agreeable, invites him to join his group, which the man gladly accepts. Meanwhile, Albrecht travels around and absorbs the scenery, but is too depressed to paint—until finally one night, as Albrecht is out brooding in solitude, the mysterious man comes to him and reveals his true identity: he is Angela's adoptive brother Emil, who is also the "tutor," who is also the "nabob," who is also, last but not least, the man Albrecht saw in the park with Angela, who had in fact at that very moment been relating to him the news of their now aborted engagement. Dumbstruck at these revelations, Albrecht spontaneously hands over to Emil his diary, in which he has documented the truth of his feelings for Angela over the course of their acquaintance. Two days later, Emil introduces Albrecht to his sister Natalie, who turns out to be the beautiful woman that Albrecht had been obsessed with at the beginning of his adventures (and the veiled figure with her at the inn outside the city thus no less than Angela herself). Natalie fills in the rest of the story: she and Emil are the children of a Boston merchant and a Parisian woman who fled revolutionary France for the East Indies, later returning to France after the Restoration with their colonial fortune in tow. Angela, meanwhile, was adopted into their family as an infant, after the young Emil, traveling in the Cévennes with his teacher, happened to stop at a roadside tavern to which the bodies of her parents, murdered that morning by highwaymen, had been brought, and decided to take the newly orphaned child (who had miraculously escaped the highwaymen's notice) home with him. Of Angela's origins, nothing further had been known—until just a few weeks ago, and indeed thanks to the unwitting actions of Albrecht himself. For Angela—"eigentlich Alexandra" (*HKG* 1,4:162; actually Alexandra)—turns out to be the long-lost identical twin of the aforementioned Russian Princess Fodor, whose resemblance to Angela in Lothar's miniature, innocently noted by Albrecht, indirectly led (though exactly how, the novella fails to explain) to the sisters' eventual reunion. The Princess, Natalie continues, in France visiting her parents' grave, learned from the locals that her sister, long thought dead, was in fact alive and well and living in Vienna, and set off directly for Austria to find Angela and bring her back to Russia to claim her birthright. But upon their eventual meeting, Angela, despite the Princess's promises of wealth and title, stood by her adopted family and sent the Russian beauty packing—leaving the field open, it is implied, for a reunion and reconciliation with Albrecht. At last, at the end of the novella, with all obstacles removed, all identities revealed, and all misunderstandings cleared up, Angela and Albrecht are wed, and as a wedding gift Albrecht's friends promise to make Albrecht's dream villa—about which he has naturally *also* written in his diary—a reality.

*Feldblumen*'s plot clearly owes a certain debt to Goethe's *Wilhelm Meisters Lehrjahre* (Wilhelm Meister's Apprenticeship, 1795–96)—not least, in Stifter's outright lifting of the character names "Lothar" and "Natalie"—and the *Turmgesellschaft* (tower society) that clandestinely presides over the young Wilhelm's fate. But the remarkable coincidences and convenient accidents of Stifter's own early *Bildungsroman* go beyond even those of Goethe's imaginings. If *Feldblumen* is not necessarily more extravagant than *Wilhelm Meister*, it is at least more extravagantly tidy: every loose thread is tied up, every chance encounter becomes a meaningful bond, every individual meets his counterpart—even down to the final chapter, in which the nameless "Sammler und Erzähler" (*HKG* 1,4:169; compiler and narrator) of Albrecht's letters announces his own imminent engagement with a member of the novella's circle. Such elaborate yet pat storylines are perhaps part of what Thomas Elsaesser describes as the particular "pressure" of the melodramatic scene: the unspoken tensions of the bourgeois milieu manifest themselves as an

THE BIRTH OF REALISM OUT OF THE SPIRIT OF MELODRAMA ♦ 147

increasingly crowded showplace of things and events, "obstacles and objects that invade [the characters'] personalities, take them over, stand for them, become more real than the human relations or emotions they were intended to symbolise."[22] Even more, however, such neatly resolved storylines are a prime example of what Brooks observes as the particular function played in melodrama by the trope of *recognition*.[23] Recognition, of course, is one of the fundamental elements of classical tragedy: the climactic moment arrives with the hero's apprehension of the awful truth of which he had previously been unaware. In melodrama, however, recognition takes on a somewhat different form. Here it is not a question of the character development entailed by traditional tragic anagnorisis, the movement from unselfconscious ignorance to terrible self-knowledge in the hero's inevitable encounter with his fate.[24] Still less is it a question of what Samuel Weber identifies as tragedy's uncanny "shock of [the] *double-take*": the realization that "what one had expected, intended, anticipated does not correspond with what actually has happened"—with the added implication that there are no longer any guarantees that one will ever get "what actually has happened" right.[25] Indeed, in contrast to tragic recognition, recognition in melodrama has to do with the revelation of *precisely* what one had expected—albeit perhaps also temporarily forgotten. Melodrama's always-already is less the implacability of fate than the restoration of the status quo: the virtuous girl will gain back her reputation; the scoundrel will get his comeuppance; the open secret will be brought to light. Even when the ending of the melodrama is an unhappy one, the unhappiness consists simply in having cleared up the confusion a moment too late. In melodrama, in other words, the message is that the true sign, truly apprehended, speaks the truth of itself. Even the cliché gestures and dualistic conflicts for which melodrama is infamous are ultimately only there to suggest that the most elusive of meanings can be communicated, that even the most complex intrigues can be boiled down to simple terms.[26] Oracles may be misunderstood, but they do not equivocate. Melodramatic recognition is thus not a move from obscurity

22   Elsaesser, "Tales of Sound and Fury," 62.

23   See Brooks, *The Melodramatic Imagination*, 53.

24   Compare Aristotle, *On Poetics*, trans. Seth Bernardete and Michael Davis (South Bend, IN: St. Augustine's Press, 2002), 30: "Recognition ..., just as the name too signifies, is a change from ignorance [*agnoia*] to knowledge [*gnosis*], whether toward friendship or enmity, of those whose relation to good or ill fortune has already been defined."

25   Samuel Weber, *Theatricality as Medium* (New York: Fordham University Press, 2004), 298.

26   Compare Elsaesser on melodrama's "'condensation' of motivation into metaphoric images or sequences" in analogy to the Freudian dream-work. "Tales of Sound and Fury," 59.

to illumination, as in tragedy, but "the liberation from misprision ... of a pure signifier," the *re*discovered knowledge of the self-identity of the sign as such.[27]

Such a rediscovered knowledge of the self-identity of the sign is performed repeatedly in *Feldblumen*. In Albrecht's first face-to-face encounter with Angela, for example, the attraction he feels for her occurs with all the necessity of a *fait accompli*: "Ob ich in sie verliebt wurde?—Nein, in diese war ich es seit meinem ganzen Leben schon gewesen" (*HKG* 1,4:64; Was I in love with her?—No, I *had* been in love with her my whole life). But even more trivial occurrences confirm this form of identity: the inn where Albrecht and Lothar happen to stop for lunch during their nature excursion is coincidently the same one that Albrecht's "model" and the veiled woman have just left; a sensitive-looking young man Albrecht notices while out on a walk turns out to be the same person he had just before been promised to be introduced to—leading Albrecht to exclaim: "Auch moralischen und sogar zufälligen Erscheinungen gehen manchmal ihre Morgenröthen vorher" (*HKG* 1,4:53; Sometimes moral and even random phenomena are also preceded by their dawns). Even the fake "editor's" annotations (cut from the *Buchfassung*) emphasize the idea of semiotic equivalency, as well as the presumed humor of daring to deviate from it: "Man wird [den Referent dieser Blätter] anfahren, er ahme in solchen Späßen J[ean] Paul nach, aber man irrt, es sind nur die Verhältnisse und Sachlagen dargestellt so und nicht anders" (*HKG* 1,1:50; One will accuse [the editor of these pages] that he is imitating J[ean] Paul with such jests, but one would be mistaken: the circumstances and facts are simply represented this way and not otherwise).[28]

Unsurprisingly, this idea of semiotic equivalency emerges in *Feldblumen* with particular starkness at those moments where art itself is at stake. In the fifteenth chapter, "Liebfrauenschuh" (Lady's Slipper Orchid), in what is easily the novella's climatic set piece, the reader finds Albrecht out on a boat on a moonlit mountain lake, still brooding over Angela's supposed betrayal and his dashed chances for domestic happiness. Suddenly, he becomes aware of a singing voice coming to him from over the waters: the song is Schubert's arrangement of Goethe's "Auf dem See" (On the Lake), a poem about being out on a boat at night, trying to heal from a broken heart—just as Albrecht is trying to heal from his broken heart, while out on a boat on a lake at night. Goethe's

---

27  Brooks, *The Melodramatic Imagination*, 53.

28  See also the end of the chapter "Ehrenpreis" (Speedwell) in the *Journalfassung*: "Der Leser quält sich ab über den Zusammenhang der Feldblumen mit dem Inhalt der Kapitel—es ist keiner—außer, wo doch ein kleiner ist" (*HKG* 1,1:108; The reader will be torturing himself over the connection between the flowers and the chapters' content—there isn't any—except when there's a little one).

words, directly mirroring Albrecht's situation, move Albrecht to tears of self-pity, which will quickly turn into tears of joy as the unseen singer reveals himself to be Albrecht's erstwhile doppelgänger and new companion Emil, the adoptive brother of Angela and the soon-to-be resolver of all Albrecht's romantic difficulties. In this way, what at first appears as a perfect example of life imitating art is—on one level—undermined: initially appropriated by Albrecht as a program of self-help, then basically rendered moot through Emil's revelations, Goethe's bittersweet message of resignation and renunciation ultimately inverts into the narcissistic certitude of never having to renounce anything.

Such an inversion leads the scholar Hartmut Laufhütte to remark that "Goethe wird extremromantisch vereinnahmt und—fast unerträglich—verbiedermeierlicht" (Goethe is ultra-romantically co-opted and—almost intolerably—Biedermeierized).[29] But it is not just the fact that Stifter transforms Goethe's wry lament into a mawkish affirmation that makes his use of the poem worthy of note. For the presence of "Auf dem See" in Stifter's novella is more than just a catalyst for the novella's happy end: it is a *template*. Restaged through a series of perfect (and perfectly unlikely) accidents, Goethe's poem becomes the literal sign of Albrecht's plight, the ready-made and as it were pre-transcendentalized sign of Albrecht's own experience. Indeed, even before Emil discloses the truth of his and Angela's backgrounds, Albrecht's identification with emotions once expressed by the "father" (see *HKG* 1,4:51) of German literature already prefigures the resolution of his troubles, insofar as his private sadness is thereby made into a universal truth, a fragment of the Olympian immortality of great art itself. In this way, Albrecht's identification with Goethe's poem functions as a kind of meta-poetical shortcut for the "cosmic moral sense of everyday gestures"[30] that melodrama aims to establish. If art, according to Stifter's late-romantic aesthetics, is both true and sublime, then seeing one's life reflected in art—or even better, making one's own life into a work of art—makes that life true and sublime by definition. The transformation of the everyday is effected in the connection to a preexisting example of that transformation. But this shortcut or second-order elevation of the everyday is itself only the *bildungsbürgerliche* transformation of melodrama's inherently tautological structure of recognition, in which, for those clear-eyed enough to see it, the humble material of an individual life emerges as a drama of transcendent significance, precisely to the extent that it becomes transparent to itself. The "effort to articulate

---

29  Hartmut Laufhütte, "*Ich bin zwar kein Gothe aber einer aus seiner Verwandtschaft:* Zur Bedeutung Goethes für Adalbert Stifters literarisches Selbstverständnis," *Jahrbuch des Wiener Goethe-Vereins,* vols. 102/103, ed. Herbert Zeman (Vienna: Fassbaender, 1998/1999), 115–31; here 116.

30  Brooks, *The Melodramatic Imagination,* 14.

the moral universe"[31] takes place as a series of confirmations that the expected is the real. Whether in life or literature, melodrama assures, the signs are all already there; the task is merely learning to read them.

## II: Through a Glass, Darkly

Brooks notably considers melodrama to be a post-revolutionary genre. "A form for secularized times,"[32] melodrama departs the realm of myth and the sacred to establish the unambiguousness of moral values now on the terrestrial plane, for an age in which those values no longer have binding force. If tragedy is the genre of sovereignty and the law, in other words, then melodrama is the genre of the law's fragility, of the restitution of moral order after its traumatic abrogation. Here Brooks speaks of the topoi of the "enclosed garden" and the "interrupted fête": idyllic physical spaces or discrete temporal units whose threatened violation—always from the outside—spurs the melodramatic plot to action.[33] Such topoi give concrete shape to melodrama's general antidisestablishmentarianism; in the face of epistemological and political uncertainty, the imperiled idyll presumes an order whose rescue requires no justification.

Many critics have analyzed Stifter's bourgeois utopias in the context of the political upheavals of nineteenth-century Europe (particularly, the revolutions of 1848), attributing his obsessive desire for harmony and tranquility to a disillusioning experience with their opposites.[34] In *Feldblumen*, of course, political events are—to say the least—not at the forefront. Nevertheless, the historical cataclysms of the time—above all, the French Revolution, but also the American War of Independence, the Napoleonic campaigns, the Russian wars of expansion, and the anti-colonial uprisings of the Indian subcontinent—figure in the spectacular biographies of Emil, Natalie, Angela, and their respective parents (and therefore, by extension, in the fortunes of Albrecht himself), and the example of *Feldblumen* clearly shows that Stifter was responding to political unrest as early as 1836 with images of aesthetic and domestic regularity. Indeed, one might even read the novella's happy ending as a kind of metahistorical melodrama, in which the classical idyll of Albrecht's

31 Brooks, *The Melodramatic Imagination*, 52.
32 Brooks, *The Melodramatic Imagination*, 205.
33 Brooks, *The Melodramatic Imagination*, 29–30.
34 See for example Carl E. Schorske, *Fin de Siècle Vienna: Politics and Culture* (New York: Vintage Books, 1981), esp. 281–83; Russell A. Berman, *The Rise of the Modern German Novel: Crisis and Charisma* (Cambridge, MA: Harvard University Press, 1986), esp. 107; and Downing, *Double Exposures*, esp. 33.

"Tusculum" (*HKG* 1,4:71),[35] made seemingly impossible by the barbarities of the contemporary age, is ironically reestablished as those barbarities' by-product. But even without these explicit connections to world-historical events, it is easy to recognize in *Feldblumen* the drama of disruption and reparation for which the "enclosed garden" and the "interrupted fête" plots are paradigmatic. In Albrecht's misplaced suspicion of Angela and Emil, the perfected microcosm constituted by Aston and his circle is *almost* destroyed, saved only at the last minute by the timely intervention of Emil himself. The certainty of Angela's sexual virtue, threatened by a moment's misreading, is definitively reestablished by her adopted siblings' filling in of the gaps that allowed her story to be misread in the first place. Truth triumphs over delusion and misinterpretation (including the latent "misinterpretation" of the portentously phallic obelisk that looms over the fateful park scene)[36] in the restoration of the original norms of goodness and forthrightness that Angela's sexual iniquities, had they proven true, would have otherwise put into question.

However, it is in more than just the sexual and moral senses that the loss of norms is at stake in *Feldblumen*. Carolyn Williams has noted the particular centrality of physiognomy to melodrama: the reinforcement of appearance-based stereotypes grounds the melodramatic text in the certitude of familiarity, reassuring the audience that their initial impressions of people correspond to those people's essences.[37] Physiognomic characterization is thus a ready form of that semiotic equivalency on which melodrama depends: beauty is virtue, swarthiness is villainy, the cold glint in his eye gives away the handsome cad. And yet, as we have seen, melodrama also often hinges precisely on the testing of such equivalency, a character's temporary misprision of a sign whose true meaning is never in doubt. In this way, melodrama is actually predicated on an interesting *double* structure of recognition: the characters may be temporarily deceived as to one another's nature, but the audience, schooled from the beginning in the language of the melodramatic sign-system, is not. The real drama, then, consists in the former's imperfect understanding coming to correspond to the latter's true one, that is to say, in the audience's recognition that the characters have finally recognized what the audience itself has known all along.

---

35   Tusculum was a city about sixteen miles outside Rome, famous in classical times for its upscale suburban villas.

36   On phallic symbolism in Stifter's *Der Nachsommer*, see Catriona MacLeod, *Fugitive Objects: Sculpture and Literature in the German Nineteenth Century* (Evanston, IL: Northwestern University Press, 2014), 141.

37   See Carolyn Williams, "Melodrama and the Realist Novel," in *The Cambridge Companion to English Melodrama*, ed. Carolyn Williams (Cambridge: Cambridge University Press, 2018), 209–23, esp. 216.

## 152 ♦ Erica Weitzman

In *Feldblumen*, this double recognition structure is also operative, but with an important twist. Early on in the novella, Albrecht—among other things, a painter of portraits—comments to his friend on the significance of the human countenance: "Wohin aber, lieber Titus (ich will jetzt ernsthaft sein), wohin kann denn ein sterblicher Mensch lieber schauen, als in ein schönes Menschenangesicht, aus dem ihm noch eine unbefleckte Seele entgegen blickt?" (*HKG* 1,1:40; But where, dear Titus [now I want to be serious], where can a mortal being look with more pleasure than at a beautiful human face, out of which another unblemished soul is looking back at him?).[38] In this "wundervolle Titelblatt der Seele" (*HKG* 1,4:48; marvelous title page of the soul), where beauty corresponds automatically to moral goodness, one can behold no less than God's own wisdom in making virtue manifest. Confronted with the possibility of Angela's betrayal, however, Albrecht comes to doubt this correspondence—only to discover in the end that it was not the correlation between Angela's beautiful face and beautiful soul that was mistaken, but the fact that Albrecht had ever thought to doubt it. The goal of Albrecht's "phisiognomischen Reisen" (*HKG* 1,1:38; physiognomic travels),[39] in which he collects beautiful faces for artistic inspiration, is simultaneously achieved and cancelled out in the reestablishment of Angela's *actually* perfect blamelessness. And yet, as Christian Begemann, for one, has observed, this seeming affirmation of the truth of physiognomic signification is fatally complicated by the existence of Angela's twin, the imperious Princess Fodor, indistinguishable from her sister to the point that, as children, their own grandfather had made them wear different necklaces in order to distinguish between them (see *HKG* 1,4:161–62). The existence of the Princess thus introduces a fundamental uncertainty into the physiognomic legibility upon which Albrecht's worldview rests. Even if the mere concept of identical twins did not already trouble the relation between appearance and ipseity, the discrepancy between the Princess's hard heart and Angela's gentle one emphasizes that appearances are, in fact, not to be trusted, destabilizing the semiotic certainty of the novella's happy end and making the story of Angela's misrecognition a potential form of misrecognition in itself, a test of the very sign system by which melodrama makes its meanings signify.[40]

Such a test becomes even more important in light of the fact that, as Albrecht specifies, the legibility of the human face is not vouchsafed to everyone, but only to the artist: "denn der Weltmensch schaut nur oberflächlich oder selbstsüchtig, und der Verliebte verfälscht, nur zu sehr am irdischen Geschöpfe hangend: aber der reine, einfältige Meister in seiner

---

38   This passage is cut from the *Buchfassung.*

39   This phrase is cut from the *Buchfassung.*

40   See Christian Begemann, *Die Welt der Zeichen: Stifter-Lektüren* (Stuttgart: J. B. Metzler, 1995), esp. 203–5.

THE BIRTH OF REALISM OUT OF THE SPIRIT OF MELODRAMA ◆ 153

Werkstätte, tagelang denselben zwei Augen gegenüber, die er bildet und rundet,—der sieht den Finger Gottes aus den todten Farben wachsen" (*HKG* 1,4:48–49; for the worldly man beholds things only superficially or selfishly, and the lover, only too attached to the earthly creature, distortedly: but the pure and simple artist in his studio, staring day after day at the same pair of eyes that he shapes and fills out—he sees emerging from the dead colors the finger of God). In the artist's act of disinterested looking—and even more, in the patient recreation of the looked-at object—the face cannot fail to disclose the spiritual essence of the one who possesses it. Indeed, the production of this disclosure is arguably the entire task of the artist (and, to an only slightly lesser degree, of the art lover): to see, in contrast to the ordinary person's interested superficialities, the reality *within* the appearance, to extract from the myriad surfaces of the phenomenal world the inner truth of its being. By these lights, the artist should in fact be impervious to misrecognition altogether, since he would have to know how to read nature's signs in order to *be* an artist in the first place.[41] But if essence is in fact untethered from appearance—as the juxtaposition of Angela's beautiful soul and the Princess's ugly one suggests—if appearance can deceive, then what is the point of art at all? In his very first letter to Titus, Albrecht describes himself as a "Schönheitsgeizhals," a hoarder of beauty, in contrast to the insensible "Metallgeizhals" (metal hoarder) of wealth and material goods (*HKG* 1,4:45–46)—but if this beauty turns out to have no moral core behind it, if aesthetic education is a dead end, what is left to the fledgling artist, or even to the would-be moral citizen and connoisseur? What is the point of the perfection of forms, if such perfection is meaningless per se?[42]

41   See Stifter, *Feldblumen* (*Buchfassung*): "Diese also ist die verschrobene Angela, sie ist aber auch die Fürstin—und wer stand denn nun vor dem Hochspiegel—wer ist denn das lebensgroße Bild, wer das kleine Abbild? ... Eine solche Aenlichkeit zwischen zwei wildfremden Menschen ist gar ganz unmöglich; das muß ich verstehen, der ich schon über hundert Angesichter malte" (*HKG* 1,4:80–81; So this is the eccentric Angela, but this is also the Princess—so who was it then who was standing in front of the convex mirror—who is the life-size image, who the little copy? ... Such a likeness among two total strangers is completely impossible; this is something I should understand, I who have already painted over a hundred faces).

42   For Begemann, this crisis of the physiognomic sign ultimately leads in *Feldblumen* to the development of a higher hermeneutics, in which Albrecht learns to read signs not just singly but in context—which however does not do away with the original interpretive difficulty "daß es identische Titelblätter der Seele gibt, unter denen grundverschiedene Bücher verborgen liegen" (that there could be identical title pages of the soul, under which completely different books lie hidden). Begemann, *Die Welt der Zeichen*, 205.

In *Feldblumen*, such aesthetic-ethical questions are quickly brushed aside, at least in the practical sense. In both the unorthodox tutelage of Angela and the reading group Albrecht forms with Angela and Aston's daughters, for example, the idea that the appreciation of beautiful works leads to both personal and collective virtue is never once put into question,[43] and even in his moments of darkest doubt, Albrecht's faith in the moral validity of his métier and the value of the creative works of great men does not ever seriously waver.[44] Still, the idea of the correspondence between appearance and essence—or rather, the uncertainty in its regard—is a theme that returns again and again in the text of *Feldblumen*, indeed often connected with the difficulties of art-making and of art-appreciating. In the fourth letter of the novella, "Glockenblume" (Bluebell)—which also narrates the first appearances of the yet-unknown Emil and the still-veiled Angela—Albrecht laments the difficulties of achieving genuine forms of perception and expression:

> Seit der ersten Kindheit, wie viel tausend verschwimmende Gestalten von kleinen Gedanken, Ahnungen,—dann halbgeborne Dichtungen, Träume, Ideen, Kleinode von Empfindungen, mögen das lange Leben eines Menschen durchwandeln, ohne daß Kunde davon wird! … Und glückselig der, der ein Ohr hat, auch nur die drei Stanzen recht zu hören, und sich ein schönes Bild zu machen—so hat er dann eine schöne Welt; es gibt aber Leute, die aus den wenigen Farbenkörnern, die dem Andern entspringen, nur Fratzen bilden— und diese bedaure ich—sie sagen freilich, sie kennen die Welt, aber es ist nicht wahr, sie bekennen nur wider Willen ihr kleines Innere, und haben noch dazu eine Zerrwelt. (*HKG* 1,4:60–61)

> [From one's earliest childhood, how many thousand vague shapes of small thoughts, intimations,—then half-born poems, dreams, ideas, little gemstones of sensation traverse a person's long life without anyone even realizing! … And happy he who has an ear to really hear even three stanzas of poetry and to make out of them a beautiful picture—then he has a beautiful world; but there are those who, out

---

43 Even the one potential note of ambiguity—when Albrecht impulsively kisses Aston's irreverent younger daughter Emma in response to her sudden realization of the value of classical literature—is still ultimately a signal of aesthetic education's essential efficaciousness: "und seit jenem Tage versäumt Emma keine einzige Vorlesung, ja, sie fing sogar an, Meßkunst zu lernen" (*HKG* 1,4:111; and from that day on Emma didn't miss a single lecture, indeed, she even began to study geometry).

44 After an early moment of crisis provoked by Angela's possible identity as the Princess Fodor, in which Albrecht suggests that beauty as such may be meaningless, Albrecht concludes: "Aber ich glaube es nun und in Ewigkeit nicht" (*HKG* 1,4:85; But I don't really believe that, not now and not ever).

THE BIRTH OF REALISM OUT OF THE SPIRIT OF MELODRAMA ♦ 155

of the few grains of color they get from others, make for themselves only grotesques—and these I pity—of course, they claim to know the world, but it isn't so, they only betray thereby the smallness of their inner life and have a distorted world to boot.]

Even the most gifted artist, Albrecht says, can barely hope to grasp the immense richness of existing thoughts and phenomena—much less, the ordinary person, who observes the world only through a distorting lens of prejudices and insensibilities. Here Albrecht speaks semi-jocularly of the human being as an "Infusionsthierchen"—the eighteenth-century classification for protozoa and similar microorganisms—a solitary, small, vulnerable creature, "fürchterlich einsam auf der Insel 'Erde'" (*HKG* 1,4:62; terrifically lonely on that island "Earth") under the bell jar of its particular situation, just as the human heart, "eben so einsam in der Insel 'Körper ...'" (*HKG* 1,4:62; just as lonely in that island "body ..."), is unable to truly connect with all the other hearts that surround it. Wistfully, Albrecht wonders if the force of love could one day bind all people together in common perception and understanding, in the same way that the planets in the heavens are bound together through gravity, and answers for the moment in the negative: "Noch sind Kriege, noch ist Reichthum und Armuth" (*HKG* 1,4:62; still there are wars, still wealth and destitution).

The utopian wish at the core of all of this is clear enough. But this utopian wish is also a double one. First, of course, it is the wish to inhabit a world ruled by harmony, equality, and affection, rather than loneliness, division, and strife (a wish rendered slightly comical in *Feldblumen* by the fact that its happy end consists of Albrecht marrying into money and building himself a private villa). But second—and for Stifter perhaps even more significantly—it is the wish to perceive both internal and external phenomena accurately, and to be able to represent those phenomena to others in such a way that they unhesitatingly acknowledge the truth of that representation. In an ideal world, writes Albrecht, people would agree with one another, in a common vision of things that moreover corresponds to exactly the way things are. Until such time, however, "Vor dem Hohlspiegel unsrer Sinne hängt nur das Luftbild einer Welt, die wahre hat Gott allein" (*HKG* 1,4:61; Before the curved mirror of our senses hangs but the phantasm of a world; the true image is possessed by God alone).

These issues already come to a head in what is effectively the initiating scene of the novella, Albrecht's first view of Angela's face in the Paradiesgarten. Still engaged in his project of beauty-collecting, Albrecht espies the shapely back of a woman standing before a curved mirror and makes an offhand remark about its "Unterweltbeleuchtung" (*HKG* 1,4:64; underworldly light) in the attempt to get her to turn around and

## 156 ♦ Erica Weitzman

show her face. When she does so, however, the result is much more than Albrecht had bargained for:

> Von meiner Kindheit an war immer etwas in mir, wie eine schwermüthig schöne Dichtung, dunkel und halbbewußt, in Schönheitsträumen sich abmühend …— —in diesem Augenblicke hatte ich das Ding zwei Spannen breit meinen Augen sichtbar gegenüber … es war mir wie einem Menschen, der in dunkler Nacht wandert in vermeintlich unbekannter Gegend—auf einmal geschieht ein Blitz—und siehe, wunderbar vergoldet steht sein Vaterhaus und seine Kindesfluren vor den Augen. (*HKG* 1,4:64)

> [Ever since I was a child there had been something in me like a melancholically beautiful poem, obscure and only half-conscious, struggling in dreams of beauty …— —in that moment I had the thing two spans wide right there in front of my eyes … it was like a person wandering in the dark of night in a supposedly unfamiliar area—all of a sudden lightning flashes—and lo, there stands his father's house and the halls of his childhood, wonderfully golden, right before his eyes.]

Angela's beautiful face, removed from the mediating effects of the mirror's smoked glass, effects a more than aesthetic disturbance in Albrecht's consciousness, at once a Freudian return of the repressed and a total break in the perceptual order of things far removed from Albrecht's usual connoisseurship of pretty faces: "Ist es ein Schönheitseindruck, den ich nur verkenne? … Schönheit war es ja nicht, was eben wirkte; … das ganze Bild liegt auf [den Nerven des Gehirns], wie eingebrannt dem Spiegel meiner Augen" (*HKG* 1,4:65; Is it an impression of beauty that I am merely failing to recognize? … But it wasn't beauty that was at work there; … the entire image lies on [the nerves of my brain] as if burned into the mirror of my eyes).[45] Less a misrecognition than a misrecognition of recognition itself, the shock of Angela's uncannily familiar (yet still exotically foreign)[46] countenance disrupts the criteria by which Albrecht had formerly been able to comprehend appearances, causing Albrecht to doubt both his judgment and his senses and for the moment putting a

---

45    In a particularly heavy-handed irony, Stifter has Albrecht write directly after these confessions that "Ich mag nun Aston's [*sic*] versprochene Angela gar nicht einmal sehen und werde auch gar nicht hingehen—mir ekelt vor den sogenannten Schönheiten" (*HKG* 1,4:66; Now I have no desire to see Anton's promised Angela and won't even go [to Aston's party]—such so-called beauties disgust me).

46    It is significant that where Natalie is described by Albrecht as a "Griechenbild" (*HKG* 1,4:57; Greek image), Angela is initially a "Morgenländerin" (*HKG* 1,1:59; Oriental woman) or a "Südländerin" (*HKG* 1,4:64; Mediterranean woman).

veil of *true* obscurity between himself and the world around him. The Latinate pun of the chapter title, "Nachtviole" (Damask Violet), partly gives away the game; what takes place in the sudden vision of Angela's face is a violation, even a rape, a traumatic interruption of vision that wipes away previous categories and sense impressions: "Alle die mir sonst so sehr gefielen … sie sind gar nicht mehr … ihr Erscheinen in dem Kreis meiner Vorstellungen wirkte, wie ein Riß in dieselben" (*HKG* 1,4:65; All those who had once so pleased me … they no longer exist … her appearance within the circle of my mental images tears open a hole in them).

The rest of the novella effectively tells the story of the gradual mending of this epistemological tear, the conversion of the violation effected by Angela's face into the familiar contours of the known and the everyday.[47] In the development and resolution of Albrecht and Angela's courtship—and even more, in the eventual clarification of Angela's backstory—Albrecht's world is slowly restored to its original ideas of beauty, identity, and simplicity, indeed to the point that the classically trained Angela, who knows Greek and Latin and plays piano "so kräftig wie ein Mann" (*HKG* 1,4:112; as powerfully as a man) becomes "ordentlich irdisch[ ]" (properly earthly) through the "liebe Wirthlichkeit, die Schürze, die Schlüssel, das hausmütterliche Auge" (*HKG* 1,4:169; charming hominess, the apron, the bunch of keys, the housewifely eye) of an afternoon in the kitchen. In other words, the end result of Albrecht's trial of misapprehension and doubt is the reestablishment of the world in its familiarity, where the obstacles that intervene between his initial and his final understanding of things are ultimately only there to ensure that understanding's more perfect realization.[48] For it is not just Angela's image that must be restored to its original purity. As Albrecht's musings on artistic judgment and expression already suggest, in the end, the miniature melodrama of Angela's purported betrayal, like the miniature of the Princess vis-à-vis her full-sized portrait, is only a *mise en abyme* for the novella's more important melodrama, the meta-melodrama of the representation

---

47 For an expanded reading of this scene in relation to questions of aesthetic-epistemological framing in *Der Nachsommer*, see Erica Weitzman, *At the Limit of the Obscene: German Realism and the Disgrace of Matter* (Evanston, IL: Northwestern University Press, 2021), esp. 43–44.

48 See also Albrecht's recollection of a traumatic childhood episode in which he mistakenly thought he had killed his brother: "In meiner Jugend geschah es einmal, daß ich mit einem Messer im Spiele meinen Bruder in die Seite stach, und als sogleich ein dunkler Blutbach das Kinderhemdlein netzte, und der rothe Fleck riesig weiter wuchs—damals verzweifelte ich, hielt mich für einen Mörder und wurde ohnmächtig" (*HKG* 1,4:131; In my youth it once happened that while playing I stabbed my brother in the side with a knife, and as a dark stream of blood immediately started to moisten his little shirt, and the red spot grew ever larger—at that moment I grew desperate, took myself for a murderer, and fainted).

of the phenomenal world as such. If, as Linda Williams has suggested, melodrama is primarily defined by the search for a "better justice,"[49] what is at stake in *Feldblumen* is the question of "doing justice" itself: the adequate depiction of a world that is in itself exactly as it should be. The loss of norms in the realm of perception and understanding—the *Zerrwelt* that only the artist sees through, and the *Luftbild* from which only God is spared—requires that these norms be once again set to rights, that the idyll of seeing is returned to its original (even if never yet actually existing) state of purity. In this sense, melodrama holds out, more even than the assurance of righting all wrongs, the promise of an undistorted and unambiguous truth—"of a morally legible universe to those willing to read and interpret properly its signs"[50]—the same hope Albrecht himself voices in his wish for "beautiful picture[s]" untouched by ignorance and partiality. *Feldblumen*'s happy end lies not just in the sentimental triumph of love over jealousy and suspicion, but also in the epistemological triumph of clarity over obscurity and confusion. The "innocence" to be vindicated in Stifter is above all the innocence of appearance itself.

# III: Reality Affects

As many critics have noted, melodrama, for all its exaggerations and improbabilities, bears an essential affinity with realism. Brooks' claim that "melodrama's mode must be centrally, radically hyperbolic, the mode of the bigger-than-life, reaching in grandiose reference to a noumenal realm"[51] also means that what is "melodramatic" in melodrama is a direct result of its naturalism: as mentioned above, melodrama's characteristic setting in the particularity of contemporary middle-class life, as opposed to the realm of the mythical and the absolute, is precisely what requires such a hyperbolic register in order to elevate it to higher meaning in the first place. Speaking in Aristotelian terms, one could say that melodrama sets the characters of comedy in the mode of tragedy: the definitional sublimity of kings and gods is replaced by the *conditional* sublimity

---

49  Linda Williams, "'Tales of Sound and Fury...' or, The Elephant of Melodrama," in *Melodrama Unbound: Across History, Media, and National Cultures*, ed. Christine Gledhill and Linda Williams (New York: Columbia University Press, 2018), 205–17; here 214. For Williams, writing with and against Brooks, the very vulnerability of melodrama's norms is also what makes it uniquely suited to progressive ends, insofar as it can, in contrast to tragedy's moral fixity, "generate outrage against realities that could and, to its creators, should be changed." Williams, "'Tales,'" 215.

50  Brooks, *The Melodramatic Imagination*, 201.

51  Brooks, *The Melodramatic Imagination*, 54.

of the virtuous bourgeois.[52] Melodrama's exaggeratedness, its tendency to grandiloquence and histrionics, is thus paradoxically also a demand for the dignity of realism. For if the ordinary can be made sublime, then the sublime must lie concealed in the ordinary; the idea of "the possibility of acceding to the latent through the signs of the world"[53] presupposes in turn that *this* world is the site of meaningful activity, that the common, the quotidian, and the concrete can possess all the transcendent power of the absolute itself.

For Stifter, in any case, this is the goal. In an early letter to Titus, Albrecht speaks in romantic tones of the dangers posed by marriage, opining that, at least for "Genies und Narren" (*HKG* 1,4:68; geniuses and fools), the beloved should remain only ever an idealized image, preserved from the disillusioning banalities of the everyday. Accordingly, in his initial imagination of his fantasy villa, Albrecht gives himself the role of the lonely bachelor artist, living side by side with three or four (exceptionally) happy married couples "als Kebsmann des Bildes meiner getrennten Zenobia, die ihrerseits wieder anderswo mit meinem Bild in geistiger Ehe lebt" (*HKG* 1,4:71; as the squire of the picture of my distant Zenobia, who for her part lives somewhere else with my picture in spiritual marriage).[54] By the end of the novella, however, this scenario will be reversed: Albrecht marries Angela, as one half of several conjugal pairs, and her portrait is no longer a chastely worshipped image, but merely a "sehr gelungenes Conterfei" (*HKG* 1,4:170; very successful likeness) framed in gold and displayed at the wedding brunch right across the table from the thing itself. What had earlier been dismissed as a danger to the ideal is now embraced as the ideal itself, and Albrecht's letters come to an end on a note of bourgeois comfort and domestic eroticism, as the suddenly fleshly Angela, whose striking beauty once ripped apart Albrecht's entire system of perception, allows herself to be kissed fondly on the cheek.

Stifter thus concludes his novella with an implicit critique of Albrecht's earlier romanticism—but only in the sense that it does not go far enough. For romanticism, Stifter implies, remains content with

---

52   On the emergence of the bourgeois image of bourgeois virtue out of the intersection of the ideas of spiritual (rather than inherited) nobility and the value of self-renunciation, see Lothar Fietz, "Zur Genese des englischen Melodramas aus der Tradition der bürgerlichen Tragödie und des Rührstücks: Lillo—Schröder—Kotzebue—Sheridan—Thompson—Jerrold," *Deutsche Vierteljahrsschrift für Literaturwissenschaft und Geistesgeschichte* 65, no. 1 (1991): 99–116, esp. 107.

53   Brooks, *The Melodramatic Imagination*, 202.

54   Admittedly, Albrecht also immediately checks himself in this fantasy, adding, in a self-ironizing commentary, "Du siehst schon daraus, Titus, daß ich sehr bald überschnappe" (*HKG* 1,4:71; You see already from this, Titus, that I'm on the verge of cracking up).

the mere *fantasy* of the ideal. In *Feldblumen*'s eminently practical happy end, on the other hand, the ideal has become the reality—and not as a compromise of the ideal, but as its even more perfect, because real, manifestation. With Albrecht's marriage to Angela, the trustworthiness of appearances, so recently put into question, is restored, and the utopian wish for accurate perception that Albrecht expresses in his early letter to Titus is fulfilled in the transformation of Albrecht's vague perceptions and uncanny intimations—"doch ist's, als wäre sie vor ungezählten Jahren in einem andern Sterne meine Gattin gewesen" (*HKG* 1,4:65; and yet it is as if she had been my wife under another star, countless years ago)—into well-nigh prophetic statements of fact. Here there is neither *Zerrwelt* nor *Luftbild*, no disconnect between appearance and essence, between perceiving and knowing, indeed between personal wish and realized truth: it is all resolved—revealed to have always already been resolved—in the frictionless denouement of fitting things into their preordained place. But it is also not simply a question of the ideal becoming the real—much less, of the real replacing or abolishing the ideal. The "ideal," such as it is, must be *domesticated* within the real, made correspondent with its own, familiar signifying forms, which are in turn revealed to have been the actual forms of the ideal all along. Indeed, for all *Feldblumen*'s convolutions and complexities, its narrative dependably stages the closing of the circle, the fulfillment of that which was and should be—not in the sense of an unknown yet inescapable fate, but in the sense of something right in front of the characters' noses the whole time.[55] "Aber gefährlich blieb es" (But it was dangerous), comments Albrecht, sitting across the table from Angela after their introduction at Aston's dinner party, "denn selbst jetzt, in dieser Prosa des Anschauens—das Himmelsbild setzte gar eine Tasse mit Rindsuppe an den Mund—verspürte ich doch gleich beim ersten Blicke wieder etwas von jener Zauberei, wie vor drei Wochen im Paradiesgarten" (*HKG* 1,4:82–83; for even now, in this prose of looking— just now the image of heaven lifted a cup of beef broth to her mouth—I nevertheless sensed, from the very first glance, something of that magic from three weeks ago in the Paradiesgarten). Melodrama's "process of investing meaning in the world"[56] manifests itself in *Feldblumen* as the removal of this danger in the discovery of the *actual* enchantment of the everyday—the final reconciliation of the "prose of looking" with the

55   This circularity is only further driven home in the novella by the two exceptions to it: (1) the fact that Lothar ends up with the unveiled woman and Albrecht with the veiled, in chiasmic opposition to their joking promise to one another at the inn, and (2) the fact that the telescope Albrecht gets in the end is not his hoped-for Fraunhofer, but a cheaper Plößl. See *HKG* 1,4:51 and 168. On the potential symbolic significance of the change in telescope brand, see Schößler, "Feldblumen," esp. 21.

56   Brooks, *The Melodramatic Imagination*, 125.

"image of heaven," in which even something as banal as the sipping of soup can become, in the words of the preface to *Bunte Steine*, one of the "Millionen Wurzelfasern des Baumes des Lebens" (*HKG* 2,2:14; millions of fibrils of the tree of life," *MS* 7) that make up the totality of cosmological and human existence. In the drama of the consummate meaningfulness of all signs, the transcendence of the world is the world as it is.

"Melodrama's relation to realism is always oblique .... It tells us that in the right mirror, with the right degree of convexity, our lives matter."[57] The strange naturalism of Stifter's later work is precisely a result of this oblique angle on "our lives," in which the everyday and the sublime are made to converge—in the end Albrecht even discovers that, contrary to Aston's reports, "[Angela] kann also doch auch kochen" (*HKG* 1,4:169; Angela can cook after all)—in the form of the everyday's total and transparent signification. In the convex or "erhabner" (*HKG* 1,4:63) mirror of Stifter's novella, the ordinary world is reflected back to the reader as a miraculous system of meaningful correspondences, as a heroic overcoming of traumatic, unreadable, or untrue signs in the establishment of the actuality of what one had always anyway already suspected to be the case. In this way, *Feldblumen* is not merely a realistic melodrama (or a melodrama shifting into realist mode), but a melodrama *of* realism, a conflict between maligned innocence and misguided skepticism on the level of the phenomenon and the signifier as such. And this, in turn, lays the foundation for Stifter's peculiar form of realism: a realism *without* drama, so to speak, in which what is real within it is no longer in question, in which the obscure and elliptical signifiers of the sensual world are resolved into evidence and unambiguous meaning as an aspect of the higher signification of semiotic transparency as a whole. That this resolution is a failed one in Stifter's work, as many have suggested, does not make it any less essential for it. Indeed, the infamous tedium of Stifter's later writings—the obsessive attention to detail and the ceremoniously self-referential dialogue—is only a continuation of the attempted resolution of the conflict between semblance and meaning already staged in *Feldblumen*'s multiply melodramatic plot. For Stifter, *Feldblumen*'s meta-melodrama of semantic legibility makes realism possible: the ideal morality of a phenomenal world whose appearance signifies nothing but itself.

57 Brooks, *The Melodramatic Imagination*, ix.

# 6: Backward Glances: Registers of the Past in Stifter's *Die Mappe meines Urgroßvaters*

*Jessica C. Resvick*

*DIE MAPPE MEINES Urgroßvaters* (My Great-Grandfather's Notebook; hereafter: *Mappe*) is perhaps the greatest example of Adalbert Stifter's notoriously finicky writing habits. The text first appeared in installments in the *Wiener Zeitschrift für Kunst, Literatur, Theater und Mode* (Viennese Journal for Art, Literature, Theater, and Fashion) in 1841–42 (hereafter *Journalfassung*), and Stifter then reworked it for inclusion in the third volume of his *Studien* collection (Studies) in 1847 (hereafter *Studienfassung*). Stifter was typical for authors of the nineteenth century in republishing his works in book form, but his republications often comprised radically different works replete with new titles and major insertions, deletions, and emendations within the text. Nevertheless, the second publication usually marked the end of his work on his stories. This is not the case with the *Mappe*. Stifter revisited the text again in 1864, hoping to turn it into a standalone, two-volume work. After scrapping the third version, he attempted a fourth version in 1867, which he continued to edit in early 1868 on his deathbed. Despite some substantial changes across all four versions, the basic plot remains the same. The unnamed narrator returns to his childhood home and discovers his great-grandfather's notebook in the attic, whose contents he excerpts and transmits to the nondiagetic reader of Stifter's text. The great-grandfather Augustinus, known simply as the Doctor, had picked up the habit of journaling from his neighbor, the Obrist (Colonel), who consoles and soon befriends him after an aborted suicide attempt. The Doctor records his thoughts and daily events, and then seals the text. After several years have elapsed, he breaks the seals and rereads his entries, and is able better to appreciate his personal growth and the unexpected directions his life has taken. While such a practice would not be out of place in the twenty-first-century self-help landscape, the Doctor's writing habits take on features unique to the nineteenth century, with the text's open-endedness and serially organized episodes emphasizing the *Mappe*'s embeddedness within the periodical publishing context.[1]

The *Mappe* is not the only work by Stifter that is preoccupied with writing and editing practices—one could easily add "Die Narrenburg" (Castle of Fools, 1842/1844), which belongs to the same originally conceived Scharnast family cycle.[2] However, the *Mappe* stands apart from every other text in the author's oeuvre due to the sheer length of time it occupied Stifter. What was it that so nagged at Stifter that he felt the need to revise the *Mappe* over a period of nearly three decades? Why did he instruct the executor of his estate to record on the manuscript pages that "This is where the poet died" (Figure 6.1)?[3] Put simply, the *Mappe* serves in many ways as a monument to Stifter's poetics and aesthetics. Beyond enabling both Stifter and his characters to achieve a kind of placidity (*Sanftmut*), the processes of writing and editing are embedded within a robust conceptual framework that encompasses some of the most important through-lines in the author's oeuvre. The reflective engagement with the past, together with the concession that such efforts will forever remain incomplete and form but partial echoes of something much greater, permeates almost everything Stifter wrote. In the *Mappe*, however, the heightened degree of self-reflexivity allows one to see more

---

1    For further detail on this point, see Nicolas Pethes, *Literarische Fall-Archive: Zur Epistemologie und Ästhetik seriellen Erzählens am Beispiel von Stifters Mappe* (Berlin: Alpheus Verlag, 2015).

2    For a comparison of the writing practices in these two texts, see Christian Begemann, *Die Welt der Zeichen: Stifter-Lektüren* (Stuttgart: J. B. Metzler, 1995), 242–59. The journal versions of "Die Narrenburg" and "Die Mappe meines Urgroßvaters" focus on different members of the Scharnast family, as does the story "Prokopus." However, Stifter's revisions to the second versions of the "Narrenburg" and "Mappe" obscure this genealogical connection, and he never revised "Prokopus" for republication in book form. For further details, see Ulrich Dittmann, *Studien: Kommentar* (*HKG* 1,9:206–7).

3    This annotation recalls the writing practices in "Die Narrenburg," where members of the Scharnast family must record their life stories and read those of all their ancestors. The protagonist reads one such text, which concludes only with the author's death. "Bei diesen Worten brach das Manuscript ab, und keine Zeile stand weiter auf dem Pergamente. Nur unten am Rande des letzten Blattes stand von fremder Hand: '† (gestorben) einundzwanzig Tage nach dem Worte: Sohne'" (*HKG* 1,4:426; With these words the manuscript broke off, and no other lines stood on the parchment. Only in the margin of the last page were the words, in different handwriting: "† (deceased) twenty-one days after the word: son"). For more on the biographical resonances with the writing process depicted in the *Mappe*, see Jessica Resvick, "The Author as Editor: The Aesthetics of Recension in Adalbert Stifter's *Die Mappe Meines Urgroßvaters*," in *Market Strategies and German Literature in the Long Nineteenth Century*, ed. Vance Byrd and Ervin Malakaj (Berlin and Boston, MA: De Gruyter, 2020), 147–70; here 160–65.

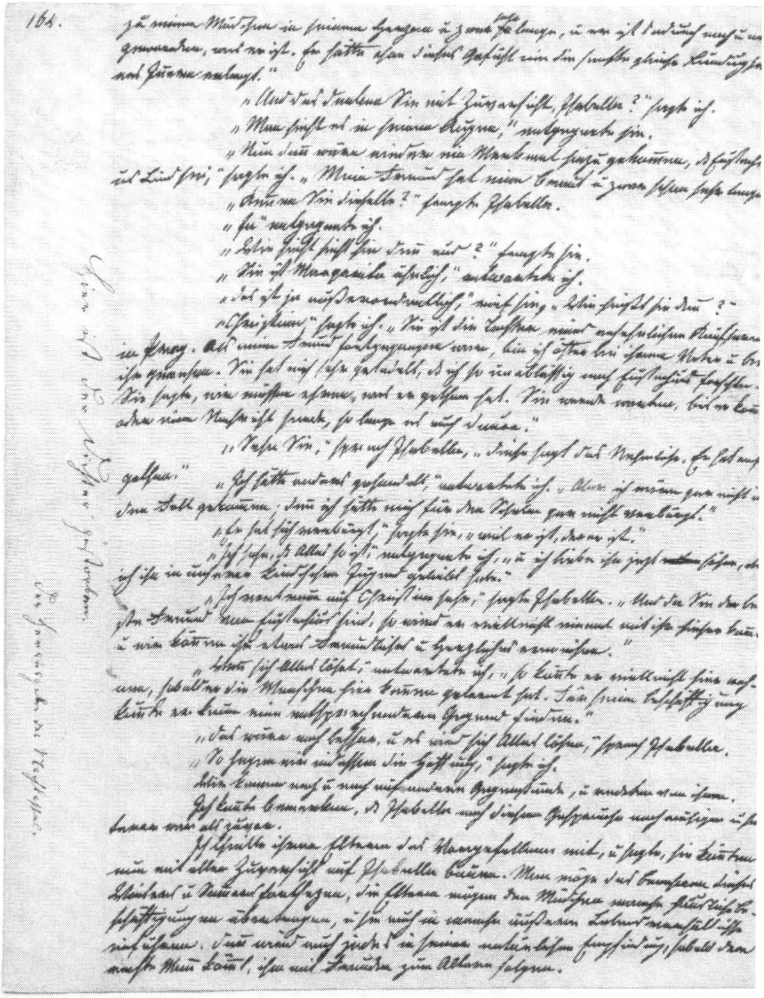

Figure 6.1. The final manuscript page of the fourth version of *Die Mappe meines Urgroßvaters*. The marginal inscription reads: "Hier ist der Dichter gestorben. / Der Herausgeber des Verfassers" (This is where the poet died. / The author's editor). The National Library of the Czech Republic. Sign. 213, Folder "F4 letzte Fassung."

clearly the subtle dispersions of force inherent to this process, with its shift from a more overt aesthetics of display to one that operates more diffusely. The key scene for understanding this shift occurs in the Obrist's narrative, specifically in the transition from the *Journalfassung* to the *Studienfassung*.[4] Here, an isolated, eruptive event is dispersed throughout the text, such that it becomes integrated and more fully enmeshed within the multiple narratives that comprise the roughly two-hundred-page tale, which, given its length and thematic complexity, might better be classified as a novel. Transferred across generations, indeed across narratives, this event allows for something imperceptible to become perceptible in its repetition. The narratives compiled under the title *Die Mappe meines Urgroßvaters*, then, collectively articulate the principles at the heart of Stifter's creative endeavors.

Writing to his publisher, Gustav Heckenast, on Christmas Day, 1844, Stifter reports on his progress on the *Studienfassung*:

> Die Erzählung des Obrists muß *graniten* sein, ich glaube, daß diese Episode das erste von mir ist, was man etwa *klassisch* nennen konnte. In anspruchloser Einfachheit und in massenhaft gedrängtem Erzählen, muß ein ganzes Leben. ... Ich habe aber gerade an der Erzählung des Obrists gefeilt, wie sonst gar nie, und aus einem Bogen Material ist ein Blatt Text geworden, damit mir die Figur so eisenfest bleibe, wie ich ihre Form beabsichtigte.[5]

> [The story of the Obrist must be *rock solid*. I believe that this episode is the first of mine that one could deem *classical*. An entire life must be contained in unpretentious simplicity and in massively condensed narration. ... I have just filed away at the story of the Obrist like I never have before, and from one sheet of material I now have one page of text, such that the figure remains as firm as I envision its form.

Stifter refers here to chapter three of the *Studienfassung* (chapter two in the *Journalfassung*), where the Obrist relates his life story to the Doctor, revealing the eruptive event alluded to above. After his brother cheats him out of his inheritance, the Obrist joins the military and takes up gambling. Eventually he begins to cultivate the habit of journaling, which he credits for helping him to develop emotional fortitude and establish

---

4    While the scene in question is present in all four versions of the *Mappe*, the greatest changes occur in the revisions from the *Journalfassung* to the *Studienfassung*. For this reason, I focus primarily on the latter version.

5    Adalbert Stifter, *Briefwechsel*, ed. Gustav Wilhelm, 2nd ed., vol. 17 of *Sämmtliche Werke* (Reichenberg: Sudetendeutscher Verlag Franz Kraus, 1929), 132–33. Emphasis in original. All translations my own, unless otherwise noted.

a gentler life. The Obrist then recounts the most devastating moment in his life. He and his wife, lost on a September hike, took a shortcut across a narrow log flume used to transport lumber out of the mountains. Nearing the end of the bridge, the Obrist turned around, but his wife, whose name the reader never learns, was nowhere to be seen. He realized in a terrifying instant that she had fallen to her death. The horror of the event derives in part from its initial imperceptibility: the wife fell gently [*sanft*], in complete silence, not wanting to endanger her husband. This ghastly event, which is rendered momentarily inaudible and whose magnitude becomes apparent only in retrospect, captures the inversion of great and small, disruption and gentleness, that Stifter would formally elaborate in the preface to his *Bunte Steine* collection (Motley Stones, 1853) just a few years later. Even more, the descriptors of the Obrist's character—*graniten* and *eisenfest*—wed the theme of gentleness to the geological themes that would underpin that latter collection.[6]

Another link between this episode in the *Mappe* and the major themes of the *Bunte Steine* collection emerges when one considers the date of Stifter's letter: December 25. While there hardly seems a Christmas miracle at stake in or with the *Mappe*, the author's famous Christmas story, *Bergkristall* (Rock Crystal), would appear the following year in *Die Gegenwart* (The Present Time) under the title "Der heilige Abend" (Christmas Eve), before its later inclusion in *Bunte Steine*. This story tracks the peril that two children face after similarly losing their way, albeit here in a fierce snowstorm amidst a more alpine, and indeed, glacial setting. If *Bergkristall* results in the children's ultimate salvation and the subsequent reconciliation of two feuding villages, the *Mappe* would seem, by contrast, to paint a bleaker picture of humankind's powerlessness vis-à-vis nature.

---

6    Stifter's descriptors call to mind Goethe's 1784 *Granit I*. There, Goethe explains that granite is a composite of other types of stone: "der erste Anblick [zeigt] daß diese Teile durch kein drittes Mittel verbunden sind, sondern nur an- und nebeneinander bestehn und sich selbst untereinander *festhalten*" (a first glance shows that these parts are not conjoined via a third medium, but rather that they exist upon and alongside one another and that they themselves hold each other *in place*). These descriptors reverberate throughout Stifter's mereological descriptors in the preface to *Bunte Steine*, which I discuss below. Additionally, the famous concluding line to *Granit I* underscores idea of solidity while recalling the principle of agglomeration: "Ich stehe auf dem Granit *fest*, und frage ihn ob er uns einigen Anlaß geben wolle zu denken wie die Masse woraus er entstanden beschaffen gewesen." (I stand *firmly* upon the granite and ask it whether it will give us cause to ponder how the mass from which it emerged was constituted). This, too, resonates with Stifter's descriptions of the Obrist's tale. See Johann Wolfgang von Goethe, "Granit I," in *Sämtliche Werke: Briefe, Tagebücher und Gespräche*, ed. Manfred Wenzel, vol. 1.25 (Frankfurt am Main: Deutscher Klassiker Verlag, 1989), 312. Emphasis added.

BACKWARD GLANCES ♦ 167

Yet Stifter's Christmastime reflections on the Obrist situate the *Mappe* within a broader conceptual and stylistic landscape. *Bergkristall* is notorious among Stifter's works for its glacial pace, with the young girl Sanna exclaiming "Ja, Konrad" (Yes, Konrad) on seventeen separate occasions. One might expect this language to have a soporific effect, but as Peter Küpper notes, the banal utterance in fact keeps the children awake during a perilous night, the plodding language thereby forming the ground of salvation.[7] The *Mappe* treats language in a similar fashion, albeit displacing its ameliorative work from text-internal speech acts to a self-reflexive register. The *Mappe* is, at its core, a text about salvation via writing, the latter of which becomes an act that is both a means of self-preservation and an artistic imperative.

One of many obvious differences between the two texts lies in the fact that the Obrist must mourn his dead wife, while the children survive their ordeal. At this elementary level of plot, the *Mappe* places far greater emphasis on retrospectivity, on the role of writing in working through the past, as opposed to the role of language in surviving the present. The depiction of the fall itself already foregrounds the significance of retrospectivity, of backward glances both literal and figurative, and this thematic focus aligns the story with the theoretical program elaborated in the preface to *Bunte Steine*. Although the first two versions of the *Mappe* would appear well before the *Bunte Steine* collection, the latter is not generally regarded as instituting a new direction in Stifter's work. The preface, rather, expresses undercurrents that are already present in his earlier pieces and Friedrich Hebbel's infamous critique of his naively mimetic style had simply prompted him to articulate his aesthetics more programmatically.[8] In this respect, the preface can be seen as a more forceful articulation of the retrospective impetus of the *Mappe*.

In the preface to *Bunte Steine*, Stifter defends his focus on ostensibly insignificant details, arguing that "small" events and phenomena—wafting air, trickling water, growing vegetation—better reveal underlying laws than do purportedly "great" events and phenomena—erupting volcanoes, storms, and the like. In order to demonstrate how attention to seemingly minor details can in fact reveal something more significant, Stifter draws on an example from geomagnetic research. Obliquely referencing research by Alexander von Humboldt and Carl Friedrich Gauss, Stifter describes the work of the natural scientist, who measures the

---

7    See Peter Küpper, "Literatur und Langeweile: Zur Lektüre Stifters," in *Adalbert Stifter: Studien und Interpretation, Gedenkschrift zum 100. Todestage*, ed. Lothar Stiehm (Heidelberg: Lothar Stiehm Verlag, 1968), 171–88; here 181.

8    For further details about Hebbel's critique and Stifter's response, see Dittmann, *Studien: Kommentar* (*HKG* 1,9:69–71).

168 ♦ Jessica C. Resvick

earth's magnetic field at various discrete points.[9] When compiled, these data points reveal the presence of a powerful magnetic storm. While the individual measurements might seem insignificant, they take on a breathtaking magnitude when viewed collectively: "aus den daraus zusammengestellten Tafeln [wird] ersichtlich ..., daß manche kleine Veränderungen an der Magnetnadel oft auf allen Punkten der Erde *gleichzeitig* und *in gleichem Maße* vor sich gehen, daß also ein magnetisches Gewitter über die ganze Erde geht, daß die ganze Erdoberfläche *gleichzeitig gleichsam* ein magnetisches Schauern empfindet" (*HKG* 2,2:11; the charts compiled from them show that certain small shifts in the magnetic needle often occur *simultaneously* and *to the same degree* in all parts of the world; that, then, a magnetic storm is passing over all the earth, that all the earth's surface *at once* is sensing *a sort of* magnetic shiver, *MS*, 4; emphases added). The repetitive use of *gleich* emphasizes and triangulates temporality (two uses of "gleichzeitig"), magnitude ("in gleichem Maße"), and approximation ("gleichsam"), while simultaneously preparing the analogy [*Gleichnis*] Stifter will soon make when he declares that the same underlying lawfulness pervades the moral as the scientific realm: "So wie es in der äußeren Natur ist, so ist es auch in der inneren, in der des menschlichen Geschlechtes" (*HKG* 2,2:12; As is outward Nature, so too is inward nature, the nature of the human race, *MS*, 4). In describing the gentle law in the realm of morality, Stifter establishes an implicit parallel between individual humans and the individual data points in the magnetic experiment. Upon witnessing a violation of ethical human relations and then working to restore them, individuals experience themselves as belonging to the whole of humanity: "wir fühlen uns noch viel höher und inniger als wir uns als Einzelne fühlen, wir fühlen uns als ganze Menschheit" (*HKG* 2,2:12; we feel far more exalted and inwardly moved than we feel as individuals, we feel ourselves as the whole of humanity, *MS*, 5). The various internal contradictions of the analogy notwithstanding, Stifter proposes an *approximate* similarity between the two realms (*gleichsam*), both of which display the same inversion of measure [*Maß*] between great and small and the same emphasis on collectivity.[10]

9    For additional historical background, see Leigh Ann Smith-Gary, "Extreme Measures: Domesticating the Sublime in German Realist Literature" (PhD diss., University of Chicago, 2012), 33–36.

10    Scholarship has addressed the numerous contradictions within the *Vorrede* at length. See for example, Alfred Doppler, "Schrecklich schöne Welt? Stifters fragwürdige Analogie von Natur- und Sittengesetz," in *Adalbert Stifters schrecklich schöne Welt: Beiträge des internationalen Kolloquiums zur A.-Stifter-Ausstellung*, ed. Roland Duhamel, Johann Lachinger, Clemens Ruthner, and Petra Göllner (Linz: Adalbert-Stifter-Institut, 1994), 9–16; Eric Downing, *Double Exposures: Repetition and Realism in Nineteenth-Century German Fiction* (Stanford, CA: Stanford University Press, 2000), 24–40; Paul Fleming, *Exemplarity and*

This *Gleichmäßigkeit,* or regularity, similarly applies to the magnetic field. In other words, changes in magnitude at a single observational point are not errant blips, but rather are widespread and indicative of the storm's presence. However, basic practicalities of measurement destabilize the analogy. For one, an unimaginable number of scientists would have to record data simultaneously to measure [*messen*] the magnitude [*Maß*] of the field at a given moment. Moreover, these scientists would have to record the changes in field strength at each point over time to ascertain whether fluctuations do indeed occur. Further, even though *gleich* as a temporal descriptor emphasizes the simultaneity of observed phenomena, the actual interpretation of the geomagnetic data occurs belatedly. It is only after the scientist compares a new measurement with an older one that she can determine whether any changes have occurred. And it is only after the fact, once all the data have been compiled into neat tables and then interpreted, that the magnetic storm in fact becomes visible. Such a time lag ensures that there is nothing *gleichzeitig* about this observational process at all.

The geomagnetic example seems, then, to break down before Stifter even concludes it. The collected data can only ever approximate the storm. No matter how many data points are collected, no matter how many locations across the globe are measured, only one will ever gain a partial view of the storm. Indeed, the otherwise imperceptible phenomenon that comes into view will, by the time the scientists compile and analyze their data, perhaps have already vanished. The scientist is forever gazing into the past but will never be able to capture the full picture. The only consolation must come from the pieces of the past that one can salvage in the present.

This basic structure of belatedness assumes a melancholic tone in the *Mappe,* linked as it is with the Obrist's mourning of his wife. Moreover, latent mythological resonances, while not generally of programmatic significance for Stifter, help to further conceptualize the links in the story between writing and retrospectivity.[11] The motif of the back-

---

*Mediocrity: The Art of the Average from Bourgeois Tragedy to Realism* (Stanford, CA: Stanford University Press, 2009), 149–54; Sean Ireton, "Adalbert Stifter and the Gentle Anthropocene," in *Readings in the Anthropocene: The Environmental Humanities, German Studies, and Beyond,* ed. Sabine Wilke and Japhet Johnstone (New York: Bloomsbury, 2017), 195–221; here 199–204; Hartmut Laufhütte, "Das sanfte Gesetz und der Abgrund: Zu den Grundlagen der Stifterschen Dichtung 'aus dem Geiste der Naturwissenschaft,'" in *Stifter-Studien: Ein Festgeschenk für Wolfgang Frühwald zum 65. Geburtstag,* ed. Walter Hettche, Johannes John, and Sibylle von Steinsdorff (Tübingen: Max Niemeyer, 2000), 61–74.

11　While Stifter occasionally refers in passing to classical texts, e.g., in *Der Nachsommer* (Indian Summer, 1857), he does not typically deploy such allusions to programmatic ends, like, for instance, his contemporaries Gottfried Keller, who

ward glance—both literal and figurative—has an obvious counterpart in the story of Orpheus and Eurydice. After Eurydice dies from a snake bite, after a misstep of sorts, Orpheus fetches her from the underworld. Provided he faces forward on his journey out of the underworld and does not look back, his wife will be returned to him. Ultimately, he is unable to resist this backward glance, and Eurydice plummets back into the depths, futilely grasping toward Orpheus and offering a faint goodbye.[12] In the *Mappe*, the account of the fall itself is sparse, given that the Obrist did not witness it. The logger later explains that he had not realized anything was amiss, "bis sie … mit der Hand in der Luft zu greifen anfing" (*HKG* 1,5:58; until she began to grasp at the air with her hand). Maintaining her silence, the wife eschews even the final goodbye that Eurydice manages to utter, disappearing wordlessly into the abyss. Despite the obvious points of divergence, both texts are testaments to the power of poetry specifically and language more generally. Eurydice's near return is brought about by Orpheus' skill as a bard, and the wife's fall, which the Obrist relays to the Doctor, fills the latter with awe at their love and the capacity of writing to engender healing. If Orpheus' journey ends in despair (and in Ovid's version, pederasty), Stifter's Obrist is altogether more successful in working through his emotional devastation.[13] While Orpheus loses his wife a second time, the Obrist gazes back into the past, repeating, in a way, the original gesture as he strives to keep his wife alive in his memory, even as she all but disappears from the narrative.

The fall episode is short, relative to the rest of the story, but it reverberates throughout the text at several key junctures.[14] As Stifter testifies in his letter to Heckenast, he condenses the *mass* of the episode ("massenhaft gedrängt[]"), and what in the *Journalfassung* was a detailed, emotionally laden text becomes in the *Studienfassung* more impersonal and

---

exploits the myth of Pygmalion and Galatea in his *Sinngedicht* cycle (The Epigram, 1881); or Theodor Fontane, who engages with the same myth when outlining his views on realism in "Unsere lyrische und epische Poesie seit 1848" (Our Lyric and Epic Poetry Since 1848, 1853).

12 "She only uttered her last 'farewell,' so faintly he hardly could hear it, and then she was swept once more to the land of the shadows." Ovid, *Metamorphoses*, trans. David Raeburn (London: Penguin, 2004), 385.

13 Sebald draws attention to the pedophilic undercurrents in Stifter's works, including in the *Mappe*. The Obrist, he notes, falls in love with his wife when she is still a child. See W. G. Sebald, "Bis an den Rand der Natur: Versuch über Stifter," in *Die Beschreibung des Unglücks: zur österreichischen Literatur von Stifter bis Handke*, 3rd ed. (Frankfurt am Main: Fischer Taschenbuch Verlag, 2003), 15–37; here 35.

14 Pethes draws attention to the recurrent use of the term *fallen* in the *Mappe*, which he sees as linking the wife's fall, coincidence [*Zufall*], and the case study [*Fallgeschichte*]. Pethes, *Literarische Fall-Archive*, 31.

detached. The Obrist and his wife lose their way on a hike, and upon turning a corner, an abyss opens before them. A logger soon appears and helps them across the flume. The Obrist walks in front, his wife walks in the middle, and the logger brings up the rear. The two men also hold a walking stick parallel with the ground, so that the wife can hold to something for support. Given the scope of Stifter's revisions, the passage is worth quoting at length:

*Journalfassung* (version 1)

Und so traten wir nun die gefährliche Brücke an, die so bedeutungsvoll, so ahnungsschwer vor uns lag, *wie eine zarte Linie* .... Die Luft des Abends war *todtenstill*, daß in ihr unsere leisen *tactgemäßen* Schritte hörbar wurden—furchtbar war es mir, daß ich nur <u>seine</u> Tritte mit den schwer beschlagenen Schuhen hörte, nicht <u>ihre</u>, und wie ich mir meine Gattinn, das geliebte, schutzlose, hierher gelockte Wesen, hinter mir gehend dachte, so war mir, *wenn ich nur ein einzigesmal umschauen könnte, so wäre Alles gut*; aber ich wagte es nicht, um den Stock nicht zu rücken, und *den Tact* des Fortschreitens nicht zu stören.—Plötzlich, kaum drey Schritte vor dem Ende der Riese, hörte ich unsern Begleiter rufen: "Sitzt nieder"—*im Momente sah ich um*—aber ich sah nur meinen Begleiter, meine Gattinn nicht—… wie Höllenblendwerk kam es mir vor, daß ich nur ihn, nur ihn, nur ihn sah, und daß Alles so *todtenstill* sey—(*HKG* 1,2:31–32; italicized emphasis added, underlined emphasis in original via *Sperrung*)

[And thus we stepped onto the bridge, which laid so portentously before us, like a tender line. … The evening air was *dead silent*, such that our quiet, *rhythmic* steps could be heard—it was terrible for me, since I could only hear <u>his</u> steps in his heavily studded shoes, not <u>hers</u>. And as I thought about my wife, the beloved, defenseless creature I had lured here, walking behind me, I felt that *if I could only look back once, then all would be well*. But I did not dare, lest I disturb the staff or interrupt our *rhythmic* progression.—Suddenly, hardly three steps from the end of the flume, I heard our companion cry: "Sit down"—*in that moment I looked back*—but I only saw my companion, not my wife—… it seemed to me a hellish illusion that I could see only him, only him, only him, and that everything was so *dead silent*—]

*Studienfassung* (version 2)

So gingen wir auf die Brücke, die in der Abenddämmerung *wie eine gezogene Linie war*. Ich hörte, da wir auf dem Holze gingen, nur seine Tritte mit den schwerbeschlagenen Schuhen, die ihrigen aber nicht. Als wir noch ein Kleines von dem Ende der Riese waren, sagte der Holzknecht leise: "Sitzt nieder,"—auch empfand ich, daß der Stock in meiner Hand leichter werde,—*ich schaute plötzlich um*— und denkt Euch: ich sah nur ihn allein. (*HKG* 1,5:57–58; emphasis added)

[Thus we stepped onto the bridge, which, in the evening twilight, was like *a drawn line*. As we walked on the wood, I heard only his steps in his heavily studded shoes, but not hers. When we were only a short distance from the end of the flume, the logger said, quietly: "Sit down,"—and I felt the staff become lighter in my hand,—*I suddenly looked back*—and imagine: I saw only him alone.]

The pathos of the *Journalfassung* is absent from the *Studienfassung*. Gone is the anticipatory language at the outset ("Die Luft des Abends war todtenstill"), which is recapitulated at the end of the trek ("daß Alles so todtenstill sey"). Gone, too, are the anticipatory descriptors once attached to the bridge ("so bedeutungsvoll, so ahnungsschwer"). The tender line of the bridge ("wie eine zarte Linie") is reduced in the *Studienfassung* with—and perhaps to—a mere stroke of the pen ("wie eine gezogene Linie"). It is as though in the progression from the first to the second version of the text, the Obrist *qua* narrator has regained control of the story, imbuing it with a kind of stability otherwise absent from the original event. The dizzying terror the wife must have felt is all but erased, the measured steps replaced by the Obrist's measured narrative tone.

The *Journalfassung* also places greater emphasis on the Obrist's sensory experience. In that version, the regular, "tactgemäß[e]" steps of the logger keep a quasi-musical time, the steady rhythm offering a sense of stability amid the precarious crossing. As desperate as the Obrist is to look back to check on his wife, since her own steps are drowned out by those of the logger, he is too afraid to interrupt their steady, rhythmic progression. If Orpheus, by contrast, succumbs to this temptation, his backward glance causing his wife to plunge back into the underworld, the Obrist's glance comes after the fact. The logger's measured command alerts him to a disruption, and only then does he look back. Indeed, this belatedness becomes his salvation.

One of the more bizarre features of the episode is the fact that the Obrist's wife falls in part because she insists on carrying her pet dog across the bridge. In a breathtaking act of self-sacrifice, she clings to the dog and remains utterly silent, so as not to endanger her husband, who might turn around and lose his balance. The dog survives the fall, without so much as a scratch. But by the time the Obrist and the workers can safely descend to the wife, the dog has become crazed and one of the workers calmly shoots it. Even if this detail serves to extend the moment of violence, with two brutal deaths in rapid narrative succession, it remains difficult to integrate with the remainder of the episode, if only because the dog is hitherto mentioned only a few times in passing. In an episode that, in W. G. Sebald's words, already sets itself off against the rest of the narrative "wie eine Traumsequenz von der Wirklichkeit" (like a dream sequence from reality), the detail of the dog remains deeply moving while also appearing somehow extraneous.[15] While not structurally superfluous in the same way as, for example, the barometer in Flaubert's "Un cœur simple" (A Simple Heart, 1877), it nevertheless makes "real" the force at the core of the gentle law.[16] Against the backdrop of an enormous trauma, a disruptive event on par with the devastating acts of nature described in the preface to *Bunte Steine*, the wife's efforts to save both husband and dog emerge as those very acts of love and communality that ordinarily seem "small," but which function as the forces that sustain humankind. Further emphasizing the great, immeasurable quality of such forces are the descriptions of the Obrist's love for his wife: "—O Herr! das könnt ihr nicht *ermessen*—" (*HKG* 1,5:60; —O Lord! This you cannot measure—).

The Obrist then describes the funerary preparations, noting that he was taken aback by the rapidity and accuracy with which his wife's coffin was constructed: "Gegen Abend kam der Sarg, der sonderbarer Weise *in dem rechten Maße* schon fertig gewesen war, und man legte sie hinein, wo sie lang und schmal ruhen blieb" (*HKG* 1,5:61; Toward evening the coffin arrived, which, strangely, was already finished *at the correct size*. She was laid inside, in a long and narrow repose). The emphasis on appropriate measure stands in sharp contrast to the immeasurable quality of the preceding events. Striking in this passage is the Obrist's shift in focus from the container to his wife: "wo *sie* lang und schmal ruhen blieb." The wife, in other words, assumes the features of the container, as the descriptors migrate from object to person in a kind of *Gleichnis*. It is difficult not to read the long and narrow wooden coffin as anything other than an approximation—to scale—of the log flume, with the wife retroactively placed back inside.

If repetition is central to the *articulation* of the gentle law—the magnetic storm echoes the "great" storms Stifter disavows at the outset of the preface, and the presence of the gentle law in the human realm echoes that in the scientific—so, too, is it central to the *depiction* of the law in the *Mappe*. The Obrist can obviously only write about his grief after the fact, but this basic fact of temporality has important theoretical implications for Stifter. As the preface to *Bunte Steine* makes clear, truly great

15  Sebald, "Bis an den Rand der Natur," 35.

16  See Roland Barthes, *The Rustle of Language*, trans. Richard Howard (Berkeley: University of California Press, 1989), 148.

events are only grasped in retrospect. At stake in this belatedness is a kind of repetition fundamental to realism, namely reality and its representation, to say nothing of the resistance to this very repetition.[17] The Obrist in fact gives his journal entries to the Doctor, who in turn recapitulates the events in his own journal, which his great-grandson then transmits to Stifter's reader. Beyond this writerly and editorial transmission and repetition, the events re-present themselves more subtly in these two (chronologically) subsequent narratives.

The Obrist soon wraps up his tale, and the bulk of the *Mappe* focuses on various moments in the Doctor's life as the local rural physician. Yet the fall echoes throughout the Doctor's narrative, even in the better-known *Eisgeschichte* of chapter four. This episode details the brutal force of an ice storm and the Doctor's harrowing efforts to reach his patients safely. The storm is one of the finest examples of Stifter's treatment of harsh natural phenomena. It builds slowly, and while the ice itself is hazardous, more threatening is the imperceptible danger below the surface. Walking is hazardous, since one does not know what lurks underneath the surface, and the inhabitants fear that melting ice and snow will later break through and flood the community.[18] Although the ice storm is absent from the *Journalfassung*, numerous descriptors from the *Journalfassung* version of the fall episode are in fact transferred onto the ice storm of the *Studienfassung*, thus establishing semantic links between the two scenes. In other words, key features of the fall are *displaced*, such that the full impact of the scene is only felt in and through repetition.

Both episodes foreground the danger of the natural environment and the potential for disorientation in a white landscape, motifs that extend into various other texts, like *Bergkristall* and "Aus dem bairischen Walde" (From the Bavarian Forest, 1868), to name just two. In Sabine Frost's assessment, the metaphors of glaciation in the depiction of the ice storm reflect the *Mappe*'s overarching preoccupation with states of freezing and flowing, preservation and transience, written text and oral speech.[19] As she argues, the acoustic phenomena during the storm generate an effect of vitality, such that flowing and freezing combine in a "meteorologische Ausnahmeerscheinung, die das Flüssige und Erstarrte miteinander

17 See on this point Downing, *Double Exposures*, 3.

18 Smith-Gary sees the ice storm as representative of what she terms Stifter's *sotto voce* sublime: "the overwhelming dimensions and furious speed of sublime storm are overwhelmingly delayed, diffused, or decelerated. The *sotto voce* reverberations of revelatory shock are rendered nearly inaudible in the measured cadences of his quintessentially prosaic style." See Smith-Gary, "Extreme Measures," 17.

19 Frost's study examines literary "whiteout" phenomena at length. For more on this motif in the *Mappe*, see Sabine Frost, *Whiteout: Schneefälle und Weißeinbrüche in der Literatur ab 1800* (Bielefeld: transcript, 2011), 117–59.

verbindet" (a meteorological anomaly that links flowing and freezing entities with one another).[20] Borrowing Frost's terminology, one can conceive of the flow of descriptors across narratives and versions as linking the episodes otherwise frozen in their respective chapters.

Many of the key links between the episodes are acoustic in nature, relating, in Walter Benjamin's terms, to the "taub[e] Raum" (deaf space) of Stifter's prose.[21] In the fall episode, the Obrist is deprived of the crucial visual and auditory clues of his wife's presence: he hears only the heavy steps of the logger and sees only what lies before him. In the *Eisgeschichte*, the Doctor, too, confronts a similarly quiet and visually obscured landscape. The Doctor takes a servant with him on his rounds, so that he has some assistance in navigating the difficult journey by sleigh through the snow: "[D]as Zerbrechen des zarten Eises, wenn das Thier darauf trat, machte ein immerwährendes Geräusch, daher aber das Schweigen, als wir halten mußten, ... desto auffallender war. Und der Regen, dessen Rieseln durch die Nadeln man hören konnte, störte die Stille kaum, ja er vermehrte sie" (*HKG* 1,5:100–1; The breaking of the delicate ice, whenever the animal stepped upon it, made a perpetual noise, thus the silence we kept, whenever we stopped, was even more apparent. And the rain rustling through the needles didn't disturb the silence, indeed, it increased it). The sonic backdrop—the horse's heavy steps breaking the tender ice, the slight rustle of the rain, and later, the delicate clinking ("das zarte Klingen," *HKG* 1,5:101) of falling ice in the forest behind them—in fact *intensifies* the men's silence.

As the men travel between the isolated homes of their patients, they repeatedly notice a muffled crashing sound that they are unable to identify. Upon reaching the forest, they suddenly recognize the source of the sound:

> Ein helles Krachen, *gleichsam wie ein Schrei*, ging vorher, dann folgte ein kurzes Wehen, Sausen, oder Streifen, und dann *der dumpfe, dröhnende Fall*, mit dem ein mächtiger Stamm auf der Erde lag. ... Man sah nur schnell *das Herniederblitzen*, hörte etwa das Aufschlagen, hatte nicht das Emporschnellen des verlassenen und erleichtertes Zweiges gesehen, und das Starren, wie früher, dauerte fort. (*HKG* 1,5:107; emphasis added)

> [After a clear crashing sound, *like a scream*, followed a short gusting, swishing, or streaking, and then *the muffled, booming fall*, after which a mighty trunk lay upon the earth. One saw only briefly *the downward*

---

20  Frost, *Whiteout*, 132.

21  Walter Benjamin, "Stifter," in *Aufsätze, Essays, Vorträge*, ed. Rolf Tiedemann and Hermann Schweppenhäuser, vol. 2.2: *Gesammelte Schriften* (Frankfurt am Main: Suhrkamp, 1991), 607–10; here 609.

*flash*, heard the thud, didn't see the lonesome and disencumbered branch shoot back up, and the fixedness, as earlier, persisted.]

Stifter evokes here something akin to the flip side of the previous fall scene. Here, the ice-laden trees fall, making a sound like the scream ("gleichsam wie ein Schrei") that the Obrist's wife suppresses. Next comes the swish of the falling stems, followed by a massive thud. Notably, all of these features are absent from the description of the wife's fall, which transpires in utter silence. The only commonality is the "Herniederblitzen" of the trees, which approximates the logger's description of the plummeting blur of white: "Wie ein weißes Tuch, sagte er, war es an seinen Augen vorüber gegangen" (*HKG* 1,5:58; He said it was like a white cloth that passed by his eyes). Only "das Starren," something like the *rigor mortis* of the landscape, persists.[22] The landscape thus takes on the features of the Obrist's wife in a kind of descriptive analogy, or *Gleichnis*. In other words, what was silenced and hidden in the fall episode reemerges, evincing, to speak with Heidegger, "das Hörenlassen des Ungesprochenen im Gesprochenen" (allowing for one to hear the unspoken in the spoken).[23]

The silence of the ice storm enables a retrospective staging of the original scene, allowing for the emergence of something otherwise inarticulable. Something truly great, lurking beneath or beyond language, finds expression in and through nature. The inexpressible violence of the wife's death, her repressed scream, the Obrist's unfathomable grief—all of this is silenced in the fall episode and its immediate aftermath, only to return in the Doctor's descriptions of violence in the natural world. If Stifter's prose oscillates, according to Eva Geulen, between "Schweigen-Wollen und Reden-Müssen" (wanting to be silent but needing to speak), a side effect of his efforts to achieve a direct equivalence between signifier and signified, the fall episode and its subsequent re-figuration illustrate the paradoxicality of the "great" and the "small."[24] The truly great cannot be expressed directly—the collected data points come too late and are too scattered, Stifter's own collected stories are dalliances ("Spielereien") of the same nature—and yet it nevertheless evokes a shudder (see *HKG* 2,2:19). The truly great is *felt*, rather than directly *articulated*, straining at the limits of both silence and language. To return to an earlier example: the dog in the fall episode now becomes readable as evoking a

22 Here I am indebted to Smith-Gary's reading of the *Eisgeschichte*. She describes "an increasing natural *rigor mortis* brought about by an atmospheric stillness." See Smith-Gary, "Extreme Measures," 46.

23 Martin Heidegger, "Adalbert Stifters 'Eisgeschichte,'" in *Aus der Erfahrung des Denkens (1910–1976)*, *Gesamtausgabe*, vol. 13 (Frankfurt am Main: Vittorio Klostermann, 1983), 185–98; here 197.

24 Eva Geulen, *Worthörig wider Willen: Darstellungsproblematik und Sprachreflexion in der Prosa Adalbert Stifters* (Munich: iudicium, 1992), 33, 34.

peculiarly Stifterian reality effect. It is not structurally superfluous, but, like Flaubert's barometer, it makes *felt* something inexpressible, in this case the bonds of love that sustain humankind.

The migration of descriptors—across narratives and realms—further extends into the *Mappe*'s tender portrayals of writing practices. The Doctor begins journaling upon the encouragement of the Obrist, who relates his own past—emphasizing the fall—after sensing the Doctor's despair. Commentators frequently note that the Doctor's notebook, which the narrator discovers in his mother's attic, is sealed with blue and red ribbons, and that Margarita—the Obrist's daughter and the Doctor's eventual wife—favors white dresses with ribbons of these very colors. Yet even before the transfer of these colors from body to book, there is first a transfer from landscape to body. In the fall episode, it is the natural world that carries these tones. On the hike, the wife collects edelweiss, which the Obrist keeps and eventually gives to the Doctor and Margarita. The edelweiss serves as a material connection between past and present, between one generation and the next. And when the couple comes to the log flume, they confront a red and blue landscape: "Als wir um einen Felsen herum wendeten, sahen wir es plötzlich vor unsern Augen luftig blauen; der Weg riß ab, und gegenüber glänzte matt röthlich eine Kalkwand, auf welche die Strahlen der schon tief stehenden Sonne gerichtet waren" (*HKG* 1,5:56; As we wound our way around a crag, we suddenly saw only blue air before us. The path came to an abrupt end, and across the abyss a limestone rock face, upon which the beams of the already deep sun shone, glimmered in a matte red). The colors of the notebook, then, resonate far beyond the romantic entanglements of the present, not least because Margarita is the spitting image of her mother. Indeed, the slippage of descriptors across time and across objects (landscape, people, books) is more broadly indicative of the diffusion of the fall episode throughout the narrative.

The transferal of the fall episode extends into the frame narrative as well, thereby knitting together the Obrist's tale (as transmitted by the Doctor), the Doctor's accounts, and the great-grandson's reflections. In this narrative, too, one finds the same migration of descriptors from one realm to another, in the service of a *Gleichnis*. This transferal of descriptors remains fairly concretized in the frame narrative, which above all foregrounds the narrator's reflective stance toward the past. The *Mappe* opens with an epigraph from Hegesippus: "Dulce est, inter majorum versari habitacula et veterum dicta factaque recensere memoria" (*HKG* 1,5:10; It is a delight to dwell in the homes of our forefathers and to reflect in memory upon their words and deeds).[25] This process, it soon becomes apparent, is more bittersweet than delightful. The narrator describes in

25  My thanks to Eunice Kim for assistance with the English translation.

rich detail the various artifacts in his childhood home, the household objects, daily accoutrements, and odd relics of the past that surrounded him in his youth. His wistful contemplation and reverence of the past carries a profound melancholy, as the holdovers from the past remind him of his own mortality:

> Wie der Mensch doch selber arbeitet, daß das vor ihm Gewesene versinke, und wie er wieder mit seltsamer Liebe am Versinkenden hängt, das nichts anderes ist, als der Wegwurf vergangener Jahre. Es ist dies die Dichtung des Plunders, jene traurig sanfte Dichtung, welche blos die Spuren der Alltäglichkeit und Gewöhnlichkeit prägt, aber in diesen Spuren unser Herz oft mehr erschüttert, als in anderen, weil wir auf ihnen am deutlichsten den Schatten der Verblichenen fort gehen sehen, und unsern eignen mit, der jenem folgt. (*HKG* 1,5:16)

> [Just as one works to ensure that what existed before him sinks, and just as he hangs on, with strange fondness, to this sinking matter that is nothing more than the rubbish of years past. It is this poetry of plunder, this sadly gentle poetry, that merely treads a path of banality and convention, but in these traces rattles our hearts more than in others, because in these we most clearly see the shadows of the deceased walking away, and our own shadow following behind.]

At play here is a physical sinking, whereby one clings to the past and sinks along with it. One follows in the footsteps of one's ancestors, tracing the same paths as the shades, whose ghostly presence among their now defunct relics serves as a memento mori. For Orpheus, who retraces his wife's path into the underworld, or for the Obrist, who can only do so in memory, the specter of death looms.

A sinking feeling—of excitement, of anticipation, of horror—recurs at a few key moments in the frame narrative. Once again, this emotional tenor is conveyed in excessively concrete terms. The narrator and his wife return to his childhood home after their wedding, and on a rainy day he ventures into the attic. There, he discovers a chest full of old papers, and he finds the second volume of the Doctor's notebook, which he fondly remembers his own father reading when he was younger. He leafs through the pages and looks for the first volume, but only finds it by chance after moving the chest and hearing the thud of the falling notebook (recall here the thud of the falling trees during the ice storm). His discovery of the volumes proceeds in reverse order, moving ever backward into the past, with the sight of the first volume evoking the narrator's memories of his long-deceased father reading the very same. During the remainder of his visit, the narrator deciphers passages from the notebook, which he then reads to his family. The wistful contemplation of the past, then, transmutes into the repetition thereof, here exemplified in the act of reading.

Eventually the narrator and his wife must return home, and their separation from the former's family is painful. Here, too, the fall episode reverberates throughout the melancholic descriptors: "Die Pferde zogen an, das durch so viele Wochen gesehene Antlitz schwand an dem Wagenfenster entlang, und wir sahen es nicht mehr—vor einer Secunde noch stand es da und in der Ewigkeit wohl werden wir es erst wieder sehen" (*HKG* 1,5:30; The horses pulled, the countenance, seen for so many weeks, disappeared along the carriage window, and we no longer saw it—a second ago it still stood there, and we will see it again only in eternity). Expected though the sudden disappearance of the mother's visage might be, it is nevertheless tinged by melancholy. This is the last time the narrator will ever see her, and thus her disappearance, from one second to the next, is linked with death. It is only in eternity that a reunion will be possible. The subsequent descriptors of the passing landscape, curiously, take on some of the spatial features of the fall scene. When the newlyweds turn around to look at the landscape fading behind them, all they see is the blue twilight of the forest gazing down upon them: "Berge und Hügel legten sich nach und nach hinter uns, und wenn wir umblickten, sahen wir nichts mehr, als den immer blauern, dämmernderen *zurückschreitenden* Wald, der so viele Tage mit seiner lieblichen Färbung auf unsere Fenster und auf uns selber *niedergeblickt* hatte" (*HKG* 1,5:30, emphasis added; Mountains and hills laid farther and farther behind us, and when we looked back we saw nothing but the ever-blue, darkening and regressing forest that for so many days had looked down upon us and our windows with its mellow hue). If the forest had once gazed down upon the couple, they now return the gaze onto the ever-receding object. The blue twilight is altogether less threatening for the couple than it was for the Obrist and his wife, who confronted a blue abyss ("plötzlich vor unsern Augen luftig blauen"), with the landscape now, in this refraction, assuming at least a temporary placidity.

In the multiple narratives collected within the *Mappe*—from the Obrist's tale, reported by the Doctor, to the Doctor's personal entries, to the narrator's efforts to edit and transmit these various tales—one finds the same basic conceptual scaffolding. All these tales feature a sudden confrontation of emptiness: the abyss in the mountains, personal despair, the eternal departure from loved ones, and, finally, the empty page. Language offers a way through the emptiness, a path toward *Sanftmut*, all the while cleaving to the relics that have managed to survive. The collected efforts, whether in the form of the Obrist's or the Doctor's journal entries, or in the collections of narratives that comprise Stifter's *Mappe*, aim, however futilely, at arresting the past. Looking backward, these various writers register and reenact the past, even as it slips through their fingers. And just as Stifter died "on" the pages of his unfinished manuscript, his final efforts remaining inexhaustible, immeasurable, so, too, did the Doctor: "Wie viele Blätter aber blieben leer, wie wenige Hefte waren beschrieben, und wie hingen an den letzteren noch die alten Siegel, weil er, damit ich seinen eigenen Ausdruck gebrauche, früher fort gemußt, ehe er sie hatte öffnen können. / Friede mit ihm!" (*HKG* 1,5:234; But how many pages remained empty, how few bound sections were written in, how the old seals still hung from the last few, because—to use his own expression—he had to depart before he could open them. / Peace be with him!)

# 7: Lessons from Stifter's *Bunte Steine*

*Zachary Sng*

THERE IS, AT the heart of Adalbert Stifter's *Bunte Steine* (Motley Stones, 1853), a fundamental emptiness. This might seem like an odd thing to say. For the most part, Stifter's world is painstakingly, perhaps even lushly described. Natural landscapes, social relations, and physical objects are depicted with a care that some might consider excessive. The plotlines are driven by activity that runs the gamut from the measured to the manic, from calm routine to strife and disaster. The text offers us a bounty on the level of both action and description, but something still seems to be missing.

For Walter Benjamin, this absence is a fundamentally linguistic one, a form of what he calls "reticence" [*Verschwiegenheit*]. Because Stifter is cut off from "the essence of the world" [*das Weltwesen*] that is language, he cannot give a persuasive account of the relationship between the natural world and the moral one.[1] The homologies that he tries to establish between the two remain restricted to the visual register and therefore mute. Because it is inarticulate, Stifter's world is also disarticulated, for an unbridgeable gulf separates material impressions from the forces that are responsible for them.[2]

So, what can we learn from the silent, imperfect world of the *Bunte Steine*? This question dovetails with a trend in Stifter scholarship since the mid-twentieth century. Moments of obscurity or difficulty in his writings have been isolated and scrutinized through various critical lenses: psychoanalysis, deconstruction, the history of science, media history, etc. The goal is often to make these moments speak for Stifter, but also in spite of him, by resituating the spareness of a text like *Bunte Steine* into a historical horizon of ideas and forms that would help to animate it, giving it a

---

1    Walter Benjamin, "Stifter," in *Gesammelte Schriften*, vol. 2.2, ed. Rolf Tiedemann and Hermann Schweppenhäuser (Frankfurt am Main: Suhrkamp, 1991), 608–10.

2    For a nuanced reading of Benjamin's remarks and a fuller account of what "silence" might mean for Stifter, see Eva Geulen, *Worthörigkeit ohne Willen: Darstellungsproblematik und Sprachreflexion in der Prosa Adalbert Stifters* (Munich: iudicium, 1992), esp. 31–56.

voice by filling in the blanks. Another common, related strategy is to read its silence as an eloquent symptom, generated by a psychic or linguistic coherence whose reconstruction is the task of the literary critic.

To even ask what the stories have to teach us is to become caught up in their poetic program, for learning is at the heart of *Bunte Steine*. Many of its most memorable scenes involve the transmission of knowledge or tradition. Often this takes place within an extended network of family ties, as in the case of the grandfather in *Granit* (Granite) who takes the child on a long walk and relates the complex histories that lie behind landmarks and features; or the grandmother in *Kazensilber* (Cat-Silver) who leads the group of children on excursions to the surrounding countryside and tells them fantastic tales. There are, however, also important scenes of learning that take place outside the family, such as the ones between the land-surveyor and the old pastor in *Kalkstein* (Limestone).

The strong interest in pedagogy in *Bunte Steine* is hardly surprising given Stifter's biography. As a student in Vienna, he supported himself as a successful private tutor, and he continued this work through his early years as a writer. His most notable pupil was Richard von Metternich, son of the Austrian Chancellor, whom he tutored from 1843 to 1846. In the wake of the 1848 Revolutions, education reform became a matter of significant public debate in the Austrian Empire, and Stifter was an enthusiastic participant. In his letters from these years as well as a series of articles published in the *Wiener Bote*, Stifter repeatedly expressed his conviction that pedagogical reform was crucial to the political emancipation and progress of the people. In 1850, he was appointed *Schulrat* (school inspector) of the province of Upper Austria, a post that he held until his retirement with full pension in 1866. Both during the period of the stories' earliest compositions (1843–48) and during the time when he reworked them for publication in book form (1848–53), Stifter was preoccupied with education in a profound way. He spent several years between 1851 and 1853 designing and compiling (with Johannes Aprent) the *Lesebuch zur Förderung humaner Bildung in Realschulen und in andern zu weiterer Bildung vorbereitenden Mittelschulen* (Reader for the Advancement of Humanist Education in Junior Highschools and in Other Continuing Educational Preparatory Middle Schools, 1854), an ambitious primer filled with a selection of biblical, classical, and modern readings for schoolchildren. To his disappointment, it was rejected for use in schools by the Ministry of Education in 1855, and Stifter had to redirect his passion for pedagogical reform elsewhere.[3]

---

3    A fine description of Stifter's engagement with school reform and pedagogy can be found in Chapter 17 of the classic biographical study, Eric Blackall, *Adalbert Stifter: A Critical Study* (Cambridge: Cambridge University Press, 1948), 275–94. For an overview of how pedagogical principles could be read as

The Preface ("Vorrede") to *Bunte Steine* opens, indeed, with a reflection on what a literary text can offer in the way of lessons. Composed in 1852, it is formulated as a response to the German dramatist and satirist Friedrich Hebbel, who had criticized Stifter for his fixation on minute details of nature and his disregard for the "larger" truths of the human condition. Stifter's reply begins by doubling down on this accusation and delivering a paean to the small and unremarkable:

> Es ist einmal gegen mich bemerkt worden, daß ich nur das Kleine bilde, und daß meine Menschen stets gewöhnliche Menschen seien. Wenn das wahr ist, bin ich heute in der Lage, den Lesern ein noch Kleineres und Unbedeutenderes anzubieten, nemlich allerlei Spielereien für junge Herzen. Es soll sogar in denselben nicht einmal Tugend und Sitte gepredigt werden, wie es gebräuchlich ist, sondern sie sollen nur durch das wirken, was sie sind. (*HKG* 2,2:9)

> [It was once said against me that I fashion only small things, and that my people are always ordinary people. If that is true, I am now in the position of offering readers something smaller and more insignificant still, namely an assortment of fancies for young hearts. Nor are they even meant to preach virtue and morals, as the custom is, but rather to work solely by what they are. (*MS*, 3)]

Stifter offers a characteristically modest take on the classical dictum that literature should 'instruct and delight' (*docere et delectare*). The stories do not transmit pieties or moral lessons as their content. They do something less, and therefore something greater.

An attention to what appears small and insignificant is central to the pedagogical program of *Bunte Steine*. It forms the basis to the famous principle known as the "das sanfte Gesetz" or "the gentle law." The Preface first sketches the idea of a powerful yet subtle law that governs natural phenomena before it extends its reach by analogy to the world of "inner nature" or moral ideas. Stifter claims that easily overlooked actions of nature such as the wafting of air and the growing of grain are no less 'great' than thunderstorms, volcanoes, and even earthquakes. These latter events might seem more spectacular, but they are nonetheless only "Wirkungen viel höherer Gesetze" (*HKG* 2,2:9; effects of much higher laws, *MS*, 4). True greatness is to be found, by contrast, in the gentlest, most inconspicuous aspects of nature's work, which are guided by the same laws. This deceptively simple observation leaves a number of questions unanswered, including the urgent one of how the gentle law might

---

influencing Stifter's writings, see the entry on "Pädagogik" by Walter Seifert in *Stifter Handbuch: Leben—Werk—Wirkung*, ed. Christian Begemann and Davide Giuriato (Stuttgart: J. B. Metzler, 2017), 275–79.

apply to the stories themselves. These are filled with examples of both great and small phenomena of nature, but what would help the reader to sort them out and interpret them, namely the connection to the so-called "higher laws," is conspicuously absent.

To return to our question: What does *Bunte Steine* have to teach us? I would like to offer some thoughts on the collection's pedagogical program, using the Preface's opening statement as a springboard. My chapter will proceed in three sections, each one based on a phrase from the above-cited passage that I will unpack and explore. The first section will consider what a pedagogy without content ("nicht einmal Tugend und Sitte") might entail. I will then move on to examine the implications of Stifter's claim that the stories work by virtue of what they are ("nur durch das wirken, was sie sind"), and then close with some reflections on Stifter's evocation of play ("Spielerei") as a mode of learning.

## "Nicht einmal Tugend und Sitte": A Pedagogy without Content

The idea of a pedagogy that works without "virtue and morals" as content is intimately connected to the "gentle law," and to understand it we have to examine further the disjunction between observable phenomena and the higher laws that guide them. Stifter sheds some important light on this disjunction when he discusses the example of magnetism. He imagines a single individual recording the fluctuations of a compass needle, which in turn tracks the minute shifts of the earth's magnetic field. The product of such an individual recording the results in a daily log over years might seem pointless. If we could, however, juxtapose countless such logs, made by different individuals distributed across the planet, an astounding picture would emerge. The compiled table would make apparent (*ersichtlich*) that "a magnetic storm is passing over all the earth," during which "all the earth's surface at once is sensing a sort of "magnetisches Schauern" (*HKG* 2,2:11; magnetic shiver, *MS*, 4).[4]

This thought experiment leads Stifter to some important qualifications about the higher laws that guide nature. Like the forces of magnetism or electricity, he notes, these laws do not directly reveal themselves to us. We lack a sense for them, just as we have no physical organ that is

---

4    Eric Downing makes the astute observation that this example evokes the figure of the storm [*Gewitter*] again, which had previously appeared in the list of spectacular natural phenomena that only appear to be great but really are not significant in themselves. This "chiastic reversal" is, Downing argues, a characteristic gesture in the text. See Eric Downing, *Double Exposures: Repetition and Realism in Nineteenth-Century German Fiction* (Stanford, CA: Stanford University Press, 2000), 27–34.

able to perceive magnetic forces. Without a "physical eye" ("leibliche[s] Auge") that can see the higher laws, we have to rely on "the mental eye" ("das geistige [Auge] der Wissenschaft") (see *HKG* 2,2:11; *MS*, 4), but even this intellectual, scientific organ, Stifter concedes, has to struggle with the task of perception:

> Weil aber die Wissenschaft nur Körnchen nach Körnchen erringt, nur Beobachtung nach Beobachtung macht, nur aus Einzelnem das Allgemeine zusammen trägt, und weil endlich die Menge der Erscheinungen und das Feld des Gegebenen unendlich groß ist, Gott also die Freude und die Glükseligkeit des Forschens unversieglich gemacht hat, wir auch in unseren Werkstätten immer nur das Einzelne darstellen können, nie das Allgemeine, denn dies wäre die Schöpfung. (*HKG* 2,2:11)

> [But since science grasps only grain upon grain, makes only observation upon observation, amasses the universal only from particulars, and finally since the multitude of phenomena and the field of facts is infinitely great, so that God has made the joy and felicity of inquiry inexhaustible, and we in our workshops can represent only the particular and never the universal, for that would be Creation. (*MS*, 4–5)]

The problem is not one of intelligibility vs perceptibility but one of a successive, serializing gaze trying to comprehend something holistic, something whose atemporal character demands that it be grasped all at once. Because of its limitations, the eye of *Wissenschaft* can only represent the individual (*das Einzelne*) and never the general (*das Allgemeine*).

The higher laws that govern both nature and man lie, ultimately, beyond our ability to either perceive with physical senses or comprehend with intellectual faculties. Where *Bunte Steine* provides a glimpse into these laws, therefore, it is only as a trace of something absconded, withdrawn into un-representability. That does not mean, however, that we should stop searching for such traces. The pursuit itself leads us to an important experience, even if its object remains elusive:

> So ist auch die Geschichte des in der Natur Großen in einer immerwährenden Umwandlung der Ansichten über dieses Große bestanden. Da die Menschen in der Kindheit waren, ihr geistiges Auge von der Wissenschaft noch nicht berührt war, wurden sie von dem Nahestehenden und Auffälligen ergriffen und zu Furcht und Bewunderung hingerissen; aber als ihr Sinn geöffnet wurde, da der Blik sich auf den Zusammenhang zu richten begann, so sanken die einzelnen Erscheinungen immer tiefer, und es erhob sich das Gesez

immer höher, die Wunderbarkeiten hörten auf, das Wunder nahm zu. (*HKG* 2,2:11–12)

[Thus the history of what is great in Nature consists in a perpetual metamorphosis of views about this greatness. When human beings were in their childhood, their mind's eye as yet untouched by science, they were enthralled by what was close at hand and striking, and were compelled to fear and admiration: but when their minds were opened, when their eyes turned toward the greater context, the particular phenomena fell away, and law rose higher and higher, the marvels ceased, and wonder increased. (*MS*, 5)]

Stifter's vision of the natural and the moral spheres involves constant change and movement. Even a term like "the great" (*das Große*), which appears to anchor one of the most important binarisms of the Preface, turns out to be less stable that we might think. Its contours are subject to a motion blur due to our constantly shifting perspective or point of view ("Umwandlung der Ansicht[ ]"). What this ends up producing is a visual lapse around the idea of relation or "Zusammenhang." As we break free from a fixation with the immediate and proximate, and turn instead to relation, a more meaningful world seems on the verge of appearing to us—as Stifter puts it: "ihr Sinn [wurde] geöffnet" (their minds were opened). At the same time, however, it is hard to miss that what is actually opening up is an ever-widening separation between the phenomenal world and the law that governs it. Both retreat from our gaze—but in opposing directions: the former sinks into profundity while the latter rarefies into lofty heights.

This double withdrawal opens up an ever-increasing interval at a pivotal moment, where we pass from a child-like to a more mature, intellectual view of things, as we leave behind marvels ("Wunderbarkeiten") and gain an appreciation for wonder ("Wunder"). The increase ascribed to wonder ("das Wunder nahm zu") aligns with the elevation of the law beyond our perception ("es erhob sich das Gesez immer höher"). Crucially, the direct object of this wonder is not the law itself, but rather the growing gap between the dissipation of phenomena and the elevation of the law that governs them. The pedagogical stakes of this passage are thus centered on a moment of not seeing, on a gaze that learns as it seeks and contemplates rather than seizing upon a definite object.

Stifter's reflections on nature and the higher laws that guide it culminate in a compelling analogy: "So wie es in der äußeren Natur ist, so ist es auch in der inneren, in der des menschlichen Geschlechtes" (*HKG* 2,2:12; As is outward Nature, so too is inward nature, the nature of the human race, *MS*, 5). With this, the Preface transports our thinking about the great and the small, about hiddenness and appearance, from the realm of natural phenomena to moral ideas. It is here that the famous "gentle law" is introduced, but significantly, framed as an object of pursuit: "Wir wollen das sanfte Gesez zu erblicken suchen" (*HKG* 2,2:12; We seek the gentle law, *MS*, 5). The German original takes up the visual register discussed earlier, and its more oblique formulation ("wollen ... zu erblicken suchen") reiterates the sense of uncertain see(k)ing.

As the Preface's argument turns to the moral sphere, its general tendency is toward increasing confidence in our ability to perceive and grasp the higher laws.[5] It is striking, however, that in the stories themselves, this gentle law—so powerful in its guidance of both the natural world and the human one—never makes an actual appearance as law. Its most profound effect on the characters is as an unobtainable object of desire, moving them to strain to catch a glimpse of it, but always in vain.

To emphasize the process of striving in the face of the law's nonavailability might make Stifter sound like a precursor to someone like Franz Kafka. Rather than being a modernist retrojection, however, this connection actually ties the Preface to a longer arc of thought that begins in German classicism. In imagining a *Sehnsucht* spanned across the divide between the sensuous and the intellectual spheres, Stifter takes up a central figure in eighteenth-century aesthetic debates.[6] Take, for example, the idea of a law that must remain unspecified and undetermined, even as we try to understand its regulative effect. In his *Kritik der Urteilskraft* (Critique of Judgment, 1790), Immanuel Kant considers this idea to be one of the central challenges in understanding aesthetic judgment. When we judge something as beautiful, we refer to a pleasure that results from the imagination operating freely and yet in accordance to some unstated law or, as Kant puts it, "in harmony [*Einstimmung*] with the understanding's lawfulness in general."[7] Faced with the difficulty of an imagination that must be both free and lawful, he therefore arrives at the description of "lawfulness without a law" (*Gesetzmässigkeit ohne Gesetz*). This plays a similar role to that of the more well-known "purposiveness without

---

5    For an excellent discussion of the Preface's account of the human, social world, see Downing, *Double Exposures*, 34–40.

6    Friedrich Schiller, whose indirect influence is legible throughout long stretches of the Preface, depicts in his *Über die ästhetische Erziehung des Menschen in einer Reihe von Briefen* (Letters on the Aesthetic Education of Man, 1795) a similar separation between the sensuous and the intellectual, the natural and the moral.

7    Immanuel Kant, *Critique of Judgment*, trans. Werner Pluhar (Indianapolis, IA: Hackett, 1987), 91. German original consulted is Immanuel Kant, *Kritik der Urtheilskraft*, in *Die Gesammelten Schriften*, vol. 5, ed. Königlich-Preussische Akademie der Wissenschaften zu Berlin (Berlin: de Gruyter, 1908–).

purpose" (*Zweckmässigkeit ohne Zweck*) in capturing a harmony among the faculties that is subjective rather than objectively given.[8]

Stifter's "gentle law" is perhaps not an actual law but lawfulness itself in the absence of a law that can be stated or represented. This distinction would explain how his prose manages to be both prolix and spare at the same time. It describes the phenomenal world in effusive, almost reverent detail, but it acknowledges that the law governing these phenomena must remain unrepresented in them.

An episode from the story *Kalkstein* illustrates how this ambivalence leaves its traces on the narrative level. The story gives us the account of land-surveyor, commissioned to conduct a long-term study of the strange rocky region in the Austrian Salzkammergut known as *Steinkar.* He is drawn to an old parson who has lived there many years and as their friendship gradually develops, he slowly learns more about the parson's life-story, the history of the land, and the character of its inhabitants. A recurrent motif throughout the text is the contrast between the scientific, objective view of nature represented by the land-surveyor and the more profound, experiential knowledge of the parson. This conflict comes to a head in a decisive episode where the two argue about whether a storm is coming:

> "Daß ein Gewitter kommen wird," sagte ich, "war wohl den ganzen Tag zu erwarten, allein wie bald die Dunstschicht sich verdichten, erkühlen, den Wind und die Elektrizität erzeugen und sich herabschütteln wird, kann man, glaube ich, nicht ermessen."
>
> "Man kann es wohl nicht genau sagen," antwortete er, "allein ich habe siebenundzwanzig Jahre in der Gegend gelebt, habe Erfahrungen gesammelt und nach ihnen wird das Gewitter eher ausbrechen als man denkt, und wird sehr stark sein. Ich glaube daher, daß es das beste wäre, wenn Sie mit mir in meinen Pfarrhof gingen und die Nacht heute dort zubrächten. ... Dort sind Sie sicher und können morgen an Ihre Geschäfte gehen, sobald es Ihnen beliebt." (*HKG* 2,2:73–74)

> ["The thunderstorm," I said, "has been brewing all day long, but how soon the layer of haze will condense, cool down, produce wind and electricity and pour itself forth, that, I believe, cannot be gauged."
>
> "It may be impossible to say precisely," he replied, "but I've lived in this area for twenty-seven years, I've made certain observations,

---

8    An overview of some connections that could be drawn between the Preface and the works of Kant, Schiller, and Goethe can be found in Sepp Domandl, "Die philosophische Tradition von Adalbert Stifters 'Sanftem Gesetz,'" *VASILO* 21, nos. 3/4 (1972): 79–103.

and they suggest that the storm will break sooner than one might think, and will be quite severe. And so I think it best that you come with me to my parsonage and spend the night there. ... You'll be safe there, and tomorrow you can go about your work as soon as you please." (*MS*, 49)]

The parson turns out, of course, to be right. Returning to the parsonage just as the storm breaks, the two enjoy a meal and a long conversation, and the surveyor spends the night as guest.

The pages following this initial disagreement are filled with the kinds of languidly expansive writing that Stifter has become known for. Furnishing, household objects, clothing are described at length, and an extended account is given of their conversation and preparation for bed. And of course, the tense anticipation of the coming storm, the slow build-up to its arrival, and its aftermath the next morning are all rendered masterfully. We never return to the question, however, that should matter most in a story about understanding the laws of nature: how did the parson know? What were the signs of the storm's impending arrival that were legible to him but not the surveyor? This is, after all, an eminently teachable moment. The limitations of the surveyor's *Meßkunst* (see *HKG* 2,2:64) or "art of measuring" have been exposed, and it only remains for the parson to provide a hint about how to integrate this experience of misreading into a better understanding of nature's law. On this point, however, the text remains resolutely, ostentatiously silent.

## "Durch das wirken, was sie sind": On Stifter's Pragmatism

It is hard to know what to make of Stifter's statement that his stories simply "work by virtue of what they are." We could take this as a strong claim about presence, as attributing to the stories an efficacy derived not from abstract moral content but from concreteness, specificity, and self-identity. It is possible, however, to read these words as a mild expression of ontological agnosticism. "Sie sollen nur durch das wirken, was sie sind," but *was sie sind* ("what they are") is placed in a black box that we might or might not know much about. Read this way, with an emphasis on *wirken* (doing) instead of *sein* (being), Stifter's statement declines to privilege essence over effect, semantics over pragmatics.

This less intuitive reading, with its focus on the pragmatic, helps us make sense of an odd passage from the "Einleitung," the short Introduction to the stories themselves that serves as a second prefatory statement. After developing a metaphorical connection between the stories in the collection and the stones that he fondly gathered as a child, the narrator appends a modest confession:

> Freilich war manchmal auch ein Stük Glas darunter, das ich auf den Feldern gefunden hatte und das in allerlei Regenbogenfarben schimmerte. Wenn sie dann sagten, das sei ja nur ein Glas und noch dazu ein verwitterndes, wodurch es eben diese schimmernden Farben erhalten habe, so dachte ich: Ei, wenn es auch nur ein Glas ist, so hat es doch die schönen Farben, und es ist zum Staunen, wie es in der kühlen, feuchten Erde diese Farben empfangen konnte, und ich ließ es unter den Steinen liegen. (*HKG* 2,2:18)

> [Of course now and then they included a piece of glass I had found in the fields, shimmering in all the colors of the rainbow. When I was told that it was just broken glass, and weathered at that, which was how it had picked up those shimmering colors, I thought: My, that might be just a piece of glass, but it has the prettiest colors, and it's a marvel how it managed to take on those colors in the cool damp earth, and I left it there among the stones. (*MS*, 9–10)]

The fact that the stones being collected might not be stones after all, is not a problem for the overall metaphor, because glass is, at the end of the day, very much like stone. But is this not an example of where effect diverges from substance, where *Wirkung* is no longer connected to *Sein*?

This passage is meant to evoke a child-like perspective, but here as elsewhere in *Bunte Steine*, the child is possessed of unexpected wisdom. The insight takes the form of an indifference to the ontological, a radical openness that does not exclude the pieces of glass by virtue of "what they are" (*was sie sind*) but instead celebrates them for their effect (*Wirkung*). This revaluation accomplishes a flattening-out of ontology: what stone or glass *is* becomes tantamount to what it *does*. Such a doing or effect is, in turn, not the product of some innate characteristic or quality of being. Our gaze is significantly directed toward exteriority and receptivity: first the color of the material, then its ability to take on color, and then our marvel (*Staunen*) in the face of this receptivity. Glass is like stone, in other words, because it *affects* the narrator the same way as stone does, and this effect is a doubling of the effect that the earth has on both glass and stone. *Wirken* is, we might say, tied to the qualities of affectability and receptivity in the receiving medium rather than to the efficacy of the agent.

Two examples from the stories might help to illuminate Stifter's interest in a pragmatic pedagogy. These examples foreground effect over content in the act of storytelling (*erzählen*). They both involve figures situated just outside the nuclear family structure, but whose storytelling helps to secure or shore up the familial in crucial ways.

The first is the grandmother from *Kazensilber*, whose storytelling is tied to her role as a tour guide to the children. She leads them on explorations of the surrounding countryside, and during these forays beyond the domestic space represented by the family home, she tells them stories filled with wild figures, strange animals, and fantastic landscapes. At some point in the plot, a strange child of unknown provenance appears from nowhere to join the group, and she is referred to only as "das braune Mädchen" or "the brown girl." With this new arrival, the grandmother's role shifts slightly: the stories that she tells and the way she directs the movements of the children through the landscape are now directed at integrating this outsider into the world of the family.

The initiating effect of the grandmother's stories have little to do with any allegorical connection between their content and the plot of the frame narrative. Attempts to connect the figures, landscapes, and plot sequences of these stories with those of the main narrative have generally been acknowledged as inconclusive and unsatisfying.[9] The stories draw from a folkloric tradition, but the content itself remains stubbornly opaque when read as reference to the framing narrative. Instead, their pedagogical value (for both the children and the reader) lies in the way they stand for the folkloric itself, as a practice of oral transmission that constitutes and reinforces a community of listeners marked as lying outside of the rational, bourgeois world represented in the story. As Albrecht Koschorke puts it, she acts as mediator in a double sense: she leads the children "beyond the boundaries of a settled order" and serves "much in the spirit of Brothers Grimm ... as initiator into the world of fairy-tales."[10]

Another example of a pragmatic storyteller would be the grandfather in *Granit*, whose role is also a double one. The story begins with a moment of crisis in the household because the child has ruined the newly cleaned wood floors by walking across it with pitch-stained feet. He receives a beating from the mother as punishment, and this is where the grandfather steps in decisively. He takes the child on a long walk to the next village and then back home again. During their journey, he points out many features of the landscape and recounts several stories about the origin of place names, the regional tree species, the lives of the villagers, etc. By the time they get home, the floors have been cleaned and all is forgiven between mother and son.

The circuitous walk, the stories told by the grandfather, and the lessons that he imparts make up the bulk of the story. One could say,

9    For a good summary of some recent approaches to the folkloric elements in the story, see Alyssa Lonner Howards, "Telling a Realist Folktale: Folklore and Cultural Preservation in Adalbert Stifter's 'Katzensilber,'" *Modern Austrian Literature* 43, no. 4 (2010): 1–21.

10    Albrecht Koschorke, "Erziehung zum Freitod: Adalbert Stifters pädagogischer Realismus," in *Die Dinge und die Zeichen: Dimensionen des Realistischen in der Erzählliteratur des 19. Jahrhunderts*, ed. Sabine Schneider and Barbara Hunfeld (Würzburg: Königshausen & Neumann, 2008), 319–32; here 320. Translation is mine.

however, it is the extension rather than the intension of these stories that enables the narrative of forgiveness to be told. That is to say: it is the time of the telling as much as the content of what is told that matters. As the grandfather says to the child about his mother's anger: "Aber lasse ihr nur Zeit, sie wird schon zur Einsicht kommen, sie wird alles verstehen, und alles wird gut werden" (*HKG* 2,2:31; Just give her time, she'll come around, she'll understand everything, and all will be well, *MS*, 17). Within the frame of the story, the time of narration (*Erzählzeit*)—that is to say, the time that it takes the grandfather to complete his walk and to share various stories with the child—serves as the main agent of healing.

This is not to suggest that the content of the grandfather's stories in *Granit* or the grandmother's folktales in *Kazensilber* can be dismissed. It is clear, however, that their main function in the stories is a *pragmatic* rather than a semantic one. It is interesting that in both of these cases, the pragmatic function leads to complications for the pedagogical program. In *Kazensilber*, the socialization of the young girl comes to an abrupt end. She mysteriously departs one day, delivering as her enigmatic farewell a line from one of the grandmother's stories: "Sture Mure ist todt, und der hohe Felsen ist todt" (*HKG* 2,2:313; Stura Mura is dead, and the high crag is dead, *MS*, 227). The reader is not given any clues about how to interpret these words in connection to any intradiegetic events or characters. Instead, they resonate as an unassimilated effect of storytelling that is neither internalized by the child nor semantically legible within the frame narrative.[11] *Granit* also ends on a discordant note that undercuts the pedagogical value of the grandfather's stories about the importance of memory and memorialization. The narrator admits that he never found out how the pitch stains were removed, and his determination to find out runs into a curious obstacle: "oft, wenn ich eine Heimreise beabsichtigte, nahm ich mir vor, die Mutter zu fragen; aber auch das vergaß ich jedes Mal wieder" (*HKG* 2,2:60; often, when I planned a trip home, I meant to ask my mother about it, but that, too, I forgot every time, *MS*, 39).

---

11   As Christoph Gardian has recently put it, the utterance is typical of the way in which the grandmother's fairy-tales are presented without contextualization and function. He reads this as a form of "absolute Poesie" and the cornerstone of what he calls Stifter's "reduced Romanticism." See Christoph Gardian, "Reduzierte Romantik: Adalbert Stifters *Bunte Steine* und das Programm einer 'Wiederherstellung in dem ursprünglichen Sinne,'" *Internationales Archiv für Sozialgeschichte der deutschen Literatur* 44, no. 1 (2019): 191–219; here 217.

## "Allerlei Spielereien für junge Herzen": On Play as Practice

The Preface attaches an interesting addendum to its statement that the stories do not transmit virtue or morals: they are offered, instead, as "fancies or past-times [*Spielereien*] for young hearts." The word *Spielerei*, which comes up at several points in the Preface and the Introduction, suggests something that is not exactly the same as a conventional *Spiel* (play or game)—perhaps something less serious, less structured. Indeed, there are few examples of what we might consider conventional games or scenes of actual playing in the stories of the *Bunte Steine*, despite its many depictions of children. What passes as *Spielerei* in the stories is instead, I propose, the many instances of oddly repetitive behavior or speech that serves no apparent practical purpose. An example would be this ritualistic exchange between grandfather and child, taken from the story *Granit*:

> "Kannst du mir sagen, was das dort ist?"
> "Ja, Großvater," antwortete ich, "das ist die Alpe, auf welcher sich im Sommer eine Viehherde befindet, die im Herbste wieder herabgetrieben wird."
> "Und was ist das, das sich weiter vorwärts von der Alpe befindet?" fragte er wieder.
> "Das ist der Hüttenwald," antwortete ich.
> "Und rechts von der Alpe und dem Hüttenwalde?"
> "Das ist der Philippgeorgsberg."
> "Und rechts von dem Philippgeorgsberge?"
> "Das ist der Seewald, in welchem sich das dunkle und tiefe Seewasser befindet." (*HKG* 2,2:33–34)

> ["Can you tell me what that is?"
> "Yes, Grandfather," I replied, "that's the alp where a cattle herd grazes in the summer and is driven back down in the fall."
> "And what is that in front of the alp?" came his next question.
> "That is the Hütten Forest," I replied.
> "And to the right of the alp and the Hütten Forest?"
> "That's Philippgeorg Mountain."
> "And to the right of Philippgeorg Mountain?"
> "That's the Lake Forest, where the dark deep lake waters are."
> (*MS*, 19)]

There is little trace here of what we usually expect from play, such as pleasure, creativity, or spontaneity. Nor is it clear what new knowledge is being transmitted to the child, despite the grandfather's unmistakably pedagogical intent. If such scenes, which can be found throughout the

*Bunte Steine*, contribute to a pedagogy of play, they do so by challenging those very terms.

One approach to understanding Stifter's intervention is via the so-called "practice" theory of play. This concept can be traced to the work of Karl Groos, the German philosopher and psychologist who wrote two major studies of play around the turn of the century: *Die Spiele der Tiere* (The Play of Animals, 1896) and *Die Spiele der Menschen* (The Play of Man, 1899). Groos undertakes a radical expansion of the concept of play as practice (*Übung*) beyond the usual sense.[12] We are accustomed to think of children's play as an imitation of the roles and conventions of the adult world, but stripped of the much higher stakes attached to them. In imitating warlike behavior or courtship rituals, for example, children would be "practicing" for their adult equivalents. Groos finds this narrow approach, however, inadequate in accounting for the relationship between play and practice. Indeed, it does not get us very far in understanding the scenes of repetition in *Bunte Steine*. It would be difficult to say that a specific convention or role is being rehearsed in the example from *Granit*; there is, so to speak, no determinate "main event" for which a scene like this might be construed as practice.

More pertinent would be Groos's key insight from his study of animals: namely, that what is being practiced in play are instincts (*Triebe*). Play as practice is about the exercise and training of these instincts. Gross distinguishes such play from play that imitates something already experienced or seen by the subject. As he turns to human games in the later *Die Spiele der Menschen*, Groos's attention shifts to this latter form of play, because it is the learning of social rituals and conventions that ensures the transmission of culture between generations. For an understanding of repetitive behavior and speech in Stifter, however, this pre-cultural, pre-mimetic sense of practice or *Übung* as the foundation of play is more illuminating. It is, in other words, practice construed not as the repetition or imitation of *content*, but as the training of *instinct*.

For Groos, this form of play should be regarded as *Vorübung* (preparatory practice) rather than serious *Ausübung* or exercise. He underscores the importance of this difference by using the same *Vor-* prefix to coin the term *Vorahmung* (as opposed to *Nachahmung*) for it:

> Denn diese Spiele … sind zum grossen Theil keine Nachahmungen, sondern—falls das Wort gestattet ist—"Vorahmungen" der ernsten Beschäftigungen des Individuums. Das "Experimentiren" kleiner

---

12   For a discussion of Groos's importance for later accounts of play by Sigmund Freud and Walter Benjamin, see Michael Powers, "The Smallest Remainder: Benjamin and Freud on Play," *Modern Language Notes* 133, no. 3 (2018): 720–42.

LESSONS FROM STIFTER'S *BUNTE STEINE* ♦ 195

Kinder und junger Thiere, ihre Bewegungs-, Jagd- und Kampfspiele, die doch die wichtigsten Grundformen des Spielens überhaupt ausmachen, sind keine Nachübungen sondern Vorübungen, sie treten vor den ernsten Thätigkeiten auf und haben offenbar den Zweck, das junge Lebewesen auf diese einzuüben und· vorzubereiten.

[For such games ... are very often not imitations (*Nachahmungen*), but rather premonitions (*Vorahmungen*)—if the word might be allowed—of the serious occupations of the individual. The "experimenting" of little children and young animals, their movement, hunting, and fighting games, which are the most important elementary forms of play, are not imitative repetitions [*Nachübungen*], but rather preparatory efforts [*Vorübungen*]. They come before any serious activity, and evidently aim at preparing the young creature for it and making him familiar with it.][13]

Imitation proper (*Nachahmung*) consists of repeating a model that has been perceived or experienced, but the form of practice that interests Groos is different, in that it "repeats" something outside of knowledge and experience.

In referring to such an act as *Vorahmung* or *Vorübung*, Groos emphasizes the honing of instinct through repetition, toward some future performance for which no model exists. The ritual of pointing, questioning, and naming in *Granit* that was discussed earlier seems to be a good example of practice that exercises some unspecified instinct. At other points in *Bunte Steine*, the word *Übung* is, in fact, used to refer to such exercises. When the narrator in *Kalkstein* runs into the old pastor at a remote location and asks if he often comes here, the latter replies: "Ich gehe gern heraus, um meine Füße zu üben, und sitze dann auf einem Steine, um die Dinge zu betrachten" (*HKG* 2,2:69; I like to go out to exercise my feet, and then sit on a rock to contemplate the things around me, *MS*, 46). The same phrase is used in *Kazensilber* to describe the perambulations of the children under the guidance of the grandmother: "Sie gingen durch die Felder, sie gingen in den Wald und übten die Füße" (*HKG* 2,2:254; They walked through the fields, they went into the woods and exercised their legs, *MS*, 181). The phrase "Füße üben" (to exercise the feet) captures the sense of practice that Groos identifies as central to play. If this practice is repetitive, it is not because it is a copy of anything other than itself, but because it exhibits a repetitive character *within* itself. Such scenes in Stifter often have an autotelic character, in that the repetitive actions seem to gesture toward no concrete goal outside of themselves.

13   Karl Groos, *Die Spiele der Thiere* (Jena: Verlag von Gustav Fischer, 1896), 6; Karl Groos, *The Play of Animals*, trans. Elizabeth Baldwin (New York: D. Appleton and Company, 1898), 7.

This sheds a different light on a passage from the Preface that I briefly mentioned earlier, one in which the word *Spielerei* also features prominently. Here, Stifter illustrates the operation of the higher laws of nature using the example of the individual who logs the movements of a compass needle:

> Wenn ein Mann durch Jahre hindurch die Magnetnadel, deren eine Spitze immer nach Norden weist, tagtäglich zu festgesetzten Stunden beobachtete und sich die Veränderungen, wie die Nadel bald mehr bald weniger klar nach Norden zeigt, in einem Buche aufschriebe, so würde gewiß ein Unkundiger dieses Beginnen für ein kleines und für Spielerei ansehen; aber wie ehrfurchterregend wird dieses Kleine und wie begeisterungerweckend diese Spielerei, wenn wir nun erfahren, daß diese Beobachtungen wirklich auf dem ganzen Erdboden angestellt werden, und daß aus den daraus zusammengestellten Tafeln ersichtlich wird, daß manche kleine Veränderungen an der Magnetnadel oft auf allen Punkten der Erde gleichzeitig und in gleichem Maße vor sich gehen, daß also ein magnetisches Gewitter über die ganze Erde geht, daß die ganze Erdoberfläche gleichzeitig gleichsam ein magnetisches Schauern empfindet. (*HKG* 2,2:10–11)

> [Suppose a man spent years observing the magnetic needle whose one end always points North, recording in a book at fixed times each day the shifts as the needle points now plainly now less plainly northward; an uninformed person would surely regard this endeavor as a small thing and a mere game; but what awe is inspired by this small thing, and what enthusiasm by this game, when we learn that these observations are in fact made across the earth's entire surface, and the charts compiled from them show that certain small shifts in the magnetic needle often occur simultaneously and to the same degree in all parts of the world; that, then, a magnetic storm is passing over all the earth, that all the earth's surface at once is sensing a sort of magnetic shiver. (*MS*, 4)]

As is the case with many well-known passages from *Bunte Steine*, this description is riven by an inherent tension. Stifter draws the reader's attention toward the awe-inspiring grandeur of the immeasurably large—in this case, the magnetic field of the entire planet. At the same time, he does not give up an attachment to the small and concrete, to the minutiae that pave the way to greatness. The moment of epiphany is not achieved at the cost of abandoning terms like *das Kleine* and *Spielerei*. Instead, we experience a conversion of affect, as we realize that the small and the frivolous are also in themselves great and worthy of awe (*ehrfurchterregend*).

An explicit connection is drawn here between play and repetition. *Spielerei* denotes an interesting conjunction of two acts: observing a phenomenon and marking it with an act of writing. It is a mere *Spielerei* because the exercise is mechanical and takes place without insight into meaning or significance. The actual universal table that would endow these iterated acts with meaning, the chart that collates all such acts of inscription from all over the world to reveal the presence of a unifying magnetic field: such things remain in the realm of fantasy. What is decisive is the individual, discrete act of repetitive marking and re-marking— which is to say, the practice of inscription itself—rather than any inscribed content.

## Conclusion

As a reflection on the act of writing, the passage leaves us with an interesting picture of Stifter's poetics. One might say that it is consistent with a pedagogy not based on content, since these acts of marking are based on registration rather than representation. What they record is *Wirkung* or effect (namely, the effect of a shifting magnetic field on a compass needle) rather than meaning, and this would also fit with the pragmatism discussed earlier. It is less clear, however, what to make of the repetitive, mechanical nature of this marking. As a form of *Übung* or practice, it supports the pedagogical program, but there is something insistent here that remains not entirely assimilable. This surplus effect is especially noticeable in the eloquent but also uncanny description with which the above-cited passage closes: "daß manche kleine Veränderungen an der Magnetnadel oft auf allen Punkten der Erde *gleichzeitig* und in *gleichem* Maße vor sich *gehen*, daß also ein magnetisches *Gewitter* über die *ganze* Erde *geht*, daß die *ganze* Erdoberfläche *gleichzeitig gleichsam* ein magnetisches Schauern empfindet" (emphases mine).

The practice of meticulous record-keeping kept up through daily routine is meant to be inspiring and salubrious, but other effects of repetition start to creep in. The most glaring is the recurring *gleich* (same) in "*gleich*zeitig," in "*gleich*em Maße," and, finally, "*gleich*zeitig *gleich*sam." Semantically, this reinforces the point being made, which is that individuals all over the world observe the fluctuations of the same planetary magnetic field. At the same time that our senses are being directed towards this hyperbolic largeness, however, the text pulls in the other direction: the repeated word *gleich* breaks down into an insistent series of initial *g*-words (*Gewitter, ganz, gehen*). We find, running counter to the momentum of gathering and unification, a peculiar tendency toward disarticulation and dispersal. "Practice" is the term that I have suggested to indicate this technique of repetition. It is derived from the same Greek root as "pragmatic," namely the word *prattein* for "to do." As a model for reading Stifter, however, this idea of practice stands in a certain tension to a pragmatic pedagogical agenda based on efficacy. Driving the technique

198 ♦ Zachary Sng

of repetition almost to an extreme, Stifter exposes a non-agential, non-teleological side of practice. This form of practice tends to remain in the purely preparatory mode that Groos designates as the *Vor-* or the "pre-". In doing so, it undercuts the idea of an active "doing" that forms the basis for any practical program of teaching and learning.

I will close with one example of where this tension reaches a breaking point, taken from the story *Turmalin* (Tourmaline), which opens with the following ominous announcement: "Der Turmalin ist dunkel, und was da erzählt wird ist sehr dunkel" (*HKG* 2,2:135; Tourmaline is dark, and what is told here is very dark, *MS*, 93). The passage in question is a young girl's account of a ritualistic exchange with her father, in which he assigns to her writing tasks that are repetitive and morbid to the point of cruelty. The two have ended up in a basement apartment in Vienna under somewhat mysterious circumstances. Years earlier, following an affair, the girl's mother abruptly disappeared from the family home in the city. After failing to find her in Vienna, the father also left the city, taking his daughter with him presumably to search for his wife. They resurface in Vienna years later. One day, the father dies in an accident, leaving the girl in the hands of strangers who then try to reconstruct her story. This is the child's account of the bizarre education she has received from her father:

> Er lehrte mich mancherlei Dinge und erzählte viel. Er sperrte immer zu, wenn er fortging. Wenn ich fragte, was ich für eine Aufgabe habe, während er nicht da sei, antwortete er: *Beschreibe den Augenblick*, wenn ich tot auf der Bahre liegen werde, und wenn sie mich begraben; und wenn ich dann sagte: Vater, *das habe ich ja schon oft beschrieben*, antwortete er: *So beschreibe*, wie deine Mutter von ihrem Herzen gepeinigt herumirrt, wie sie sich nicht zurückgetraut, und wie sie in der Verzweiflung ihrem Leben ein Ende macht. Wenn ich sagte: Vater, *das habe ich auch schon oft beschrieben*, antwortete er: *So beschreibe es noch einmal*. Wenn ich dann mit der Aufgabe, wie der Vater tot auf der Bahre liegt, und wie die Mutter in der Welt umherirrt und in der Verzweiflung ihrem Leben ein Ende macht, fertig war, stieg ich auf die Leiter und schaute durch die Drahtlöcher des Fensters hinaus. Da sah ich die Säume von Frauenkleidern vorbeigehen, sah die Stiefel von Männern, sah schöne Spitzen von Röcken oder die vier Füße eines Hundes. Was an den jenseitigen Häusern vorging, war nicht deutlich. (*HKG* 2,2:173–74)

> [He taught me things, and told me many stories. He always locked the door when he went away. When I asked what lesson I should do while he was gone, he'd reply: Describe the moment when I'll lie dead on the bier, and they'll bury me; and when I said: Father, I've described that lots of times, he'd reply: Then describe your mother in the torment of her heart, how she wanders about the world

because she doesn't dare come back, and how she puts an end to her life in despair. When I said: Father, I've described that lots of times too, he'd reply: Then describe it again. When I was finished with the lesson of Father lying dead on the bier and Mother wandering about the world and putting an end to her life in despair, I'd climb up the ladder and look through the mesh of the window. There I saw the hems of women's dresses pass, saw the boots of the men, saw pretty coattails or the four paws of a dog. What went on by the houses across the street was unclear. (*MS*, 121–22)]

Of all the pedagogical exchanges in *Bunte Steine*, this is by far the strangest. To borrow from Groos's vocabulary, we might say that the instinct (*Trieb*) that has been inculcated and honed with perverse success in the child is the repetitive drive. It comes across not just in the scenes narrated by her but in the actual narration itself. Her account of the father's lessons in repetition turns out, in other words, to be itself an exercise in repetition. Its goal is not to recapitulate and refine some previous experience, nor is it (contrary to Groos's model) to prepare the child for some future activity. In fact, its sole drive is toward death.

The acts that the child is called upon to perform in these exercises involve something more than the mere visualization of death. The imperative *Beschreiben* exhorts her to imagine, but also to *in-scribe* or to put into writing (*Be-schreiben*). This remarkable scene thus invites us to rethink two gestures that are central to Stifter's poetics: writing (*Schreiben*) and description (*Beschreiben*). As in the case of the passage on magnetism, *Schreiben* is neither primarily about subjective expression nor about objective representation. Instead, it is a mechanical activity taken here to an absurd and pathologized extreme. Rather than supporting a pedagogical agenda devoted to wholeness and fullness, it can only lead to an emptying-out and a breaking-up. Looking out through the window of the basement apartment, what the girl sees is meaningless, fragmented, and always the same: glimpses of hems and boots and feet whose insistent tread stamps out meaning. That is perhaps why the lush descriptions (*Beschreibungen*) in Stifter's *Bunte Steine* do not unequivocally succeed at bringing a world to life—underlying their rich rendition of the world of nature and men, there runs a tendency that is counter to animation, meaning, and life. The last words of the passage, "war nicht deutlich" could be read as a reference to this. "It was unclear," but also: something has moved beyond the reach of *Deutung*. It can no longer be pointed to, brought back into the order of signification, or interpreted.

# 8: Absence and Omnipresence: On the Significance of Waste in Stifter's *Der Nachsommer*

*Lars Rosenbaum*

SEARCHING FOR WASTE in Stifter's *Der Nachsommer* (Indian Summer, 1857), a novel in which everything glistens in cleanliness and orderliness, may seem like an odd endeavor.[1] The domestic spaces that the protagonist inhabits as a child and visits as an adult are veritable paragons of orderly households. These include the city apartment and subsequent suburban domicile of his parents in Vienna as well as the two country estates that help shape his later development: the Asperhof belonging to his paternal friend and mentor Risach and the Sternenhof, where his future wife Natalie and her mother Mathilde reside. Not a single speck of dust sullies these abodes, nothing lies purposeless within their confines; furniture is looked after with care, household items treated with deference. The same holds true for the extramural gardens and their harmoniously arranged grounds, particularly at Risach's Rosenhaus, where every fallen leaf is instantly removed, sandy pathways are regularly raked smooth, and trees receive a thorough bark-scrubbing every spring. Indeed, even in the otherwise detritus-generating realm of labor—here for instance the Asperhof's artisanal workshop—order and tidiness remain a top priority. Thus, given this initial sampling of hygienic examples drawn from the novel, what is the point of pursuing traces of waste therein?

But critical inquiry into the issue of waste requires detailed and extra scrupulous scrutiny; after all, the very things that one strives to interpret are often stripped of their identity through normative narrative processes of creating order.[2] As Michael Thompson, for instance, states in

---

1    This is a translation and updated modification of my previously published article: "Allgegenwärtig und nirgends zu sehen? Die Bedeutung von Abfällen in Adalbert Stifters *Nachsommer*," *Zeitschrift für deutsche Philologie* 133 (2014): 197–218.

2    For examples of such scholarly inquiry into the importance of waste, dirt, and pollution in Germanophone literature and film, see the following special journal issues: *Entsorgungsprobleme: Müll in der Literatur*, ed. David-Christopher

his seminal study *Rubbish Theory*: "We make things important by making other things unimportant. That which we discard, shun, abhor, wash our hands of, or flush away we are consigning to the rubbish category."[3] Commonplace objects such as used facial tissues or half-eaten apples, left lying on a table, are bothersome because they do not belong there. They are matter "in the wrong place"[4] and we tend not to "waste" so many words on them. If we then dispose of them in the trash bin, we deprive them of their visibility and thus no longer find them bothersome, indeed we can all the better ignore them. Nevertheless, they continue—secretly, yet verifiably—to exist. Based on such everyday examples, it seems clear that waste *can* be present without being visible or mentioned in conversation. Waste, in other words, is subject to a collective "conspiracy of blindness,"[5] even though we are always already aware of its existence.

Though waste may seem to be absent on the semantic level of the novel, this is not necessarily the case from a conceptual standpoint. Indeed, the crucial significance of waste in *Der Nachsommer* becomes—paradoxically—apparent insofar as all ambits of life in the text answer to the primacy of sanitary order, an order that is constituted and conserved through specific (here colloquial-gerundial) acts of "cleaning up," "putting away," "sorting out," and "getting rid of," all of which reflect a basic attitudinal aversion toward disorder and contamination. While it may seldom receive explicit mention, waste nevertheless exhibits an oblique yet oftentimes distinct presence through some of the aforesaid narrated actions. And when it thereby becomes circumvented, its absence can be attributed to a heightened attentiveness on the part of the novel's

---

Assmann, Norbert Otto Eke, and Eva Geulen, *Zeitschrift für deutsche Philologie* 133 (2014); and *Verschmutzung/Pollution*, ed. Sean Ireton, *Literatur für Leser* 37, no. 2 (2014). Altogether, these two volumes contain eighteen articles dealing with a wide range of authors, directors, eras, and methodological approaches. The former special issue contains of course the original version of this chapter. It also features an article on waste in Jeremias Gotthelf's *Die Wassernot im Emmental* (1837) by Samuel Frederick, which has since been reworked in his recent monograph as a chapter titled "Divine Debris." See Samuel Frederick, *The Redemption of Things: Collecting and Dispersal in German Realism and Modernism* (Ithaca, NY and London: Cornell University Press, 2021), 137–71.

3   Michael Thompson, *Rubbish Theory: The Creation and Destruction of Value*, 2nd ed. (London: Pluto Press, 2017 [1979]), 101.

4   Thompson, *Rubbish Theory*, 101. In his fundamental structural deliberations on waste, according to which pollution can be defined as "something that is out of place," Thompson expands on arguments raised by Mary Douglas in her classic 1966 study, *Purity and Danger: An Analysis of Concepts of Pollution and Taboo*, which has been reprinted several times since. For the latest edition, see Mary Douglas, *Purity and Danger: An Analysis of Concepts of Pollution and Taboo* (London: Routledge, 2002).

5   Thompson, *Rubbish Theory*, 20 and passim.

202 ◆ LARS ROSENBAUM

characters toward refuse and its byproducts. As I will demonstrate in this chapter, *Der Nachsommer* outlines criteria according to which "things" become evaluated as wastage, whether in households (section I), gardens (section II), or the Asperhof workshop (section III). The novel further presents the human agents responsible for the removal of all such accrued remnants, scraps, and other impurities, along with their requisite skills in a preoccupation that can best be described as "waste management."[6] As an added interpretive consequence, my focus on *waste* will yield an outcome of *worth*, especially in view of the artisanal and indeed artistic objects that undergo transformation in the Asperhof workshop (section IV). Ultimately, all such interrogative ventures into the category of waste and its associated processes help elucidate Stifter's underlying conception, and resultant execution, of realism (section V).

# I.

In the novel's brightly polished domestic spaces one finds hardly any indication of waste or impurity. Indeed, such spaces consist of clearly structured interiors that are not only isolated from the outside world[7] but also remain impervious to the infiltration of waste materials or any other form of commingled contamination.[8] These hermetic household conditions already become apparent at the beginning of the novel, where the

6    I borrow this term from Erica Weitzman, whose reading of rubbish, decay, and their aesthetic revaluation in *Der Nachsommer* shares certain commonalities with my own. See Erica Weitzman, *At the Limit of the Obscene: German Realism and the Disgrace of Matter* (Evanston, IL: Northwestern University Press, 2021), 25–48.

7    For an analysis of spatiality in general and, more concretely, of the domestic rooms depicted in the novel across multiple households, see Herbert Seidler, "Gestaltung und Sinn des Raumes in Stifters *Nachsommer*," in *Adalbert Stifter: Studien und Interpretationen; Gedenkschrift zum 100. Todestage*, ed. Lothar Stiehm (Heidelberg: Stiehm, 1968), 203–26. Compare also Saskia Haag, *Auf wandelbarem Grund: Haus und Literatur im 19. Jahrhundert* (Freiburg im Breisgau: Rombach, 2012), esp. 146–69.

8    On the importance of purity and the diverse contaminants, intermixtures, and remainders that are filtrated out of the novel, see the following articles: Barbara Thums, "Adalbert Stifters *Der Nachsommer*: Reste-lose Poetik des Reinen?," in *Was übrig bleibt: Von Resten, Residuen und Relikten*, ed. Barbara Thums and Annette Werberger (Berlin: trafo Wissenschaftverlag, 2009), 79–97; Sabina Becker, "Nachsommerliche Sublimationsrituale: Inszenierte Ordnung in Adalbert Stifters *Nachsommer*," in *Ordnung, Raum, Ritual: Adalbert Stifters artifizieller Realismus*, ed. Sabina Becker and Katharine Grätz (Heidelberg: Universitätsverlag Winter, 2007), 315–38; and Cornelia Zumbusch, "'rein und anfangsfähig'" Stifters Reinigungsarbeiter (*Narrenburg* und *Die Mappe meines Urgroßvaters*)," *Zeitschrift für Kulturwissenschaften* 1 (2013): 53–64.

small-scale apartment in which Heinrich spends his youth together with his parents and sister is described:

> Überhaupt durfte bei dem Vater kein Zimmer die Spuren des unmittelbaren Gebrauches zeigen, sondern mußte immer aufgeräumt sein, als wäre es ein Prunkzimmer. Es sollte dafür aber aussprechen, zu was es besonders bestimmt sei. Die gemischten Zimmer, wie er sich ausdrückte, die mehreres zugleich sein können, Schlafzimmer, Spielzimmer und dergleichen, konnte er nicht leiden. Jedes Ding und jeder Mensch, pflegte er zu sagen, könne nur eines sein, dieses aber muß er ganz sein. Dieser Zug strenger Genauigkeit prägte sich uns ein, und ließ uns auf die Befehle der Eltern achten, wenn wir sie auch nicht verstanden. So zum Beispiele durften nicht einmal wir Kinder das Schlafzimmer der Eltern betreten. Eine alte Magd war mit Ordnung und Aufräumung desselben betraut. (*HKG* 4,1:11)

> [For Father, every room always had to be in immaculate order, showing no traces of its immediate use, as if it were a state reception hall. Its function should also be obvious. He couldn't stand "mixed rooms" as he called them—rooms that were used for several things, such as a combination bedroom-playroom or the like. He used to say: everything and every man can be only one thing, but he must be that with all his heart and soul. We were quite impressed by this quality of strict preciseness and obeyed our parents' instructions even if we didn't understand them. For example, we children were not even allowed to enter our parents' bedroom. An elderly maid took care of cleaning and tidying up there. (*IS*, 11; translation modified)][9]

Stately order prevails throughout the apartment; only the above references to cleanliness and tidiness lead one to the conclusion that things (at least occasionally) might need to be cleaned and tidied up in the first place. This logic may seem tautological, but it points to the deeper "conspiracy of blindness" within the novel; that is, it reveals the otherwise invisible existence of waste and disorder and further helps disclose their attendant mechanisms. As the above passage implies, tidiness is predicated on things not being in their proper place. The clearly delineated order of things,[10] as enforced by the father's "Zug strenger Genauigkeit" or

---

9    Translator's note: As I do here, I will often modify Wendell Frye's otherwise admirable translation of *Der Nachsommer* but will not continue to make note of this practice, except in glaring instances (SI).

10    On the "order of things" and the importance of signs/semiotics in *Der Nachsommer*, see, for instance, Axel Fliethmann, *Stellenlektüre Stifter-Foucault* (Tübingen: Niemeyer, 2001); Christian Begemann, *Die Welt der Zeichen:*

"quality of strict preciseness," thus strives for holism over fragmentation with respect to the material allocation of the household. The fastidious adherence to this order becomes apparent in his personal library, each volume of which occupies its fixed yet concealed place behind the glass panes and green silk curtains of the specially constructed book cabinets which, in turn, adorn the walls of a specially kept room (see *HKG* 4,1:10; *IS*, 10). When finished with a given book, the father returns it forthwith to its original location such that no sign remains of its temporary use or, for that matter, of any lingering human presence. Thus, even objects that are properly situated yet bear signs of previous use—here, for example, the activity if not utility of reading—also fall under the novel's imperative of tidiness and orderliness.

Nevertheless, since a perused book can be neatly snapped shut and tidily returned to its rightful place, it does not outright belong to the category of waste. This category is, rather, reserved for things that either diverge from the novel's envisaged *ordo*—namely, its titular late-summerly atmosphere of tranquility—or that represent borderline cases, fragments, and amalgams beyond clear categorization. These so-called *Undinge* (non-things)[11] are also subsumed under the imperative of tidiness, however they cannot be reintegrated into the household order as easily as a book. Due to their domestic incompatibility, they must first be deprived of their identity, which effectively means that they become eliminated through (not-so-random!) acts of neatness.

Although household refuse is never overtly mentioned in *Der Nachsommer*, one would assume it to appear in at least some narrative form; after all, we are dealing with a "realistic" novel that does not simply suspend biological and physical laws. Why is this the case? And can the existence of such refuse perhaps be corroborated in the end? Recall here the "elderly maid" who "took care of cleaning and tidying up" the parents' bedroom. Given her day-to-day duties, she would undoubtedly be well informed about the private waste byproducts generated by the family that employs her. Indeed, if *she* rather than Heinrich (or any other Drendorf family member) were the narrator, she would surely be able to report on used bedsheets, sweat-stained clothes, and even more unpleasant things. As Thompson notes, "no one is a hero in the eyes of their servant," whereby he places emphasis on the obvious sociological implications of waste: "An understanding of rubbish is essential if we are to

---

*Stifter-Lektüren* (Stuttgart: J. B. Metzler, 1995); and Hans Joachim Piechotta, *Aletorische Ordnung: Untersuchungen zu extremen literarischen Positionen in den Erzählungen und dem Roman "Witiko" von Adalbert Stifter* (Giessen: W. Schmitz Verlag, 1981).

11 See in this regard Vilém Flusser, *Dinge und Undinge: Phänomenologische Skizzen* (Munich Hanser, 1993).

uncover the mechanics of this sliding scale that relates private and public, informality and formality, expediency and principle. Without this key, we must inevitably focus either on the valet or on the hero and never on the relation between them."[12]

Any inquest into waste in *Der Nachsommer* cannot ignore the social hierarchy that reigns in the Drendorf home, revealing the extent to which its family members "conspire *not* to see the soiled linen and the soggy handkerchiefs,"[13] while their servants dutifully remove all vestiges of domestic disorder behind, so to speak, closed doors. And given that the first-person narrator Heinrich has taken over the paternal order as a matter of course, not once questioning it, even in retrospect as a fully matured adult, *his* narration of events never manages to penetrate these proverbial closed doors. Consequently, waste goes unmentioned in the text and the procedures for its removal are alluded to at best in abstract fashion—indeed, through the recurring use of nouns containing abstract grammatical *-ung* suffixes, particularly the key words *Ordnung* and *Aufräumung*. Moreover, everyday objects related to these very concepts of orderliness and tidiness—for instance brooms and rubbish bins, cleaning rags and soapsuds—likewise elude reference, at least here in the context of the Drendorf household.

In view of the "social implications" of waste, Heinrich's mother assumes an intriguing and critical role. As evidenced in the following passage, she exercises control over (almost) all domestic activities in their new and much larger suburban home:

> Die Mutter, welche über die Erwerbung des Vorstadthauses außerordentlich erfreut war, widmete sich mit gesteigerter Thätigkeit dem Hauswesen. Alle Samstage prangte das Linnen "weiß wie Kirschblüthe" auf dem Aufhängeplaze im Garten, und Zimmer für Zimmer mußte unter ihrer Aufsicht gereiniget werden, außer denen, in welchen die Kostbarkeiten des Vaters waren, deren Abstäubung und Reinigung immer unter seinen Augen vor sich gehen mußte. ... Sie bekam einen Ruf in der Umgebung, daß Nachbarinnen kamen, und von ihr Dienstboten verlangten, die in unserem Hause gelernt hätten. (*HKG* 4,1:15–16)

> [Mother, who was ecstatic about the new house in the suburbs, devoted herself even more enthusiastically to housekeeping. Every Saturday our linen gleamed "white as cherry blossoms" on the clotheslines in the yard and every room had to be cleaned under her supervision save for the rooms where Father's treasures were kept. These could be cleaned and dusted only under his personal

---

12 Thompson, *Rubbish Theory*, 102–3.
13 Thompson, *Rubbish Theory*, 102 (my emphasis).

supervision. ... Mother's reputation as an excellent housekeeper grew; servants who had been trained in our home were in great demand among the ladies in the neighborhood. (*IS*, 13)]

The mother is here stylized as the *keeper* of cleanliness and order;[14] she does not carry out the chores herself but rather coordinates and supervises these labors. The text, accordingly, foregoes any narration concerning how the linen became soiled or by what precise procedures it was then washed; all that matters is the result, namely "cherry-blossom white" laundry gleaming on the clothesline for all to see.[15] Such a sight, a veritable paragon of purity, serves as a kind of job advertisement whose message seems effective enough given the piqued public interest in the Drendorf's domestic help.[16] This passage proves especially illuminating for readers concerned with the issue of waste, the existence of which can clearly be deduced on the narrative level of the novel. Dirt particles may well go unmentioned in its pages, but they must have been removed perforce in the laundering process, otherwise there wouldn't be so much emphasis placed on the whitened result. Similarly, given the meticulous "Abstäubung" of the father's unnamed treasures, dust constitutes yet another invisible yet deducible waste product that permeates the subtext of the novel.

While Heinrich's parental household is managed in exemplary fashion, an even more vigilant adherence to cleanliness and orderliness holds sway in Risach's Rosenhaus. When Heinrich, after a long walking tour through the Upper Austrian countryside, first sets foot into this unique domicile that will come to play an increasingly important role in

14 This "idealized" yet practically identity-deprived image of an acquiescent woman concerned with, if not consumed by, household order qua purity correlates with other female figures in the novel, for instance Mathilde and Risach's deceased mother, about whom he reminisces in the following fashion: "Ich hatte mich daran gewöhnt, die Mutter als das Bild der größten häuslichen Reinheit zu betrachten als das Bild des Duldens der Sanftmuth des Ordnens und des Bestehens" (*HKG* 4,3:161; I had gotten used to regarding my mother as the epitome of cleanliness in housekeeping, as the very image of patience, gentleness, order, and steadfastness, *IS*, 410).

15 For further background on the significance of white laundry in works by Stifter and Gottfried Keller, see Elsbeth Dangel-Pelloquin, "Weiße Wäsche: Zur Synthese von Reinheit und Erotik bei Keller und Stifter," in *Die Dinge und die Zeichen: Dimensionen des Realistischen in der Erzählliteratur des 19. Jahrhunderts*, ed. Sabine Schneider and Barbara Hunfeld (Würzburg: Königshausen & Neumann, 2008), 143–56.

16 Interestingly, laundry detergent commercials always make a point of showing the before-and-after difference between stubborn dirtiness and wondrous spotlessness. In *Der Nachsommer*, however, this original condition of grime is tellingly dismissed.

his personal and social development, Risach makes two rather unusual requests: (1) that his guest wear specially provided "felt slippers" over his boots so as not to besmirch the ammonite-marble floors of the entrance hall; and (2) that he then clean his original footwear on a "straw mat" by means of a "shoe brush." These conscientious and quasi-ceremonial measures ensure that no outside substances find their way into the interior of the home and thereby harm the precious (read: pristine) floors, furniture, and other household accessories. Waste is thus averted *a priori* in the Rosenhaus. Heinrich, accustomed to similar codes of conduct from his childhood, not only readily complies with the above but remains "convinced ... of the necessity" (*IS*, 34)—"von der Nothwendigkeit überzeugt" (*HKG* 4,1:52)—of such sanitary sanctions.

Nevertheless, his sudden intrusion seems to threaten the order of the home,[17] for which reason Risach first conducts him into a sitting room, leaving him there alone for an interval. This room resembles a kind of airlock, one in which Heinrich can gradually acclimate to the special atmosphere of the Rosenhaus. Compare the following passage, the many details of which underscore a more naturally aerated than artificially airtight chamber:

> Als ich eine Weile gesessen war, bemächtigte sich meiner eine seltsame Empfindung, welche ich mir Anfangs nicht zu erklären vermochte. Es war mir nehmlich, als size ich nicht in einem Zimmer, sondern im Freien und zwar in einem stillen Walde. ... Ich spürte eine reine freie Luft mich umgeben. Die Ursache davon war, daß die Fenster des Zimmers in ihren oberen Theilen offen waren. Diese oberen Theile konnten nicht nach Innen geöffnet werden, wie das gewöhnlich der Fall ist, sondern waren nur zu verschieben, und zwar so, daß einmal Glas in dem Rahmen vorgeschoben werden konnte, ein anderes Mal ein zarter Flor von weißgrauer Seide. Da ich in dem Zimmer saß, war das Letztere der Fall. Die Luft konnte frei herein strömen, Fliegen und Staub waren aber ausgeschlossen. (*HKG* 4,1:55)

> [After I had sat for a while, a strange sensation came over me which at first I wasn't able to explain. It seemed to me that I wasn't sitting in a room at all, but outdoors in a quiet patch of woods. ... I felt pure fresh air around me. The reason was that the upper parts of the windows were open. These couldn't be opened inward, as is

---

17 This issue of intrusion, which seems especially flagrant here during Heinrich's initial visit to the Rosenhaus, recurs throughout the novel. Given his incessant coming and going within this domestic demesne, Heinrich must repeatedly adjust to the hygienic regime imposed by Risach. Indeed, such ongoing adjustments remain a crucial component of his *Bildung* or education.

usually the case; rather, they could only be slid in or out and were so arranged that at one time they could put in glass, at another, a light gauze of light gray silk. The latter was the case at the time I was sitting in the room. The air could come in freely, but all the flies and dust were kept out. (*IS*, 35)]

The "pure fresh air" that Heinrich experiences in the Rosenhaus is the result of a filtration technology that effectuates an unadulterated flow of natural ventilation such that the integrity of the household order remains uncompromised by any admixture of foreign substances. The same holds true for the birdsong that fills the room, which creates the effect of a secluded space devoid of domiciliary din (see *HKG* 4,1:55–56; *IS*, 36). This absence of waste, disorder, and human hubbub superimposes itself upon reality insofar as all remnants of individuality and domestic activity are erased.

It is interesting to note, especially given his father's fastidiousness regarding his personal library, that Heinrich commits a major faux pas while waiting in the sitting room: he casually places a book, in which he had previously been browsing, on a chair when summoned to dinner by his host. Risach, for his part, immediately returns it to the shelf "damit das Zimmer die ihm zugehörige Gestalt behalte" (*HKG* 4,1:58; so that the room is kept in its proper organization, *IS*, 37). This seemingly innocuous scene illustrates Risach's deep-seated mentality of order, which posits any out-of-place object as a disturbing factor in need of rectification or, here more precisely, relocation. His corrective action of restoring the book to its assigned place sends a message to his guests that they are obliged to conduct themselves according to the "Sitte" (*HKG* 4,1:58) or "custom" (*IS*, 37) of the house. Since Heinrich henceforth accepts and indeed affirms this customary practice, promising not to "cause any disorder" (*IS*, 78; "keine Unordnung machen" [*HKG* 4,1:130]), he can be accommodated by Risach as a regular Rosenhaus visitor and eventual lodger.[18]

Under Risach's guidance, Heinrich becomes familiar with a household that is even more comprehensively structured and functionally arranged than that of his parents. And, of course, the absence of waste (at least on the surface) and the dearth of disorder are key characteristics

18   It should be noted that the prevailing order of the Rosenhaus does not deny its residents ample freedoms, except perhaps in the case of its (largely unseen) service staff. Compare for instance Heinrich's following remark, one of many to this effect: "In diesem Hause war jeder unabhängig, und konnte seinem Ziele zustreben. Nur durch die gemeinsame Hausordnung war man gewissermaßen zu einem Bande verbunden" (*HKG* 4,1:218; In this house everyone was independent and could pursue his own interests. We were only bound somewhat by the general house rules, *IS*, 127).

of both domains. In the case of the much larger Rosenhaus, some examples of the predominant orderliness include the following rooms and their respective furnishings, fixtures, and other appurtenances. In what is supposedly Risach's study, or more literally workroom (*Arbeitszimmer*), "waren doch keine unmittelbaren Spuren von Arbeit sichtbar. Alles schien in den Laden verschlossen oder auf seinen Plaz gestellt zu sein" (*HKG* 4,1:90; there were no visible signs of the room having been used. Everything seemed to be kept in drawers or was in its proper place, *IS*, 55). The same applies to other apparent workspaces including a room equipped for scientific experiments, another special room in which Risach stores his systematically ordered botanical collection in apothecary cabinets, and the so-called "bookroom" (*Bücherzimmer*) whose holdings are catalogued in archival-like fashion. Curiously, the separate reading chamber (*Lesegemach*) does not contain any books—for that is evidently the function of the bookroom—but nor does anything within its confines evoke "den Zweck des Lesens" (*HKG* 4,1:93; the purpose ... of reading, *IS*, 57). Heinrich is further struck by the utter lack of clutter in either of these librarial spaces, which are devoid of such typical furniture and paraphernalia as ladders, tables, seats, benches, books, papers, writing materials, or even cleaning utensils. As a result, he perceives in them the systematic "Geist der Ordnung und Reinheit" (*HKG* 4,1:222; spirit of order and purity, *IS*, 129). Furthermore, whereas he finds most other libraries comparable to churches that conduct their services with junk (*Trödel*), he regards Risach's well-ordered bookroom as a "Tempel" (*HKG* 4,1:221; temple, *IS*, 129) in which books are safeguarded from their impending economic depreciation—and perhaps ensuing cultural deterioration.

Risach further leads Heinrich into the private chambers of the Rosenhaus, all of which come across as sterile spaces bereft of personal touches or even traces. Risach's own separated bedroom and "dressing room" (*Kleiderzimmer*) are arranged according to pure "Zweckmäßigkeit" (*HKG* 4,1:91; utility, *IS*, 56); neither evinces any discernible qualities of what should ordinarily be spheres of privacy if not intimacy. Articles of clothing are conspicuously absent, and the lavatories seem perfunctory at best. Even the guest rooms, as occupied by Natalie and Mathilde and viewed by Heinrich later in the novel, are superlatively laid out "in der musterhaftesten Ordnung" (*HKG* 4,1:171; in the most exemplary order, *IS*, 101). More notably, Mathilde's so-called "Rosenzimmerchen" or "little rose room," which Risach considers the most sacrosanct of all and refuses to defile by uttering a humanly profane word within its walls, bears absolutely no signs of use: "*Kein* Merkmal in dem Gemache zeigte an, daß es bewohnt sei. *Kein* Geräthe war verrückt, an dem Teppiche zeigte sich *keine* Falte, und an den Fenstervorhängen *keine* Verknitterung" (*HKG* 4,1:173; There was *no* sign that the room was lived in. *No* piece of furniture was out of place; there *wasn't* a wrinkle on the carpet *nor* a crease in the draperies, *IS*, 102). Here Stifter employs a narrative strategy of negation (all the above emphases are mine), one that creates the impression, if not illusion, that these vacant, immaculate rooms are governed by a quiescent, immutable, and timeless order. Aside from the physical presence of its residents and guests, there is no indication that the Rosenhaus is in fact occupied: its rooms lack any traces of privacy or inhabitancy and the narration itself is almost equally lacking in depictions of the kind of cleaning activity that logically must have transpired prior to Heinrich's recurrent entrances into these well-ordered spaces. As he remarks in one such case, here regarding his own allocated sleeping quarters: "Alles *war* gefegt und gereinigt [worden]" (*HKG* 4,3:115; Everything *had been* swept and cleaned, *IS*, 385). As my emphases here intend to show, the removal of household waste remains an activity that always refers to an unnarrated, often pluperfect, past.

Circumstantial evidence of cleaning can be discerned at certain other junctures in the novel. For instance, the floor mat on which Risach and his guest brush their shoes must surely be scrubbed of grime every now and then, the dust-collecting and bug-repelling window screens in the sitting room as well. The same can be said of clothes in need of washing, washtubs in need of scouring, books and furniture in need of dusting, etc. This sample list of reader-inferred rather authorially narrated acts of cleaning is not meant to dispute the hygienic regime of the Rosenhaus but rather to point out the complex household and strict hierarchical processes at work within it. And the reader does eventually gain some insight into these workings, for instance in some of the following character constellations and managerial configurations. When visiting the Asperhof, Mathilde orchestrates many of the same housekeeping procedures that she carries out at her own estate of the Sternenhof. She thus oversees "den weiblichen Antheil des Hauswesens" (*HKG* 4,1:306; the feminine part of the household, *IS*, 176) and often takes part in the actual work herself (see for example *HKG* 4,1:256; *IS*, 148). Subordinate to her (and of course Risach) is the caretaker, who makes sure that within the realm of the Rosenhaus "keine Verwirrung … zu sehr sichtbar ist" (*HKG* 4,2:191; no disarray … will be overly apparent, *IS*, 280). To this end, he coordinates a whole team of service personnel who are in turn responsible for taking care of all the "dirty work," but in the most discrete fashion possible since Risach tends to be bothered by the close presence of domestic attendants. Throughout his narration, Heinrich also remains distant from the maids and servants, according little attention to their activities and duties. Granted, during his initial visit he is given a tour through the various operational facilities such as the pantry, bakery, laundry room, and root cellar and he even witnesses staff members at work there, but he never seems truly cognizant of the precise nature of their labor. As a result, any potential waste that might be generated in such critically functional recesses of the Rosenhaus goes almost entirely ignored.

In conspicuous contrast to the orderliness of the Rosenhaus rooms discussed up to this point, the sleeping chambers of the attendants lie in complete disorder. In Heinrich's simple way of stating matters: "es lagen Dinge herum" (*HKG* 4,1:171; things were lying around, *IS*, 101). Thus, while the domestic employees are forced to deal with the refuse produced by their bourgeois lord and his privileged guests, their own standards of hygiene lag far behind. This visible disparity, which legitimizes the hierarchy of the Rosenhaus, assures Heinrich's own uncritical stance with respect to the deeper social mechanisms that operate behind the regnant Asperhof order and its waste-denying ways. Just as the everyday problems of the servants go unnoticed, social and political upheavals—indeed, conflicts of any kind—remain blatantly absent from Heinrich's narrative. These social-realistic aspects belong to the category of waste; their narrative potential is (practically) unexploited in the novel.

# II.

Like its interior rooms, the Rosenhaus garden also appears in a perfect state; there is no organic waste to be seen and all the plants look luxuriant and healthy. During his initial visit, as Heinrich is admiring the roses that not only envelop the trellis attached to the house exterior but practically dominate the entire garden, he notices not a single "unvollkommene Blume kein dürrer Zweig kein unregelmäßiges Blatt" (*HKG* 4,1:145; imperfect flower, not one dead twig, not even an irregular leaf, *IS*, 86). As he reflects on the colorfulness of this profuse display:

> Auch das Grün der Blätter fiel mir auf. Es war sehr rein gehalten, und kein bei Rosen öfter als bei andern Pflanzen vokommender Übelstand der grünen Blätter und keine der häufigen Krankheiten kam mir zu Gesichte. Kein verdorrtes oder durch Raupen zerfressenes oder durch ihr Spinnen verkrümmtes Blatt war zu erblicken. Selbst das bei Rosen so gerne sich einnistende Ungeziefer fehlte. (*HKG* 4,1:48).

> [I also noticed the green of the leaves. It was kept very nice, and none of the leaf diseases that occur more frequently with roses or any of the more common plant ailments were visible. You couldn't see a dead leaf or one that had been eaten by caterpillars or bent by their spinning. Even the bugs that usually make their nests in roses were missing. (*IS*, 31)]

When Heinrich assures his host that he has never seen such a living perfection of florae, the latter enlightens him about the diverse "Anstalten" (*HKG* 4,1:145) or "set-ups" (*IS*, 86) necessary for such successful cultivation of his roses. When planting them, for instance, one must seek out a location with southern exposure and mix that sun-warmed soil with the compost of long-perished rosebushes, thereby creating optimal conditions for growth. And since the entire household has developed a profound aesthetic appreciation for the roses as well as an acute awareness of their wellbeing,[19] any visible anomalies are dealt with right away. Compare for instance the following measures, which seem more surgical than horticultural: "Man reinigt die Rinde, pflegt sie, verbindet ihre Wunden, knüpft die Zweige an, und schneidet das Untaugliche weg" (*HKG* 4,1:146; We clean the bark, take care of it, bind up any wounds, tie up the twigs, and cut off the unsuitable parts, *IS*, 87). Severely ailing plants are removed, replanted in a special garden dubbed "das Rosenhospital" (*HKG* 4,1:146; the rose hospital, *IS*, 87), and replaced by healthy specimens from the nursery; dying plants are disposed of without delay. The perfect condition of the roses is thus the result of elaborate efforts on the part of Risach and his experienced staff. The intricacies of their labors prove especially instructive—indeed organically productive—when it comes to the issue of waste. Through the various cultivation procedures outlined above, ranging from cleaning to pruning, from removal to disposal, an array of accrued plant material can be reprocessed and reused. In a word: recycled. As Risach summarizes this painstaking procedure:

> Da wir nicht wissen, welches denn der lezte Grund des Gedeihens lebendiger Wesen überhaupt ist, so schloß ich, daß den Rosen am meisten gut thun müsse, was von Rosen kömmt. Wir ließen daher seit jeher alle Rosenabfälle sammeln, besonders die Blätter und selbst die Zweige der wilden Rosen, welche sich in der ganzen Gegend befinden. Diese Abfälle werden zu Hügeln in einem abgelegenen Theile unseres Gartens zusammengethan, den Einflüssen von Luft und Regen ausgesezt, und so bereitet sich die Rosenerde. Wenn in einem Hügel sich keine Spur mehr von Pflanzenthum zeigt, und nichts als milde Erde vor die Augen tritt, so wird diese den Rosen gegeben. (*HKG* 4,1:145)

19 During the rose-blooming season, the house members gather daily to celebrate this event in near ritualistic fashion. Indeed, people from around the region are drawn to the spectacle. Mathilde, however, displays the most observance if not reverence—compare Heinrich's earlier remark regarding the so-called "Rosendienst" (*HKG* 4,1:177; rose homage, *IS*, 104) that epitomizes Risach's estate— toward the roses during their period of blossoming. See especially the paragraph detailing such devotion in *HKG* 4,1:268; *IS*, 155.

[Since we don't know what is actually the cause of growth in living things, I concluded that what would do roses the most good are things that come from roses. Therefore, we had all the dead parts of roses collected, especially the petals and even twigs of wild roses found in this region. These were put into mulch mounds in out of the way places in the garden, exposed to the influence of wind and rain, and in this way our 'rose earth' was developed. When there was no longer any sign of a plant and our eyes could see nothing more than a fine soil in the mound, then it was used for the roses. (*IS*, 86–87)]

Several important points emerge from this passage. First, the assorted rose remnants are secreted to a place where they remain unseen and do not compromise the aesthetic integrity of the garden, resulting in a spatial hierarchy between center and periphery. In this vein, Risach draws Heinrich's attention to the former (focal) rather than to the latter (marginal) space, hinting at the existence of the compost pile but not actually showing it to his guest. Despite this diversionary tactic, Risach fully recognizes the intrinsic value of such moldered green waste and its biochemically modified, nutrient-rich humus, which is transferred to the center of the garden, fostering new crops of roses and thereby participating in the cycle of growth and decay. These narrated organic processes undermine the common definition of waste as something that possesses only privative or negative value and thus proves inadequate—in Thompson's words "hopelessly inadequate"[20]—in regulating our everyday attitude toward the environment. Such a definition only obscures the potential for objects deemed as waste to be revalued, whether through internal or external processes. Again, Risach is aware of this potential and capitalizes on it with respect to his recycled roses, yet he goes to great lengths to ensure that his garden idyll is not marred by noticeable signs of rosebush waste. Things that are perceived as aesthetically worthless or even dismissed as a nuisance and are consequently sorted out as waste can nevertheless possess or gain economic value in covert fashion. After a certain lapse of time, they can even be reinvested in the scenic design of the garden.

Like the roses, all the other growth in Risach's garden—which is a mixture of an ornamental and kitchen garden—finds itself in a flawless state. The fruit trees, for instance, abound with lush foliage, the leaves of which are larger and darker than normal, and no signs of caterpillar damage are anywhere to be seen (see *HKG* 4,1:62–63; *IS*, 40). Moreover, their bark is completely free of moss and, in the case of the cherry trees, looks "fast so fein wie graue Seide" (*HKG* 4,1:150; almost as fine as gray silk, *IS*, 89). All this is the result of extensive maintenance and care

---

20 Thompson, *Rubbish Theory*, 124.

on the part of Risach's workers, who scrub the tree trunks and lower boughs with soapy water every spring, thereby removing any potentially harmful foreign matter. The fact that they also trim the trees of all dead and excess branches further attests to the constant generation of waste throughout the Rosenhaus garden. Though such waste accumulates, so to speak, between the lines of the narrative, it seems to vanish amidst its stylized-hygienicized rhetoric.[21] At best, it is named only upon its removal, thereby violating only minimally the aesthetics of order upheld in the novel.

And yet Rosenhaus garden waste does not just accumulate for the sake of being forever eliminated. Beyond its somewhat muted presence in the case of the rosebushes and the fruit trees, it reappears in more manifest fashion elsewhere in the novel. One such example concerns the discarded remnants of cabbage and other crops that Risach collects and stores in the cellar; that is, in a realm of the household that, significantly, remains hidden from casual view. During the winter months, these scraps are then brought out to the fields "*beyond*" (*außerhalb*) the garden for the wild rabbits to consume, thereby deterring them from nibbling on the young plant shoots closer to the Rosenhaus (see *HKG* 4,1:167; *IS*, 99; my emphasis). The creative (re)utilization of garden waste in the above examples reflects the efficient management of the Asperhof and suggests one of the reasons for its greater economic profitability relative to the neighboring farmsteads.

As demonstrated earlier in the context of the Drendorf households, both urban and suburban, hierarchical structures play an important role. Here, in the established order of the Asperhof, Risach presides over all aspects related to its economic management. And though he presides over the labor carried out in both garden and field, he employs a horticulturalist to take care of practical matters, who in turn coordinates a small workforce to perform the necessary manual tasks. Thus, all are ultimately involved in the outdoor waste control that contributes to the productivity of the estate. Indeed, Risach fancies himself as a kind of *primus inter pares*, but this proves only partially true. In a key scene, one in which he and Heinrich survey the garden from an elevated vantage point, he remarks that "ich hier unter meinen Arbeitern bin" (*HKG* 4,1:72; here I am among my workers, *IS*, 46). Given that Heinrich just pointed out the "groß[e] Entfernung" (*HKG* 4,1:72; great distance, *IS*, 45) separating them from the farmhands toiling below and making it difficult to discern the precise nature of their labors, Risach's understanding of workplace solidarity seems problematic. Indeed, a later remark to Heinrich reinforces the hierarchy between landowner and manual laborer: "der, welcher wiederholt den Anordnungen nicht nachkömmt, [wird] des

---

21   See here Thums, "Adalbert Stifters *Der Nachsommer*," 83.

Dienstes entlassen" (*HKG* 4,1:125; whoever repeatedly fails to follow my directions is discharged of his service, *IS*, 75). On the other hand, at a subsequent point in the novel, a sense of worker-employer concord seems to carry the day: "Hierzu kam noch eine gewisse Fröhlichkeit und Heiterkeit der untergeordneten Leute, die bei jeder sachgemäßen Führung eines Geschäftes, bei dem sie betheiligt sind, und bei einer wenn auch strengen doch stets freundlichen Behandlung nicht ausbleibt" (*HKG* 4,1:281; In addition to this the laborers were happy and cheerful, something never lacking when any work is properly directed and they are treated strictly but kindly, *IS*, 162).[22]

As Risach further explains to Heinrich, he effectively employs an additional team of "Arbeiter" (workers), namely the semi-domesticated songbirds that have been enticed to inhabit his garden and protect it from rapacious caterpillars and other harmful insects. In fact, their usefulness in this regard exceeds that of any other possible agent or deterrent: "Diese sind es, welche die Bäume Gesträuche die kleinen Pflanzen und natürlich auch die Rosen weit besser reinigen, als es Menschenhände oder was immer für Mittel zu bewerkstelligen im Stande wären" (*HKG* 4,1:152; It's they who cleanse the trees, bushes, little plants, and, naturally, the roses too, far better than human hands can, or whatever other means might be applied, *IS*, 90). This utter absence of caterpillar damage is the result of an organized enterprise that is structured according to flexible yet efficient job-sharing principles.[23] For although the birds themselves may inflict a degree of damage by consuming some of the fruit crop, such damage remains negligible in relation to the overall profit. Similarly, according to Risach's estimation, the extra trouble ("Mühe") and not inconsiderable costs ("Kosten") that come from caring for the birds do not outweigh the benefits afforded by their domestication and pest-eliminating implementation. His more precise calculations run as follows:

---

22  In this vein, the novel has been read by several scholars as a social-conservative utopia. Compare for instance, in chronological order, the following studies: Walther Killy, *Wirklichkeit und Kunstcharakter: Neun Romane des 19. Jahrhunderts* (Munich: Beck, 1963), esp. 83–103; Horst Albert Glaser, *Die Restauration des Schönen: Stifters "Nachsommer"* (Stuttgart: J. B. Metzler, 1965); Dieter Borchmeyer, "Stifters *Nachsommer*: Eine restaurative Utopie?," *Poetica* 12 (1980): 59–82; Peter Uwe Hohendahl, "Die gebildete Gemeinschaft: Stifters *Nachsommer* als Utopie der ästhetischen Erziehung," in *Utopieforschung: Interdisziplinäre Studien zur neuzeitlichen Utopie*, vol. 3, ed. Wilhelm Voßkamp, (Stuttgart: J. B. Metzler, 1982), 333–56; and Robert Leucht, "Ordnung, Bildung, Kunsthandwerk: Die Pluralität utopischer Modelle in Adalbert Stifters *Der Nachsommer*," in *Figuren der Übertragung: Adalbert Stifter und das Wissen seiner Zeit*, ed. Michael Gamper and Karl Wagner (Zurich: Chronos, 2009), 289–306.

23  See here Ansgar Mohnkern, "Ordnung, Wachstum, Zins: Zu Stifters *Nachsommer*," *Weimarer Beiträge* 59, no. 3 (2013): 416–30; here 420.

"allein wenn ich die edlen Früchte eines einzigen Pflaumenbaumes, welchen mir die Raupen der Vögel wegen nicht abgefressen haben, verkaufe, so deckt der Kaufschilling die Nahrungskosten der Sänger ganz und gar" (*HKG* 4,1:169; when I sell the fine fruit of a single plum tree that hasn't been ravaged by caterpillars because of the birds, then the proceeds completely cover all the costs of their food, *IS*, 100). Though local growers remain skeptical of Risach's financial claims let alone his unorthodox gardening practices, his correspondence with business partners confirms that his cost-benefit analyses of waste and pest management are both economically and ecologically sound.

Nevertheless, there is a flip side to this process, one that involves an anthropocentric intervention that belies Risach's otherwise environmentally friendly ethos. In his incessant explanations to Heinrich about the workings of his estate, he admits to applying violent tactics such as outright killing a particular species—the *Rotschwanz* or redstart—that preys on useful honeybees rather than on the caterpillars that despoil his precious rosebushes. (Apiculture is, after all, a crucial component of Risach's sustainable estate.) These birds must therefore be dealt with, in Risach's words, "ohne Gnade mit der Windbüchse zu tödten" (*HKG* 4,1:170; by killing them without mercy with the air rifle, *IS*, 100). That is, unlike the troublemaking sparrows that plague other spheres of his agronomic endeavors, nuisances that Risach merely scares away with percussive shots from the air rifle, he feels compelled to outright gun down the redstarts. The "order" of the Rosenhaus thus seems to devolve into a kind of military order, whereby disruptive elements are summarily eliminated.[24] The waste-relevant question of what then happens with the carcasses of these slaughtered creatures is unfortunately not addressed.

# III.

After Heinrich's tour of the house and garden, he is conducted to the "cabinetmaker's workshop" (*Schreinerwerkstätte*). So as not to disrupt either the daily routine or the aesthetic appeal of the Rosenhaus, this workplace remains hidden behind dense bushes and tall trees and can only be reached via a narrow winding path. From a grassy clearing one then espies a single-storied structure, its chimney releasing a fine fume ("feiner Rauch") and woodworking sounds emerging from its interior (see *HKG* 4,1:95; *IS*, 58). In contrast to a typical nineteenth-century factory, with its clamor of production and sooty smokestack emissions, the Asperhof workshop represents

---

24 For more detailed discussions of the violence underlying Risach's agronomic regime, see Begemann, *Die Welt der Zeichen*, 343–49; and Klaus-Dieter Sorg, *Gebrochene Theologie: Studien zum Bildungsroman von Goethe bis Thomas Mann* (Heidelberg: Universitätsverlag Winter, 1983), 105.

an idealized image of early industrial manufacturing. Once inside, Heinrich is struck by the brightness of the space and its "übersichtliche Ordnung und Einheit" (*HKG* 4,1:96; clear sense of order and unity, *IS*, 59). Each of the cabinetmakers is granted his own separate workstation, where he keeps his tools and any wood-pieces still in progress; anything not needed right away is stored on shelves located along the side wall of the room. Initially, nothing seems to indicate the presence of waste.

As Risach emphasizes to Heinrich, his woodworkers strive for "das Genaue und Zweckmäßige" (*HKG* 4,1:101; precision and utilitarianism, *IS*, 61); he also admits that it is difficult to find such employees given that the working classes tend to suffer from complacency or carelessness. Nevertheless, he has found the perfect worker in Eustach, who has not only augmented his carpentry skills with studies in the natural sciences but also refined his sensibilities by reading belles-lettres. In close collaboration with Risach, Eustach produces and continually revises drawings that serve as prototypes for woodworking projects that are then carried out by his assistants, who are the ones most involved in the daily operations of the workshop. The social hierarchy of this realm is hence also tripartite and reflects, more broadly, Risach's view of society in which a limited number of specialists must be complemented by a plurality of members,

> bei denen sich eine gewisse Richtung nicht ausspricht, die das Alltägliche thun, und deren eigenthümliche Anlage darin besteht, daß sie gerade keine hervorragende Anlage zu einem hervorragenden Gegenstande haben. Sie müssen in großer Menge sein, daß die Welt in ihren Angeln bleibt, daß das Stoffliche gefördert werde, und alle Wege im Betriebe sind. (*HKG* 4,3:59)

> [who show no particular direction, who perform the everyday tasks and their distinctive predisposition lies in the fact that they have none in any particular field. Of necessity, these are in the majority; that way the world stays on its axis, that way the material world is advanced and everything continues to function. (*IS*, 354)]

Although this "material world" is being "advanced" within the very workshop that Heinrich visits, he does not provide any further details concerning the activities of the assistants or the residues and remnants that must inevitably litter such a workshop environment, not least wood scraps and shavings left strewn on the floor or scattered on the work benches. Again, reader logic might dictate that such textually nonexistent scrapings had already been swept up and used to feed the flames of a (here explicitly mentioned) "Herd, auf welchem das zu Schreinerarbeiten unentbehrliche Feuer brannte" (*HKG* 4,1:96; a hearth in which the fire that is indispensable for carpentry and cabinetmaking was burning, *IS*, 59). Heinrich's retrospective narration, however, brackets out this work-related waste and other credible—yet here invisible—work-world realities. Nevertheless, waste underlies the workings of the workshop in a different fashion. As a site of transition, whereby old and dilapidated objects deemed worthless are repaired and refurbished, their value thereby restored, the Asperhof once again demonstrates that its lack of detectable waste does not necessarily mean that it lacks an effectual waste management plan.

# IV.

Risach's workshop does not just produce new items out of the raw material of wood; in fact, its main purpose lies in the refurbishment of antique furniture. The contrast between these two artisanal activities becomes linguistically apparent in the compounds "Schaffungslust" versus "Bewahrungslust" (*HKG* 4,3:143, 144; the creative urge, the urge to save and preserve, *IS*, 400). In more precise terms, the objective is to prevent old, damaged, and deteriorating furniture, artworks, and everyday household objects from definitive decline and make them usable again for domestic use. The workshop is thus a site of cultural transition, where objects change over from their status as ephemeral waste to a condition of more stable permanence.[25] According to Thompson, a transition of this nature involves

> the transfer across two boundaries, that separating the worthless from the valuable and that between the covert and the overt. Things may drift into obscurity but they leap into prominence. For an item to cross these boundaries it must begin to acquire value and it must emerge from its obscurity. It must leave its timeless limbo and acquire a real and increasing life-span, and since it has become visible it must also discard its polluting properties. Either an item is invisible or visible, is timeless or has an expected life-span, is polluting or is pure, is an eyesore or a sight for sore eyes.[26]

The objects refurbished in the Asperhof workshop are mainly "Plunder und Trödel" (*HKG* 4,1:297; rubbish and junk, *IS*, 171), the kind of things one would find stored away in an attic yet that the ardent collector Risach somehow manages to procure while on his travels. Long neglected or considered worthless by their original owners, they have been relegated to the category of waste. Risach, however, rescues them from oblivion and

25  See here also Saskia Haag, "Versetzt: Restaurierung als Entortung in Stifters *Nachsommer*," in *Figuren der Übertragung*, ed. Gamper and Wagner, 77–86. Haag's essay generally probes the nexus of transportation and restoration in the novel and more specifically argues that cultural transition is always connected to changes of place.

26  Thompson, *Rubbish Theory*, 41.

restores—both literally and figuratively—their value. This process is both lengthy and involved: before they can be integrated into the interior of the Rosenhaus or Sternenhof, they must first be divested of their "polluting properties" within the walls of the restoration workshop. Here Risach and his team draw up plans and sketch out designs for each item of furniture and its appropriate overhaul, ranging from the initial cleaning process to the actual repair work, from essential replacements to stylistic embellishments. These elaborate procedures are necessary in order to erase all signs of age and deterioration and reinstate the household functionality of each furnishing—remake it, in other words, into both a serviceable and appealing "sight for sore eyes." Only then can these restored objects find repose within the quiescent and timeless order of the novel, whereby their cultural transition from evanescence to intransience is concluded.

Risach's patented practice of transforming worthless waste into valuable *objets d'art* makes it "clear that one man's rubbish is another man's desirable object; that rubbish, like beauty, is in the eye of the beholder. Yet it would be wrong to explain away this distinction ... between matters of fact and matters of opinion, since on both sides there would seem to be exactly the same certainty that characterizes matters of fact."[27] While his detractors reproach him for his obsession with "old things" (see *HKG* 4,1:297; *IS*, 171) his orientation toward such antiquated artefacts stems from a firm conviction that the present age is suffering from artistic decline. Thus, in his experienced estimation, the objects that he routinely seeks out and smartens up possess both the beauty (*Schönheit*) and spirit (*Geist*) that is sorely lacking in the modern era. He furthermore insists that he is not bound to the trend of merely "collecting" antiques, which he criticizes as a pastime that indiscriminately esteems things according to their calculable age:

> Statt der neuen Mode mit neuen Gegenständen kam die neueste mit alten Gegenständen. Man raffte Schreine Bethschemel Tische und dergleichen zusammen, weil sie alt waren, nicht weil sie schön waren, und stellte sie auf. Da standen nun Dinge beisammen, die in ihren Zeiten weit von einander ablagen, es konnte nicht fehlen, daß ein Widerwärtiges herauskam. (*HKG* 4,1:297–98)

> [Instead of the latest fashion being modern things, the fad was antiques. They collected cabinets, hassocks, tables, and such things only because they were old and not because they were beautiful, then they arranged them in their houses. Thus, things far removed in time from each other were put together; inevitably the result was repulsive. (*IS*, 171)]

27  Thompson, *Rubbish Theory*, 106–7.

Risach, in other words, considers himself competent enough to judge things more appropriately, indeed intrinsically, based on their aesthetics and pragmatics—in contrast to the average antique collector beholden to whatever taste happens to be in vogue. He also knows how to achieve "die größte Wirkung" (the maximum effect) with refurbished objects. In any given room, furnishings must be arranged such that their collective age and purpose are harmonized and they exhibit "denselben Geist" (*HKG* 4,1:298; the same spirit, *IS*, 172) as a result. Risach's aesthetic notion of order thus strives for an uncompromising purity of style, and he will simply not tolerate anything less.[28]

Risach's art collection also consists of items that were initially restored in his workshop, yet, as with his attitude toward antiques, he differentiates himself from a "Sammler gewöhnlicher Art" (collector of the common sort) who has no conception "von der Tiefe der Kunst von ihrem Ernste und von ihrer Bedeutung für das menschliche Leben" (of the profundity of art, of its gravity, of its significance in the life of man). Guided by this self-understanding of art, Risach's aesthetic acumen remains uncompromising. When offered a collection of copper engravings for purchase, he has no difficulty discerning the difference between artistically "worthless" ("wertlos[-]") products made solely for profit and works of more intrinsic artistic merit (*HKG* 4,3:131; *IS*, 393). His ultimate decision to acquire this collection, which has been passed down from the original owner to his heirs, none of whom have any apparent appreciation of art, is based on both aesthetic and economic factors. Risach, that is, knows exactly how to match artistic value with a commensurable monetary price, thereby demonstrating that he is not some dreamy aesthete with his head in the clouds but rather a pragmatic-minded connoisseur who is well-versed in art market rates and regularities.[29] He is, after all, perfectly primed for marketplace success: beyond an aesthetic education and keen sense for lucrative investments (some of which his well-trained eye discovers in old junk), he possesses a sufficient inheritance to be able to afford expensive works of art. As a case in point, his collection of "masters" that hangs in the Rosenhaus as if in a museum,[30] far removed from the financial bustle of the art market, attests to his successful transactions, not least according

28   On this issue of idealized harmony in the *interieurs* of the Rosenhaus, see Haag, *Auf wandelbarem Grund*, 149.

29   Compare here Thums, "Adalbert Stifters *Der Nachsommer*," 93; and Mohnkern, "Ordnung, Wachstum, Zins," 424–25.

30   Such masters include Titian, Domenichino, and Guido Reni. The art collection belonging to Heinrich's father is far more impressive and includes paintings by Titian, Domenichino, Reni, Veronese, Carracci, Rosa, Poussin, Lorrain, Dürer, both Holbeins, Cranach (unclear whether the elder or younger), Van Dyck, Rembrandt, Ostade, Potter, van der Neer, Wouwerman, and Ruisdael (See *HKG* 4,2:154; *IS*, 260).

to Thompson's rubbish-theoretical reflections on art and economics: "The complete transfer of a class of items to museums and public collections is consonant with a general belief that, if only those items were in circulation, they would be increasing in value. In other words, they are so durable they are priceless."[31] Risach thus makes sure that only valuable paintings end up in his collection. In this vein, he retains the "good" copperplates mentioned above but has the "bad" ones destroyed so that they do not adversely affect the aesthetic experience of the art-appreciative beholder. His traditional concept of eternal and immutable beauty thus blinds him from rediscovering potential *objects*, which he here—perhaps too hastily—downgrades to *rejects* of art. This preemptive move would seem to contradict his otherwise productive practice of unearthing valuable art through random discoveries, whether in the realm of unwanted waste or highbrow taste.

A prime example of this practice occurs with a painting dubbed *Heilige Maria mit dem Kinde* (Madonna and Child), which Risach considers the prize of his collection. This work, which Eustach's brother Roland happened to find stashed away in someone's attic, undergoes a long and complicated transformation from the category of waste to that of permanence and value. The details of this radical renovation are rich and extensive. Some partial indications of the painting's initial state of disrepair can be gleaned from the following citation:

> Das Bild war ohne Blindrahmen, und war nicht etwa zusammengerollt, sondern wie ein Tuch zusammengelegt, und lag im Staube. Roland konnte nicht genau erkennen, ob es einen Werth habe, und kaufte es dem Manne um ein Geringes ab. Ein Soldat hatte es einmal aus Italien geschickt. Er hatte es als bloße Packleinwand benüzt, und hatte Wäsche und alte Kleider in dasselbe gethan, die ihm zu Hause ausgebesssert werden sollten. Darum hatte das Bild Brüche, wo nehmlich die Leinwand zusammengelegt gewesen war, an welchen Brüchen sich keine Farbe zeigte, da sie durch die Gewalt des Umbiegens weggesprungen war. Auch hatte man, da wahrscheinlich die Fläche zum Zwecke einer Umhüllung zu groß gewesen war, Streifen von ihr weggeschnitten. (*HKG* 4,2:103–4)

> [The painting had no provisional stretcher, it wasn't even rolled, but was folded like a cloth and was lying in the dust. Roland couldn't tell exactly if it were valuable or not and bought it from the man for a trifle. A soldier had sent it from Italy. He had simply used it as a package liner for wrapping old clothing and underwear which were to be mended for him at home. For that reason the painting had breaks where the canvas had been folded, consequently there was no

---

31 Thompson, *Rubbish Theory*, 112–13.

222 ♦ LARS ROSENBAUM

color since it had fallen off because of the pressure of folding. Since
the surface apparently had been too large for wrapping purposes
they also had cut away strips from one side. (*IS*, 231–32)]

The itemized list of "Mißhandlungen" (mistreatments) goes on. Suffice
it to say that the painting has persisted in a condition of abject waste for
decades and it thus takes years for the Asperhof workshop to reverse these
effects of neglect—indeed, abuse—through their tried and tested restoration techniques, which are arguably as artistic as they are artisanal. As
a result of such tireless efforts, the repaired Madonna seems to take on
a renewed life of its own: "Wenn nach und nach die Gestalt eines alten
Meisters vor uns aufstand, so war es nicht blos das Gefühl eines Erschaffens,
das uns beseelte, sondern das noch viel höhere eines Wiederbelebens eines
Dinges, das sonst verloren gewesen wäre" (*HKG* 4,2:107; As the form
done by an old master slowly took shape before our eyes, it wasn't just
the feeling of having created something that permeated our very beings; it
was even loftier, a feeling of having made something alive again that otherwise would have been lost, *IS*, 233).[32] Moreover, the social contingency of
waste also becomes apparent in this greater transactional process. The individual from whom Risach purchased the renaissance painting presumably
lacked the financial resources to refurbish it (he of course also lacked the
aesthetic judgment to recognize its potential value in the first place) and
Risach uses this situation to his advantage, converting what is essentially
attic junk into the coveted object of his desire. As he sums up this successful
investment and, at bottom, waste management ploy: "Dem Manne, von
welchem das Bild in seinem verstümmelten Zustande gekauft worden war,
gab ich noch eine Summe, mit welcher er weit über seine Erwartung abge-
funden war; denn das Bild hätte er doch nie herstellen lassen können, er
wäre auch auf den Gedanken nicht gekommen, und ohne Roland wäre das
Bild nicht verkauft worden, bis es immer mehr verfallen, und einmal vernichtet worden wäre" (*HKG* 4,2:110–11; I gave the man from whom the
painting had been bought in its mutilated condition a sum with which he
was satisfied far beyond his expectations because he never would have even
thought of it; and without Roland the painting wouldn't have been sold; it
simply would have continued to deteriorate until it was finally completely
ruined, *IS*, 235).

Another central work of art, namely the Greek statue of a maiden
adorning the marble staircase of the Rosenhaus, came into Risach's pos-
session under similar circumstances. This statue, also of marble, has an
intriguing history in terms of transactional revaluation. Risach came

---

32   As Weitzman aptly notes in her extended reading of this scene: "The rescue of objects from the state of trash provides an even greater pleasure than the
creation of beauty alone." Weitzman, *At the Limit of the Obscene*, 40–45; here 40.

upon it by chance in Italy, where it was stowed in a shed as an apparent plaster figure that had outlived its decorative purposes for the various social festivities organized by the local landowner. Purchased at no small price, the statue is transported to the Asperhof, whereupon its actual value comes to the (physical) fore, once again by chance. As it turns out, efforts to remove the long-accumulated grime from the statue's surface reveal, beneath the plaster shell, a core of solid white marble. Thanks to this "werthlosem Stoffe" (worthless material), the ancient statue has remained protected from "Unreinigkeiten" (impurities) and spared from "den Unbilden folgender Zeiten (*HKG* 4,2:81, 82; the inclemencies of subsequent times, *IS*, 219). Once this plaster coating—which essentially functions as packaging waste—is removed, the preserved form of the marble maiden emerges in its original beauty and takes its valued place within the aesthetic order of the Rosenhaus.

## V.

Dust and dirt, decayable compost and animal carcasses, wood shavings and packaging waste—though largely absent in the narrative, they are nevertheless present in the narrated world of *Der Nachsommer* and furthermore evident in the concerns of its characters, all of whom strive to preserve *and* optimize the Stifterian *ordo* enforced throughout the novel. Such preservation requires that waste be avoided or eliminated; that is, removed from the narrative field of vision, as implicitly carried out by the various servants that operate behind the scenes. The reusability of waste, however, remains the responsibility of the masters of the house; in Risach's case, this entails improving the operations of the Asperhof and increasing the quality of his art collection. During his educational journey, Heinrich, too, learns how to become more attentive toward waste and more selective in distinguishing between worthless and potentially valuable objects. One example of this learning process concerns the remnants of an antique wall paneling that he discovers in the home of a woodcutter and, after having it refurbished in Risach's workshop, presents to his father as a gift (see *HKG* 4,2:13–15; *IS*, 182–83).[33] The "transformation of yesterday's rubbish into tomorrow's durables"[34] thus becomes an important facet of Heinrich's *Bildung* or, more specifically in this case, his aesthetic education.

---

33  For further analysis of this episode, one that addresses the problem of adequately restoring an incomplete wall paneling and thereby producing a finished product in the original style, see Haag, "Versetzt: Restaurierung als Entortung in Stifters *Nachsommer*," 81–82.

34  Weitzman, *At the Limit of the Obscene*, 41.

Given that the characters of the novel tend to exhibit such a heightened awareness of waste in its various forms, it is striking that this otherwise omnipresent phenomenon remains consistently ignored in the text. This absence points to Stifter's unique understanding of realism: on the one hand, the ambition to recreate the details of reality as closely as possible; on the other, the adherence to classicist ideals. As Gerhard Plumpe has argued, Stifter shared—at least formally—the basic premises of the contemporary realism debate by combining realist and idealist tendencies in his work, thereby creating a literary aesthetic according to which not all aspects of reality are held to be worthy of artistic representation and transfiguration.[35] I have explored this issue of realist aesthetics in greater depth, focusing on the historical semantics of dirt in the so-called "long nineteenth century." As I argue, along similar lines as Plumpe but in far more expansive fashion, Germanophone bourgeois realists issued a variety of programmatic writings during the 1850s that outline creative techniques designed to help literary texts better overcome the discrepancy between idealism and realism. Such techniques are numerous but can be subsumed under three basic categories: "Ordnungs-, Idealisierungs-, and Läuterungstechniken" (techniques of order, idealization, and purification).[36] Stifter, for his part, not only applied these ideal-realistic compositional methods to *Der Nachsommer* (which was, after all, written precisely during this decade) in a narrative-technical fashion but indeed embedded them within the very content of the novel, as most readers of this chapter will by now readily discern.

Stifter himself once wrote that "jede Nebensache und jede andere Tendenz eines Kunstwerkes, als daß es schön sei, ausgeschlossen [bleiben müsse]" (*HKG* 8,1:27; one must rule out any minor aspect and any other tendency of an artwork, besides its beauty). By virtue of its disruptive and disorderly properties, waste proves to be precisely such a minor "matter" within the pages of *Der Nachsommer*. On a literary level, it thus remains a *non*-communicable phenomenon, while the processes that seek to prevent or at least overcome it—whether cleanliness, orderliness, or beautification—constitute a recurring motif within the plot of the novel.

—Translated by Sean Ireton

35 See Gerhard Plumpe, "Adalbert Stifter: Ordnungsrufe des Seins," in *Bürgerlicher Realismus und Gründerzeit 1848–1890*, ed. Edward McInnes and Gerhard Plumpe (Munich: Hanser, 1996), 606–25 and 796–97; here 607–8.

36 Lars Rosenbaum, *Die Verschmutzung der Literatur: Zur historischen Semantik der ästhetischen Moderne im "langen 19. Jahrhundert"* (Bielefeld: transcript, 2019), 206.

# Part III

# Elements and Environments

# 9: Stifter's Stones

*Jason Groves*

EVEN MORE SURPRISING than the recent spate of publicity given by international Anglophone newspapers to Isabel Fargo Cole's translation of *Bunte Steine* (Motley Stones, 2021 [1853]) is their common celebration of Adalbert Stifter as the defining European writer of the more-than-human world.[1] This is a writer whose friends characterized his work as "kleinliche Detailmalerei unwesentlicher Dinge" (petty detail paintings of unimportant things) and whose reception outside of Central Europe has been largely restricted to academia.[2] This recent embrace of Stifter by a broader audience owes something to the renewed recognition by contemporary pandemic-stricken readers of the ecological importance of the dimensionally insignificant (relative to human magnitude). The insights that Stifter makes into these relationships and the awe that he reserves for small things are derived in no small part from his engagement with geological matters and methodologies through which inquiry into everyday stones leads to earth-magnitude phenomena. In the following, I scrutinize Stifter's motley, multi-faceted stones as they inform his aesthetic geology but also as they are informed by and deformed under the political duress, in particular regarding the public debate around Jewish emancipation and assimilation, that becomes manifest in his novella *Abdias* (Abdias, 1842).

Stones are frequent companions of the characters in Stifter's stories. They play with, walk with, speak with, live with, and even sleep with stones. Their affinity for stones extends to an affinity *with* stones, as the narrator of "Ein Gang durch die Katakomben" (A Walk through the Catacombs, 1844) writes: "durch vervielfältigte geistige und leibliche Communicationsmittel sind wir feiner, glatter, geschmeidiger geworden, wie Kiesel, die sich an einander abreiben" (*HKG* 9,1:49; through the proliferating spiritual and material means of communication, we have become finer, smoother, and more malleable, like pebbles that abrade one another). But for all the conspicuousness of stones in Stifter's fiction (and

---

1    Martin Riker, "'Motley Stones' Review: More Than Human," *The Wall Street Journal*, May 7, 2021.

2    Emil Kuh, *Zwei Dichter Österreichs: Franz Grillparzer—Adalbert Stifter* (Pest: Hecknast, 1872), 456.

painting), from the titles of his most-read novellas to some of the most pivotal passages in his longest novel, the prominent position of these discrete lithic objects belies his frequent depictions of mineral materials, like the above pebbles, that are subjected to extreme abrasion or that resist consolidation into stone in the first place. Accordingly, my title, "Stifter's stones," is something of a misnomer. In the following pages, the term "stones" refers to a wide range of mineral materials and magnitudes, from grains of sand to monolithic granite blocks; similarly, "lithosphere" here refers to everything from subsurface rock to soil and surface rocks, whereas geologists typically differentiate the latter into the pedosphere. In Stifter's stories, the lithosphere undergoes incessant composition and decomposition, and his depiction of these processes touch on important issues of narration and description, poetologies of knowledge, and the temporalization of perception—issues which are not only germane to Stifter's writing but also more broadly to nineteenth-century literary realism. His literary depictions of the lithosphere are noted for being informed by, and meaningfully contributing to, geological knowledge that "undermines the symbolic meaning of stone as the emblem of durability," as Timothy Attanucci observes in a recent book that brings together Stifter's interests in monument restoration and geology.[3] Recent developments in Stifter scholarship reflect a growing awareness of the importance of the processual in his fiction, which has often been dismissed for its lack of discrete events, coherent plots, and narrative development. Description and narration of a dynamic lithosphere in Stifter has furthered an appreciation for the presence of these supposedly missing story elements—and moreover the attempts of those stories to present durations and magnitudes greater than many of his contemporaries.

From the largest monolith to the smallest grain, Stifter's stones straddle a divide between the cultural and the geological that is itself subject to erosion. His depictions of transient geological formations certainly owe something to the image of stone's impermanence as it emerges from a geohistorical perspective, but they also owe something to the ways in which stone, stoniness, and geology were politically coded. Given that, as Richard Block observes, "the oppressive conditions of the Austrian empire prevented Stifter from directly speaking about its practice" and that Stifter therefore "writes about the political in terms other than the political," it follows that depictions of even the most inhuman of landscapes are susceptible to politicization, that is to say, implicated in and complicated by

---

3    Timothy Attanucci, *The Restorative Poetics of a Geological Age: Stifter, Viollet-le-Duc, and the Aesthetic Practices of Geohistoricism* (Berlin and Boston, MA: De Gruyter, 2020), 32.

political inscriptions.[4] What is more, just as Attanucci advises readers to expect a certain degree of mediation and displacement of Stifter's geological discourse—"in examining the geologics of Stifter's narratives, one must have as much of an eye for hidden structures and aesthetic forms as to the more obviously 'geological' signs"—so too does one need an eye for the traversal of even those inconspicuous geologics by an equally inconspicuous politics.[5] Werner Micheler has shown how the natural sciences in general and the earth sciences in particular were politicized—and politics geologized—in and around the uprisings of 1848, as exemplified in the revisions that Stifter made to the stories collected in *Bunte Steine* in the wake of these events.[6] But as much as the idyllic landscapes in that collection bear evidence of revision, restoration, and politics (not to mention the countermovements of obliteration and disruption that also take shape in those stories), there are antecedents of these dynamics. Stifter's granular realism lends support to the granular readings needed to make these hidden structures and forms legible.

## Appreciating *Abdias*

The novella *Abdias*, first published in 1842 in the *Osterreichischer Novellenalmanach für 1843*, revised in 1845–46, and published in 1847 in the fourth volume of Stifter's *Studien*, occupies a stratum underlying the more obvious geologics of *Bunte Steine* and *Der Nachsommer* (Indian Summer, 1857). Scholars have long recognized how *Abdias*, which brought Stifter early critical acclaim, inaugurates important philosophical lines of inquiry and aesthetic issues. First, both the metaphysical speculation on the nature of nature and the geophysical speculation on natural laws in the novella's introduction prefigure the preface to *Bunte Steine*. Second, in the story of Abdias's daughter Ditha becoming sighted, the description of individual acts of visual perception are a major narrative event, and this challenge to the binary of description and narration will persist throughout his work. Third, the lengthy descriptions of natural phenomena, combined with the inscription of ideological values in these descriptions, is one of the earliest pronounced examples of what will become the hallmark of his complicated realist aesthetic. That *Abdias* combines observation of the natural world and aesthetic responses to it in

---

4    Richard Block, "Stone Deaf: The Gentleness of Law in Stifter's 'Brigitta,'" *Monatshefte* 90, no. 1 (Spring, 1998): 17–33; here 18.

5    Attanucci, *The Restorative Poetics of a Geological Age*, 9.

6    Werner Micheler, "Vulkanische Idyllen: Die Fortschreibung der Revolution mit den Mitteln der Naturwissenschaft bei Moritz Hartmann und Adalbert Stifter," in *Bewegung im Reich der Immobilität* (Vienna: Böhlau, 2001), 472–95.

230 ♦ JASON GROVES

the form of an aesthetic geology is less commonly appreciated.[7] Though it was written a few years before Stifter's acquaintance with the mountaineer and geologist Friedrich Simony, who will prove to be highly influential in Stifter's embrace of literature as a vocation and whose expeditions will serve as a model for texts ranging from *Bergkristall* (Rock Crystal, 1853) to *Der Nachsommer*, *Abdias* nevertheless belongs to Stifter's geologics what with its depictions of an austere, mineral-rich environment whose exposure to geological and meteorological forces rivals that of the alpine regions in these later stories.[8]

Stifter's familiarity with the work of naturalist and explorer Moritz Wagner helps to account for the rich descriptions of the desert environment, and his use of that source text also helps to account for the peculiar depiction of Jews in that environment.[9] Notably, *Abdias* is Stifter's only text that features Jews prominently and that engages with contemporaneous debates regarding the emancipation of European Jews, and interspersed among the rich descriptions of the desert environment are toxic descriptions of "schwarze, schmutzige Juden" (*HKG* 1,5:240; dark, dirty Jews).[10] Such descriptions may be one reason that few scholars of literature and the environment have touched the story. But the text contains

---

7    I take the term "aesthetic geology" from Noah Heringman, *Romantic Rocks, Aesthetic Geology* (Ithaca, NY and London: Cornell University Press, 2004).

8    On Stifter's relationship to Simony, see Georg Braungart, "Der Hauslehrer, Landschaftsmaler und Schriftsteller Adalbert Stifter besucht den Gletscherforscher Friedrich Simony. Hallstatt, im Sommer 1845," in *Bespiegelungskunst: Begegnungen auf den Seitenwegen der Literaturgeschichte*, ed. Georg Braungart, Friedmann Harzer, Hans Peter Neureuter, and Gertrud M. Rösch (Tübingen: Attempto, 2004), 101–18.

9    The opening sentence of Wagner's ethnographic account of "die Juden der Berberei' (the Jews of Barbary) in his travelogue, with its focus on rubble, diasporic movement, and misfortune, already contains major elements of Stifter's depiction of Jews in *Abdias*: "Die Juden der Berberei haben sich dort wahrscheinlich nach der Zerstörung Jerusalems, wo die Trümmer des unglücklichen Volkes Israel den Boden ihrer Väter verliessen und über alle Welttheile sich zerstreuten, niedergelassen" (The Jews of Barbary settled there, likely following the destruction of Jerusalem, where remnants of the unfortunate people of Israel forsook the soil of their fathers and scattered across all parts of the world). Moritz Wagner, *Reisen in die Regentschaft Algier in den Jahren 1836, 1837 und 1838*, vol. 2 (Leipzig: Verlag von Leopold Voss, 1841), 93. This reference to Wagner as a source text for *Abdias* is made by Eva Geulen in *Stifter Handbuch*, ed. Christian Begemann and Davide Giuriato (Stuttgart: J.B. Metzler, 2017), 36.

10    Adalbert Stifter, *Abdias*, in *Brigitta, with Abdias, Limestone, and The Forest Path*, trans. Helen Watanabe-O'Kelly (New York: Angel Books; Chester Springs, PA: Dufour Editions, 1990), 21–95; here 23 (translation modified). Further references to Watanabe-O'Kelly's translation of *Abdias* will appear parenthetically in the text, abbreviated as *A*.

ample material for an ecocriticism that concerns itself with how disgust constitutes an environmental discourse, or an ecocriticism that attends to how geological discourse has been mobilized by a dehumanizing racial discourse.[11] A study of the geological and racial imagination in *Abdias*, and points of intersection between the two, offers an impetus for a reevaluation of stones and geological formations in Stifter's subsequent writings. There are many facets to Stifter's motley stones, and while their racialization may be a minor aspect, it is also an under-theorized one.

Before embarking on a discussion of the geological and racial imagination of *Abdias*, I offer a brief note on terminology. The extent to which it is appropriate to speak of race in *Abdias* in something approximating its contemporary usage hinges on descriptions of Abdias and his fellow Jews, the genesis of the novella, and a felicitous translation. In terms of its genesis, it is important to observe that Stifter was working on the *Journalfassung* of *Abdias* at the same time as *Die Narrenburg* (The Castle of Fools, 1842), a novella that chronicles a racially diverse family line and which, as Joseph Metz argues, "announces the beginning of the problem of the visibility of race in the Austrian inner-colonial context."[12] The concurrence of their composition helps to explain the contiguity of this problematic, albeit in a different geographical context in the case of *Abdias*. A felicitous reference to the Jewish "race" in the opening pages of Watanabe-O'Kelly's translation of *Abdias* makes the contiguity visible. In this and another instance, "race" translates "Geschlecht," which brings together in one polysemous word the "idea of 'peoples,' 'nations,' 'classes' and 'races'" that Kenan Malik identifies as the imprecise notion of race in the early nineteenth century.[13] A third instance of race, in the line "Thus was the nature of the race from which Abdias was descended," also makes the racialization of Abdias explicit, though the corresponding term in German is not "Geschlecht" but "Volk": "So war dies Volk, und von ihm stammte Abdias her" (*HKG* 1,5:241; *A*, 23–24). For all of the embellishment involved in that translation, an essential nature is attributed to Jews—whether as a "people," a "nation," or a "race"—in *Abdias*, a nature that is inorganic and stone-like, and not only metaphorically. Here we have the attribution of an essential nature to a "Volk" who is defined by inherited physical characteristics and cultural behaviors that make them culturally inferior in the narrator's eyes. Accordingly, I

---

11   Regarding the former, see Sarah Jaquette Ray, *The Ecological Other: Environmental Exclusion in American Culture* (Tucson: University of Arizona Press), 2013.

12   Joseph Metz, "Austrian Inner Colonialism and the Visibility of Difference in Stifter's 'Die Narrenburg,'" *PMLA* 121, no. 5 (2006): 1475–92; here 1477.

13   Kenan Malik, *The Meaning of Race: Race, History, and Culture in Western Society* (New York: New York University Press, 1996), 80.

situate the depiction of Jews in proximity to a modern discourse of race, no matter how inconsistent and crude those depictions are. As protean as Abdias's racial identity is, it is a racialized identity. For example, the Jews and Abdias are disparagingly introduced in their opening description as "schwarz" in a way that comports with anti-Blackness, even when it is doubtful that the narrator means to say that they are racially Black, a dubiousness that Watanabe-O'Kelly amplifies in the translation of "schwarz" as "dark": "Düstre, schwarze, schmutzige Juden gingen wie Schatten in den Trümmern herum, gingen drinnen aus und ein, und wohnten drinnen mit dem Schakal, den sie manchmal fütterten" (*HKG* 1,5:240; Dark, melancholy, dirty Jews moved around in the rubble like shadows, went in and out among it and lived in it with the jackal which they sometimes fed, *A*, 23). Even when it is perhaps less crucial for the narrator what Abdias is and more crucial what he is not, namely a white European and a Christian, he is racially othered throughout the text and in a way that draws on geological discourse.

## *Abdias*'s Inhuman Geologies

While *Abdias* stands as Stifter's earliest sustained literary depiction of the lithosphere, the novella does not feature prominently in scholarship on Stifter's environmental imagination.[14] This is somewhat curious, as the setting, located in the ruins of a Roman town "Tief in den Wüsten innerhalb des Atlasses" (*HKG* 1,5:240; deep in the deserts behind the Atlas Mountains, *A*, 23) in the Maghreb, is a geologically interesting one, as the two mountain ranges encountered in the story, the Austrian Alps and the Atlas Mountains, share a common origin in the collision of the African and Eurasian tectonic plates. Though much of this story will take place outside of the mountainous regions whose descriptions feature so prominently in Stifter's work and thought, the arid desert in the shadow of the Atlas is nevertheless as dynamic as any mountainous region. While the description of this desert backdrop traffics in primitivist stereotypes of Kabyles and Jews living in a land that time forgot, the narrator also offers a nuanced perception of this landscape that distinguishes between fine desert sand, soft sand, and blown sand. In this "Sandland" (sandy

---

14   Two notable exceptions are Franziska Frei Gerlach, "Die Macht der Körnlein: Stifters Sandformationen zwischen Materialität und Signifikation," in *Die Dinge und die Zeichen: Dimensionen des Realistischen in der Erzählliteratur des 19. Jahrhunderts*, ed. Sabine Schneider and Barbara Hunfeld (Würzburg: Königshausen & Neumann, 2008), 109–22; Alexander Phillips, "Adalbert Stifter's Alternative Anthropocene: Reimagining Social Nature in *Brigitta* and *Abdias*," in *German Ecocriticism in the Anthropocene* ed. Heather I. Sullivan and Caroline Schaumann (Palgrave Macmillan, New York, 2017), 65–85.

country) with its atmosphere of "Sandluft" (sandy air), sand surpasses any mere framing effect and any colonial cartographical impulse (*HKG* 1,5:297, 288; *A*, 63, 57). Sand is not a thing but an ongoing event: it settles, it unsettles, and it also does so as a verbal event. Sand agglomerates itself to everything, including Stifter's language: *Sandland, Sandluft, Sandwege, Sandhaufen* (*HKG* 1,5:297, 288, 333, 262). In one of the opening lines describing Abdias's home, the narrator, in calling attention to the resonance of *Sand* in *sandten* (the preterite of "send"), indicates a ubiquity of sand in language that parallels its ubiquity in the atmosphere: "Das Licht sandten von oben herab mit Myrten verrankte Fenster, die manchmal der gelbe Wüstensand verschüttete" (*HKG* 1,5:242; Windows overgrown with myrtle sent light down from above, sometimes letting in the yellow desert sand, *A*, 24–25). In this passage, the ambivalence of the verb *verschütten*, which encompasses a range of flows from "to let in" particles to "to bury" in debris, further underscores a menacing capacity of sand to infiltrate every space and medium. (Stifter will use *verschütten* in the latter case in the introduction to *Bunte Steine* when, in the important passage on great and small events, he writes of "das Erdbeben, welches Länder verschüttet" (*HKG* 2,2:10; the earthquake that buries whole lands, *MS*, 4). The event that Stifter describes in *Abdias* is certainly on the smaller end of the magnitudes encompassed by *verschütten*, but the threat of an overwhelming event, like the earthquake in the preface to *Bunte Steine*, should be audible in a text in which, it seems, even language is *versandet*, "filled with sand" and pervaded by an inorganic materiality.

Though the ubiquity of sand in *Abdias* is unmatched in Stifter's oeuvre, processes of erosion in geological and cultural spheres play out in many if not most of his stories.[15] The proliferation of dust in *Der Hagestolz* (The Bachelor, 1845/1850) is another vivid example of the diminution and obliteration to which things are subjected in Stifter's stories.[16] Even where erosion is not present, the susceptibility of both landscape and culture to erosional forces informs Stifter's varied cultural practices, as Timothy Attanucci has shown in his wide-ranging reading of Stifter's geohistorical restorative poetics. What is notable about *Abdias* is its depiction of a setting and a community subject to such an extreme degree of erosion and abrasion. The Austrian landscapes that feature in Stifter's stories, for all their vulnerability to catastrophic erosion, are

15 See Sabine Schneider, "Kulturerosionen: Stifters prekäre geologische Übertragungen," in *Figuren der Übertragung: Adalbert Stifter und das Wissen seiner Zeit*, ed. Michael Gamper and Karl Wagner (Zurich: Chronos, 2009), 249–69.

16 See Kevin A. Gordon, "Historical Rupture and the Devastation of Memory in Adalbert Stifter's *Der Hagestolz*," *Journal of Austrian Studies* 45 nos. 3/4 (2012): 87–112.

234 ♦ Jason Groves

sites where deposition and sedimentation have been possible for longer stretches of time. It would be difficulty to underestimate the importance of such historical processes of slow and uninterrupted accumulation for his art. By contrast, in *Abdias*, the former Roman town now occupied by Abdias and other Jews is a site of historical and geological abrasion and erosion without end, as we read in its opening description: "Sie ist nach und nach zusammengefallen, hat seit Jahrhunderten keinen Namen mehr, wie lange sie schon keine Bewohner hat, weiß man nicht mehr" (*HKG* 1,5:239; It has gradually fallen into ruins, has been nameless for centuries, and it is unknown how long it has had no inhabitants, *A*, 23). The few structures that do persist, though not at all intact, are remarkably eroded and weathered, as in the opening narration of Abdias's home:

> Durch einen römischen Triumphbogen hindurch an zwei Stammen verdorrter Palmen vorbei gelangte man zu einem Mauerklumpen, dessen Zweck nicht mehr zu erkennen war. Jetzt war es die Wohnung Arons, des Vaters des Abdias. Oben gingen Trümmer einer Wasserleitung darüber, unten lagen Stücke, die man gar nicht mehr erkannte, und man mußte sie übersteigen, um zu dem Loche in der Mauer zu gelangen, durch welches man in die Wohnung Arons hinein konnte. Innerhalb des ausgebrochenen Loches führten Stufen hinab, die Simse einer dorischen Ordnung waren und in unbekannter Zeit aus unbekanntem zerstörenden Zufalle hierher gefunden hatten. Sie führten zu einer weitläufigen Wohnung hinunter, wie man sie unter dem Mauerklumpen und dem Schutte von außen nicht vermutet hätte. (*HKG* 1,5:241)

> [Through a Roman triumphal arch, past two trunks of withered palms, one reached a clump of walls whose purpose could no longer be recognized. Now it was the dwelling of Aaron, Abdias's father. Atop were the ruins of an aqueduct; at the bottom lay unrecognizable pieces over which one had to pass to get to the hole in the wall through which one entered Aaron's home. Within the breached hole, the opening steps led down; these were cornices of the Doric order, and had in an unknown time and through the agency of an unknown destructive chance found their way here. They led down to a spacious dwelling such as one would not expect to find under the bulk of walls and debris outside. (*A*, 23–24, translation modified)]

This scene, too, belongs to Stifter's geologics. For one, the language describing the subterranean dwelling denotes both manufactured and geological forms: clumps, ruins, holes, fragments, debris. These may be cultural objects, but their form is a result of unabated erosion. As such, *Abdias* seems to be an outlier from the robust narrative pattern of "*natural order—disruption—restored order*" that Sean Ireton has identified in

*Bunte Steine.*[17] Stifter's gentle law (*sanftes Gesetz*), which posits a state of underlying equilibrium in nature and in culture, and between them as well, does not seem to apply to this Jewish community. But it is precisely in its status as an outlier to the gentle law—which might also be characterized as a gentile law to mark its cultural specificity—that this story of abrasion is central to Stifter's realism, which is, as Paul Fleming concludes in a study of Stifter, "a realism of the irregular and out of the ordinary."[18]

The extraordinary erosion and degradation of the dwelling and its surroundings could be accounted for by strictly immanent physical laws and processes but for the fact that a Jewish community is the subject of such acute exposure. That is, this anomalous level of exposure—of Abdias in particular and Jews and Kabyles in general—to geological forces cannot be accounted for solely by geological processes. The phenomenon of erosion as depicted in *Abdias* is a good example of what Eric Downing characterizes as Stifter's realist practice of "inscribing a specific set of subjective and ideological values onto the site of these phenomena and then presenting them as immanent natural laws."[19] Just as the level of exposure is extremely high in *Abdias*, so too is the inscription of subjective and ideological values more heavy-handed here than in the subsequent stories collected in *Bunte Steine*. For example, in the novella's opening inquiry into personal misfortune that results from unfathomable series of events, an inquiry which is followed by the story of the inordinate exposure of Abdias to such events, the narrator speculates on the possibility of insight into the natural laws that underlie these events with the following language: "haben wir dereinstens recht gezählt, und können wir die Zählung überschauen: dann wird für uns kein Zufall mehr erscheinen, sondern Folgen, kein Unglück mehr, sondern nur Verschulden" (*HKG* 1,5:238; if someday we have counted correctly and if someday we can comprehend what we have counted: then chance will not exist for us anymore but consequence, not misfortune but guilt, *A*, 22). For Joseph Metz and other readers of the novella attentive to antisemitic tropes in circulation at the time, this seemingly nonpolitical speculation on the limits of intelligibility is thoroughly political: "With its resonances of moral guilt, causal blame, and monetary debt, this word is the very marker of an anti-Semitic discourse of the Jew, especially appearing as it does in this

---

17 Sean Ireton, "Adalbert Stifter and the Gentle Anthropocene," in *Readings in the Anthropocene: The Environmental Humanities, German Studies, and Beyond*, ed. Sabine Wilke and Japhet Johnstone (New York: Bloomsbury, 2017), 195–221; here 198.

18 Paul Fleming, *Exemplarity and Mediocrity: The Art of the Average from Bourgeois Tragedy to Realism* (Stanford, CA: Stanford University Press, 2008), 162.

19 Eric Downing, *Double Exposures: Repetition and Realism in Nineteenth-Century German Fiction* (Stanford, CA: Stanford University Press, 2000), 25.

sentence about counting."[20] The implication that there will be no more chance (*Zufall*) but consequences certainly invites the reading that the domestic, geographic, and geological disarray to which these Jews and their environments are subjected is not, ultimately, an unknown chance (*Zufall*) but rather a consequence of what the narrator does not presume to know, though some of the usual suspects crop up throughout the text: the murder of Christ, ethnic exclusivity, resistance to modernity. But even if Jews' misfortune might one day be traced to an anthropogenic cause, it plays out geologically in what could be called its geosocial formations.[21]

The single-most destructive event in the novel—the ransacking of Abdias and Deborah's house by his nemesis Melek-Ben-Amar while Abdias is traveling on business—can be accounted for by material events and so cannot be attributed to unknown chance. However, the depiction of the dwelling and surrounding landscape upon Abdias's return involves an image of devastation whose catastrophic magnitude seems to surpass the destruction caused by the pillaging:

> Er bog um den Triumphbogen und abgelegene Trümmer herum, und als er auf den hohen Schutthaufen, der über seinem Hause lag, gekommen war, stieg er auf den noch höheren hinan, der sich hinter demselben befand, wo Sand und weitgedehnte Blöcke lagen und eine große Umsicht auf alle Dinge und auf das Dämmerrund der Wüste sich eröffnete. (*HKG* 1,5:263)

> [He went round the triumphal arch and the outlying ruins, and when he had ascended the high pile of rubble that lay above his house, he climbed the even higher one situated behind it, where there was sand and a great expanse of scattered blocks and which afforded a wide view of everything and of the overcast desert around it. (*A*, 40, translation modified)]

While this passage precedes Abdias's encounter with anything relating to the new damage, the description of the ruins, heaps of debris, and scattered blocks suggests a massive upheaval that, compared to the initial description of the dwelling in the opening lines, appears to be in an even more advanced state of devastation, and one that has advanced perceptibly within the span of a few years. An additional layer in this palimpsestic

---

20   Joseph Metz, "The Jew as Sign in Stifter's *Abdias*," *The Germanic Review: Literature, Culture, Theory* 77, no. 3 (2002): 219–32; here 223.

21   *Abdias* offers an opportunity to consider how, as Nigel Clark and Kathryn Yusoff propose, "social and political agency is both constrained and made possible by the forces of the earth itself." Nigel Clark and Kathryn Yusoff, "Geosocial Formations and the Anthropocene," *Theory, Culture & Society* 34, nos. 2–3 (2017): 3–23; here 3.

landscape might be discerned by observing the similarity of these descriptors (*Trümmer ... Schutthaufen ... Sand und weitgedehnte Blöcke*) to those that Stifter uses to depict glaciated landscapes and terminal moraines in the Austrian Alps that were familiar to him. In this environment hostile to all organic life, even the few items of organic origin—wooden structural beams, palm fronds that provide roofing, carpets and mats—have been obliterated. By the time Abdias departs for Austria, little more remains inside than the earth and the bare stones of the thousand-year-old walls.

This extraordinary degree of devastation trails Abdias to Austria, where it is graver yet less perceptible. In her 1936 essay on the depiction of Jews in European art, Margarete Susman reads domestic space in Abdias's home in Austria as "unterirdisch erschüttert" (subterraneously shattered).[22] The same could be said of his home in North Africa, and Susman's following remark would also hold true for both domiciles, with the exception of the description of his childhood world as placid: "überall spüren wir ein kaum merkliches Beben unter seiner abgeschlossenen, ruhevollen Welt" (everywhere we sense a scarcely perceptible quaking underneath its closed, placid world).[23] The underground convulsions to which Susman draws attention might be perceptible not only in scenes of ruined structures like the one above but also in the (counter)form of disarray of the *Haufen*, or heap, that looms over his North African home and also constitutes most materials in it. Already in the opening description of the interior of Aron's house, the narrator, emphasizing the disheveled state of it, observes that "Haufen alter Stoffe" (*HKG* 1,5:241; heaps of old cloths, *A*, 24) form the sole furniture for sitting and leaning. Over the course of the story, the heaps proliferate in domestic spaces, in the lithosphere, and in language: *Erdhaufen, Sandhaufen, Schutthaufen*, but also *Menschenhaufen* (see *HKG* 1,5:262, 262, 263, 270; heaps of earth, heaps of sand, heaps of rubble, and heaps of humans). It is as though no material is capable of maintaining a consolidated form, as though everything is unsettled by a force that, tectonic or not, nevertheless belongs to Stifter's geologics. There is, perhaps, in Susman's suggestive description a recognition that these landscapes were formed and continued to be formed by tectonic processes. However, if the literal and figurative subduction of Abdias from North Africa into Europe makes something of Stifter's seismological unconscious manifest, the instability of the ground that Stifter is elsewhere more successful in regulating also reveals unconscious biases, which are geologically elaborated but socially and politically motivated. That the erosiveness and instability of the ground surpasses any strictly geological account does not make it any less geologically interesting.

22  Margarete Susman, "Nachwort," in *Abdias: Erzählung von Adalbert Stifter* (Berlin: Shocken Verlag, 1935), 108–13; here 110.
23  Susman, "Nachwort," 110.

## Racial Formations

Abdias could almost count himself among Stifter's stones. His affinity for gold and other metals extends into an affinity with metals in the metallurgical metaphor of tears flowing from his eyes following the death of his wife Deborah "wie geschmolzenes Erz" (*HKG* 1,5:268; like melted bronze, *A*, 44). In the wake of her death, his long-standing proximity to stone becomes almost ontological in his stillness and the indefinite time that elapses in this description: "Er blieb immerfort auf den Steinen sitzen, auf die er sich niedergelassen hatte" (*HKG* 1,5:268; He remained sitting on the stones onto which he had sunk, *A*, 44). His immersion into the lithosphere persists in Austria, where he and his dwelling are so incongruous that they are viewed in lithic terms, namely "wie die Steine, die hie und da aus dem Grase hervorstanden" (*HKG* 1,5:304; as … the stones that stuck up here and there out of the grass, *A*, 67). An affinity for stones is shared by several characters in Stifter's fictions, not to mention Stifter himself, but in the case of Abdias, the eroded distinction between organic life and inorganic nonlife has a significance that differs from other lithophiles.

Abdias's affinities for and with the inorganic run deeper than individual characteristics. While his tears are "like" melted bronze, while his metallic inclination is visible in his love of gold coins, and while, from a certain perspective, he could be likened to a stone, Abdias's is lithicized in a way that is intimately linked to his status as a racialized subject. His lithification stems from his Jewishness, a Jewishness that is marked by a stone-like obstinacy. As one of the "Kinder jenes Geschlechtes, welches das ausschließendste der Welt [ist]" (children of the most exclusive race in the world), namely Jews, Abdias is described already in the opening pages as stonily—the German word is "starr" which Watanabe-O'Kelly translates as "rigidly"—fixated on a distant homeland (*HKG* 1,5:240; *A*, 23). As the narration of his life progresses, antisemitic tropes and stereotypes involving other forms of rigidity increase and develop in a way that cannot be separated from its depictions and discourses of inorganic nature. Exclusiveness and excludedness are stock figures of antisemitic discourse in the 1830s and 1840s, where they were mobilized in the debates around Jewish emancipation and assimilation known as the "Jewish Question," debates which frequently reference the mythic figure of the Wandering Jew, or Ahasverus, to whom the globe-trotting Abdias shares more than a passing resemblance and more than a nominal resonance. As the writer Karl Gutzkow posits in a screed from 1838 that intercalates an ardent anti-Jewish sentiment into a pro-emancipation position, "Ahasver ist der Jude in alledem, was ihm von dem Berufe, an der Geschichte theilzunehmen, ausgeschlossen hat, der Jude gerade in seine Missionsunfähigkeit" (Ahasverus is the Jew in everything that excludes him from the vocation of participating in history, the Jew precisely in his incapacity to have a mission).[24] Paul Rose's commentary on this passage illuminates the association between Jews and stone, and it is a commentary that resonates in the novella's combination of racial exclusivity, Ahasverus-like itinerancy, and Abdias's desert-like nature: "The curse of Ahasverus and the Jews is their refusal to have died at the appointed hour, hanging on instead in a sterile, restless immortality that excludes them from the organic flow of history."[25] Though *Abdias* is in this way very much a product of its time, with its ossified Jewish community living in rubble, it also participates in a long-standing "tendency to think Jewish difference in lithic terms," as Jeffrey Cohen elaborates in *Stone: The Ecology of the Inhuman*.[26] *Abdias* exhibits this tendency when it mobilizes geological figures of stoniness, sandiness, erosiveness, and aggregativity in the service of a racialized dehumanization of Jews, if not as explicitly as Cohen's medieval sources The novella thereby offers material for the study of the entanglement of racial and geological formations that scholars of the Anthropocene have raised in recent years.[27] If the Jew in *Abdias* is a racial formation, understood as a product of "the sociohistorical process by which racial identities are created, lived out, transformed, and destroyed," that formation is also a geosocial one, informed by geohistorical processes and, no matter how rudimentary, geohistorical discourses.[28]

Martha Helfer's chapter on *Abdias* in *The Word Unheard: Legacies of Anti-Semitism in German Literature* offers an important basis for understanding the antisemitic discourse of biological nature in the novella, while also offering a starting point to appreciate its racialized discourse of geological nature. Beyond taking stock of the numerous epithets, stereotypes, canards, and themes in *Abdias* (as well as numerous pro-Jewish gestures), and beyond compellingly demonstrating how the novella's narrative evinces an anti-assimilationist political agenda that makes it a significant document in contemporaneous debates around the "Jewish Question," Helfer argues how at the discursive level the construction of the "Jew" in the novella is entangled in its construction of "nature," such

24   H. H. Houben, *Gutzkow-Funde* (Berlin: Wolff, 1901), 237.

25   Paul Lawrence Rose, *German Question/Jewish Question: Revolutionary Antisemitism from Kant to Wagner* (Princeton, NJ: Princeton University Press, 1990), 29.

26   Jeffrey Jerome Cohen, *Stone: An Ecology of the Inhuman* (Minneapolis: University of Minnesota Press, 2015), 150.

27   See especially the chapter "Geology, Race, and Matter," in Kathryn Yusoff, *A Billion Black Anthropocenes or None* (Minneapolis: University of Minnesota Press, 2018), 1–22.

28   Michael Omi and Howard Winant, *Racial Formation in the United States* (New York: Routledge, 2014), 109.

240 ♦ JASON GROVES

that antisemitism is cast as a natural phenomenon.[29] As Helfer and other commentators have noted, framing the story of this "dirty Jew" with an introduction that engages in metaphysical speculation on the nature of nature puts the life of the protagonist in the position of illustrating natural systems—or rather, as the case may be, the inscrutability of those systems.

Helfer focuses mostly on the biological and meteorological forms through which these laws and systems become discernible: Jews and jackals presented as subhuman co-species, nature metaphors that render Abdias's predatory economic activity innate, the naturalization of his otherness in climatic terms that also legitimize Austrian xenophobia (like the "öde afrikanische Sonne" [bleak African sunlight] that hangs over his residence in Austria), and repeated comparisons of his daughter Ditha to a flower that, given her death by lightning strike, ultimately demonstrate her and his (and Jews') inability to flourish on Austrian soil (see *HKG* 1,5:334; *A*, 89). Through the inborn inadaptability of Jews, their predilection for arid climates, Ditha's vulnerability to electrical storms and the frequency of these in Austria, Helfer shows how in *Abdias* "nature itself—or, more precisely, the higher principle that orders nature—opposes Jews' assimilation" in Europe.[30] The narrator shares this view and surely helps to shape it. In a passage from the *Journalfassung* that did not make it into the *Studienfassung*, even though the sentiment still holds, he observes that Abdias "war ein fremder Baum in diesem Lande und seine Tochter ein fremder Apfel auf diesem Baume" (*HKG* 1,2:150; was an exotic tree in this land and his daughter an exotic apple on this tree). Of course, these introduced species fail to take hold and in effect become invasive species.

The anti-assimilationist political agenda that Helfer sees in the novella's othering of Abdias, as well as its casting of antisemitism as a natural phenomenon, are also evident in its depiction of inorganic nature—and Abdias's proximity to it. Despite the association of Abdias and Ditha with botanical and arboreal figures, the nature of Jews in *Abdias* is largely inorganic. The dehumanizing aspect of these descriptions should also be considered as part of the novella's political and geological agenda. Paul Rose's observation that in the 1840s the debates around the "Jewish Question" in Europe were motivated by a "fear of 'the other' that refuses to be absorbed into the organic whole" is literalized in the lithic and geophilic

---

29  Martha B. Helfer, *The Word Unheard: Legacies of Anti-Semitism in German Literature and Culture* (Evanston, IL: Northwestern University Press, 2011), 114. Unlike Helfer and other scholars cited in this essay, I write "antisemitism" without a hyphen and all lower case, in accordance with an increasing number of style guides from Jewish organizations. For a discussion of the terminology of antisemitism, see Helfer, *The Word Unheard*, xviii–xix.

30  Helfer, *The Word Unheard*, 135.

Jews of *Abdias*.[31] The depictions of Abdias in the opening sections as soiled, dirty, digging for coins in the rubble, living under a diamond sun, and strangely recalcitrant demonstrates the status of Jews as others who are, Helfer observes, depicted as "at best subhuman beings."[32] Even when Abdias is present, the narrator often remarks that no human was to be seen, only a crooked form, a shadow, or a stone. Even more explicitly, the reference in the opening pages to Jews as an exclusive race positions them separate from "das menschliche Geschlecht" (*HKG* 1,5:238; the human race, *A*, 22) that is mentioned just a few paragraphs earlier. While Jews' subhuman status is established in comparisons to predatory animals, that status, or lack thereof, is even more pronounced and extreme in comparisons to nonliving thing, for example in what the narrator of the *Journalfassung* refers to as Abdias's "Wüstennatur" (*HKG* 1,2:150; desert nature). The unsighted Ditha, too, occupies a shadowy zone between the nonliving and the living for much of her childhood, only fully joining the latter upon being struck by a lightning bolt and suddenly becoming sighted, at which point her face comes alive, as the narrator tersely notes: "es begann auch zu leben" (*HKG* 1,5:327; she also began to live, *A*, 84). The vitality of Jewish people is tenuous in *Abdias*, and the lithosphere in which they are often immersed is neither accorded the vibrancy nor subjected to the gentle law that it will be in Stifter's later stories set in Europe. Frequently stuck in his unchanging ways, often unreceptive to his environment, Abdias's provisional assimilation into the cultural life of Austria is a temporary one, as he and his offspring are only fully assimilated when no longer living. If it is possible to speak of a natural antisemitism in *Abdias*, then surely it is also possible to speak of its geological form.

This co-construction of the discourse of the Jew and the stone is not Stifter's invention. As indicated above, Jeffrey Cohen has shown how the depiction of Jewish difference in lithic terms was already developed in "the geology of medieval anti-Judaism."[33] The tradition of regarding Jews as inveterately obdurate is one that resonates with their depiction in *Abdias*, even if Stifter does not directly draw on Cohen's medieval sources. Cohen's account of medieval anti-Judaism, in which Jewish intransigence is "repeatedly figured through unyielding rock, a materialization of spiritual deadness and historical anachronism," persists in *Abdias*.[34] Moreover, the association of Jews with rubble in the medieval Christian narratives celebrating the destruction of Jewish Jerusalem, which Cohen elaborates while drawing on Suzanne Conklin Akbari's account of this "narrative of

31    Rose, *German Question/Jewish Question*, 28.
32    Helfer, *The Word Unheard*, 130.
33    Cohen, *Stone*, 153.
34    Cohen, *Stone*, 150–51.

242　◆　JASON GROVES

triumphant Christian domination on the razed ground of Jewish history" in Jerusalem, resonates in the narrator's deprecative description of the ruined and dead town that is Abdias's birthplace.[35] Allusions to geological racial differences in *Abdias* and elsewhere may not acquire the power and perniciousness as ideas of biological racial difference, but they are still forces to be reckoned with.

Abdias and Ditha's ill-fated assimilation into Austria will end with their burials. During their tenancy there, they made a desolate valley prosper, but their legacy is largely confined to feeding a patch of flowers and grass—and the narrator's curiosity. Martha Helfer takes Abdias's return to nature to entail that he grounds Austrian nature, but Susman's essay raises the question: Is there an intact ground to return to? It might be more accurate to say that Abdias *un*grounds and abrades Austrian nature. While Abdias peacefully enters the lithosphere, the lithic formations and counterformations that feature in *Abdias* and that persist in Stifter's later depictions of Austrian landscapes—shifting sands, displaced stones, talus fields and other unconsolidated piles of matter—are unsettled by this association. Narrators will continue to express disgust when encountering these strange, exotic, disturbing, and incompatible formations in successive writings, which suggests that they continue to be encoded, no matter how inconspicuously, as Jewish. If Jews are inorganic and inhuman, they are so in the highly ambivalent sense that Cohen elaborates in *Stone: An Ecology of the Inhuman*: both as "difference ('in' as a negative prefix) and intimacy ('in' as an indicator of estranged interiority)."[36] For all of Abdias's differences and othering, he is the estranged interior of Stifter's literary lithology.

## Afterlives of *Abdias*: Shifting Sands, Motley Stones, Debris Flows

With Abdias's death, Jews go underground in Stifter's Austria. But traces of the stratum deposited in this novella resurface in Stifter's subsequent stories. The overwhelming "sand country" of Abdias's birthplace crops up in the tidy paths of sand that Ditha traverses in Austria, and it also appears, in isotope form, in the desolate steppeland in *Brigitta*; in the sandbanks of the Kar landscape in *Kalkstein* (Limestone, 1853) and the heap of sand on which the pastor is perched in his first encounter and which nearly engulfs him in later descriptions; and in the prominent sandy slope introduced in the opening scene in *Kazensilber* (Cat-Silver,

---

35　Suzanne Conklin Akbari, *Idols in the East: European Representations of Islam and the Orient, 1100–1450* (Ithaca, NY and London: Cornell University Press, 2009), 114.

36　Cohen, *Stone*, 10.

1853) and that is frequented by the racialized "brown girl" whose affinities with sand and extreme weather are highly reminiscent of Ditha. Part of my argument for regarding the sand in these later stories as an isotope of the desert sand in *Abdias* comes from Franziska Gerlach, who traces a line from the sandy path in the European garden in *Abdias* to the clean and well-ordered courtyard of sand in front of the Rosenhaus in *Der Nachsommer*; this landscaping project entails a steady dismantling of the threatening associations of sand in the North African desert and the remediation of sand from an amorphous, threatening mass into a legible sign of refined Austrian culture.[37] Neither the eradication nor the remediation of the amorphic landscapes of sand in *Abdias* have been placed by scholars in the context of the "Jewish Question," but bringing together Gerlach's and Helfer's arguments, it would follow that an anti-assimilationist—or a violently assimilationist—subtext could figure into these acts of highly charged landscaping. That is to say, the cultural anxiety that masses of drifting sand provoke in *Abdias*, and which cannot be separated from the attitude toward the diasporic "dirty Jews" in that story, helps to account for the emphatic presentation of clean and well-ordered beds and paths of sand in later stories. Not only sand, but other forms of unconsolidated material that are troped as Jewish in *Abdias* appear in texts ranging from *Bunte Steine* to *Der Nachsommer* in ways that retain traces of these racial formations and as such suggest an ongoing mediation of the "Jewish Question," no matter how mediated and displaced, in literary depictions of the lithosphere. If, following Helfer, *Abdias* can be said to stage the introduction of "the Jew" into Austrian society and nature, and if we can also understand "the Jew" metatextually and metaphysically as an "unstable disrupter of meaning" that hinders the attribution of events to a higher cause or to a deeper significance, we might also trace this racialized disruption textually and narratively in the proliferation of unstable forms and literal disruptions in the physical ground—in a word, in the transience of stones and proliferation of unconsolidated counter-formations in later stories.[38] Tove Holmes' argument in a recent article on Stifter's erosive geologies—"in the face of the unfathomable past and unstable earth, both landscapes and narrative itself are continually eroded, recomposed, and restructured"—also opens up the further possibility of

37   "Mit dem Sandweg im europäischen Garten beginnt aber auch die stete Arbeit am Bannen der bedrohlichen Sandmassen und ihre Transformation zu gereinigten Kulturzeichen" (But with the path of sand in the European garden also begins the ongoing labor of warding off the menacing sand masses and transforming them into cleansed signs of culture). Gerlach, "Die Macht der Körnlein," 117.

38   Helfer, *The Word Unheard*, 141.

considering Stifter's legendary revisionary practices as an aspect of his geologics, one not untouched by the anxieties displayed in *Abdias*.[39]

In terms of formations, the heap may be the most threatening one of all, as it is inimical to the idea of a formation. It is also a characteristically Jewish counterform. When the narrator of *Abdias* introduces, in an uncharacteristically lapidary sentence, heaps of cloth as the sole furniture for sitting and reclining, it is an emphatically Jewish feature, as the preceding sentence emphasizes: "überall waren die vielen Päcke und Ballen und Krämereien verbreitet, daß man sah, mit welchen schlechten und mannigfaltigen Dingen der Jude Aron Handel trieb. … Zum Sitzen und Lehnen waren Haufen alter Stoffe" (*HKG* 1,5:241; numerous packs and bales and odds and ends lay about everywhere, showing with what inferior and diverse objects the Jew Aron traded. … To sit and lean against there were heaps of old cloth, *A*, 24). Heaps serve as a principal support for the main events in the part of the story set in North Africa. The first thing that Abdias does upon returning home from his first journey, after embracing his father at the threshold, is to throw himself on a heap of mats. Upon returning home from his second journey, he finds Deborah lying, with the newborn Ditha, on a heap of loose earth. The most prominent and frequently referenced heap, of course, is the one of stone that looms over their home, provides the panoramic view of their surroundings, and serves as the hiding place for Abdias's gold.

For all the ubiquity and prominence of heaps in Jewish life in North Africa, not a single *Haufen* appears in the narrative segment of *Abdias* set in Austria. However, even in the absence of any discernible Jewish community, heaps do resurface in subsequent stories. As Holmes observes, Stifter's stories are "littered with such *Geröllhalden*, talus deposits or accumulations of broken rock debris that elude his narrative attempts to bring order to nature and human civilization alike, de- and reconstructing the stories told about them or evading significance entirely."[40] If Helfer's characterization of the "Jew" in *Abdias* as an "unstable disrupter of meaning" resonates in Holmes' characterization of these heaps as "evading significance entirely," it might be because the disruptions introduced by *Abdias* reverberate throughout successive stories. Moreover, even when the accumulations of debris in later stories are distinct from those in *Abdias*, the disgust and disparaging attitudes that they elicit and that cleave to them over the course of *Abdias* persist. Continuing this convention established in *Abdias*, heaps (particularly those described as *Haufen*) are, almost without exception, negatively coded throughout Stifter's oeuvre. "Der Gang durch die Katakomben" contains the most horrifying

---

39   Tove Holmes, "An Archive of the Earth: Stifter's Geologos," *Seminar: A Journal of Germanic Studies* 54, no. 3 (2018): 281–307; here 281.

40   Holmes, "An Archive of the Earth," 285.

instance of a heap in the image of a wheelbarrow full of bones that the narrator encounters at the paved-over cemetery outside St. Stephen's Cathedral. On a narrative level, he is disturbingly precise about the mineralized contents—upper arms, pieces of skull, a jawbone with teeth, a shoulder blade—while, on an emotional level, he is disturbed by the re-paving of the square above the cemetery that displaced the contents of several graves into the wheelbarrow. Here, as in *Abdias*, the heap is a kind of cairn for an incessant process of erosion. *Ver-* verbs of deterioration predominate in the description of the obscured and displaced cemetery, whose holdings have "verschwunden … verstummt … verwittert" (*HKG* 9,1:51; disappeared … fallen silent … weathered).

Heaps are no less a matter of concern in *Bunte Steine*. As Isabel Fargo Cole's new translation of *Motley Stones* alludes, the title itself presents the collection as an aggregation of disparate things, even if, as Lori Wagner argues, the individual titles are organized according to the mineralogical structure of granite, the title of the initial story.[41] As much as the title might signal an embrace of aggregate counterforms, the preface codes such collections negatively in an extended analogy between natural history and moral history, where Stifter describes belligerent encounters with "feindselige Haufen" (*HKG* 2,2:15; hostile bands, *MS*, 7) during one of the earlier stages in the development of the species. The belligerent horde is superseded, the passage continues, by "ein völkerumschlingendes Band" (*HKG* 2,2:15; a bond embracing the peoples, *MS*, 7). (*Bunt*, which has been traced to an Indo-European root shared by Sanskrit *bandh* via *binden* ["to bind"], might also signal Stifter's formal investment in the title *Bunte Steine* over and against formless hoards of materials and money, like those found in Aron's home in *Abdias*.) Though the primitivism of Abdias's world was already made adequately apparent by the narrator's descriptions and epithets, here it becomes particularly apparent that the *Haufen* is inimical to the human as such, just as the Austrian landscape—"der ihm ungewohnte, feindselige Landstrich" (*HKG* 1,5:318; the region which was inimical to him, *A*, 78)—is to Abdias. In *Kazensilber*, which is in some ways a foil to *Abdias* and where, not coincidentally, heaps crop up most frequently in all of the *Bunte Steine* collection, they form in the wake of a catastrophic hailstorm, a devastating environmental disaster that leaves numerous massive heaps of hailstones amidst bushes and trees stripped of leaves and badly damaged structures. Heaps also appear during the fire that devastates the family manor: the "mound of embers" (*Gluthaufen*) that the firefighters attempt to pull from the ceiling to prevent the fire from spreading to the roof, the "flaming heap" (*Feuerhaufen*) of beams on the floor that block the entrance to

---

41 Lori Wagner, "Schick, Schichten, Geschichte: Geological Theory in Stifter's *Bunte Steine*," *VASILO* 2 (1995): 17–41.

Sigismund's room, and, ultimately, the disarray of the incinerated manor: "Die Mauern des Hauses waren schwarz und beschmutzt, der Sandplatz und der Rasen vor dem Hause waren schwarz wie ein Kohlenmeiler, die Stätte des Brennholzes war ein Haufen nasser Kohlen und Asche" (*HKG* 2,2:308; The walls of the house were black and begrimed, the sandy yard and the lawn in front of the house were black as a charcoal pile, the firewood shed was a heap of wet coal and ash, *MS*, 223). The scene of Abdias's ransacked house and fire-blackened stones haunts this description, as does the threat posed by a form of disarray that was peculiar to Jews, a threat that is here intensified and made far more volatile by its seeming naturalization in the catastrophe-prone elements themselves.

Martha Helfer's claim regarding Abdias's burial in Austria—though "nature itself … opposes the Jews' assimilation," "the Jew becomes part of Austrian nature"—also bears out in the proliferation of heaps in these stories.[42] The nature that disorders, the nature that reduces well-ordered structures to heaps and piles, the anomalous nature that is neither supernatural nor unnatural, is an *ab*natural nature: the nature of Abdias. I take the term "abnatural" from Jesse Oak Taylor who coins it in order to account for how "nature in the Anthropocene exists in a state of perpetual withdrawal" in which the designations of natural and unnatural both fail to stick. [43] Observing that the prefix *ab-* means both "away from" and "derived from" (which also holds in many cases for the German prefix *ab-*), Taylor remarks that "'abnatural' speaks to both nature's absence and its uncanny persistence" and "characterizes those moments in which nature appears other to itself, beside or outside itself."[44] The latent persistence of an ungentle nature becomes manifest in these *Abdias*-esque heaps, even after the threat of interminable abrasion and erosion has been contained by the institution of the gentle law. In individual stories, these heaps of detritus may be temporary disturbances that are able to be rapidly eradicated, but their continued outcropping in Stifter's oeuvre might require a reevaluation of the reigning concept of nature subordinate to the gentle law, given how integral heaps are to an otherwise invisible Jewish life and a decidedly ungentle—and un-gentile—law of nature.

When these disparate passages are aggregated, a sustained if intermittent engagement with the disarray of the heap in Stifter's writing emerges. While many of the heaps are only marginally geological, and seemingly only marginally pertinent for a study of Stifter's stones, the interest in heaps and the attendant investment in containing the outfall from them

---

42   Helfer, *The Word Unheard*, 282, 285.

43   Jesse Oak Taylor, *The Sky of Our Manufacture: The London Fog in British Fiction from Dickens to Woolf* (Charlottesville: University of Virginia Press, 2016), 5.

44   Taylor, *The Sky of Our Manufacture*, 5.

in *Bunte Steine* bears upon one of the most celebrated and pivotal passages on stone in *Der Nachsommer*—or any of Stifter's stories for that matter. Occurring in the first chapter of the second volume, the encounter by protagonist Heinrich Drendorf with this heap catalyzes some the most significant reflections on earth history in all of Stifter:

> Als ich in dem Frühling die Hauptstadt verlassen hatte und dem langsam über einen Berg empor fahrenden Wagen folgte, war ich einmal bei einem Haufen von Geschiebe stehen geblieben, das man aus einem Flußbette genommen und an der Straße aufgeschüttet hatte, und hatte das Ding gleichsam mit Ehrfurcht betrachtet. Ich erkannte in den roten, weißen, grauen, schwarzgelben und gesprenkelten Steinen, welche lauter plattgerundete Gestalten hatten, die Boten von unserem Gebirge, ich erkannte jeden aus seiner Felsenstadt, von der er sich losgetrennt hatte und von der er ausgesendet worden war. Hier lag er unter Kameraden, deren Geburtsstätte oft viele Meilen von der seinigen entfernt ist, alle waren sie an Gestalt gleich geworden, und alle harrten, daß sie zerschlagen und zu der Straße verwendet würden. (*HKG* 4,2:27–28)

> [In the spring, when I had left our capital and was walking slowly up a grade behind the coach, I once stopped by a pile of stones they had taken from a riverbed and strewn by the road. I regarded this with a sense of awe. In the red, white gray, dark yellow, and speckled stones all with flat rounded shapes, I recognized the harbingers of our mountains; I could tell the craggy home of each one, where it had been separated and from whence it had been sent out. Here it lay among comrades whose birthplaces were often many miles distant from its own; all of them had assumed the same shape, and all were waiting to be broken apart and used on the road. (*IS*, 190)]

Given that *Der Nachsommer* can be characterized as a *Bildungsroman*, or novel of self-formation, it is probably not surprising that this is the only *Haufen* in the entire multivolume work. As in virtually every other instance in *Bunte Steine*, the heap is presented as an anomaly and registered by the narrator with concern. And as in most every other instance, the heap is dismantled or otherwise eradicated, as they are anathemas to formation, whether individual or cultural. In *Abdias*, the heaps, as markers of Jewish life, disappear upon his immigration to Austria; in the preface to *Bunte Steine*, the earlier stage of human society, marked by warring hordes, is superseded by transnational alliances; in *Kazensilber*, the heaps of hailstones melt, and the piles of burned rubble are quickly removed and composted. (The never-ending displacement of the piles of bones in "Der Gang durch die Katakomben" is one exception, but this is registered with horror by the narrator.) Here, the operation is more complicated but follows a similar outcome: first, the threatening disarray of the heap is neutralized by being granted the coherence of a *Ding* (and, following Stifter's realist aesthetics, accorded an exceptional kind of perception he calls awe) and from there the disarray is undone in two distinct scenarios, both of them anti-assimilationist in their own way: first, by imaginatively repatriating the comrades to distant points of origin and second by projecting a near-future scenario where the heap has been flattened and incorporated into a road.

Though this formation is not explicitly racial, the narrator's approach to this displaced assemblage (as he departs the multi-ethnic capital) is reminiscent of the narrator's description of the diasporic Jews in *Abdias* as children of the race "starr bloß auf einen einzigsten Punkt derselben hinweisend, doch in alle Länder der Menschen zerstreut" (*HKG* 1,5:240; rigidly taking one place as their sole point of reference, yet scattered in every land known to man, *A*, 23). This is not to equate these motley stones with motley Jews—any consideration of this scene in terms of the convention of presenting Jewish difference in lithic terms would have to account for a considerable degree of mediation and displacement here— but rather to remark on an analogical relationship between these disparate heaps and to propose the possibility of a morphological relationship between Stifter's engagement with the "Jewish Question" in *Abdias* and the geological question and questions raised by displaced stones and unconsolidated materials in later writings including *Der Nachsommer*. The question that the vicissitudes of Abdias's life pose for that narrator and given the situation that immediately rises in the wake of this question—"Warum nun dieses? und man wird in ein düsteres Grübeln hinein gelockt über Vorsicht, Schicksal und letzten Grund aller Dinge" (*HKG* 1,5:240; Why did this happen exactly? and [one is] tempted into a gloomy brooding about providence, destiny, and the ultimate cause of all things, *A*, 22)—prefigure the question that occurs to Drendorf immediately in the wake of the confrontation with this roadside heap in *Der Nachsommer*: "Besonders kamen mir die Gedanken, wozu dann alles da sei, wie es entstanden sei, wie es zusammenhänge, und wie es zu unserem Herzen spreche" (*HKG* 4,2:28; In particular the thoughts came to me: why is all that here, how did it come to be, and what does it tell us, *IS*, 190). Here, too, the narrator's introduction to the life of Abdias and the request to pass judgement on him "wie es ihm sein Herz nur immer eingibt" (*HKG* 1,5:240; according to the promptings of his heart, *A*, 23) parallel Drendorf's introduction to this heap and his response (literally: "how it speaks to our hearts"). The accumulation of geological questions that follow Drendorf's encounter with this heap greatly outstrip the anthropocentric questions that open *Abdias*, both in length and breadth. And yet the geological objects that prompt those questions in *Der Nachsommer*—colossal masses of rock, piles of deposits, debris fields—are those unconsolidated or destratified formations that were so characteristic of Abdias's dwelling and of Jewish life in general. Viewing the heaps and deposits of sand as a constellation, one can draw a line of inquiry into geophysical processes that runs from *Abdias* to *Der Nachsommer*, and it is haunted by the questions of assimilation in *Abdias*.

While intersecting lines of inquiry into Jewish assimilation and the workings of geophysical systems that were first developed in *Abdias* crop up in subsequent writings, the mountaineers and mountainous formations that populate stories in *Bunte Steine* and *Der Nachsommer* take Stifter's work in different directions. To give an adequate account of Stifter's mountains, which are certainly germane to the topic of Stifer's stones, would necessitate another study entirely.[45] That said, in *Der Nachsommer* in particular, the Alps serve as a privileged site for intellectual and cultural formation (*Bildung*), and this, combined with the extent to which Drendorf's self-formation emerges out of his encounters (as geologist and mountaineer) with geophysical formations, might not be unrelated to the concomitant absence in *Abdias* of geological formations and *Bildungsbürger* in the erosive and atemporal "sand land" that Abdias inhabits. In this way, the isomorphism of *Bildung*—as a term for personal growth that emerges out of observation of natural processes and that, in the case of Drendorf, emerges out of the encounter with geophysical formations in a mountainous region—is maintained *ex negativo* in *Abdias*. The heaps are counterformations, and Abdias, who follows in his people's constrained lifeways, is himself abradable (as his pock-marked face attests) but hardly formable, as each instance of personal and cultural development is eventually countered by regressive behaviors or calamitous events precipitated by human actions. The exception that Ditha's remarkable development poses is all too short lived, and the promise of Austria is never fully realized. Yet even in those writings far removed from *Abdias*, like *Der Nachsommer*, and in those alpine spaces farthest removed from the desert and the "Jewish Question" hotly debated in Vienna, the threats posed by Abdias—the threats of societal disarray, interminable erosion, and social formations coming undone—are not absent. They might in fact signal a point of departure for Stifter's turn to remote alpine regions and distant geological times in the first place.

---

45 On this topic, see in particular Sean Ireton, "Geology, Mountaineering, and Self-Formation in Adalbert Stifter's *Der Nachsommer*," in *Heights of Reflection: Mountains in the German Imagination from the Middle Ages to the Twenty-First Century*, ed. Sean Ireton and Caroline Schaumann (Rochester, NY: Camden House, 2012), 193–209.

# 10: Stifter's Glaciers

*Matthew H. Birkhold*

ADALBERT STIFTER, "THE greatest landscape-painter in literature," as Hannah Arendt famously described the Austrian author, is renowned for his evocative prose describing the meadows, forests, and mountains of his Central European home, which encompassed both his native Bohemian Forest and the Upper Austrian Alps that he frequented later in his adult life.[1] Yet, glaciers, one of the most striking geological features of the Alps, are largely missing from his oeuvre. The icy masses appear prominently in only two of Stifter's works: the 1845/53 short story *Bergkristall* (Rock Crystal) about two children who go missing in the mountains on Christmas Eve and *Der Nachsommer* (Indian Summer), the 1857 three-volume *Bildungsroman* that follows Heinrich Drendorf up and down the Austrian peaks as part of his ideological and aesthetic development. In a third text, *Das alte Siegel* (The Ancient Seal, 1844/1847), a glacier is briefly mentioned in one paragraph when the titular seal is thrown into a crevasse.

This dearth of glaciers is particularly surprising in light of Stifter's otherwise deep interest in geology and "lifelong obsession" with wintery landscapes.[2] Indeed, from contemporary reports, we know that Stifter did not ignore glaciers out of a lack of interest—he was fascinated by the frozen forms. He just never stepped foot on a glacier himself. This may explain why he never painted glaciers in his visual works and why he largely omitted them from his literary texts.[3] It makes the instances in which glaciers do appear, however, all the more remarkable. This chapter is not interested in the narrative or symbolic role of glaciers in Stifter's stories, but rather the act of depicting the ice itself. How did Stifter manage to portray glaciers? What do they tell us about his prose and the Austrian landscape he so carefully sought to describe?

---

1 Hannah Arendt, "Great Friend of Reality: Adalbert Stifter," in *Reflections on Literature and Culture*, ed. Susannah Young Ah-Gottlieb (Stanford, CA: Stanford University Press, 2007), 110–14; here 111.

2 Eva Geulen, "Depicting Description: Lukács and Stifter," *The Germanic Review* 73, no. 3 (1998): 267–79; here 270.

3 Geulen, "Depicting Description," 275. Snow-covered mountains, however, appear in the background of some of his paintings, for example *Im Gosautal: Die Holzmeisteralm mit dem Dachstein* from 1834.

To answer these questions, this chapter first offers a brief overview of the growing interest in glaciers during the eighteenth and nineteenth centuries. As land surveyors, artists, adventurers, and scientists climbed the Alps, they had new opportunities and impetus to describe the ice but were confronted with the same obstacle: How to make the enormous, dynamic, white forms comprehensible. Many pronounced glaciers impossible to understand unless one personally saw them. No secondhand account could properly capture the ice; after all, glaciers are difficult to portray in any medium. They can be hidden under a blanket of snow and can assume a variety of colors or be uncompromisingly monotone. The ice is always in motion, constantly growing and shrinking, and it continually transforms the landscape through which it slithers. As Stifter proclaims in *Bergkristall*: "Was das Starrste scheint, und doch das Regsamste und Lebendigste ist, [ist] der Gletscher" (*HKG* 2,2:227; the glacier, that thing that seems most unyielding, and yet is most astir and alive, *MS*, 161). Further compounding the complexities, most glaciers inhabit inhospitable locations that are difficult to reach by all but the most intrepid mountaineers. Despite these difficulties and his own inexperience, Stifter tackled the mimetic challenge of representing glaciers head on.

Like other German-language realist writers of the period, Erica Weitzman succinctly summarizes, Stifter had to "square the demands of art with new and potentially incompatible developments in the physical and natural sciences."[4] He did so, as the next part of this chapter details, by turning to Friedrich Simony. Through conversations with the Austrian alpinist and a careful study of his expressive written accounts of trips in the Dachstein mountains, Stifter gathered information about glaciers that enabled him to represent the ice.

The final part of this chapter highlights the manner in which Stifter adds his own narrative voice to Simony's reports and deploys a variety of literary tools to render glaciers legible. Like his other narrative constructions, Stifter's glaciers are self-consciously reflective of their own creation. Accordingly, by focusing not on a particular text but on the appearance of glaciers across Stifter's works, this chapter uncovers how the author weighs in on the contemporary debate about how to depict the enormous ice masses and critically examines the role of language in the process. Throughout his literary works, Stifter sought to teach people how to read and interpret landscapes. Glaciers may be the biggest task he faced.

Ultimately, this chapter uncovers the literary legerdemain of Stifter's glaciers. Although the author never saw the ice up close himself, he conjures a glacier out of prose, showing the power of the written word to portray this evasive subject. Aware that he has produced an illusion, however, Stifter is not confident in his own magic act. Nevertheless, the

---

4    Erica Weitzman, *At the Limit of the Obscene: German Realism and the Disgrace of Matter* (Evanston, IL: Northwestern University Press, 2021), 26–27.

author leaves the reader with an incredible gift that he himself could not have conceived. As the planet warms and glaciers continue to melt, the ice will resist representation in a new way, namely, by vanishing. In the end, Alpine glaciers may only exist as artistic representations like Stifter's own.

## Background: Seeing Glaciers

Stifter makes no secret that he is interested in the question of how one sees a glacier. *Bergkristall* is itself a text about seeing, or more precisely, the limits of sight. Through Konrad and Sanna's gradually expanding perception of their glacial environment, the story invites the reader to try to see the ice, as well. As the children trek back alone to Gschaid from their grandparents' home in a neighboring village, they get lost in the snow-covered forest. The path has been obscured, the usual signposts buried, and eventually the sky and earth blend together in an impenetrable—and unreadable—white. "Wenn ich nur mit diesen meinen Augen etwas zu erbliken imstande wäre," Konrad laments, "daß ich mich darnach richten könnte" (*HKG* 2,2:214; If only I could see something with these eyes of mine … so that I could get my bearings, *MS*, 151). In the uniform environment, the children's eyes fail them. Acutely aware of this sensory challenge, the lost pair attempts to gain information about their surroundings through other means. At one point Konrad implores his sister to wait: "wir wollen ein wenig stehen bleiben, und horchen, ob wir nicht etwas hören können, was sich im Thale meldet, sei es nun ein Hund oder eine Gloke oder die Mühle" (*HKG* 2,2:214; let's stay where we are for a moment and listen, and see if we can't hear some sign from the valley, perhaps a dog or a bell or the mill, *MS*, 43). But it is to no avail; the children hear nothing and they are stuck with their sight. Thus, Konrad leads his sister "in dem weißen, lichten, regsamen undurchsichtigen Raume fort" (*HKG* 2,2: 215; the light white restless opaque space, *MS*, 44).

In this setting, the children's senses are fully taxed. Sanna complains that her eyes hurt. Konrad corroborates and the children press on: "Es war wieder nichts um sie als das Weiß, und ringsum war kein unterbrechendes Dunkel zu schauen. Es schien eine große Lichtfülle zu sein … alles war, wenn man so sagen darf, in eine einzige weiße Finsternis gehüllt" (*HKG* 2,2:215–16; Again there was nothing but whiteness surrounding them, and all around no intervening darkness could be seen. There seemed to be a great wealth of light … everything was swathed, if this can be said, in one great white darkness, *MS*, 152). The literal next steps of Konrad and Sanna make clear the object undergirding this overpowering whiteness. "Sie merkten auch, daß ihr Fuß, wo er tiefer durch den jungen Schnee einsank, nicht erdigen Boden unter sich empfand, sondern etwas anderes" (*HKG* 2,2:216; And they found that their feet, sinking deeper through the fresh snow, did not feel the ground beneath them, it was something else, *MS*, 45). The children get closer to inspect. "Es war Eis—lauter Eis" (*HKG* 2,2: 217; It was ice—sheer ice, *MS*, 153). As the children endeavor to make sense of this foreign Alpine environment, the narrator is tasked with a new and more specific challenge: how to portray the ice. How can the reader experience a glacier without actually climbing a mountain and seeing it firsthand?

Most Austrians, like other Europeans in the nineteenth century, did not regularly encounter glaciers at close proximity. The mountains had only recently become a place to visit for those who did not live in the Alps. According to the traditional account, mountains slowly transitioned from a fearful place to a desirable retreat in the eighteenth century.[5] Albrecht von Haller, a Swiss naturalist and poet, is often identified as a key transitional figure. In 1729, he first published his forty-nine-stanza work "Die Alpen" (The Alps) glorifying the range. It was quickly translated into several European languages and sparked both scientific and literary interest in the mountains. The line, "Der Berge wachsend Eis" (ice growing from the mountains), even raised curiosity about glaciers as far away as Scotland.[6] Consequently, more naturalists began to visit the mountains to make sense of the landscape. Glaciers, however, proved a special conceptual challenge. Joseph Walcher, one of the first Austrians to systematically study glaciers, acknowledged of the dynamic ice in 1773, "daß man sich, ohne es gesehen zu haben, nicht leicht ächten Begriff davon machen wird" (that without having seen it, one will not easily get a real idea of it).[7] The judgment identifies not just the strangeness of the ice, but also the failure of the written word to adequately express it. In fact, it would take more than half a century and many personal visits to the ice for learned naturalists to agree about the basic properties of glaciers, including their composition, formation, and dynamics.

Walcher's assessment that to understand a glacier one must see it notwithstanding, there was increasing demand for representations of the ice. The Swiss artist Caspar Wolf (1735–83) made a career selling images of

---

5    For foundational accounts, see: Marjorie Hope Nicolson, *Mountain Gloom and Mountain Glory: The Development of the Aesthetics of the Infinite* (Seattle: University of Washington Press, 1959); Fergus Fleming, *Killing Dragons: The Conquest of the Alps* (New York: Grove, 2000). More recently, scholars have begun to challenge this traditional narrative, for example, Dawn Hollis and Jason König, "Introduction," in *Mountain Dialogues from Antiquity to Modernity* (London: Bloomsbury, 2021), 1–20.

6    For more on Haller and his influence on glaciology, see: Heinz J. Zumbühl, "'Der Berge wachsend Eis …': Die Entdeckung der Alpen und ihrer Gletscher durch Albrecht von Haller und Caspar Wolf," *Mitteilung der Naturforschenden Gesellschaft in Bern* 66 (2009): 105–32.

7    Joseph Walcher, "Vorrede," in *Nachrichten von den Eisbergen in Tyrol* (Vienna: Kurzböcken, 1773), n.p.

the frozen Alps. His paintings and engravings were exhibited far from the mountains in places like Amsterdam and Paris, and in Switzerland he was commissioned to paint more than two hundred landscapes, including several glaciers, to be reproduced for tourists.[8] There was also a growing need for accurate depictions of glaciers on maps for members of newly formed climbing associations and the military.[9] The shimmering ice, though, proved difficult to capture. For instance, the first military mapping survey of the Austrian Empire, known as the *Josephinische Landesaufnahme* from 1764 to 1787, was intended to produce the most precise map ever created of the Habsburg territories. Its creators, however, struggled with glaciers.[10] Often the ice is depicted as abstract crystallizations, appearing like *Eisblumen* crawling across the map, only vaguely hinting at where the "[e]wiges Eis und Schnee" (eternal ice and snow) as the map labels it, might be (Figure 10.1). In other locations, the mapmakers seem to have given up entirely. As the coordinates climb higher and higher up the Alps, the hyper-detailed depictions, which include individual buildings and trees at lower altitudes, simply cease and give way to unmarked white space. The abstract glacier becomes nearly indistinguishable from the negative space of the blank white page (Figure 10.2).

For the second military survey, the so-called *Franziszeische Landesaufnahme* from 1806 to 1869, the mapmakers filled in some of the white spaces and added new details. In the Steiermark section from 1821–36, for instance, the same "eternal ice" depicted on the first military survey (Figure 10.1) now appears as cerulean puddles, like pools collected in the depressions of a craggy rock (Figure 10.3). With little indication of their topography provided, many of the glaciers even appear indistinguishable from the nearby lakes.

---

8    Willi Raeber, *Caspar Wolf: 1735–1883: Sein Leben und Werk* (Munich: Sauerländer, 1979).

9    For more on the history of mountaineering, see Caroline Schaumann, *Peak Pursuits: The Emergence of Mountaineering in the Nineteenth Century* (New Haven, CT: Yale University Press, 2020).

10    The Josephinische Landesaufnahme did not include Tyrol and Vorarlberg because detailed maps already existed of these mountainous regions. In particular, the *Atlas Tyrolensis*, produced between 1760 and 1770 by Peter Anich and Blasius Hueber and published in 1774, was lauded as a breakthrough in the depiction of glaciers—though, only for the achievement of indicating their approximate locations. As Hans Kinzl summarizes: "Die Gletscherflächen sind auf der Karte weder der Form noch dem Umfang nach genau, sie entsprechen einander aber recht gut in ihren relativen Ausmaßen" (The glacial surfaces on the map are not accurate in either shape or scope, but they correspond to one another quite well in terms of relative dimensions). Hans Kinzl, "Die Darstellung der Gletscher im Atlas Tyrolensis von Peter Anich und Blasius Hueber (1774)," *Raimund-von-Klebelsberg-Festschrift der Geologischen Gesellschaft in Wien* 48 (1955): 89–109; here 102–3.

Figure 10.1. Innerösterreich (1784–85)—*Josephinische Landesaufnahme* (original map). Österreichisches Staatsarchiv [B IX a 54].

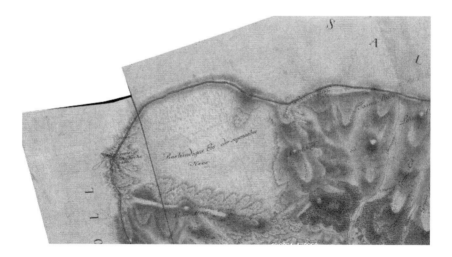

Figure 10.2. Innerösterreich (1784–85)—*Josephinische Landesaufnahme* (original map). Österreichisches Staatsarchiv [B IX a 54].

Figure 10.3. Steiermark (1821–36)—*Franziszeische Landesaufnahme* (original map). Österreichisches Staatsarchiv [B IX a 290].

By the mid-nineteenth century, cartographers began adding contour lines to glaciers to make them more legible, as in the maps included in the first issue of the *Jahrbuch des Oesterreichischen Alpenvereins* (Yearbook of the Austrian Alpine Club) in 1869. According to Kurt Brunner, however, "die erste exakte Gletscherkarte" (the first exact glacier map), was not made until 1883, when Eduard Richter published his "Beobachtungen an den Gletschern der Ostalpen I. Der Obersulzbach-Gletscher 1880–82" (Observations on the Glaciers of the East Alps) in the *Zeitschrift des Deutschen und Österreichischen Alpenvereins* (Journal of the German and Austrian Alpine Club).[11]

In the century and a half between the publication of Haller's epic poem and Richter's cutting-edge map, the question of how to make glaciers legible to those who could not see them up close lingered around the Alps. It is therefore no surprise that an Austrian author like Stifter, who was greatly invested in understanding and portraying the natural world—and the difficulties such an effort entailed—tackled this question, too.

---

11 Kurt Brunner, "Karten dokumentieren den Rückzug der Gletscher seit 1850," *Wiener Schriften zur Geographie und Kartographie* 17 (2006): 191–200; here 192.

## Simony's Glaciers

Before turning to Stifter's glaciers, it is necessary to make a brief detour to those portrayed by Friedrich Simony. Co-founder of the Österreichischer Alpenverein in 1862, Simony was the first professor of geography at the University of Vienna and the first person to overnight on the summit of the Hohe Dachstein among other notable accomplishments. This "prime practitioner of nineteenth-century Alpinism"[12] also enjoyed a meaningful friendship with Stifter. In particular, much has been made of an 1845 hike the pair undertook in the lower altitude of the Dachstein massif. On this outing, Stifter—who was decidedly not a mountaineer—would still have only observed glaciers from a distance. Consequently, the author relied on Simony's personal reports of the ice. Analyzing Stifter's glaciers in light of Simony's works thus helps to highlight the narrative strategies Stifter utilizes to craft the landscapes later featured in *Der Nachsommer* and *Bergkristall*.

In an 1871 letter to the author Emil Kuh, Simony describes sharing his experiences with Stifter. "Eine Erwähnung [des Gletschers] … gab den Anstoß, von meinem ersten winterlichen Besuches des Karls-Eisfeldes zu sprechen und dabei eine Eishöhle zu schildern" (a mention of the glacier … gave impetus to speak of my first winter trip to the Karl icefield and to describe an ice cave).[13] Stifter was purportedly so enraptured he even compelled the naturalist to later retell his "Winterfahrt nach dem Gletscher" (winter trip to the glacier).[14] Simony reports, too, that Stifter carefully examined the former's landscape sketches: "Eingehend verfolgte er Strich um Strich in jeder neuen Zeichnung" (in depth he followed each new drawing line by line).[15] In addition, Stifter heavily relied on Simony's 1843 essay "Drei Dezembertage auf dem Dachsteingebirge" (Three December Days on the Dachstein Mountains) published in the *Wiener Zeitschrift für Kunst, Literatur, Theater und Mode* (Viennese Journal for Art, Literature, Theater, and Fashion) and "Zwei Septembernächte auf der Hohen Dachsteinspitze" (Two September Nights on the High Dachstein Pinnacle) published in the same journal in 1844.

---

12   Sean Ireton, "Geology, Mountaineering, and Self-Formation in Adalbert Stifter's *Der Nachsommer*," in *Heights of Reflection: Mountains in the German Imagination from the Middle Ages to the Twenty-First Century*, ed. Sean Ireton and Caroline Schaumann (Rochester, NY: Camden House, 2012), 193–209; here 199.

13   Letter from Friedrich Simony to Emil Kuh from August 19, 1871, in *Adalbert Stifters Leben und Werk in Briefen und Dokumenten*, ed. Kurt Gerhard Fischer (Frankfurt am Main: Insel, 1962), 150.

14   Fischer, *Leben und Werk*, 152.

15   Fischer, *Leben und Werk*, 151.

Compared to texts by other early glaciologists of the era, Simony's writing sparkles with poetic expression. While walking across the Karls-Eisfeld, today known as the Hallstätter Glacier, Simony and his team are blinded by the white, much like Stifter's fictional Sanna and Konrad in *Bergkristall*: "Keine andere Farbe als das blendende Weiß des Schnees und das Grau der ringsrum abgelagerten, senkrechten Felsmassen ... erblickten unsere Augen" (our eyes saw no other color besides the blinding white of the snow and the gray of the upright rock masses deposited all around).[16] In the most vivid passage of the two essays, Simony describes "das Kristallgewölbe eines Gletschers" (the crystal dome of a glacier), informing readers that they can have no idea of the "wahrhaft feenhaften Anblickes" (truly fairylike sight) created by the "herrliche Blau, Grün und Weiß, welches ... von allen Seiten in allen Graden der Intensität und Durchsichtigkeit ... strahlt" (*HD*, 36; splendid blue, green, and white, which ... radiates from all sides in all degrees of intensity and transparency). Simony goes on to describe the cavern, again later recognizable in Stifter's *Bergkristall*, as the "geheimnisvolle[r] Palast des Alpenkönigs ..., der aus dem schönsten und reinsten Lazur, Saphir, Smaragd und Bergkristall erbaut ist" (*HD*, 36; mysterious palace of the king of the Alps ... which is built from the most beautiful and purest lazur, sapphire, emerald, and rock crystal). To communicate the supernatural atmosphere created by the glacier, Simony portrays the landscape like something out of a fairytale, evoking magic and jewels.

Further underscoring the otherworldliness of the glacier, Simony shares an anecdote about a member of his team who was enchanted by the ice. The captivated alpinist broke off a piece of the glacier to bring back to Hallstatt to show others its magical qualities. But the removed chunk, "von der herrlichen blauen Masse abgeschlagen, sich im kleinen als völlig farblos ausweis" (*HD*, 37; chipped off the glorious blue mass, in miniature proved itself as completely colorless), so the fellow climber threw it away. Simony's assessment seems correct: his "werten Leser" (dear readers), like the residents of Hallstatt, can have "keine Ahnung" (no idea) about the marvelous sight of the glacier without trekking up the mountain themselves (*HD*, 36).

The glacier otherwise plays only a minor role in these two texts. Simony recounts how he and his team took temperatures around and atop the glacier and drove stakes into the ice so they could measure it. He quotes his friend Eduard Weiß to share how the glacier made him

---

16  Friedrich Simony, *Auf dem Hohen Dachstein* (Vienna: Österreichischer Schulbücherverlag, 1921), 31. Unless otherwise noted, quoted passages from Simony come from his essay "Drei Dezembertage auf dem Dachsteingebirge." Subsequent references to this source will be by the abbreviation *HD* and page number.

feel: "Ich möchte weinen über meine Winzigkeit, die ich nie so tief emp-
funden wie hier, auf diesem Obelisk der Schöpfung, wo eine Welt wie ein
Staubkörnchen mich verschlingt" (I want to cry about my minuteness,
which I never felt so deeply as here, on this obelisk of creation, where a
world devours me like a speck of dust).[17] And he mentions legends about
growing glaciers, but only to explain that he will not comment on them.
In the end, Simony explains, "das Karls-Eisfeld war bald überschritten
und über seine untere Abdachung ging es im pfeilschnellen Fluge hinab"
(*HD*, 41; the Karl Icefield was soon crossed and we went at lightning
speed down its lower slope). The appearance is brief but spectacular.

It is no wonder that Simony's prose proved an inspiration to Stifter.
Even travel guides at the time pale in comparison. Adolph Schaubach's
*Die deutschen Alpen: Ein Handbuch für Reisende* (The German Alps: A
Handbook for Travelers) is representative. In the 1846 text, Schaubach
enumerates several paths to the Dachstein glacier and notes the difficulty of
the climb. And though he claims "herrlich war hier die Aussicht" (the view
here was glorious), the writer does little to describe the glacier.[18] Julius
von Schröckinger-Neudenberg's *Reisegefährte durch Ober-Oesterreichs
Gebirgsland* (Travel Companion through Upper-Austria's Mountain
Region) is similarly thin on detail. In the 1856 text, published one year
before *Nachsommer*, Schröckinger-Neudenberg identifies the paths to the
Dachstein glacier, which he could not reach himself because of inclement
weather. Still, he claims the sight of the ice is astonishing, though does
little to describe it besides enumerating the size: "der Gletscher misst über
10,000 Klafter im Umfange" (the glacier measures more than ten thousand
fathoms in circumference).[19] Writers like Schaubach and Schröckinger-
Neudenberg possibly wanted to leave the experience a surprise for the
would-be traveler, or perhaps Wachler's eighteenth-century assessment
remained true: despite the power of the written word, without seeing glaciers firsthand, it is hard to truly get a sense of them.

## Stifter's Glaciers: *Bergkristall*

Inspired by Simony's descriptions, Stifter wrote *Bergkristall* and *Der
Nachsommer*. In *Das alte Siegel*, first written before Simony published the
essays recounting his Dachstein escapades, Stifter atypically sets the story
in the Tyrolean Alps and invents the Morigletscher. Besides naming the

---

17 Friedrich Simony, "Zwei Septembernächte auf der Hohen Dachsteinspitze," in *Auf dem Hohen Dachstein*, 46–97; here 75.

18 Adolph Schaubach, *Die deutschen Alpen: Ein Handbuch für Reisende, drit-
ter Theil* (Jena: Fromann, 1846), 326.

19 Julius R. von Schröckinger-Neudenberg, *Reisegefährte durch Ober-Oesterreichs Gebirgsland*, 4th ed. (Linz: Vinzenz Fink, 1856), 112.

ice into which the titular old seal is hurled, the author does not offer any description of the landscape. Consequently, Stifter's first attempt to portray glaciers comes in *Bergkristall*. Among other scholars, Stefan Braun has carefully analyzed the influence of Simony's works on Stifter's prose, identifying passages Stifter borrows nearly verbatim from the alpinist.[20] Some have found the author lacking in comparison. Sean Ireton, for instance, rightly argues that Stifter's account "comes across as restrained and objective compared to Simony's emotionally charged and putatively scientific report."[21] Simony's splendid descriptions of glaciers, however, are scant. And the renowned mountaineer repeatedly denies the possibility of ever truly understanding the ice without personally visiting it. Stifter, by contrast, attempts to produce a glacier out of his prose that is comprehensible to his reader. The original 1845 version of *Bergkristall*, published under the title "Der heilige Abend" (Christmas Eve) in the journal *Gegenwart* (Present), includes rich descriptions of glaciers, marking Stifter's first published attempt to depict a glacier. For the revised text included in the collection *Bunte Steine* (Motley Stones) in 1853, Stifter further expands the scenes of the children on the glacier. In addition, he revises the language to emphasize his awareness of the difficult literary task. Examining the narrative techniques the author deploys not only reveals his literary prowess, it uncovers Stifter's participation in the broader discourse about the representation of glaciers. Unsurprisingly, Stifter is cognizant of the role of language in the effort. In the end, he seems to concede the inherent failure of this mimetic act, confirming that glaciers resist reproduction in the written word despite his own magical creation.

Through shifting narrative perspectives and a surfeit of description, Stifter creates a specific topographical space in *Bergkristall* for the children to traverse and the reader to imagine.[22] The text itself early demonstrates the importance of embracing this approach to gain a complete

20  Stefan Braun, *Naturwissenschaft als Lebensbasis? Adalbert Stifters Roman Der Nachsommer und weitere Schriften Stifters als Dokumente eines Versuches der Daseinsgestaltung auf der Grundlage naturwissenschaftlichen Forschens* (Linz: Stifterhaus, 2006), 104–8.

21  Ireton, "Geology," 201. Georg Braungart similarly describes Simony's writing as "eine Synthese aus Wissenschaft und Poesie." Georg Braungart, "Der Hauslehrer, Landschaftsmaler und Schriftsteller Adalbert Stifter besucht den Gletscherforscher Friedrich Simony. Hallstatt, im Sommer 1845," in *Bespiegelungskunst, Begegnungen auf dem Seitenwegen der Literaturgeschichte*, ed. Georg Braungart, Friedmann Harzer, Hans Peter Neureuter, and Gertrud M. Rösch (Tübingen: Attempto, 2004), 101–18; here 102.

22  For a discussion of the careful construction of the topography of the mountains in *Bergkristall* see: Kathrin Geist, *Berg-Sehn-Sucht: Der Alpenraum in der deutschsprachigen Literatur* (Paderborn: Wilhelm Fink, 2018), 119–21.

understanding of a landscape. The nameless narrator explains that it appears no path leads in or out of the children's village, "wenn man so ziemlich mitten in dem Thale steht" (when you stand in the middle of the valley). It is, however, merely a "Täuschung" (*HKG* 2,2:192; illusion, *MS*, 133). From a higher vantage point, the various trails reveal themselves, including the way from Gschaid to Millsdorf. For the first third of the novella, the narrator carefully traces the path Konrad and Sanna will later follow to their grandparents' home. The reader thus learns where the children must climb up and down the mountain, which meadow they will cross, and through which forest they will trek. In the words of Martin Wagner, Stifter creates a "material, visual reality" using these narrative tools.[23]

This reality is intelligible until a storm brings falling snow that temporarily obscures the landmarks that indicate the path. The children then inadvertently wander onto the nearby glacier, which obliterates the carefully constructed space. They attempt to turn around "wo sie hinauf geklettert waren, aber sie kamen nicht hinab. Es war lauter Eis, als hätten sie die Richtung, in der sie gekommen waren, verfehlt" (*HKG* 2,2:221; where they had climbed up, but they could find no way to come down. There was nothing but sheer ice, as though they had mistaken the direction they had come from, *MS*, 156). Sanna and Konrad are instantly disoriented, as if they have wandered onto one of the unfinished corners of the *Landesaufnahme*. Fittingly, perhaps, cartographic blank spaces are meant to allow the eye to rest as the reader processes information. Atop the ice, the children's eyes are undeniably given a break, but they have frighteningly little to interpret as they attempt to navigate the blank white glacier.

Stifter fills in the details. Contrasting both Simony, who is largely bound to first-person reports, and visual artworks with a single fixed viewpoint, Stifter uses an omniscient narrator and shares the impressions of numerous characters to offer a multidimensional view of the icy landscape. Through the children, the reader experiences the ice at close proximity, as when the former feel the glacier underfoot. In addition, the narrator alternately describes how the ice appears from far away: "es wird das unbestimmte Schillern von Bläulich und Grünlich sichtbar, das das Geschiebe von Eis ist, das dann blos liegt" (*HKG* 2,2:189; the indistinct shimmer of blue and green grows visible, the shifting ice that then lies bare, *MS*, 131); and how it looks up close: "glimmerte es seitwärts grünlich und bläulich und dunkel und schwarz und selbst gelblich und röthlich" (*HKG* 2,2:220; the sides glimmered from within, shades of green and blue and dark and black and even yellow and red, *MS*, 155). Beyond

---

23 Martin Wagner, *The Narratology of Observation* (Berlin: De Gruyter, 2018), 54.

communicating how the ice looks and feels, the shifting views enable a better understanding of the size of the glacier. Assuming a bird's-eye perspective, the narrator explains: "Sie waren winzigkleine, wandelnde Punkte in diesen ungeheuern Stüken" (*HKG* 2,2:219; They were miniscule moving dots amidst these monstrous fragments, *MS*, 154). Through the mouth of Konrad, the text reaffirms the power of these shifting perspectives. "Das ist das Eis," the boy explains to his sister as they attempt to make sense of the glacier, "das unten nur so klein ausschaut, weil man sehr weit entfernt ist" (*HKG* 2,2:218; that's the ice, it only looks so small from below because we're so far away, *MS*, 154). The multiple views ultimately aid in identifying and properly perceiving the glacier, which is simply "etwas anderes" when the children and reader first encounter it.

Unlike their appearance on early-nineteenth-century maps, most alpine glaciers are not smooth white masses. Instead, they have wild topography. Stifter gives the glacier shape with his words as the children wander over its surface. But his mimetic act is limited by his apparent inability to find precise terminology. Stifter describes vague "Platten" (plates), "Blöcke" (blocks), "Kugeln" (balls), and "Hügel" (mounds) on the glacier, eventually resorting to "Körper" (bodies), a term so indistinct it is nearly meaningless in terms of helping the reader visualize the landscape. The shortcoming, however, is not entirely the author's fault. Since glaciology was in its nascent stages as a discipline, many features of a glacier did not yet have standardized terms and few readers anyway would have been familiar with the little specialized vocabulary already established.[24]

Stifter compensates for the terminological deficit by utilizing rich metaphoric language to help visualize the glacier. Borrowing fairytale language from Simony, he compares the ice to glimmering "Edelstein[e]" (gemstones) and describes it "wie zusammengeschobener Schaum" (*HKG* 2,2:217; foam pushed together, *MS*, 153). At times, Stifter also veers into the otherworldly—literally. Sanna and Konrad find themselves in a cavern "so blau, wie nichts in der Welt" (*HKG* 2,2:219; as blue as nothing on earth, *MS*, 155). Simultaneously, the author grounds his description in the quotidian details of mountain life. The bodies growing on the glacier are "so hoch wie der Kirchthurm in Gschaid" (as high as the church steeple ... in Gschaid), and the cavern is so large that one

---

24  Stifter is likely describing what are today known as seracs (from the Swiss French: *sérac*), large blocks or columns of glacial ice, whether in their intact or collapsed states, i.e., whether as glacial formations or glacial debris. At the time he wrote *Bergkristall*, this term was still being defined for scientific readers and would not have been widely understood outside the Swiss Alps See for instance: Albert Mousson, *Die Gletscher der Jetztzeit: Eine Zusammenstellung und Prüfung ihrer Erscheinungen und Gesetze* (Zurich: Schulthess, 1854), 34.

could pass through it "mit einem ganzen großen Wagen voll Heu" (*HKG* 2,2:217; a great cartload of hay, *MS*, 153, translation modified). The mundanity of these objects is in direct opposition to the unearthliness upon which the narrator insists. This is no place for a hay wagon and no church could actually stand so high in the mountains. Yet by invoking incongruent ideas, the metaphorical language emphasizes the strangeness of the place while making it legible, giving the reader a sense of the size and shape of these frozen bodies to paint a fuller image of the scene.

The written word, accordingly, enables both the children and reader to better understand the mountain landscape. It solves the problem faced by Simony's companion who could not physically bring a piece of the glacier home because it would lose its magical luster. Without climbing a mountain, the reader can see the jewel-like ice. And just by reading *Bergkristall*, the reader can vicariously hear "den Schall, der entsezlich war, als ob die Erde entzwei gesprungen wäre, der sich nach allen Richtungen im Eise verbreitete, und gleichsam durch alle Aderchen des Eises lief" (*HKG* 2,2:227–28; the report, appalling, as though the earth had cracked in two, the sound spreading throughout the ice in all directions, seeming to course through all its fine veins, *MS*, 161). In addition to rendering the otherworldly glacial landscape comprehensible, Stifter's words act as new landmarks around which the children can orient themselves. The constant repetition of phrases, including Sanna's persistent echo, "Ja, Konrad" (Yes, Konrad), help the children make sense of their new environment and navigate it. Kathrin Geist observes that "die immer gleiche Struktur der Sätze, vorwiegend Haupt- und Relativsätze, schafft so Orientierung in einem unbekannten Raum, dessen Struktur gänzlich vom gewohnten Raum des Dorfes abweicht" (the constant structure of the sentences, predominantly main and relative clauses, creates orientation in an unknown space, the structure of which deviates completely from the familiar space of the village).[25] While filling in the blank space of the white page, Stifter's words begin to fill in the blank white space of the glacier.

Stifter's manuscript for *Bergkristall* (Figure 10.4), which is full of signs and directions that allow his words to be read, becomes a sort of map itself. Consistent with his editorial practice, Stifter tinkered with his portrayal of glaciers in "Der heilige Abend," rearranging details and elaborating his descriptions. In the final 1853 version, after the miraculous night in which the northern lights appear, the children struggle longer to get off the ice. Konrad advises "wir werden gar nicht mehr in das Eis hinein gehen, weil wir in demselben nicht fortkommen" (*HKG* 2,2:231; let's not go into the ice again; we can't make any headway there, *MS*,

---

25  Geist, *Berg-Sehn-Sucht*, 132.

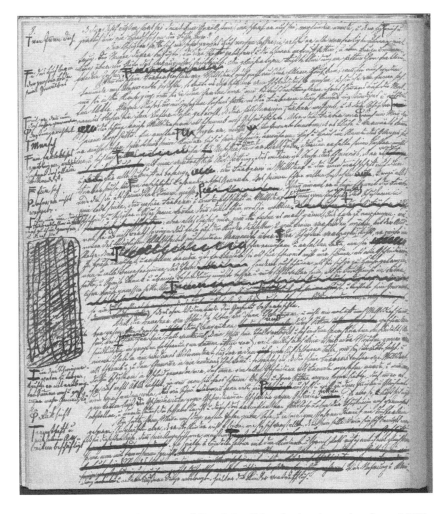

Figure 10.4. Manuscript page of *Bergkristall* for the book version from 1853. Bayerische Staatsbibliothek, Signatur Cgm 8071 (2, Handschrift S. 14).

164). He seems to sense it is a sort of maze that he cannot escape of his own volition.

Stifter self-consciously plays with this linguistic power. As the children climb over the glacier, they grow desperate to get off of it. Their efforts, however, repeatedly fail. "Da kamen sie wieder in das Eis. Sie wußten nicht, wie das Eis daher gekommen sei, aber unter den Füssen empfanden sie den glatten Boden" (*HKG* 2,2:230; Then they entered the ice again. They did not know how the ice had come to be there, but they felt the smooth footing, *MS*, 163). They cannot explain or make sense of it, but no matter where they go, the ice reappears. "Aber da fanden sie wieder Eis" (*HKG* 2,2:232; But there they found more ice, *MS*, 164). The narrator clarifies that the predicament it is not the result of the children's perceptual or navigational shortcomings. The problem is stated in a momentum-killing sentence: "Aber es gab kein Jenseits" (*HKG* 2,2:220; But there was no beyond, *MS*, 156, translation modified). In the 1845 version, the narrator explains more concretely, as the children climb an ice ridge: "Aber das Jenseits, wo es nun sogleich hinabgehen sollte, war nicht da, der Wall hatte kein Jenseits" (*HKG* 2,1:163; But the beyond, where it was supposed to go down, was not there, the wall had no beyond). As the narrator further explains: "Wo es sich abwärts neigte, war nicht hinunter zu kommen, ohne zu stürzen" (*HKG* 2,1:164; where it tilted downward, it was impossible to come down without falling). The earlier version ties the dilemma to a specific, impassable topography; the later version makes it an existential condition. Whereas Simony's companion Eduard Weiß felt small on top of the mountain while visiting the Dachstein glacier, Konrad and Sanna in *Bergkristall* are faced with the infinite. Stifter places the children into dimensionless, negative space. These words, Martin Swales claims, "brutally negate the parameters of the familiar world" as the "children have strayed into a world where all the coordinates of normal living, normal perception, have gone into abeyance."[26] These words also underscore the author's absolute control over the landscape. Only Stifter's evocative metaphors, shifting perspectives, and careful details give shape to the glacier and make it graspable.

While reducing the landscape to words, Stifter acknowledges the instability and artificiality of language as a foundation for the representation of the natural world. In "Der heilige Abend," Konrad says that the children will "da gerade von dem Eise hinunterlaufen" (*HKG* 2,1:162; there just run down from the ice). But in *Bergkristall* he declares "so werden wir über die blaue Farbe hinab gehen" (*HKG* 2,2:218; so we'll go

---

26  Martin Swales, "Homeliness and Otherness: Reflections on Stifter's *Bergkristall*," in *The German Bestseller in the Late Nineteenth Century*, ed. Charlotte Woodford and Benedict Schofield (Rochester, NY: Camden House, 2012), 115–126; here 120–21.

downhill across the blue color, *MS*, 154). By focusing on the color, and suggesting that they should walk over it, Konrad emphasizes the abstract nature of their surroundings: the children are walking over a linguistically constituted environment and not a real physical space. Koschorke and Ammer long ago noted the tendency of Stifter's description to push "die Referentialität der Wörter gegen Null, bis sie statt ursprünglicher Lebensfülle bloß noch eine Schemenwelt und zuletzt allein ihre eigene Exitenz, ihren Materialcharakter als Wörter demonstrieren" (the referentiality of the words towards null, until, instead of the original abundance of life, they demonstrate a shadow world and ultimately their own existence and their material character as words).[27] Stifter, however, is uneasy about the language of this *Gletscherwelt*. The narrator quickly adds a qualifier to the apt if oxymoronic description of the "white darkness" that envelopes the children: "wenn man so sagen darf" (*HKG* 2,2:216; if this can be said, *MS*, 152). In Adorno's formulation, Stifter here "[blickt] in den Abgrund … in welchen die Sprache einstürzt, die sich selbst aufheben möchte in Namen und Bild" (look[s] into the abyss into which language collapses when it tries to become name and image) and he is not confident about what he sees.[28]

When the children are rescued and finally escape the white void, their perception is restored. They can again hear the bells and see the flags and signs, as if they stepped foot back onto a completed section of the *Landesaufnahme*. As they regain these other senses, Konrad and Sanna, together with the narrator, seem to lose their ability to make sense of the glacial mountain and it reverts back to uniform, blank space: "Bald gingen sie nach einer Richtung, bald schlugen sie die entgegengesetzte ein, bald gingen sie abwärts bald aufwärts. Immer ging es durch Schnee, immer durch Schnee, und die Gegend blieb sich beständig gleich" (*HKG* 2,2:234–35; Now they went in one direction, now they turned in the other, now they went downhill now uphill. The way was always through the snow, always through the snow, and the surroundings never changed, *MS*, 167). Standing at lower altitudes far from the glacier, the children's father even denies their self-knowledge that they were on the ice at all:

27 Albrecht Koschorke and Andreas Ammer, "Der Text ohne Bedeutung oder die Erstarrung der Angst: Zu Stifters letzter Erzählung *Der fromme Spruch*," *Deutsche Vierteljahrsschrift für Literaturwissenschaft und Geistesgeschichte* 61, no. 4 (1987): 676–719; here 711.

28 In his persuasive reading of *Granit*, Jason Groves cites the same passage in a similar context. See *The Geological Unconscious: German Literature and the Mineral Imaginary* (New York: Fordham University Press, 2020), 85. Theodor W. Adorno "Über epische Naivetät," in *Noten zur Literatur* (Frankfurt am Main: Suhrkamp, 1981), 34–40; here 37. English translation from: Theodor W. Adorno, "On Epic Naiveté," in *Notes to Literature*, vol. 1, trans. Shierry Weber Nicholsen (New York: Columbia University Press, 1991) 24–29; here 27.

"Sie sind über das Gletschereis und über die Schründe gegangen, ohne es zu wissen" (*HKG* 2,2:237; They crossed the glacier and the crevasses without knowing it, *MS*, 169), he explains, despite the children's explicit discussion of the glacier with each other. Back in the village, the experience of the glacier is thus further destabilized through language.

In *Bergkristall*, Stifter both answers the question of how to represent a glacier and simultaneously undermines it. Words can constitute a glacier, but also destroy it. The author uses a variety of literary tricks to make the ice visceral to his readers, conjuring a glacier out of prose. However, he contritely acknowledges that the glacier he has produced is no more than a linguistic illusion, for which he must almost apologize to the reader.

## Stifter's Glaciers: *Der Nachsommer*

Stifter confirms this artifice and his apparent discomfort with it in *Der Nachsommer*, the only other text in which he describes glaciers in any detail. As the protagonist Heinrich takes ever-longer trips into the mountains, he assumes new challenges including a winter visit to the Simmi glacier (a linguistic homage to Simony). Typical of Stifter's works, the novel's three volumes are not full of "twists and turns of plot, but rather extensive description" as Timothy Attanucci notes.[29] Through these details, the reader is intended to appreciate the landscape, or as Robert Holub puts it: "As readers, we too are supposed to experience the word-paintings that characterize [Stifter's] prose as enrichments of the story, as an element of depth and beauty."[30] The reader of *Der Nachsommer*, however, is largely denied such an experience of the glacier. Yet the reader is not meant to be uninterested in the ice—in fact, the text inspires the opposite.

As in *Bergkristall*, the glaciers in *Der Nachsommer* demand inspection and contemplation. When he first reaches the ice, Heinrich explains that it "mich sehr anregte, und zur Betrachtung aufforderte" (*HKG* 4,1:40; excited me very much and stimulated my desire to observe it, *IS*, 26), but little description follows. Others want to see the ice, too. In one of the next instances a glacier is mentioned, Heinrich visits a local princess who "nahm ... besonderen Anteil" (was particularly interested) when he spoke of the Simmi glacier. As he shares his drawings and she fastidiously studies them. He remarks: "Ich mußte ihr genau beschreiben und zeigen, wo wir gewesen und was wir getan haben. ... Sie ließ sich jedes,

---

29  Timothy Attanucci, *The Restorative Poetics of a Geological Age: Stifter, Viollet-le-Duc, and the Aesthetic Practices of Geohistoricism* (Berlin: De Gruyter, 2020), 80.

30  Robert C. Holub, *Reflections of Realism: Paradox, Norm, and Ideology in Nineteenth-Century German Prose* (Detroit, MI: Wayne State University Press, 1991), 71.

auch das Kleinste an diesen Zeichnungen beschreiben und erklären" (*HKG* 4,3:44; I had to describe precisely where we had been and what we had been doing. ... She had me describe and explain even the most minute details on these drawings, *IS*, 345). Despite the princess's demand for description and careful study, the text never details the object of her attention, leaving the reader in the dark about the appearance of the glacier. The narrator's own engagement begins to feel perfunctory, too. In his next visit to the glacier, Heinrich describes how at daybreak he and his sister, Klotilde, reached the dome of the glacier and then merely explains "wir betrachteten hier nun, was zu betrachten war, und ... traten ... den Rückweg an" (*HKG* 4,3:91–93; we enjoyed the view, and ... set out on the way back, *IS*, 372). The reader is repeatedly told the glacier is worthy of contemplation but is refused a robust description, thereby heightening curiosity about the ice.

When the reader is finally offered a literary look, linguistic uncertainty dominates. In the chapter that begins volume two, Heinrich describes how he "saß in der Einsamkeit und schaute auf die blau oder grüne oder schillernde Farbe des Eises" (*HKG* 4,2:10; sat in the solitude contemplating the blue, green, or iridescent colors of the ice, *IS*, 180). The more definite conjunction "und" (and) connecting the adjectives in *Bergkristall* are replaced in *Der Nachsommer* with the less certain "oder" (or), leaving a nebulous impression of the ice. The most detailed description is found in volume three, when Heinrich visits the glacier in winter. Though the snowpack blankets the ice in a monotonous mantle of white, Stifter shows us that the glacier is still open to narrative description: "Wo die Eismengen geborsten und zertrümmert waren, hatte sie an ihren Oberflächen der Schnee bedeckt, mit den Seitenflächen sahen sie grünlich oder bläulich schillernd aus dem allgemeinen Weiß hervor" (*HKG* 4,3:109; Where the ice masses were burst or there was rubble, it was covered by snow, at least the upper surfaces; the sides peered out from the general white in iridescent blue or green, *IS*, 381). Here, again, language does not seem to be able to capture what the ice looks like. These descriptions are atypical for Stifter. They are not an example of Stifter's "technique of telling less by telling more,"[31] since the reader is hardly flooded with specifics about the glacier. Nor does the portrayal of the ice comport with the author's tendency to paint scenes by giving detailed information about what something is not, which Helena Ragg-Kirkby names "the heart of Stifter's narrative technique."[32] The glacier is instead mostly kept out of sight in Stifter's prose.

31  Helena Ragg-Kirkby, "'Eine immerwährende Umwandlung der Ansichten': Narrators and Their Perspectives in the Works of Adalbert Stifter," *The Modern Language Review* 95, no. 1 (2000): 127–43; here 130.

32  Ragg-Kirkby, "'Eine immerwährende Umwandlung,'" 134.

The written word is not alone in this failure. Through Heinrich, Stifter suggests that visual representation is also not up to the task of representing glaciers. Following his trip to the Simmi ice with his sister, the protagonist shows her "mehrere Zeichnungen, die ich von Gletschern, ihren Einfassungen, Wölbungen, Spaltungen, Zusammenschiebungen und dergleichen gemacht hatte, vor, damit sie in der frischen Erinnerung das Gesehene mit dem Abgebildeten vergleichen konnte" (several drawings I had done of the glaciers, their fringes, curvatures, crevices, how they push together and such things, so she could compare the drawings with the actual formations while they were still fresh in her memory). Without waiting for her to weigh in, he acknowledges "wie sehr die Abbildung hinter der Wirklichkeit zurück bleibe" (*HKG* 4,3:92; how very much the drawings fell short of reality, *IS*, 372). It is a foregone conclusion that the drawings could not capture reality. In an effort to demonstrate the equation of literature and the visual arts, Holub observes, "the narrators in Stifter's prose works ... vie with their artistic heroes; the former paint with words and phrases, and the latter utilize brush and palette."[33] When it comes to glaciers, it seems both have failed. In *Der Nachsommer*, Stifter does not even give us expressive let alone confident words to describe a glacier. Like Heinrich, he seems to know how much they would lag behind the real glaciers in the Alps. Through this omission, the glacier in *Der Nachsommer* creates another void, this time a blank space in the novel.

Compared to other glacier writings of the period, including *Bergkristall*, Stifter's portrayal of the "eternal ice" in *Der Nachsommer* is strange because Heinrich's winter visit is ultimately a non-event.[34] Simony, from whom Stifter practically plagiarizes these glaciers, describes avalanches, near-deaths, and wonderous landscapes in addition to conveying new scientific knowledge. Stifter offers neither an aesthetic account nor a glaciological report. And Heinrich's ascent is certainly not a gripping tale of harrowing physical adventure or exciting environmental adversity. The episode atop the glacier is reduced to a few sentences. In one of the more descriptive passages, Heinrich narrates: "Wir verweilten einige Zeit auf dem Eise und nahmen auf demselben auch unser Mittagmahl, in Wein und Brod bestehend, ein" (*HKG* 4,3:109; We spent some time on the ice and had our noon meal of bread and wine up there, *IS*, 382). Such a non-event is not unusual in Stifter's works, like the looming thunderstorm

---

33  Holub, *Reflections*, 71.

34  Sean Ireton analyzes the shifting human interactions with the Alps and the variety of narratives such interactions produce, including hybrid texts like Simony's poetic-scientific essays. See Sean Ireton, "Dialektik der Erschließung: The German-Austrian Alps between Exploration and Exploitation," *humanities* 10 (2021): https://doi.org/10.3390/h10010017.

that never materializes in *Der Nachsommer*. However, the encounter with the glacier does not precipitate a plot development or even result in rich description for the reader to enjoy.

As Austrians were grappling with the challenge of how best to represent glaciers, Stifter joined the effort in *Bergkristall*, using multiple perspectives and rich metaphoric language to create a glacier out of his prose. His return to the ice in *Der Nachsommer*, however, is less of a second attempt and more of a renunciation of the endeavor. Despite his renown for painstaking detail and lavish descriptions, Stifter glosses over the glaciers in his sprawling epic while simultaneously insisting that they are objects worthy of our attention. The text consequently reads as an announcement of the failure to depict glaciers, confirming Stifter's ostensible discomfort with what he produced in the earlier story.

# Conclusion

Stifter's reluctance to portray glaciers seems to be the consequence of his awareness of the limitations of language as a mimetic medium. Throughout his works and in *Bunte Steine*, in particular, Stifter questions the capacity of language to represent the natural world. For example, Erica Weitzman has shown how Stifter in *Turmalin* "recognizes that language … [has] no necessary connection to the things that it signifies" and thus falls apart.[35] And Jason Groves contends that in *Granit* Stifter "not only knows or senses but transitively writes the inadequacy of language and its inability to obtain the sovereignty over the world."[36] In many cases, this allows language in Stifter's works to constitute its own reality, as Eva Geulen has persuasively argued. Stifter's "verbalrealistische[s] Gesetz" (verbal-realist law), according to Geulen, means that "Worte bedeuten nichts mehr, sondern werden Ereignis. Sie bezeichnen keine Geschehnisse, sondern sie sind das Geschehen" (words no longer mean anything, but become an event. They do not denote occurrences but are the occurrence).[37] In *Der Nachsommer*, however, the words mark the missing event. Stifter's later works and his revisions of earlier works, Brigid Haines notes, are "characterized by the increasing use of impassive, non-reflective narrators and a tightening of the gaps and uncertainties in the stories."[38] The ambiguities that do remain in Stifter's texts

---

35   Erica Weitzman, "Despite Language Adalbert Stifter's Revenge Fantasies," *Monatshefte* 111, no. 3 (2019): 362–79; here 373.

36   Groves, *Geological Unconscious*, 87.

37   Eva Geulen, *Worthörig wider Willen Darstellungsproblematik und Sprachreflexion in der Prosa Adalbert Stifters* (Munich: iudicium, 1992), 35.

38   Brigid Haines, *Dialogue and Narrative Design in the Works of Adalbert Stifter* (London: MHRA, 1991), 5.

are often about human actions and unreachable cosmic truths; the natural world, however subjectively portrayed, is not plagued by the same indeterminacy.[39] But glaciers, when traced across "Der heilige Abend," *Bergkristall*, and *Der Nachsommer*, appear to have been Stifter's stumbling block. The ice remained beyond his climbing capability and beyond the reach of what he thought language could achieve. The author thus confirms the general consensus that glaciers resist representation.

Yet Stifter accomplishes more than he recognizes in his texts. His glaciers are more evocative than coeval travel guides, and they deliver more than Simony manages in his colorful essays, since Stifter does not deny the possibility of experiencing a glacier without a firsthand encounter. Stifter takes the reader across the blank space of the map and fills it in, showing the ice and creating the feeling of being atop a glacier even if it is an illusion created by words. Contemporaries agreed. One unnamed reviewer, writing in the *Österreichische Blätter für Literatur und Kunst* (Austrian Pages for Literature and Art) in 1853, claimed that the glaciers in *Bergkristall* were "mit der entschiedensten Kraft des Meisters und einer bis in das Kleinste gehende Virtuosität geschildert" (portrayed with the decisive power of the master and a virtuosity that goes to the smallest detail).[40] Another critic even praised the comparatively hastily sketched glaciers in *Der Nachsommer*. "Dazu kömmt die Großartigkeit schriftlicher Landschaftsmalerei, worin Stifter von jeher unübertroffen war und die nur er selbst übertreffen konnte, namentlich in der Schilderung einer Gletscherbesteigung mitten im Winter" (in addition there is the brilliance of written landscape painting, in which Stifter has always been unsurpassed and which only he himself could surpass, namely in the description of climbing a glacier in the middle of winter).[41] Even if this enthusiasm is simultaneously a testament to the otherwise poor descriptions of glaciers circulating at the time, it speaks to a larger aesthetic achievement. The Austrian author Emil Kuh asserted in 1868 that portraying the white monotony of snow-covered glacial mountains was near impossible: "Die[se] Stille darzustellen, mit Worten darzustellen, hat gewiß Jeder bisher für eine nicht zu lösende Aufgabe der Poesie gehalten. Stifter hat diese Aufgabe gelöst" (to portray this silence, to portray it with words, has certainly been considered by all to be an unsolvable task of poetry.

---

39   See Ragg-Kirkby, "'Eine immerwährende Umwandlung,'" 141.

40   *Österreichische Blätter für Literatur und Kunst: Beilage zur Österreich-Kaiserlichen Wiener Zeitung*, January 10, 1853, no. 2. Cited in *HKG* 2,4: 69.

41   Hieronymous Lorm, "Adalbert Stifter: 'Der Nachsommer'—eine 'Erzählung,' in *Wiener Zeitung*, no. 294: 23 (December 1857), 3642, cited in *HKG* 4,4:127.

Stifter has solved this task).[42] Despite such praise, Stifter did not seem as enthused about his glaciers.

The author's unease is due to his awareness of the "Schemenwelt" that his powerful words inevitably create and its implicit comparison to the real world of the mountains. When Stifter wrote *Bergkristall* and *Der Nachsommer*, he assumed that glaciers would perpetually occupy the Alps. Konrad espouses this pervasive belief when he attempts to explain the glacier to his sister: "das ist das Eis, das ... wie der Vater sagte, nicht weggeht bis an das Ende der Welt" (*HKG* 2,2:218; that's the ice ... father says it will never be gone until the end of the world, *MS*, 154). Just as the *Landesaufnahme* officially labelled the "eternal ice" of the Habsburg Empire, Stifter failed to understand that glaciers could disappear. Consequently, he misjudged the import of his magical words. As the *Gletscherwelt* of the Austrian Alps transforms, Stifter's words take on new meaning. Already in 1857, at least one reviewer recognized the potential of Stifter's enduring legacy. He pronounced the glacier descriptions as bearing "das Siegel der Unvergänglichkeit" (the seal of immortality) and suggested they be "in Mustersammlungen aufbewahrt noch der spätesten Nachwelt zum Genuß gereichen" (kept in collections of samples for future generations to enjoy).[43] Stifter's glaciers may be a mere linguistic illusion, a white abyss, compared to the glittering glaciers that Simony visited, but they could eventually be all we have left of this beautiful otherworldly ice.

---

42  Emil Kuh, *Adalbert Stifter* (Vienna: Tendler, 1868), 31–32.
43  Kuh, *Adalbert Stifter*, 31–32.

# 11: Cheerful Terror: Stifter and the Aesthetics of Atmosphere

*Alexander Robert Phillips*

To the extent that it is about anything at all, Heiner Goebbels's theater installation *Stifters Dinge* (Stifter's Things) is as much about the atmosphere in the theater as it is about the things on the stage. In a press release upon its 2007 premier, the Théâtre Vidy in Lausanne, Switzerland, described it as a "composition for five pianos with no pianists, a play with no actors, performance without actors—one might say a no-man show."[1] Music from mechanically played pianos is interspersed with sounds from archival recordings, while lights illuminate a pool of dry ice, from which smoky tendrils curl into the air. The Théâtre Vidy says of *Stifters Dinge* that the things (they list "light, pictures, murmurs, sounds, voices, wind and mist, water and ice") do not function in a merely illustrative role, but rather become the protagonists.[2] The installation is, in that sense, uncanny, but its uncanniness is an atmospheric effect because it arises out of the interplay between the solid objects, components of the atmosphere as a geophysical system, and both pictures and sounds. Goebbels himself says that his aim was to afford the audience "die Entdeckung des freien Raums" (the discovery of free space).[3] "Free space" is not empty space because the theater is not a vacuum. Rather, what the "discovery of free space" means in practice is that the atmosphere in the theater is both a part of and a result of the composition.

In facilitating a "discovery of free space," *Stifters Dinge* captures not only Stifter's fascination with things in general but his fascination with the atmosphere and the experience thereof. This is a recurring theoretical problem running throughout Stifter's oeuvre, from his first published story

---

1    Théâtre Vidy, "Heiner Goebbels, *Stifters Dinge*," September 13, 2007, 3, https://vidy.ch/wp-content/uploads/2022/11/dv-13-14-stifters-eng-1.pdf.

2    Théâtre Vidy, "Heiner Goebbels, *Stifters Dinge*," 3.

3    Marc Perroud and Heiner Goebbels, *The Experience of Things, Heiner Goebbels: Stifters Dinge*, 2008, 2:25; http://edu.medici.tv/movies/the-experience-of-things-heiner-goebbels. Translations are mine unless otherwise indicated. *The Experience of Things* documents the installation and the work that went into creating it.

"Der Condor" (The Condor, 1840/44), to the famous preface to *Bunte Steine* (Motley Stones, 1853), to his last writings in the 1860s. According to Stifter himself, atmospheric phenomena were central to his writing from his earliest juvenilia. In a letter to Leo Tepe dated 26 December 1867, for instance, he notes: "meine ersten Schriftstellerversuche liegen in meiner Kindheit, wo ich stets Donnerwetter beschrieb" (my first attempts at writing were back in my childhood, when I was constantly describing thunderstorms).[4] In his mature work, the atmosphere persists as a thing carefully described, but also as a realm of sometimes contradictory aesthetic experiences. As one of Earth's systems, it can be predictable and knowable, and as such may signify stability and order, but because of its scale and sheer dynamism it contains within it the threat of chaos. The atmosphere as physical reality and "the atmospheric" as subjective experience are largely determinative of Stifter's aesthetics, both where it is explicitly theorized or implicitly staged within the stories themselves.

The atmosphere's special aesthetic status for Stifter becomes apparent in comparison to the lithosphere, that other system that plays such a significant role in his writings.[5] Stone might epitomize materiality as such for its solidity and weightiness, as opposed to the seemingly ethereal nature of atmosphere. Yet it is air that presses down constantly and inexorably on every body on the Earth's surface. In addition, air has no specific form, being a compound of gases, and it is transparent or not, depending on its aerosol content. And despite its material aspects, the atmosphere is not just air and thus not exactly a "thing": energy also constitutes the atmospheric system, as does light, which, under the sign of the then dominant wave theory, was its carrier.[6]

For Stifter, "atmosphere" cannot be thought of as separate from its aesthetic connotations. Historically the word stands with "ambience,"

---

4    Adalbert Stifter, *Sämmtliche Werke*, ed. August Sauer, Franz Hüller, Kamill Eben, Gustav Wilhelm, vol. 22 (Prague: Calve; Reichenberg: Kraus, 1904), 179. (This first critical "Prague" edition of Stifter's collected works is hereafter abbreviated, per scholarly convention, as *PRA*, along with respective volume and page number.) For an overview of the topic of weather in Stifter's works, see Michael Gamper, "Meteorologie/Wetter," in *Stifter-Handbuch: Leben—Werk—Wirkung*, ed. Christian Begemann and Davide Giuriato (Stuttgart: J. B. Metzler, 2017), 253–56.

5    For two recent studies on the function of stone in Stifter's work, see Timothy Attanucci, *The Restorative Poetics of a Geological Age: Stifter, Viollet-Le-Duc, and the Aesthetic Practices of Geohistoricism* (Berlin: de Gruyter, 2020); and Jason Groves, *The Geological Unconscious: German Literature and the Mineral Imaginary* (New York: Fordham University Press, 2020), 67–92.

6    Stifter writes in the "Winterbriefe aus Kirchschlag" that light and warmth consist "fast gewiß" (almost certainly) of waves, leaving open other possibilities, such as particle theory (*HKG* 8,2:322).

"milieu," and "mood" (*Stimmung*) within the same semantic field, such that a distinction between aesthetic feeling and the physical qualities of the air become impossible to disentangle, as Timothy Attanucci observes.[7] This concomitance is not an accident of language but instead reflects the fact that human beings are embodied creatures in an environment, the implications of which Gernot Böhme explores in *Atmosphäre: Essays zur neuen Ästhetik* (Atmosphere: Essays on a New Aethetics).[8] For Böhme, thinking about aesthetics from the perspective of ecology takes us back towards its etymological meaning, *aisthesis*, or sensible perception, because humans perceive the effects of a changed natural environment through their bodies.[9] Atmosphere as a "new aesthetics," as Böhme calls it, is thus a return by way of ecology to the old-old aesthetics, so to speak. Atmospheric aesthetics as *aisthesis* legitimates, he argues, the semantic association between atmosphere as geophysical reality and the "atmospheric" descriptors that common parlance might deploy to describe aesthetic effects and affects, as when an evening is said to have a melancholy atmosphere.[10] "Heiter" as an atmospheric descriptor is emblematic of this convergence, in general and for Stifter. Translated as "bright," "heiter" describes an aspect of the literal atmosphere, namely the level of light; when rendered as "cheerful," "heiter" reflects atmosphere in the sense of mood. And what is "heiter" can also be ominous, for instance in the opening of *Brigitta* (1843/47), when the narrator explains powers of human perception and judgment beyond rationality through the oxymoronic metaphor of a "heiterer unermeßlicher Abgrund," (*HKG* 1,5:411; bright/cheerful immeasurable abyss).[11]

Atmospheric aesthetics takes us away from questions about whether, for Stifter, nature really matters in its own right, or whether it only matters to the extent that it has meaning for human perception and the social world.[12] It is, simply put, a false dichotomy. Stifter did indeed take an

7    Timothy Attanucci, "Atmosphärische Stimmungen: Landschaft und Meteorologie bei Carus, Goethe und Stifter," *Zeitschrift für Germanistik* 24, no. 2 (2014): 282–95; here 283.

8    Gernot Böhme, *Atmosphäre: Essays zur neuen Ästhetik*, 7th ed. (Berlin: Suhrkamp, 2013). See also Urs Büttner and Ines Theilen, "Einleitung," in *Phänomene der Atmosphäre: Ein Kompendium literarischer Meteorologie* (Stuttgart: J. B. Metzler, 2017), 1–25; here 9–19.

9    Böhme, *Atmosphäre*, 14–15.

10    Böhme, *Atmosphäre*, 34.

11    See Adalbert Stifter, *Brigitta, with Abdias, Limestone, and The Forest Path*, trans. Helen Watanabe-O'Kelly (London: Angel Books; Chester Springs, PA: Dufour Editions, 1990), 97. Here the translation reads: "bright and unfathomable abyss."

12    For examples of the argument that, in spite of Stifter's extensive descriptions of nature, what is really at stake is the human and the social, see Wolfgang

interest in the natural sciences, and the fact that he stages the aesthetic experience of atmosphere does not negate the ways in which that interest manifests itself in his writing. In the case of *Der Condor* Stifter included a set of notes explaining the science behind the description of the sky, giving a scientific dimension to the story's realism.[13] While the perceiving subject might be the link between atmosphere in its physical and aesthetic senses, subjective experience does not eliminate the fact that the atmosphere possesses a reality in Stifter's essays and fiction, and that such reality conditions aesthetic experience.[14] Aesthetic experience, however, does circumscribe scientific consciousness, which reflects Stifter's critical stance toward an equally reductive positivism.[15] Furthermore, from a contemporary perspective, reading Stifter with an eye toward his atmospheric aesthetics illuminates the longer history of atmospheric representation to which the so-called "climate fiction" of today is heir.

Stifter wrote at a historical moment that witnessed the beginning of modern meteorology. The middle years of the nineteenth century saw advancements in the atmospheric sciences; statistics-based practices carried out in observatories lent weather forecasting a methodological framework. The electronic telegraph, in turn, connected weather observatories in a way that made it possible to track atmospheric phenomena across larger distances. These developments led to the emergence of the modern synoptic weather chart, familiar to consumers of modern meteorological reports today, leading in turn to the decline of almanacs

---

Preisendanz, "Die Erzählfunktion der Naturdarstellung bei Stifter," *Wirkendes Wort* 16, no. 6 (1966): 407–18; here 410; Horst Albert Glaser, *Die Restauration des Schönen: Stifters "Nachsommer"* (Stuttgart: J. B. Metzler, 1965), 7; and Eric Downing, *Double Exposures: Repetition and Realism in Nineteenth-Century German Fiction* (Stanford, CA: Stanford University Press, 2000), 27.

13  See especially Ulrich Johannes Beil, "Sterne und Fußnoten: Medialität, Physik und Phantastik in Stifters *Der Condor*," in *Figuren der Übertragung: Adalbert Stifter und das Wissen seiner Zeit*, ed. Michael Gamper and Karl Wagner (Zurich: Chronos, 2009), 187–207.

14  See, by contrast, Elisabeth Strowick's position that "Stifters Texte Wirklichkeit als wahrgenommene Wirklichkeit generieren" (Stifter's texts generate reality as perceived reality). Elisabeth Strowick, "'Dumpfe Dauer': Langeweile und Atmosphärisches bei Fontane und Stifter," *The Germanic Review: Literature, Culture, Theory* 90, no. 3 (2015): 187–203; here 193.

15  Martin Selge, *Adalbert Stifter: Poesie aus dem Geist der Naturwissenschaft* (Stuttgart: W. Kohlhammer, 1976), 14. For a discussion of science versus aesthetic perception in Stifter's essay "Wiener-Wetter," see Timothy Attanucci, "The 'Gentle Law' of Large Numbers: Stifter's Urban Meteorology," *Monatshefte* 112, no. 1 (2020): 1–19. For a more general discussion of science and art in light of meteorology, see Michael Gamper, "Stifters Elektrizität," in *Figuren der Übertragung*, ed. Gamper and Wagner, 209–34; here 212–13.

and "weather prophets."[16] On the political front, the Austrian Empire and later Austria-Hungary was, as Deborah Coen argues, a state where "the essential elements of the modern understanding of climate arose as a means of thinking across scales of space and time." Because of its size and the diversity of its vast territories, "such thinking was a political imperative."[17] Stifter was cognizant of meteorology as an emergent science, having had as a textbook at Kremsmünster physicist Andreas Freiherr von Baumgartner's *Die Naturlehre nach ihrem gegenwärtigem Zustande mit Rücksicht auf mathematische Begründung* (The Natural Sciences in Their Current State with Regards to Their Mathematical Foundations, 1824–31), which included chapters on meteorology. During his time as a student at the University of Vienna, Stifter also attended Baumgartner's lectures.

On the cultural front, all of these developments gave rise to a consciousness of the dynamism and non-localizability of atmospheric systems. The atmosphere is an example *par excellence* of what Timothy Morton calls "hyperobjects," things so massively distributed across time and space that they effect an expansion of geospatial consciousness beyond one's subjective "world."[18] Sixty-two years after Stifter's death, another Austrian author, Robert Musil, worked the same problems of large-scale geospatial consciousness into the famous opening of his novel *Der Mann ohne Eigenschaften* (The Man without Qualities, 1930). Musil's narrator begins with a lengthy scientific description of atmospheric conditions over Europe on an average late summer day, which he then sums up in a more subjective register, remarking, "Mit einem Wort, das das Tatsächliche recht gut bezeichnet, wenn es auch etwas altmodisch ist: Es war ein schöner Augusttag des Jahres 1913" (In a word that characterizes the facts fairly accurately, even if it is a bit old-fashioned: It was a fine day in August 1913).[19] The humor here hinges on the shift from the scientific register and geographically wide perspective to the particularity of individual-embodied subjective experience. For all these reasons, representing the atmosphere is a major challenge for Stifter's realist poetics,

---

16  Katherine Anderson, *Predicting the Weather: Victorians and the Science of Meteorology* (Chicago, IL: University of Chicago Press, 2005), 131–69.

17  Deborah R. Coen, *Climate in Motion: Science, Empire, and the Problem of Scale* (Chicago, IL: University of Chicago Press, 2018), 2.

18  Timothy Morton, *Hyperobjects: Philosophy and Ecology after the End of the World* (Minneapolis: University of Minnesota Press, 2013), 38–54.

19  Robert Musil, *Der Mann Ohne Eigenschaften*, vol. 1 (Reinbek bei Hamburg: Rowohlt, 1978), 9; *The Man without Qualities*, trans. Sophie Wilkins, vol. 1 (New York: Vintage, 1995), 3.

as Kathrin Maurer for example demonstrates in her analysis of Stifter's novella *Kalkstein* (Limestone, 1853).[20]

## Atmospheres between Physics and Aesthetics: "Winterbriefe aus Kirchschlag" and *Die Mappe meines Urgroßvaters*

Stifter explores the dynamic relationship between the atmosphere as a material reality and atmosphere as an aesthetic effect in "Winterbriefe aus Kirchschlag" (Winter Letters from Kirchschlag), first published in the *Linzer Zeitung* in 1866. Following the humanist and European Enlightenment tradition of educational letters to the reading public (see *HKG* 8,2:359–61), Stifter blends the personal with the scientific, with sections on light, heat, electricity, air, water, and finally reflections on beauty and aesthetic sense. In the essay's more scientific parts, Stifter describes the properties of the various phenomena: for example, electricity flows between positive and negative poles; gas will expand to fill its container; water exists in liquid, solid, and gaseous states; and so on (*HKG* 8,2:327, 331, 335). Some of the letters reflect a shift away from classical Aristotelian physics: water, Stifter points out, used to be understood as an element, but modern science has "taken [it] apart" (*zerlegt*), showing it to be a compound of different chemical elements (*HKG* 8,2:335). This discovery contributed to the decline of the classical notion of the four elements.[21] Stifter's rhetoric of dissection, that science has "taken apart" water, carries a sense of loss, as if the discovery of the empirical truth of water came at the expense of a sense of holism.

Elements in the atmosphere were very much on Stifter's mind during his visits to Kirchschlag, a town located in the heights above Linz. He spent considerable time there in the fall and winter of 1865/66, hoping that the putatively therapeutic properties of the mountain air would improve his declining health, and in so doing, he was one of many tourists traveling through the Austrian Empire in pursuit of "climatotherapy." Since the 1850s, such tourism had come to be an important part of the Habsburg economy.[22] Thus the discussion of basic physics in the "Winterbriefe" is met with Stifter's own reflections on the effects of physical phenomena on the human body and mind. In one key moment in the section on air, Stifter describes standing on the heights of Kirchschlag looking down at Linz, whereby his perspective implicitly recalls Caspar

---

20 Kathrin Maurer, "Adalbert Stifter's Poetics of Clouds and Nineteenth-Century Meteorology," *Oxford German Studies* 45, no. 4 (2016): 421–33.

21 Gernot Böhme and Hartmut Böhme, *Feuer, Wasser, Erde, Luft: Eine Kulturgeschichte der Elemente* (Munich: C. H. Beck, 1996), 136–40.

22 See Coen, *Climate in Motion*, 61.

David Friedrich's representation of the sublime experience in his iconic 1818 painting *Der Wanderer über dem Nebelmeer* (Wanderer above the Sea of Fog). We know from his letters that the view he describes is the same as the view from the room he occupied in Kirchschlag, but the salient difference between Friedrich's wanderer and Stifter in the "Winterbriefe" has to do with the air quality in the landscapes before them.[23] Stifter writes: "Wir sehen an den heitersten Tagen von unserem Berge hinab über der Donau-Ebene und namentlich über Linz einen schmutzig blauen Schleier schweben, die Ausdünstung der Niederung und insbesonders die Ausdünstung der Menschen, Tiere, Schornsteine, Unratkanäle und anderer Dinge der Stadt" (*HKG* 8,2:320; Looking down from our mountain on the most cheerful days we see above the Danube plain and especially above Linz a dirty blue veil hovering, the emission of the lowland but especially the vapor of people, animals, chimneys, sewage canals, and other things of the city). "Dirty," of course, is an aesthetic complaint, but the "veil" has an ambiguous status, being both a "natural" feature of the atmosphere over the Danube plain as well as the noxious result of the concentration of people, animals, and industry in an urban environment. This is smog in the etymological sense, a portmanteau of "smoke" and "fog," and as such an atmospheric result of both human and non-human processes. Anyone taking in such a view, Stifter claims, thinks "mit einer Art unheimlichen Gefühles" (*HKG* 8,2:320–21; with a certain uncanny feeling) about all the people below. The dynamic of the familiar and the unfamiliar that would later constitute Freud's definition of the uncanny is at work here, making this scene a late example of a larger pattern in Stifter's atmospheric aesthetics.[24]

Today we understand the negative health effects of smog to be the result of toxic gases, volatile organic compounds, and particulate matter that constitute exhaust, but in the middle of the nineteenth century there were still scientists casting doubt on its harmful effects. Important scientific figures such as Jacob Henle and Rudolf Virchow, for instance, published studies questioning whether the black lungs of coal miners were caused by particulate inhalation.[25] Stifter does indeed see air quality as connected to physical health, but he grasps smog's ill effects through the lens of miasma theory, which at the time had not yet given way to germ theory as the origin of disease (see *HKG* 8,2:333) Thus the main problem

23   See his letter to Amalia Stifter from October 18, 1865, in *PRA* 21,5:39.

24   On the relation between the sublime and the uncanny in Stifter, see Michael Minden, "Stifter and the Postmodern Sublime," in *History, Value, Text: Essays on Adalbert Stifter; Londoner Symposium 2003*, ed. Michael Minden, Martin Swales, and Godela Weiss-Sussex (Linz: Adalbert-Stifter-Institut, 2006), 9–21.

25   See Franz-Josef Brüggemeier, *Das unendliche Meer der Lüfte: Luftverschmutzung, Industrialisierung und Risikodebatten im 19. Jahrhundert* (Essen: Klartext, 1996), 252–55, esp. 252.

with smog in the "Winterbriefe" is that it obscures light, hence the metaphor of the veil. The veil is part of a pattern in both the "Winterbriefe" and in Stifter's greater oeuvre of drawing on textile metaphors both to make air visible as a medium through which light waves pass and to make light appear as a material thing, a pattern Jana Schuster sketches out in her own study of Stifter's aesthetics of atmosphere.[26] Indeed, the notion of an ether persisted with the wave theory of light.[27] From that perspective, the veil of smog is the terrible inverse of ether as the medium of light: both have a material existence, but whereas ether is thought to carry light waves, smog actually obscures light. Smog for Stifter is therefore bad because dullness (*Dumpfheit*) of light is dullness of the soul (see *HKG* 8,2:319). The stakes of a lack of light, as Stifter imagines them, hinge on the corollary between outer nature and the inner nature of the human soul, a problem that recurs in Stifter's fiction and reflection on realist aesthetics.

The discussion of physics ultimately leads Stifter back to aesthetics as a philosophical discourse in the final part of the "Winterbriefe," where he considers the category of the beautiful. Stifter's terms reflect the inflation that Enlightenment aesthetic categories like "beauty" and "the sublime" had undergone by the mid-nineteenth century. He identifies as "beautiful" what for Kant would have been "sublime": when looking at the night sky, he states it is beauty that "enflames" (*beseligt*) and "destroys" (*vernichtet*) the soul (*HKG* 8,2:340). Atmospheric formations are Stifter's key examples of the beautiful, and he describes in detail both fog and Alpine clouds. Works of art, for, Stifter are helpful in seeing these formations as beautiful insofar as they sensitize the viewer to the far grander beauty of nature itself (see *HKG* 8,2:342–44).

If art functions to cultivate a sense for the beauty of nature in general, then the atmosphere would only be one natural thing among many, having a prominent, but otherwise not particularly special status as an object of representation. But atmospheric forces also exert an effect on other things, which in turn determines atmosphere as an aesthetic effect. We might consider the description of the things in the house of the narrator's father in *Die Mappe meines Urgroßvaters* (My Great-Grandfather's Notebook, 1841; revised 1847, 1864, 1867), acquired by previous generations of the family. Before relating the episodes that are themselves related in Augustus's—the titular great-grandfather's—notebook, the narrator recalls his past pleasures exploring the collection of antiquated things accumulated in his father's house. In his description of his household

---

26 Jana Schuster, "'Lichtschleier': Stifters Ästhetik der Atmosphäre," in *Fleck, Glanz, Finsternis: Zur Poetik der Oberfläche bei Adalbert Stifter*, ed. Thomas Gann and Marianne Schuller (Paderborn: Wilhelm Fink, 2017), 35–60; here 42–43.

27 Böhme and Böhme, *Feuer, Wasser, Erde, Luft*, 160–61.

collection, we glimpse the dialectical relation between the physical atmosphere and atmosphere as a mood generated from the aura of the objects. The image of St. Margaret gives off "einen so drohenden Schein" (such a threatening glow), while some of the objects contained in a trunk "in der Dunkelheit so geheimnisvoll leuchtete[n]" (shone in the darkness so mysteriously). The sum effect of these "Denkmalen" (monuments) is a "schauerliche innere Freude" (an eerie inner joy). An "eerie inner joy," one of many oxymorons that occur throughout Stifter's works, is an inner aesthetic response to objects that, like the saint with the threatening glow, exude an ambivalent aura. That aura is largely the effect of atmospheric forces over time. The "verwitterte Hutfeder" (weathered hat feather) is one of the many things that have become "immer verkommener und trüber" (ever more decayed and darkened) over the years. (For all of the above references, see *HKG* 1,5:13–14.) Exposure to oxygen and light are the primary atmospheric culprits that cause objects to fade with time. The aura of history that the collection exudes does not come from the mere fact that they are old things that once belonged to the narrator's ancestors. Instead, it is the signs of atmospheric exposure that reflect their age and thus give the collection their historical aura.

The contents of Augustus's notebook further reflect the paradoxical experience of atmospheric phenomena and the aesthetic experience thereof. Warm weather and clear skies, for instance, contrast with, and even portend, catastrophe. In the story of Augustus's mentor, the Colonel, the latter's wife plummets to her death while crossing a flume spanning a gorge, and during her fall she stifles her scream in order not to startle and thereby endanger the Colonel and the lumberjack who guides them. The reflecting red sunlight on the facing chalk cliff seems to signal danger, but the silent catastrophe takes place under a breezy blue sky (see *HKG* 1,5:56–58). And in the far more famous episode of the winter storm, the real danger comes only after the clouds have dissipated (see *HKG* 1,5:96). Opening his window, Augustus realizes the destructive potential of atmospheric unpredictability as he imagines the sudden rise in temperatures, which will melt the accumulated layers of ice and snow and inundate streams, causing widespread avalanches and floods (see *HKG* 1,5:120). After the extensive description of the ice- and snowstorm, it is ironically the warmer temperatures that cause terror in Augustus's imagination and inflict the greater environmental damage. This comes as Augustus thinks through the chain of cause and effect, reflecting an awareness of weather not as an isolated, localized event, but as the product of a larger atmospheric system.

Such a concatenation of disruptive environmental events as part of atmospheric systems constitutes a pattern in Stifter's oeuvre.[28] The vastness of the atmosphere and the long spatial reach of causality would, from the perspective of Enlightenment aesthetics, seem to be the key components for arriving at an adequate definition of the sublime. But unlike, say, for Kant, the vastness does not lead in this case to any such "sublime" experience. Instead, the result is closer to a remark Stifter makes when describing an epochal snowstorm in his final completed and posthumously published piece, "Aus dem bairischen Walde" (From the Bavarian Forest, 1868): "Was anfangs furchtbar und großartig erhaben gewesen war, zeigte sich jetzt anders, es war nur mehr furchtbar" (What had been at the beginning frightening and enormously sublime now revealed itself to be different, it was now only frightening).[29] The collapse of the sublime into sheer terror in the face of atmospheric realities is a point of fascination for Stifter, one that binds all the phases of his writing career.

## Atmospheres of Terror: *Der Condor* and "Die Sonnenfinsternis am 8. Juli 1842"

The collapse of the sublime into simple terror in the face of the atmosphere is a pattern that appears as early as *Der Condor*. The first two chapters narrate Cornelia's flight in the titular hot air balloon "Condor," which she undertakes as a way of asserting herself against the bonds that society places on women. Ascending from Vienna, the balloon rises so high that the aeronauts can see over the Alps to the Mediterranean, an experience that overwhelms Cornelia and causes her to collapse in the basket. This experience ultimately thwarts Cornelia and her love interest, the painter Gustav, from entering into a romantic relationship, as the former insists on returning to domestic life, while the latter departs for South America.

Cornelia's flight becomes a way of comparing the subjective experience of the atmosphere at incredibly high altitudes (or, at least, Stifter's imagination thereof) to the way it is perceived on *terra firma* below in Vienna. In the first chapter of the story, "Ein Nachtstück" (A Night

---

28   See, for instance, the discussion of the wolf scene in my essay: Alexander Robert Phillips, "Adalbert Stifter's Alternative Anthropocene: Reimagining Social Nature in *Brigitta* and *Abdias*," in *German Ecocriticism in the Anthropocene*, ed. Caroline Schaumann and Heather Sullivan (New York: Palgrave Macmillan, 2017), 65–85; here 73–75.

29   *PRA* 15,2:342. For a more recent and accessible version of this tale, see Adalbert Stifter, "Aus dem bairischen Walde," in *Sämtliche Erzählungen nach den Erstdrucken*, ed. Wolfgang Matz (Munich: Deutscher Taschenbuch Verlag, 2005), 1515–43; here 1533.

Scene), Cornelia's suitor Gustav peers out his window through a telescope, waiting to observe the balloon's rise. Once the voices on the street below have died down and he sits alone with his telescope and the tomcat Hinz, Gustav praises the Viennese "Nachtstille" (the silence of the night), "die die Philosophen, Dichter und Kater lieben" (*HKG* 1,4:18; that hour, beloved of philosophers, poets, and tomcats).[30] But the apparent pleasantness of the atmosphere is belied by the light emanating from a neighbor's window, a brightness that breaks the darkness of the night, and yet signifies loss, because it emanates from a room where a poor washerwoman's child lies dying. The *Journalfassung* of 1840 makes the relation between the child's death and the night atmosphere even more explicit: the pleasant quiet of "Nachtstille" becomes "die tödtlichste Stille" (*HKG* 1,1:13; the deadliest stillness). The sky into which the balloon rises turns out to be similarly ambivalent: it is both "clear" (klar) and "cheerful" (heiter), but also "empty" (leer) and "immense" (ungeheur)—the latter term connoting not just immensity, but also monstrosity.

The second chapter, "Tagstück" (Day Scene), shifts to the balloon basket. Each of the characters, Cornelia and the two scientists Richard and Coloman, exhibit very different responses to the universe as it presents itself at that altitude. The narrator frames the flight as an encounter with the sublime and the "Urgewalt" (primordial power) of the space (see *HKG* 1,4:25; *C*, 7). The scene subtly ironizes Kant's analytic of the sublime: the balloon's rise literalizes the moment of transcendence, but as it goes up, Cornelia falls down.[31] Her fainting spell is an extreme aesthetic response, in the etymological sense, as the enormity of the scene overwhelms her senses, causing panic. For the elder scientist Coloman, the experience is the exact opposite. The scientific goals of the flight entirely determine his experience of the space; he displays no emotion as he peers through his optical devices while Cornelia reels. How are we to interpret Cornelia's collapse? The answer the text supplies is one of gendered failure, summed up in the male chauvinism behind Coloman's remark: "das Weib erträgt den Himmel nicht" (*HKG* 1,4:28; the woman cannot bear the heights of heaven, *C*, 10). "The woman," as opposed to just "she," insinuates that any such effort to defy patriarchal limits is doomed

---

30  Adalbert Stifter, "The Condor," in *Tales from Old Vienna and Other Prose*, trans. Alexander Stillmark (Riverside, CA: Ariadne Press, 2016), 1–20; here 2. The translation is of the *Buchfassung*, and is hereafter referenced in the main text of this chapter as *C* along with appropriate page number.

31  For a reading of Stifter as an ironic author, against a consensus in Stifter scholarship that holds otherwise, see Jochen Berendes, *Ironie—Komik—Skepsis: Studien zum Werk Adalbert Stifters* (Tübingen: Niemeyer, 2009), esp. 3. Berendes argues that Stifter's supposed reach for a "classical style" effects a structural elevation of irony, subverting the texts' superficial formal goals and producing a radicalization of irony itself.

to failure. The narrator also appears to subscribe to Coloman's view, as did Stifter himself.[32] Cornelia also internalizes the belief that the heavens are no place for a woman, telling Gustav she was blind to try to rise above her gender (see *HKG* 1,4:35; *C*, 15–16). But it is also possible to read the story against the grain of its stated gendered politics and understand the scene in terms other than those of feminine failure. Coloman's judgment about the weakness of her gender, as Jochen Berendes points out, is only possible because his telescope and other scientific instruments mediate between him and the atmosphere, blocking his receptivity to the multiplicity of meaning Cornelia is able to see in the sky.[33] As for the younger Richard, his imperious "majestätischen Blick" (*HKG* 1,4:28; majestic glance, *C*, 9–10) likewise stands in contrast to Cornelia's receptiveness to the nature before her. The crucial difference, meanwhile, is the contrast between the coldness of the universe as seen up in the air with the sentimental view of the people in the city below who regard the sky from a position of distance and safety.

On the plot level, Cornelia's voyage into the air seems to have given her a new appreciation for domesticity, while Gustav plans to travel across land and sea. But the third chapter strongly intimates that the atmosphere is the stumbling block preventing their union. Obviously, Cornelia's trip into the sky brought about her change in perspective, but the role that the atmosphere and atmospheric aesthetics play in this plot development is more complicated than that. Gustav, for his part, is moved by a desire to experience other environments and, specifically, the atmosphere in other places. As he for instance exclaims to Cornelia: " draußen [ist] eine andere Welt andere Bäume, andere Lüfte—und ich ein anderer Mensch" (*HKG* 1,4:38; there is another world out there, other trees, other airs—and that I am another human being, *C*, 16). For Gustav, the experience of the physical atmosphere is matched by his desire to express in art something of the atmospheric within his own person, as evidenced in his follow-up plea: "O Cornelia, hilf mir's sagen, welch' ein wundervoller Sternenhimmel in meinem Herzen ist" (*HKG* 1,4:36; O, Cornelia, help me utter what a wonderful star-filled heaven is in my heart, *C*, 16). Such euphoria about the "wonderful star-filled heaven" appears

---

32  Kurt Mautz, "Natur und Gesellschaft in Stifters 'Condor,'" in *Literaturwissenschaft und Geschichtsphilosophie: Festschrift für Wilhelm Emrich*, ed. Helmut Arntzen, Berndt Balzer, Karl Pestalozzi, Rainer Wagner, and Kurt Mautz (Berlin: De Gruyter, 2018), 406–35; here 410. Stifter was apparently inspired by the real-life case of André-Jacques Garnerin, who undertook a balloon journey with a young woman in 1798. The police deemed the ride with a woman immoral and forbade it from happening again. See Franziska Schößler, "'Der Condor,'" in *Stifter-Handbuch: Leben—Werk—Wirkung*, ed. Christian Begemann and Davide Giuriato (Stuttgart: J. B. Metzler, 2017), 15–19; here 17.

33  Berendes, *Ironie—Komik—Skepsis*, 8.

doubtful in contrast to the cold universe that Cornelia witnessed and he did not. The revised *Studienfassung* attributes the failure of the relationship more strongly to something atmospheric than the *Journalfassung*. Stifter introduced a passage in which the narrator senses an ineffable atmospheric presence between him and Cornelia, what he calls a "Geist des Zwiespalts" (spirit of discord) that cannot be swept away "mit einem Hauch des Mundes, mit einer Falte des Gewandes" (by a mere breath of their lips or the flick of a garment), until it becomes an "ungreifbarer Riese wolkig, dunkel" (*HKG* 1,4:33; unassailable giant, cloudy and gloomy, *C*, 13). For Gustav, this thing in the air emanates from Cornelia, specifically from a pride and desire for freedom which he detects beneath all of her self-accusatory rhetoric about overstepping the bounds of her gender. In the same passage, this mood makes itself palpable as, watching Cornelia and listening to her breathing, the room suddenly becomes humid. The narration here is focalized through Gustav, so that it is unclear whether or not there was an objective rise in the concentration of water vapor there in the room. Nor does it matter as much as the simple fact that Gustav experienced a shift in the physical atmosphere together with a particular mood in the room, both of which determine the romantic failure.

The subject of atmospheric aesthetics in *Der Condor* ends, finally, with aesthetics as relating to artworks specifically. The final chapter takes place years later, when Gustav is still in the Andes, following, not incidentally, in the footsteps of Alexander von Humboldt. The narrator is attending an art exhibition in Paris, where two of Gustav's paintings are on display. Both paintings are atmospheric "moonscapes," that is, scenes bathed in moonlight, one a birds-eye view of a large city, the other a boating party on a night that, besides being moonlit, is cloudy, humid, and electrified. The atmospheric forces in these paintings are rendered on canvas, contained within a frame, creating for the narrator the safe pleasure of the familiar: he recognizes the cat, Hinze, whose strutting Gustav observed at the opening of the story. In the *Journalfassung*, the only response Gustav's works evoke is celebration by the Parisian art scene and tears from Cornelia over their aborted relationship, but in the *Studienfassung* the events of the story haunt her: "gelassen und kalt stand die Macht des Geschehenen vor ihrer Seele" (*HKG* 1,4:41; the [power] of past events reared up calmly and coldly before her inmost soul, *C*, 20).

Like *Der Condor*, "Die Sonnenfinsternis am 8. Juli 1842" (The Eclipse of the Sun in 1842), an essay published in the *Wiener Zeitschrift für Kunst, Literatur, Theater und Mode* (Viennese Journal for Art, Literature, Theater, and Fashion) during the same month as the eclipse itself, stages an encounter with the cosmos in order to consider the possibilities for an experience of the sublime. Insofar as the light and energy from the sun are part of the atmospheric system, and that sudden darkness in the middle of the day evokes feelings of awe and terror, "Die

Sonnenfinsternis" is another text in which Stifter reflects on atmospheric aesthetics. The argument of the essay is that the eclipse is ultimately indicative of God's existence and his role as a guarantor of the stability of the universe. The puzzle, however, is that the eclipse can be both awe inspiring but also eminently predictable, such that Stifter remarks that he could have described it without ever having seen it.[34] Stifter's resolution to that apparent contradiction is that the meaning of the event lies precisely in its predictability because we can see therein the workings of God: "Durch die Schrift seiner Sterne hat er versprochen, daß es kommen werde nach tausend und tausend Jahren, unsere Väter haben diese Schrift entziffern gelernt" (He promised through the writing of His stars that it would come about many thousands of years later; our ancestors learned to decipher this writing).[35]

In "Die Sonnenfinsternis" the predictability of the solar eclipse inspires awe as a code from God. In his reading of the essay "Wiener-Wetter," Timothy Attanucci points out that Stifter's thinking about the sublime breaks with Kant, because for Stifter it is the law behind the workings of nature that is sublime, not human rationality measured against the greatness of nature.[36] Reason does indeed triumph momentarily in Stifter's account, when the populace looks up at the sun through their optical instruments and remembers that they are looking at God's writing in the heavens. But, as in *Der Condor*, reason only triumphs when optical devices serve to mediate between the viewer and the thing itself. In any event, God's promises as encoded in the stars are not what Stifter calls sublime. Instead, he feels the sublime when the lights go out, a feeling that comes from the onset of darkness without the atmospheric reddening at sunset. Stifter reports being "von Schauer und Erhabenheit [...] erschüttert" (shaken by [eeriness] and sublimity) together, and for the two minutes when the moon blots out the sun, the scene is "geisterhaft," and there is a sense of "ein lastend unheimliches Entfremden unserer Natur" (phantom-like; a burdensome, uncanny estrangement of nature).[37] For Kant, the experience of the sublime ends with the triumph of individual rationality, but in "Die Sonnenfinsternis" the sublime is decoupled from rationality and becomes twinned instead with the spectral and the alienating. The insistence that through events such as eclipses we can know a benevolent God does not carry through to the description of the eclipse itself. This is another instance of what Michael Minden

---

34 See *PRA* 15,2:5; Adalbert Stifter, "The Eclipse of the Sun in 1842," in *Tales from Old Vienna and Other Prose*, 145–58; here 145.

35 *PRA* 15,2:6; Stifter, "The Eclipse of the Sun in 1842," 146.

36 Attanucci, "The 'Gentle Law' of Large Numbers: Stifter's Urban Meteorology," 5.

37 *PRA* 15,2:10; Stifter, "The Eclipse of the Sun in 1842," 149.

CHEERFUL TERROR ◆ 287

calls the "postmodern sublime" in Stifter, whereby the sublime becomes the uncanny.[38] God reappears for Stifter in the middle of this uncanniness. When the moon completely covers the sun and everyone removes their protective eyewear, Stifter reports a sudden silence when God speaks now not through cosmic signs, but directly to the people.[39] In spite of its conspicuous absence in the eclipse itself, we could still privilege rational reflection, as Stifter does in concluding that this exceptional event is itself a sign of stability and order. But to do so is also unsatisfyingly compensatory in the face of the uncanniness and alienation of witnessing the world plunged into darkness.

## The Limits of Science:
### *Der Nachsommer* and *Bunte Steine*

The problem of predictability versus first-hand experience in "Die Sonnenfinsternis" raises the problem of scientific knowledge and its relation to aesthetics in all senses of that term. In the balloon scene in *Der Condor*, the two were separated out between the scientist characters on the one hand and Cornelia on the other. In "Die Sonnenfinsternis" and the "Winterbriefe" the two strands are brought together and mediated through Stifter's own embodied perspective. This mediating function is given over to the figure of the scientist or, as is more often the case, the scientific layperson.

The scientific layperson, for Stifter, is poised to perceive the world in a more holistic way because their grasp of science does not come at the expense of other ways of knowing the world, such as the aesthetic or more loosely heuristic. A prime example of this importance is a pivotal scene early in Stifter's magnum opus, *Der Nachsommer* (Indian Summer, 1857), in which the opposition between a scientific approach to weather prediction and an older almanac-style "weather wisdom" is staged. Seeking shelter from what he is certain is an oncoming storm, the protagonist Heinrich Drendorf calls at a nearby house that will turn out to be the estate of Baron von Risach. After hearing his reason for seeking shelter, Risach tells Drendorf that he is welcome to stay, but that the storm will not, in fact, break. A disagreement ensues, the crux of which has to do with forms of knowledge of local natural systems, in general, and atmospheric forces, in particular. Drendorf justifies his insistence that the storm will break in an hour by claiming both scientific knowledge of clouds and storms, as well as the familiarity with the region gained from his many hikes through its landscapes. On both counts, Risach effectively one-ups him, declaring that he also knows a thing or two about the local

38  See again Minden, "Stifter and the Postmodern Sublime."
39  *PRA*, 15,2:11; Stifter, "The Eclipse of the Sun in 1842," 149–50.

weather, but, being older and having resided there longer, possesses more environmental knowledge and is thus more qualified to make veracious claims to this effect (see *HKG* 4,1:49–50; *IS*, 32–33). After the storm does not, in fact, take place, Risach reveals to Drendorf that the reason he was able to accurately predict the weather was through his observations of animal behavior (see *HKG* 4,1:120–22; *IS*, 72–73). Here Risach is engaging in his own form of "weather prophecy,"[40] which is not exactly pseudoscientific but still rests more on a heuristic approach than a precise methodology. Risach seems to appreciate that his way of knowing the area is not strictly methodological. He disavows the title "scientist" (*Naturforscher*) but still keeps abreast of the most recent scientific literature, owns a collection of scientific instruments for predicting weather, and maintains a library in which the works of Alexander von Humboldt feature prominently (see *HKG* 4,1:51; *IS*, 33–34).[41] But then, that Risach would fall back on the non-methodological and the heuristic in order to make a prediction about the weather is hardly surprising given that the weather cannot be predicted with absolute certainty. His role model Humboldt, as it happened, was skeptical that the irregularity of atmospheric forces could ever be squared with the need to base prognoses on statistical norms.[42] Urs Büttner and Ines Theilen point out that while nineteenth-century meteorologists regarded weather prophecy as charlatanism, their own predictions were like the weather prophets insofar as they were also based on analogies to past observations.[43] In this sense, meteorology relates to weather prophecy in much the same way as chemistry relates to alchemy, and Risach merely represents the persistence of an older epistemology within the context of modern atmospheric science.

Risach's holistic knowledge of his region is part of what figures him as an ideal type living in apparent harmony with his environment. Taken at face value, such harmony might seem to be politically progressive. In fact, however, it reflects Stifter's post-1848 conservative turn insofar as Risach's deep knowledge of the non-human systems in and around his estate attests to its exclusivity as a utopia of conservative order.[44] While

40 See here Michael Gamper, "Rätsel der Atmosphäre: Umrisse einer 'literarischen Meteorologie,'" *Zeitschrift für Germanistik* 24, no. 2 (2014): 229–43; Anderson, *Predicting the Weather*, 175–76.

41 On the parallels between Risach and Humboldt in relation to weather prediction, see Oliver Grill, "Unvorhersehbares Wetter? Zur Meteorologie in Alexander von Humboldts 'Kosmos' und Adalbert Stifters 'Nachsommer,'" *Zeitschrift für Germanistik* 26, no. 1 (2016): 61–77.

42 Grill, "Unvorhersehbares Wetter?" 65.

43 Büttner and Theilen, "Einleitung," 4–5.

44 In his classic study of *Der Nachsommer*, Horst Glaser characterizes Stifter's "restorative utopia" as a caste society, one that wants capitalism without class conflict. See Glaser, *Die Restauration des Schönen*, esp. 1–3. More recently, by

waiting to see whether the storm will actually break out, for instance, Drendorf observes workers cutting grass. If they are working the field, he deduces, then they must also believe as Risach does, that the storm will not come. Drendorf says as much to Risach, and Risach gives a blunt reply: the fieldhands know nothing about the weather but are just doing as they are told (see *HKG* 4,1:75; *IS*, 47). In the narrative universe of *Der Nachsommer*, environmental knowledge is connected to social hierarchy.

The political ambivalence of Risach's character notwithstanding, he remains an ideal type in Stifter's narrative universe largely because of his careful observation of the natural world. Observation, in turn, is the core problem at stake in Stifter's most famous statement of his realist aesthetics, namely the preface to the 1853 novella cycle *Bunte Steine*. Here, too, atmosphere as a physical and an aesthetic 'thing' serves as a medium through which Stifter illustrates his literary program. According to the thesis of the preface, what the "Unkundigen und Unaufmerksamen" (ignorant and inattentive) take to be great—massive events such as storms and volcanic eruptions—are, in fact, small. Seemingly small events prove to be great because they are constant and universal, they are "das Welterhaltende" (*HKG* 2,2:10; what sustains the world, *MS*, 4). The "Forscher" (scientist/researcher), in contrast, recognizes what is truly great because "der Geisteszug des Forschers vorzüglich auf das Ganze und Allgemeine geht" (*HKG* 2,2:10; the scientist's mind tends chiefly toward what is whole and universal, *MS*, 4). This universal is what Stifter calls, again oxymoronically, "das sanfte Gesetz" (the gentle law), an overarching moral structure that governs all things in both external as well as inner, human nature.

As a universal principle, the gentle law is not limited to the atmosphere, but Stifter seems to think that it is a good place to look for signs of its existence: "Das Wehen der Luft das Rieseln des Wassers das Wachsen der Getreide das Wogen des Meeres das Grünen der Erde das Glänzen des Himmels das Schimmern der Gestirne halte ich für groß" (*HKG* 2,2:10; The wafting of the air the trickling of the water the growing of the grain the surging of the sea the budding of the earth the shining of the sky the glimmering of the stars is what I deem great, *MS*, 3–4)— these all contrast with singular, dramatic events such as storms, volcanoes, and earthquakes. The phenomena on his list of the small are atmospheric

---

contrast, Robert Leucht has argued against a reading of Risach's estate as being *merely* a conservative utopia, showing instead that a variety of utopian concepts come together in the novel. Risach's attitude toward his workers, however, constitutes a moment of conservative sentiment because of its investment in the maintenance of social hierarchy. See Robert Leucht, "Ordnung, Bildung, Kunsthandwerk: Die Pluralität utopischer Modelle in Adalbert Stifters *Der Nachsommer*," in *Figuren der Übertragung: Adalbert Stifter und das Wissen seiner Zeit*, ed. Michael Gamper and Karl Wagner (Zurich: Chronos, 2009), 289–306; esp. 291.

either in the first order, such as the gentle breeze and the brightness of the sky; or as effects predicated to some extent on the influence of the atmosphere, such as crop growth and soil fertility (both of which require air, sunlight, and rain); ocean swells (which require wind, combined with gravity); or twinkling starlight (an atmospheric effect of interstellar refraction). In terms of punctuation, Stifter's idiosyncratic omission of commas from this lengthy list not only has the effect of mimicking the regularity and rhythm that typifies the gentle law but also forces us to read these phenomena as bound together in a greater totality.

The one who recognizes that greater totality is the researcher (*Forscher*). Armed with a compass, he collects individual readings from all over the Earth's surface, revealing a magnetic storm, which proves "ehrfurchterregend" (*HKG* 2,2:10–11; awe inspiring, *MS*, 4). The figure of the researcher here marks one of the many direct and indirect allusions in Stifter's works to Alexander von Humboldt, who coined the very term "magnetic storm" and perceived its visible manifestation as the *aurora borealis/aurora australis*, herein a stricter meteorological idiom.[45] Once again, the totality of the atmosphere produces a specific aesthetic effect of reverence and horror, both of which are contained in the word "Ehrfurcht" (awe).[46] But unlike in *Der Condor*, where Coloman's instruments make him impervious to the horror of the sky, the awe in the preface to *Bunte Steine* is predicated on knowledge gained through instruments, the sum of minute pieces of data that the researcher gathers methodically, "Körnchen nach Körnchen" (*HKG* 2,2:11; grain upon grain, *MS*, 4).

The researcher is supposed to illustrate a program for realist fiction that makes the gentle law visible through its depiction of the small: "Wir wollen das sanfte Gesez zu erbliken suchen, wodurch das menschliche Geschlecht geleitet wird" (*HKG* 2,2:12; We seek to glimpse the gentle law that guides the human race, *MS*, 5). This programmatic statement rests on what Eric Downing calls "rhetorical tactics of chiastic mimetic equivalence" between non-human and human natures.[47] The problem with this equivalence, and the argument in the preface more generally,

45  On Humboldt and the northern and southern lights, see Marie-Theres Federhofer, "Nordlicht: Tellurische Deutung und ästhetische Darstellung bei Alexander von Humboldt," in *Phänomene der Atmosphäre: Ein Kompendium literarischer Meteorologie*, ed. Urs Büttner and Ines Theilen (Stuttgart: J. B. Metzler, 2017), 222–32; here 228–29.

46  According to the Grimms' *Wörterbuch*, the connotation of "scheu" as "reverential horror" was still present in Old High German *êra*; when that connotation fell away, its meaning was assumed with the new compound "ehrfurcht." See "Ehrfurcht," in *Deutsches Wörterbuch von Jacob Grimm und Wilhelm Grimm*, vol. 3 (Leipzig: S. Hirzel, 1859), www.woerterbuchnetz.de/DWB/ehrfurcht.

47  Downing, *Double Exposures*, 27.

has been the subject of frequent critique. Closer examination reveals it is not a universal law guiding humans and nature, but, as Paul Fleming argues, "a moral imperative dressed up as statistical regularity."[48] Alfred Doppler, for his part, argues that it breaks apart due to the violence of both nature and its own coercive force as a moral imperative.[49] There is a further contradiction, I would add, in Stifter's statement that the stories in the collection will somehow make the gentle law visible. That we "seek" to glimpse the gentle law implies the possibility that we might fail and see nothing at all, and even if we do see something, we are only promised a partial and fleeting view, a mere "glimpse."

In the novellas that make up *Bunte Steine*, however, atmospheric forces work in characteristically conflicting ways. *Kalkstein* (Limestone) and *Kazensilber* (Cat-Silver) feature violent storms as key plot elements, but these turn out to be part of greater atmospheric cycles and are themselves a precondition for regeneration.[50] Atmospheric forces in these stories function as "disruptive nature" in what Sean Ireton identifies as a narrative pattern in Stifter of "order—disruption—reinstated order."[51] By contrast, the most significant atmospheres in *Turmalin* (Tourmaline)— for instance, the dust and stillness of the pensioner's abandoned apartment and the dampness of the one he subsequently moves into—mystify more than they reveal. As the narrator announces from the start, the story is titled *Turmalin* because its plotline is as dark as the eponymous stone, and while he claims that there is a universal law at work in the novella, just as there is in the *Bunte Steine* preface, he offers it as a negative, for we glimpse what happens when a man turns away "von dem innern Geseze, das ihn unabwendbar zu dem Rechten führt" (from the inner law that unfailingly leads him to do what is right). The narrator likewise reaches for an atmospheric metaphor to describe the turn away from rationality, "wenn er das Licht seiner Vernunft trübt" (*HKG* 2,2:135; when he clouds the light of his reason, *MS*, 93).

48 Paul Fleming, *Exemplarity and Mediocrity: The Art of the Average from Bourgeois Tragedy to Realism* (Stanford, CA: Stanford University Press, 2009), 153.

49 See Alfred Doppler, "Schrecklich schöne Welt? Stifters fragwürdige Analogie von Natur- und Sittengesetz," in *Adalbert Stifters schrecklich schöne Welt: Beiträge des internationalen Kolloquiums zur A.-Stifter-Ausstellung*, ed. Roland Duhamel, Johann Lachinger, Clemens Ruthner, and Petra Göllner (Linz: Adalbert-Stifter-Institut, 1994), 9–15; here 10–11.

50 See especially Sean Ireton's reading of *Kazensilber* in "Between Dirty and Disruptive Nature: Adalbert Stifter in the Context of Nineteenth-Century American Environmental Literature," *Colloquia Germanica: Internationale Zeitschrift für Germanistik* 44, no. 2 (2011): 149–71; here 164–67.

51 Ireton, "Between Dirty and Disruptive Nature," 161.

Dust and dampness in the story literalize the metaphor of clouding one's own reason. After his wife's infidelity leads to the breakup of the family, the pensioner abandons his apartment in central Vienna and disappears. When the authorities open it up two years later, they find a layer of dust pervading an apartment that has remained unchanged since the moment of abandonment, the stopped clock signaling a literal representation of the temporal signature that Elisabeth Strowick finds in Stifter's atmospheres.[52] As we learn in the second half of the story, the pensioner has taken up a suburban residence in a dank basement apartment in Perron House. To the extent that they are intended to illustrate universal laws of rationality in the negative, darkness, dust, and dampness in *Turmalin* would seem to contrast with light as a metaphor for rationality and a healthy development of the soul more generally. In the second half of the story, the narration is taken over by a woman who lives not far from Perron House. After the Pensioner is found dead, she adopts his daughter. Life in the basement apartment has left the girl with an abnormally large head and speaking a language that is somehow highly literary and yet nonsensical (*HKG* 2,2:163–64; *MS* 114). After taking her into her own bright, airy house, the woman begins instructing the girl in language and domestic work, during which time the girl's language begins to make sense and her head shrinks down to a "normal" size. But these improved atmospheric conditions turn out to be ambivalent at the close of the story, when the first narrator, speaking from a long time after the events of the story, remarks that the houses have been replaced by a "glänzende Häuserreihe" (*HKG* 2,2:179; gleaming row of houses, *MS*, 126). Even as he describes the brightness of the new neighborhood, the narrator suggests that this cheerful atmosphere comes at the expense of historical memory: all the characters are either dead or have moved away, Perron House has been demolished, and the younger people have no idea what took place there.

## Conclusion

The experience of atmosphere, then, raises many of the tensions and contradictions that structure Stifter's writing: scientific rationality versus aesthetics (in all senses), regularity versus chaos, and meaning versus meaninglessness, to name a few. Rather than reading such contradictions as signs of texts that are "in einem unschlichtbaren Widerstreit mit sich selbst" (in an irreconcilable conflict with themselves),[53] we are alerted to the double character that the atmosphere and non-human nature, more

52  See Strowick, "'Dumpfe Dauer,'" 188.
53  Christian Begemann, *Die Welt der Zeichen: Stifter-Lektüren* (Stuttgart: J. B. Metzler, 1995), 2.

generally, exhibit in Stifter's narrative universe. If we understand Stifter strictly according to the moral-didactic terms that appear on the mere surface level of the preface to *Bunte Steine*, then he might seem to be emblematic of the gradualist thinking about nature that Amitav Ghosh, in his book *The Great Derangement*, argues has left the European realist tradition fundamentally ill-equipped to represent the realities of fast-moving climate breakdown.[54] But if we admit that the moments of doubt and disruption in Stifter's works are more than mere byproducts of a conservative worldview willfully blind to its own precariousness, then Stifter appears as something other than an author whose assumptions about the world are belied by the contemporary climate emergency. In his texts, what we take to be a pleasant atmosphere can suddenly reveal itself to be an object of terror, the possibility of which persists even after the disruptive moment has passed. Rather than being a retrograde antithesis to what has, in the twenty-first century, come to be called "climate fiction" or "cli-fi"—that is, literature dealing in some fashion with anthropogenic global warming—Stifter's work crystallizes a moment within a longer history of literary thinking about an earth system and the field of associations it occupies.[55] His atmospheric aesthetics bind together art, ethics, and their relation to non-human systems in ways that critically reflect nineteenth-century shifts in ecoaesthetic discourses, discourses that still reverberate, for better and for worse, in today's environmental politics.

54  Amitav Ghosh, *The Great Derangement: Climate Change and the Unthinkable* (Chicago, IL: University of Chicago Press, 2016), 15–24.
55  See, for instance, Axel Goodbody and Adeline Johns-Putra, *Cli-Fi: A Companion* (Oxford: Peter Lang, 2019). Of thirty works discussed across the various essays in their collection, only six appeared before the year 2000, the earliest in 1962.

# 12: Stifter's Bavarian-Bohemian Bioregionalism

*Sean Ireton*

## Watershed Moments

IN THE OPENING segment of *Der Waldgänger* (The Forest-Goer, 1846), one of his few stories that Stifter did not revise and reissue in book format,[1] the autofictional narrator reminisces on his definitive departure from his Bohemian homeland. Somewhere near Kirchschlag in the foot-hills above Linz, "der Verfasser" or "der Wanderer" (the author/the wan-derer), as Stifter alternately refers to himself in the third person, crosses a divide separating the Mühlkreis region from the Danube basin of Upper Austria. In the process, he surveys numerous natural features on either side of the ridgeline, including those pertaining to the geosphere (moun-tains, rolling hills, vales), the hydrosphere (rivers, streams, rivulets), the biosphere (forests, bushes, orchards), and the atmosphere (the meteoro-logical differences between the overcast skies to the north and the sunny climes to the south). Whereas the distant dark-blue strip of the Bohemian Forest blends with the gray ceiling of clouds behind him, the sunlit river basin below seems to beckon toward a new and figuratively bright future. This pivotal point of his journey from Bohemia to Vienna, where he will spend the next twenty-two years of his life, significantly occurs upon a point of partition or *Scheidepunkt* in the physical landscape. Indeed, this eight-page section of the text (see *HKG* 3,1:95–102) is punctuated by a leitmotif-like complex of *scheiden* (to divide/separate) and its linguistic variants, all of which serve to underscore a variety of interconnections between Upper Austrian geography and Stifter's early autobiography. Thus, the wandering-narrating analogue of Stifter crosses a *Scheidelinie* (dividing line) but tarries at the abovementioned *Scheidepunkt*, reflect-ing on his recent separation or *Scheiden* from both his hometown of Oberplan and love interest Fanny Greipl, who resided in the nearby town of Friedberg and whose parents saw little if any professional promise in the likes of the young and dreamy "Bertl" Stifter. The creative compound

---

1    Although the story was written and published in 1846, it appeared with the imprint 1847 in *Iris: Deutscher Almanach auf das Jahr 1847.*

*Schneidelinie* also appears here, designating the "edge"-like "line" at which the crest of the Bohemian Forest and the blanket of clouds looming over it converge on the northern horizon. If one were to read on in this long—and later more fictionalized—narrative centered not around Stifter but the titular "forest-goer" Georg, one would soon note that the aspect of *scheiden* expands into a full-fledged motif that reinforces both the natural and anthropological divisions thematized in the text. The local topography is, for instance, full of geographical and hydrographical wrinkles that demarcate the arboreal and fluvial subzones within the greater compass of southern Bohemia. And the eventual divorce (*Scheidung*) between Georg and his first wife Corona instigates an abrupt juncture in the storyline, one that has already been riven by human separations of various kinds, for instance hometown departures, family deaths, and a general sense of alienation (on the part of Georg) from humanity.

This polyvalent deployment of the basic morpheme *scheid-* can, from an environmental standpoint and especially in the initial loco-descriptive episode of *Der Waldgänger*, best be interpreted along the "lines" of *Wasserscheidelinien* or "watersheds." The narrator, after all, passes several such hydrographical boundaries and intersectional points (*Scheidepunkte*), oftentimes pausing to peruse the mixed terrain that extends in all directions beneath and beyond him. A watershed is a rather intricate geophysical concept, as is apparent in the terminological variants used to designate it and further differentiate its diverse phenomenal types. Thus, "drainage divide," "water divide," "water parting," and "height of land" are all synonymous terms for a literal-topographical site at which "water" gets "shed." But different topographies shed water in differing ways and in varying scales. Compare, for instance, "triple divides" or "hydrological apexes," from which *three* rather than merely two drainage systems originate from a single identifiable highpoint; and "continental divides," which separate major drainage basins, each of which feeds into an ocean or sea. In German, scientific watershed nomenclature is similarly rich, but the basic term *Wasserscheide* means precisely what it morphologically professes: a "water-separation." Its English counterpart, however, tends to conflate the well-defined high divide separating catchments with those lower-lying catchments themselves. Such minor differences of language usage aside, Stifter is, for his part, acutely aware of the "critical" (from Greek *krínein* = to separate, divide) function of watersheds, both in his broader oeuvre and especially here in *Der Waldgänger*. Though he employs such technical terms as *Scheidelinie* and *Scheidepunkt* without their hydro-prefixes *Wasser-* (*Wasserscheidelinie* being the full German word for *Wasserscheide* and *Wasserscheidepunkt* being the standard designation for "triple divide" or "hydrological apex"), it seems clear from the text and its broader transliterary environmental context that he is describing a network of watersheds in Upper Austria, more precisely in the Mühlkreis and the environs of Linz. If there were any doubt about this panoramic perception and the narrator's eventual immersion in an actual watershed, one only need compare the following excerpt, which traces the course of an ever-swelling drainage flow somewhere in the heights above Linz:

> Ganz oben, wo das Thal mit noch geringer Tiefe anfängt, begann auch ein winziges Wasserfädlein, neben dem Wanderer abwärts zu gehen. Es ging in dem Rinnsale neben dem Wege unhörbar und nur glizzernd vorwärts, bis es durch die Menge des durch die Höhen sickernden Wassers gestärkt vor ihm plaudernd und rauschend einher hüpfte, als wollte es ihm den Weg durch die Thalmündung hinaus zeigen, und bis es endlich durch die ungeheure Wucht des in die Tiefe gedrückten Wassers genährt, und von manchem aus dem Bauche des Berges hervor springenden Brünnlein begrüßt, und von manchem schwarzen Steine aufgehalten schäumte und tobte, und ihn ermunterte zu folgen. (*HKG* 3,1:98)

> [Far above, where the valley already starts its descent, a tiny trickle of water also began its course downward, alongside the wanderer. Silent and sparkling, it flowed forth in the runnel alongside the pathway, until, reinforced by waters seeping down from higher elevations, it hopped along, prattling and swishing, as if it sought to show him the way through the valley exit and beyond; and, when it was eventually nourished by the enormous force of the water pressured into the depths and greeted by many a wellspring issuing from the belly of the mountain, and hindered by many a dark rock, it frothed and seethed onward, animating him to follow suit.]

This final chapter of the volume functions, at least to some degree, as a summative conclusion or kind of literary-bioregional bookend to my earlier intellectual-biographical introduction. After all, the correlations between biography and bioregion, between identity and inhabitancy, are intimately entwined with certain authors, especially so-called environmental ones. Through the interpretive lens of bioregionalism, one of many modes of ecocritical inquiry that has emerged in recent decades, I intend to examine Stifter's pronounced and oftentimes profound place-based writing. After a preliminary, albeit robust, overview of North American bioregional theory, I will explore the Bavarian-Bohemian Forest as a physical and cultural bioregion. My chapter will culminate with a close reading of a select tale, *Der beschriebene Tännling* (The Inscribed Fir-Tree, 1846/1850) whereby I probe its potential as a productive example of literary bioregionalism or what has also been called "bioregional poetics." More narrowly, the subgeneric category of "narrative reinhabitation" has been proposed and applied to bioregional-inflected literature, particularly in the Anglophone world, and I will follow this interpretive cue with respect to Stifter's sample text.

More generally, such an approach will help shed further light on Stifter's enduring sense of place as manifested in the dozen or so other stories set in his native-narrative terrain. These range, chronologically, from his second journal publication "Das Haidedorf" (The Village on the Heath), serialized in 1840 and later included as the third tale in *Studien I* (1844), to his final opus *Aus dem bairischen Walde* (From the Bavarian Forest), completed shortly before his death in January 1868 and released posthumously thereafter. In the end, although Stifter's lifelong attachment to the Bavarian-Bohemian Forest largely transpired in physical absentia, as forty-two of his sixty-two years of life were spent elsewhere (namely, in Vienna and Linz), he never narratively abandoned his "life-place" or literal "bio-region." His work thus presents an instructive example, or at least intriguing case study, of bioregionalism. At the very least, it serves as a testing ground for the limits versus possibilities of literary bioregional approaches.

To be sure, Stifter has long been considered a "regional" writer, which is a label that carries at least two implications. On the one hand, it neutrally implies that he adheres to what, or in this case *where*, he knows best and capitalizes on this personal-local background. On the other hand, regionalism in the Germanophone tradition is often construed as provincialism and, even more artistically damning, as *Heimatliteratur*. The finer literary lines between rustic parochialism and rurally situated universalism have been well articulated by Charles Hayes, the editor of a didacticized version of *Der beschriebene Tännling* intended for an American college-level readership (back in the day when students of language were principally primed to read literature). Out of deference to Hayes and his excellent edition of Stifter's story, I cite his observations here at greater length: "Stifter himself was much more than just a *Heimatdichter*. His interests as a storyteller extended beyond the borders of his native Bohemia. The characters who figure in his works are like the people he grew up with, but they represent more than just themselves, and although most of his stories are situated in the Bohemian forest he never portrayed provincial life for its own sake but only as a means to an end."[2] This crucial interplay between micro-places and macro-spaces, between backwoods (backwards?) village life and worldly (progressive?) bourgeois-humanistic ideals, lies at the heart of Stifter's oeuvre and constitutes one of its many inner tensions if not chronic contradictions. Lawrence Buell, one of the premier ecocritical scholars of American literature, has formulated this perennial problem in the following terms: "the bioregional horizon must extend beyond a merely local horizon: the locale cannot shut itself off from the translocal forces even if it wanted to."[3] More specifically, one of the crucial differences between

2    Charles Hayes, "Introduction," in Adalbert Stifter, *Der beschriebene Tännling*, ed. Charles Hayes (Waltham, MA: Blaisdell, 1970), vii–xxi; here x.

3    Lawrence Buell, *The Future of Environmental Criticism: Environmental Crisis and Literary Imagination* (Malden, MA: Blackwell, 2005), 88.

*bio*regional-minded as opposed to regional-beholden writing is the post-Edenic awareness of environmental precariousness. As Buell further notes in more socio-historical terms: "Perhaps what especially differentiates modern bioregionalism, be it rural or urban, from traditional regionalism is the sense of vulnerability and flux."[4] Stifter's precise niche in such a sliding traditional-versus-modern scale of human-nature relations remains to be seen. First, however, a summary of bioregional thought and practice will help elucidate this decisive dilemma of ecological integrity versus fragility—and what role humans play in the process.

## Bioregionalism, Reinhabitation, and Watershed Consciousness

Bioregionalism is both a theory and a practice that emerged during the 1970s in American countercultural circles and, to a lesser degree, in academic discourse, particularly in the field of human geography. While a new generation of postwar geographers began to theorize about questions of place and, increasingly, our modern predicament of placelessness,[5] the San Francisco-based free spirits Gary Snyder and Peter Berg laid the literary, philosophical, and practical foundations for the "reinhabitation" movement, which would become synonymous with bioregionalism for decades to come. Indeed, Berg's 1977 essay "Reinhabiting California," coauthored with the scientist Raymond Dasmann and published in *The Ecologist*,[6] has become *the* foundational document of this new environmental direction. Inspired by Allen Van Newkirk, who established the Institute for Bioregional Research in 1975, Berg not only leaned on but

---

4    Buell, *The Future of Environmental Criticism*, 88.

5    For some seminal studies that anticipate or otherwise complement bioregionalist thinking, see (in chronological order): Yi-Fu Tuan, *Topophilia: A Study of Environmental Perception, Attitudes, and Values* (Englewood Cliffs, NJ: Prentice-Hall, 1974); Edward Relph, *Place and Placelessness* (London: Pion, 1976); Edward S. Casey, *Getting Back into Place: Toward a Renewed Understanding of the Place-World* (Bloomington: Indiana University Press, 1993); and J. E. Malpas, *Place and Experience: A Philosophical Topography* (Cambridge: Cambridge University Press, 1999). For two convenient overviews of place-based geographical inquiry and its increasing convergence with bioregionalism, see Tim Cresswell, *Place: A Short Introduction* (Malden, MA: Blackwell, 2004); and Michael Vincent McGinnis, ed., *Bioregionalism* (London and New York: Routledge, 1999).

6    Dasmann came to Berg's succor when the latter's original essay, titled "Strategies for Reinhabiting the Northern California Bioregion," was rejected for publication by the peer-reviewed journal. This proto-version has since been published, as an illuminating appendix, in Peter Berg, *The Biosphere and the Bioregion: Essential Writings of Peter Berg*, ed. Cheryll Glotfelty and Eve Quesnel (London and New York: Routledge, 2015), 263–70.

also elaborated on Van Newkirk's neologism, expanding it beyond its ecological ambit to include human existence. For Berg, a bioregion refers "both to geographical terrain and a terrain of consciousness."[7] In other words, it is as much a scientifically determined as an anthropologically relative notion, which seems inevitable given the added human factor involved. Unlike for instance an ecosystem, the physiographical parameters of which most scientists can agree upon (at least in conventional twentieth-century ecological theory), a bioregion cannot be definitively circumscribed but is always subject to interpretation by the humans that inhabit it. Berg's argumentative point of departure remains, in the end, literalist: bioregionalism entails "living-in-place" according to the natural processes and cycles of a given area based on its climate, topography, and other unique environmental factors. As evident in the original solo-authored title of his essay, "*Strategies* for Reinhabiting the Northern California Bioregion," Berg's objective is solution-driven and praxis-oriented, not unrealistic let alone atavistic. In the final collaborative version with Dasmann, he outlines his bioregional vision as follows:

> *Reinhabitation* means learning to live-in-place in an area that has been disrupted and injured through past exploitation. It involves becoming native to a place through becoming aware of the particular ecological relationships that operate within and around it. It means undertaking activities and evolving social behaviour that will enrich the life of that place, restore its life-supporting systems, and establish an ecologically and socially sustainable pattern of existence within it. Simply stated it involves becoming fully alive in and with a place. It involves applying for membership in a biotic community and ceasing to be its exploiter.[8]

In more concrete geographical terms, Berg and Dasmann argue that northern California constitutes a plausible and viable bioregion. Definitions of "northern" California can of course vary, but from the bioregional perspective of Berg and Dasmann it comprises a vast expanse encircled by mountain ranges (the Sierra Nevada to the east, the Coast Ranges to the west, the Cascades to the north, and the Tehachapi Mountains to the south) and furthermore encompasses a major watershed, namely the Sacramento-San Joaquin Rivers drainage system. Watersheds are indeed one of the key factors for determining a given bioregion from both an ecological and historical standpoint; that is, with respect to the dual realms of the natural and

---

7   Peter Berg and Raymond Dasmann, "Reinhabiting California," *The Ecologist* 7, no. 10 (1977): 399–401; here 399. See also, among several other reissued versions: Berg, *The Biosphere and the Bioregion: Essential Writings of Peter Berg*, ed. Glotfelty and Quesnel, 35–40; here 36.

8   Berg and Dasmann, "Reinhabiting California," 399/36.

the human. On the one hand, a "network of springs, creeks and rivers flowing together in a specific area exerts a dominant influence on all non-human life there"; on the other, native tribal boundaries "were often set by the limits of watersheds"—as were the pioneer settlements that usurped the land and ousted its aboriginal inhabitants.[9] In addition to its hydrology, the northern California bioregion is defined by the fertility of its soil (especially in the Central Valley) and the abundance of its vegetation (especially in the form of montane forests). Thus, the sustainability of watersheds, topsoil, and plant species has become compromised by a territorial concoction that exceeds its bioregional capacities, whether through water diversion, agricultural malpractices, or clearcutting. Like most American states, California is a politico-historical construct whose cartographical contours simply do not correspond to the natural lay of the land. To cite but one reinhabitory proposition put forward by Berg and Dasmann, a separate state of northern (or more officially: Northern) California could redraw its counties and other administrative districts to create "watershed governments appropriate to maintaining local life-places."[10] Such bioregionally organized units would benefit *all* resident species, both human and nonhuman, that share this distinctive swath of land and, by extension, the entire interspecial planet.

The above ideas expounded by Berg and Dasmann in their seminal article are echoed, almost to the word, by Gary Snyder: "People are challenged to become 'reinhabitory'—that is, to become people who are learning to live and think 'as if' they were totally engaged with their place for the long future. This doesn't mean some return to a primitive lifestyle or utopian provincialism; it simply implies an engagement with community and a search for the sustainable sophisticated mix of economic practices that would enable people to live regionally and yet learn from and contribute to a planetary society."[11] Given his wide-ranging endeavors and accomplishments as a Pulitzer Prize-winning poet, wide-ranging essayist, UC-Davis professor, Zen Buddhist, environmental activist, erstwhile Forest Service employee, and longtime (re)inhabitant of the northern Sierra Nevada, Snyder embodies bioregionalism on multiple levels. In the words of one scholar: "He arguably has become the single most practical proselytizer of a uniquely hybrid intellectual/spiritual/rural bioregional vision."[12] In 1977, the same year that Berg and Dasmann's article appeared in *The Ecologist*, an analogous reflection by Snyder was featured in a far different forum, namely in a homespun collection of essays

9    Berg and Dasmann, "Reinhabiting California," 400/38.

10    Berg and Dasmann, "Reinhabiting California," 401/40.

11    Gary Snyder, "The Rediscovery of Turtle Island," in *A Place in Space: Ethics, Aesthetics, and Watersheds* (Berkeley, CA: Counterpoint, 1995), 236–51; here 247.

12    Doug Aberley, "Interpreting Bioregionalism: A Story from Many Voices," in *Bioregionalism*, ed. Michael Vincent McGinnis (London and New York: Routledge, 1999), 13–42; here 18.

called *The Old Ways* and published by City Lights Books. In this piece, simply titled "Re-Inhabitation," Snyder paints a broad anthropological picture of inhabitory peoples over the millennia and around the globe. For most of human history, Snyder maintains, people have dwelled in and adapted to their particular environment, all the while developing "local ecosystem habitation styles" and accumulating intimate knowledge about their respective "local bioregion system, from cirrus clouds to leaf mold."[13] Only recently, with the rise of industrial society, has this close bond to the land and autochthonous sense of place been severed, at least in many parts of the world—and not least in North America. Granted, Snyder's above observations are standard historical fare, but he embeds his argument in an autobiographical framework and then embellishes it along bioregional lines. After all, for Snyder autobiography is at bottom autobioregionality; "who we are" is always tied to the question of "where we are."

Tracing his familial migratory roots from parts east and south to the Pacific Northwest, Snyder recounts his budding sense of place while growing up among the patchwork fields and forests of western Washington. Apparently also influenced by contact with a local Salish elder, he began to identify less with his white American heritage and ever more with the ecologically rich natural-cultural landscape around him, as an eventual result of which "I defined myself by relation to the place."[14] Following this nostalgic narrative springboard, Snyder inflects his otherwise staid anthro-historical essay with newer notions coined by Raymond Dasmann, namely "ecosystem-based cultures" and "biosphere cultures." These essentially synonymous terms offer another, and perhaps more illuminating, way of understanding inhabitory peoples and their cultural clashes with imperialist powers that exploit nature and its resources. Thus, while there have always been "societies whose life and economies are centered in terms of natural regions and watersheds,"[15] there have, conversely, often been forces (for instance the Roman Empire) that conquer and colonize these self-subsistence populations through resource acquisition, extraction, and even depletion. This form of environmental imperialism extends from deforestation to species extinction but also includes water diversion or, in extreme cases, what might best be called "watershed manipulation," a grander form of hydrological engineering that reroutes water sources from one major drainage system to another. Though one might assume this to be a modern western practice (controversial examples in California include the Hetch Hetchy

---

13  Gary Snyder, "Re-Inhabitation," in *The Old Ways* (San Francisco, CA: City Lights Books, 1977), 57–66; here 59. Republished as "Reinhabitation," in *A Place in Space: Ethics, Aesthetics, and Watersheds* (Berkeley, CA: Counterpoint, 1995), 183–91; here 185.

14  Snyder, "Re-Inhabitation," 58/"Reinhabitation," 184.

15  Snyder, "Re-Inhabitation," 61/"Reinhabitation," 186.

Project and the Owens Valley-Los Angeles Aqueduct), Snyder notes that it extends back thousands of years to ancient China, the Middle East, and the Mediterranean. (An interesting example with respect to Stifter and the Bavarian-Bohemian Forest is the 51.9 km floating canal or *Schwemmkanal* that was constructed between 1789 and 1793 and again between 1821 and 1823 to transport wood from the Vltava/Moldau watershed across the continental divide to the Danube drainage basin, and then onward to Vienna. This innovative canal project, which effectively circumvented a major Central European watershed and was at the time, at least regionally, dubbed "the eighth wonder of the world," is mentioned only once in Stifter's entire oeuvre—namely in the *Journalfassung* of *Der beschriebene Tännling* [see *HKG* 1,3:269]. Nevertheless, he must have crossed its narrow course multiple times on his forest hikes throughout the years, as anyone perforce does today.[16]) As Snyder elsewhere notes, such a network of bio/eco-based settlements can form the basis of "watershed councils"[17] that work together in the greater cause of environmental sustainability. This idea recalls Berg and Dasmann's advocacy for "watershed governments" in the de facto state, but still unrecognized bioregion, of (northern) California. Snyder's reflections on watersheds, however, run deeper and inundate his writings. For Snyder, watersheds enlace the earth like "a kind of familial branching, a chart of relationship,"[18] thereby manifesting an almost human notion of kinship. Though one might dismiss this analogy as an overly anthropomorphic projection of interrelatedness, the fundamental importance of watersheds for biotic life and human habitation cannot be denied. Bioregionalism thus requires, and is perhaps even predicated on, "watershed consciousness,"[19] both in theory and practice. And, as evidenced in his sundry reinhabitory writings and further evinced by his decades-long resettlement efforts, Snyder was the consummate representative of both.

Bioregional thought in the wake of Snyder and Berg and Dasmann has striven, and often struggled, to establish an adequate definition of itself and its precise purview. An early follow-up essay from 1981 by Jim Dodge, titled "Living by Life: Some Bioregional Theory and Practice,"

16   For detailed historical-pictorial accounts of this floating canal, see Erhard Fritsch, "Der Schwarzenberg-Schwemmkanal im Wandel der Zeit," *Mitteilungen des Landesvereins für Höhlenkunde in Oberösterreich* 39, no. 1 (1993): 43–74; and Fritz Lange, *Von Böhmen nach Wien: Der Schwarzenbergische Schwemmkanal* (Erfurt: Sutton, 2004). For brief and basic facts, see Reinhold Erlbeck, "Die Waldwelt Oberplans zur Zeit Adalbert Stifters," *Bayerische Landesanstalt für Wald und Forstwirtschaft, LWF Aktuell* 2018, 20–24, https://www.lwf.bayern.de/mam/cms04/service/dateien/a116_inhalt.pdf (accessed July 30, 2022).

17   Gary Snyder, "Coming into the Watershed," in *A Place in Space*, 219–35; here 229.

18   Snyder, "Coming into the Watershed," 229.

19   Snyder, "Coming into the Watershed," 235.

was a key catalyst for pushing the parameters of the discussion and generating further debate. On the one hand, Dodge relativizes the burgeoning movement with the claim that "bioregionalism is hardly a new notion; it has been the animating cultural principle through 99 percent of human history, and is at least as old as consciousness."[20] On the other, he enumerates a handful of criteria, beyond, for instance, watersheds, that can help determine a given bioregion. Watersheds, while crucial, can often be ill-defined or exceedingly large in scope. Dodge lists five additional factors that contribute to a more holistic view of bioregional boundaries. These include "biotic shift" (the percentual change in flora and fauna species, which should not exceed 15 to 25 percent); "land form" (geomorphological distinctions that admittedly tend to follow watershed patterns but are not subsumed by them); "elevation" (geospatial verticality versus horizontality, which implies that hill people might differ from flatlanders even though they both inhabit the same greater watershed); "cultural/ phenomenological perceptions" (human-based understandings of placehood regardless of more objective scientific findings); "spirit places" (psychophysical influences that transcend descriptive geography and, even more so, elude scientific grasp). To his credit, Snyder, the antithesis of a reductionist, later qualified his view of bioregions along the very same lines as Dodge, stating that: "Biota, watersheds, landforms, and elevations are just a few of the facets that define a region."[21] And Dodge, to his own credit, adopts a pragmatic stance like that of his predecessor Snyder, admitting that: "Bioregionalism, whatever it is, occupies that point in development (more properly, renewal) where definition is unnecessary and perhaps dangerous. Better now to let definitions emerge from practice than impose them dogmatically from the git-go."[22]

Given that the concept of a bioregion, in contrast to that of an ecosystem, places equal emphasis on human traces as on naturally occurring phenomena, a certain degree of anthropological bias is bound to obtain. Many widely agreed-upon bioregions are in fact the product of collective human endeavor more than of detached scientific inquest. That is, they have been articulated and demarcated not only by certain individuals— whether Berg, Dasmann, Snyder, Dodge, or other spokespeople who have received less attention here—but by popular regional movements that hold regular congresses, publish newsletters and periodicals, host websites, and

---

20   Jim Dodge, "Living by Life: Some Bioregional Theory and Practice," *The CoEvolution Quarterly* 32 (1981): 6–12; here 6. Reprinted in *Home! A Bioregional Reader*, ed. Van Andruss, et al. (Philadelphia, PA: New Society Publishers, 1990), 5–12; here 5.

21   Gary Snyder, *The Practice of the Wild* (Berkeley, CA: Counterpoint, 1990), 41.

22   Dodge, "Living by Life," 8/8.

304 ♦ SEAN IRETON

engage in other methods of outreach.[23] Examples of bioregions that have become defined at least as much by human initiative as scientific survey include, in rough order of establishment: the Shasta Bioregion, Cascadia (the Pacific/Inland Northwest, including southern British Columbia), Ozarkia (the Ozark Plateau of southern Missouri/northern Arkansas), the Great Lakes Basin (aka Laurentia Bioregion), the Ohio River Watershed, the Gulf of Maine, the Hudson River Valley (aka Hudsonia), the Texas Hill Country, the Piedmont (the foothills of North Carolina, South Carolina, and Georgia), the more comprehensive Katúah Bioregion (after the Cherokee name for the entire southern Appalachians), and the Kansas Area Watershed. This is but a small, indeed infinitesimal, sampling of the larger picture. According to one of the few bioregional studies published in German, by the mid-1990s some 250 such initiatives, whether in the form of organized groups or more freelance publication organs, were in existence throughout North America, including Mexico.[24]

The movement of bioregionalism came later to Europe and still seems to have gained less of a foothold than its North American counterpart.[25] The reasons for this are varied. In the broadest of terms, a preexisting mentality of cultural regionalism has prevailed throughout much of European history, thus perhaps inhibiting the need for an explicit or novel brand of *bio*regionalism. In Germany, more specifically, regionalism and the more recent phenomenon of "neo-regionalism" harbor their share of right-wing if not ecofascist tendencies, ranging from the "green-brown" politics of the Third Reich to postwar ideologies espoused by the likes of the Ökologisch-Demokratische Partei (Ecological Democratic Party) and their more extremist offshoot Unabhängige Ökologen Deutschlands (Independent Ecologists of Germany).[26] Bioregionalism can, in other words, be coopted by nationalistic, nativistic, and deep-down racist

---

23  For a brief overview of such organizations and their diverse activities, see Aberley, "Interpreting Bioregionalism," 26–28. For a more thorough enumeration, see Eduard Gugenberger and Roman Schweidlenka, *Bioregionalismus: Bewegung für das 21. Jahrhundert*, 2nd ed. (Osnabrück: Packpapier Verlag, 1996), 43–60.

24  See Gugenberger and Schweidlenka, *Bioregionalismus*, 46, 179. On the latter page, Peter Berg himself provides this statistic in an interview translated here into German.

25  For some early bioregional movements launched during the 1980s and 90s in Europe, see Gugenberger and Schweidlenka, *Bioregionalismus*, 172–74.

26  For representative book-length studies of these two trends, see Frank Uekötter, *The Green and the Brown: A History of Conservation in Nazi Germany* (Cambridge: Cambridge University Press, 2006); and Oliver Geden, *Rechte Ökologie: Umweltschutz zwischen Emanzipation und Faschismus*, 2nd ed. (Berlin: Elefanten Press, 1999). With specific respect to the ecofascist potential of bioregionalism, see Jonathan Olsen, "The Perils of Rootedness: On Bioregionalism

factions. According to this mindset, outsiders are not welcome in(to) a long-settled and self-fancied autochthonous zone; the "eco-boat is full," so to speak, as is the local *ethnic* rather than—per its original definition—*ecological* carrying capacity.[27] As Udo E. Simonis, a research professor of environmental policy in Berlin, argues more concretely: the "long tradition of political regionalism in Europe; major European countries are administratively based on the principle of subsidiarity; and the European Union also largely functions on the basis of that principle."[28] Thus, while environmental protection in Europe has become ever more politically relevant, *bio*regionalism per se remains "a demanding concept"; indeed, "depending upon the expectations implied in the concept, and the efforts made to implement it, no real bioregion may be found in Europe."[29] This bold and blanket statement should of course be understood, in accordance with the subtitle of the cited article ("A Pragmatic European Perspective"), from a present-day realistic rather than future-oriented quixotic perspective. The basic argument advanced by Simonis, is that any kind of realizable bioregional functionality is compromised by the intergovernmental structures that have been put in place throughout much of contemporary Europe. This infrastructural issue even extends to eco-conscious Germany, some 21 percent of whose total land mass is officially protected in some fashion, whether as nature parks, national parks, or biosphere reserves. (The maps reproduced in Simonis's study prove especially helpful in conveying the totality of these "green" spaces.) Interestingly, one of these protected areas, and in fact the first national park established in Germany, forms an integral part of Stifter's literary landscape: der Nationalpark Bayerischer Wald or Bavarian Forest National Park. Here, near the so-called *Dreiländereck* or triangular convergence of Bavaria, Bohemia, and Austria one finds an integrative ecosystem that transcends national boundaries; or, in the case of Stifter's oeuvre, a trans-territorial and natural-cultural bioregion that can be best be labeled the "Bavarian-Bohemian Forest."

## The Bavarian-Bohemian Forest as Bioregion

The Bavarian-Bohemian Forest can be considered an ecological-cultural bioregion according to the various criteria outlined by Berg and Dasmann,

---

and Right Wing Ecology in Germany," *Landscape Journal* 19, nos. 1–2 (2000): 73–83.

27 For these general arguments and specific terms, I am indebted to Gugenberger and Schweidlenka, *Bioregionalismus*, 121–25.

28 Udo E. Simonis, "Bioregionalism: A Pragmatic European Perspective," *Ekistics* 64, nos. 382, 383, and 384 (1997): 67–72; here 67.

29 Simonis, "Bioregionalism," 70.

306 ◆ SEAN IRETON

Snyder, Dodge, and others. However, it also functions as a literary bioregion, one in which Stifter dwells as a kind of narrative reinhabitant, chronicling its natural history, its anthropogenic alterations, and its moments of environmental recovery. One of many remarkable aspects of Stifter's tales set in his immediate homeland is that they were all written from afar, whether in Vienna during the 1840s or in Linz during the subsequent two decades of his life. These works include: *Das Haidedorf*, *Der Hochwald*, *Die Mappe meines Urgroßvaters*, *Abdias* (the final third of which takes place there), *Der beschriebene Tännling*, *Der Waldgänger*, "Die Pechbrenner" (later revised as *Granit*), *Kazensilber*, *Der Waldbrunnen*, *Der Kuß von Sentze*, *Witiko*, and *Aus dem bairischen Walde*. During his twenty-two years in the Austrian capital and an additional twenty years spent in the more proximate city of Linz, Stifter visited Oberplan and environs only a handful of times yet he continued to write about the region with an apparent photographic memory, which, combined with his authorial eye for detail and general mania for minutiae, enabled him to produce accurate but also vivid evocations of the landscape that he left behind in 1826, at the age of twenty-one. One thus finds in Stifter, like in Snyder, a rich admixture of autobiography and autobioregionality. In Stifter's case, this creative combination is predicated more on nostalgia than on a genuine back-to-land mode of living. Nevertheless, one should not underestimate the bioregional relevance of this premodern "disease" which physicians in the sixteenth and seventeenth centuries believed "could result in death if the patient could not be returned home."[30] Though Stifter was never in mortal danger of this psychosomatic kind, he did suffer from obesity, alcoholism, and a fatal cirrhosis of the liver, no doubt due to his sedentary and gluttonous urban lifestyle. Such an existence could not contrast more sharply with that of the many perambulatory and outdoorsy figures depicted in his fiction—or, for that matter, with Stifter's own youthful ramblings through which he gained firsthand knowledge of the countryside around Oberplan. Hence, perhaps, the palpable sense of nostalgia that permeates his oeuvre and the deeper psychological urge to idealize his Bavarian-Bohemian Heimat, for nostalgia in the end "demonstrates ... the importance of attachment to place"[31] and would thus seem to operate as one of Stifter's primal narrative drives.

From a purely physical rather than presumptive psychological standpoint, the Bavarian-Bohemian Forest is a unique bioregion insofar as it fosters two major European watersheds. The crest that runs through its middle forms, in fact, a continental divide. The western Bavarian side belongs to the vast Danube/Black Sea drainage basin while the eastern Bohemian flank feeds the Vltava/Moldau River, which flows into the Elbe and then onward into the North Sea. With respect to climatology,

30  Relph, *Place and Placelessness*, 41.
31  Relph, *Place and Placelessness*, 41.

the watershed separates the moister, maritime-influenced weather of western Europe from the drier continental climes to the east. Culturally, this region is also dichotomous, at least from a linguistic and ethnic perspective: Slavic Czech-speaking peoples are predominant in the Bohemian Forest whereas German-speakers inhabit the Bavarian Forest and the Mühlviertel of Upper Austria. This population makeup has, however, fluctuated throughout history and in Stifter's day the Bohemian Forest was an entirely German-speaking region. Indeed, during the nineteenth century some ninety percent of greater Bohemia had been settled by Germans. After the Second World War this area was reconfigured in both human and environmental terms: the Bohemian side of the divide was resettled by Czechs and the very *Wasserscheide* that forms the backbone of this wooded expanse became, in effect, a geopolitical *Menschenscheide* as manifested by a fortified border known as the Iron Curtain. Thus, a military restricted zone or proverbial "no-man's land" cut through the core of this landscape, adding a geopolitical rift to its longstanding cultural and environmental complexity. Such a convoluted concatenation of natural factors and historical events testifies to the singularity of this region but would also seem to undermine its status as a bona fide bioregion, at least as defined by North American visionaries and pragmatists, especially given their emphasis on watersheds. Nevertheless, a more nuanced appraisal of the Böhmerwald and the Bayerische Wald as one continuous rather than two merely contiguous bioregions is necessary, whether from an ecological, cultural, or literary approach. Kirkpatrick Sale offers some guiding words toward this end: "There is an advantage in keeping borders vague, even if it goes against the scientistic love of fixedness, for it tends to encourage a blend, a cross-fertilization of cultures at the bioregional edges …. That is why I think the final distinctions about bioregional boundaries … can be safely left to people who live there, providing only that they have undertaken the job of honing their bioregional sensibilities and making acute their bioregional consciousnesses."[32]

As Stifter emphasizes at the beginning of *Witiko*, this entire pan-forested region should best be called "der bömisch-bayerische Wald" (see *HKG* 5,1:13, 14), such is its natural cohesion. This Bohemian-Bavarian arboreal domain remains the principal, and in many cases primeval, setting of Stifter's fiction. Some of his works, most notably *Der Hochwald* and *Witiko*, open with lengthy and hyper-detailed surveys of the forest and its pristine premodern state. However, *all* of his works situated here feature at some point, oftentimes at multiple narrative junctures, scrupulous descriptions of the naturally given but also humanly tended terrain. More precisely, peripatetic figures roam the heights and depths of

---

32 Kirkpatrick Sale, *Dwellers in the Land: The Bioregional Vision* (San Francisco, CA: Sierra Club Books, 1985), 59, 61.

the forest, usually on the eastern side of the crest (which was, after all, Stifter's own vantage point from Bohemian Oberplan) but also on the Bavarian and Upper Austrian side, with occasional watershed crossings in between. Such characters and texts include the roving woodsman Gregor in *Der Hochwald*; the wayfaring woodcutter Hanns in *Der beschriebene Tännling*; the melancholic and nomadic Georg in *Der Waldgänger*; the rambling (both physically and verbally) grandfather and accompanying grandson in *Granit*; and the frolicking family of nature-goers, here a grandmother and her three grandchildren, in *Kazensilber*. But Stifter's most comprehensive—both in terms of textual breadth and topographical scope—portrayal of the Bavarian-Bohemian Forest can be found in his lifelong literary project *Die Mappe meines Urgroßvaters*, the protagonist of which is a country doctor and thus the perfect narrative vehicle for an exploration of the vicinity and its denizens.[33]

As I have demonstrated elsewhere and will only summarize here,[34] the posthumously published third and fourth drafts of the *Mappe* offer a unique solution to the problem of deforestation and general ecological degradation that accelerated in this region during the eighteenth and nineteenth centuries. The so-called "Fürstengarten" blurs the boundaries between nature and culture to such a degree that the narrator's initial stroll through a well-ordered park soon turns into a long trek through dense woods and rugged terrain. This "Fürstengarten" is a radicalized version of the English landscape garden; its parameters encompass an immeasurable tract of land and a wide range of topographies. Indeed, the "Fürstengarten" is not a garden per se, neither according to the text (see *HKG* 6,1:236; 6,2:217) nor based on the etymological origin of the term (Proto-Germanic *gardaz* = a "fenced enclosure"). Here the human and natural realms are not physically partitioned or even markedly distinct but rather fluid and interconnected. As the narrator himself observes from precisely such an imbricated organic-anthropogenic prospect, namely

---

33 Similar characters ambulate through the landscape of what I would call Stifter's "secondary literary bioregion," namely the foothills and high mountains of Upper Austria, south of the Bavarian-Bohemian Forest. These include the Alpine explorer Heinrich in *Die Narrenburg*; the teenage Victor on his long trek to his uncle's refuge of solitude in *Der Hagestolz*; the wandering-convalescing hypochondriac Tiburius Kneigt in *Der Waldsteig*; the errant children amidst snow and ice in "Der heilige Abend"/*Bergkristall*; the land surveyor of the remote limestone landscape in "Der arme Wohltäter"/*Kalkstein*; and, above all, Heinrich Drendorf in *Der Nachsommer*, who hikes up and down the Austrian topographical map over the course of several hundred pages.

34 See Sean Ireton, "Adalbert Stifter and the Gentle Anthropocene," in *Readings in the Anthropocene: The Environmental Humanities, German Studies, and Beyond*, ed. Sabine Wilke and Japhet Johnstone (New York: Bloomsbury, 2017), 195–221; esp. 214–17.

the overgrown ruins of a mountaintop tower: "Eine Begrenzung des Gartens, wie etwa eine Mauer ein Gitterwerk oder auch nur ein Zaun ist, konnte ich nirgends erbliken" (*HKG* 6,1:236; Nowhere could I descry a boundary to the garden such as a wall, latticework, or even a fence might serve). A later remark to the prince and proprietor of this infinite estate underscores, more than the mere visible continuity, the underlying unity of this extensive and integrative landscape project: "[es] war mir ... als sei das alles Eines, so groß es ist" (6,1:240; To me it seemed ... as if everything were One, despite its scale). The "Fürstengarten" thus operates as a non-demarcated demesne—signposts, trail markers, and other manmade conveniences are barred from its grounds—of human activity and ecological integrity. One is always-already within its ambit, or, as the narrator learns from a fieldworker upon inquiring into its whereabouts: "Ihr seid ja schon drinnen" (*HKG* 6,1:232; 6,2:209; You are already inside it). In alternative terms, the "Fürstengarten" represents a fully functioning bioregion, a stable-sustainable space in which flower gardens and wildflower patches, fruit orchards and vegetable fields coexist with endemic tree species such as maples, oaks, elms, alders, lindens, beeches, birches, aspens, spruces, firs, and pines. With respect to its greater topographical territory, the "Fürstengarten" incorporates cultivated acreage, forested foothills, rocky outcroppings, and the abovementioned highpoint that affords panoramic vistas of the greater region, including the homesteads and hamlets that seem to occupy a harmonious niche within what might best be called Stifter's Bavarian-Bohemian Bioregion.

Stifter could hardly have envisioned a more seamless sphere of human-nature symbiosis than in this ecotopian version of his otherwise blighted bioregional backyard. His visionary model of a pan-Bavarian-Bohemian province that extends across cultural-ethnic (German versus Czech) and geographical-hydrographical (the Danube/Black Sea versus Vltava/North Sea watersheds) boundaries anticipates, in its own literary-imaginative way, the two national parks and adjoining conservation zones that currently protect the very environment he incessantly wrote about. The *aristocratically* supervised "Fürstengarten," which Stifter loosely based on the Rothenhof summer palace of the Schwarzenberg princes located near Krumau/Český Krumlov, corresponds even more loosely to the *federally* administered areas that make up the largest forested biosphere in Central Europe: der Nationalpark Bayerischer Wald, established in 1970 as (West) Germany's first national park, and the much larger Národní Park Šumava,[35] founded in 1991 after the fall of European

---

35 In Czech, *šumava* means "rushing" or 'rustling," as in the sound made by wind. Stifter often alludes to this atmospheric phenomenon, employing the German verb *rauschen* or its articular infinitive *das Rauschen*. At times in his oeuvre, these rustling winds turn into hurricane-like windstorms that wreak havoc

Communism. In 1997 the former was significantly expanded, in fact almost doubled in size, and in 2020 some additional acreage was added. Adjacent to the latter lies the Chráněná Krajinná Oblast Šumava (Šumava Protected Landscape Area), which constitutes, together with the Národní Park Šumava, what is known in English as the "Biosphere Reserve Šumava." The more precise areal coverage of all three German-Czech environmental sectors can be summed up as follows: der Nationalpark Bayerischer Wald encompasses 250 km$^2$; Národní Park Šumava 681 km$^2$; and Chráněná Krajinná Oblast Šumava 996 km$^2$. All totaled, this safeguarded space amounts to nearly 2,000 km$^2$. Under the larger aegis of the Arbeitsgemeinschaft Europäischer Grenzregionen (Association of European Border Regions), founded in 1971, the bilateral sub-organization Euregio Bayerischer Wald-Böhmerwald was established in January 1993 and a mere nine months later expanded to comprise the trilateral Euregio Bayerischer Wald-Böhmerwald-Mühlviertel. These three regions neatly correspond to Stifter's Bavarian-Bohemian-Upper Austrian homeland and thus offer further bioregional correlations between past and present, between narrative fiction and administrative fact. Although they would later undergo minor reconfiguration—whereby in 2004 the latter "Euro-region" was expanded to include an Austrian district along the Lower Inn River and was thus renamed "Bayerischer Wald–Böhmerwald–Unterer Inn"; and the Mühlviertel became its own self-defined (and self-marketed) bioregion in 2014—the upshot of these recent bioregional initiatives is that they strive to unite as many transliminal cooperative endeavors as possible, including in such diverse realms as transportation, labor, agriculture, economy, ecology, environment, tourism, education, sports, culture, technology, and energy use.[36] With especial regard to Stifter and his literary-bioregional legacy, it only seems appropriate that the Adalbert Stifter Verein (Adalbert Stifter Society) is a cosponsoring member of the Euregio Bayerischer Wald–Böhmerwald–Unterer Inn.

## Narrative Reinhabitation in *Der beschriebene Tännling*

During the summer of 1845, Stifter revisited Oberplan for the first time in several years, reacquainting himself with the local landscape and

---

on the Bavarian-Bohemian Forest. For a dynamic sketch of the aftermath of such a storm, see his "Windbruch im Böhmerwald" (Deadfall in the Bohemian Forest, ca. 1845), https://www.gettyimages.ae/detail/news-photo/schriftsteller-%C3%B6sterreichzeichnung-windbruch-im-b%C3%B6hmerwald-news-photo/542859601?adppopup=true (accessed July 30, 2022).

36 For the above information I rely on the following websites and their informative links: https://euregio.bayern/wir-ueber-uns; and https://bioregion-muehlviertel.at (accessed July 30, 2022).

its inhabitants, including his own family members. Later that fall *Der beschriebene Tännling* appeared in *Rheinisches Tagebuch auf das Jahr 1846* and was eventually revised as the final tale for the concluding sixth volume of *Studien* (1850). Within the greater spectrum of variances between *Journalfassungen* and *Buchfassungen*, the tale underwent an average amount of modifications but none that affected its core content or moral message. In both cases, *Der beschriebene Tännling* is Stifter's most unmediated and unabashed homage to his hometown and its sylvan backdrop. It contains less fictitious filters and storytelling devices than *Das Haidedorf* or "Die Pechbrenner"/*Granit*, both of which take place in the exact same locale. In the *Journalfassung*, Oberplan is in fact mentioned right from the start (as the fourth word in the text) and although this proper noun does not occur until the end of page two in the *Buchfassung*, Stifter begins this reworked version of the tale with a cartographic overview of the region that invokes other place names, albeit more folkloric ones: "zum Hochficht" (The Tall Spruce), "zum schwarzen Stoke" (The Black Stump), "zur tiefen Lake" (The Deep Pond), "zur kalten Moldau" (The Cold Moldau), and "zum beschriebenen Tännling" (The Inscribed Fir Tree). These weird and wonderful names—"seltsame und wunderliche Namen" in the original (*HKG* 1,6:381)—all refer to landscape features located in the forested fringes of Oberplan and, though Stifter may well have known them from his own experience, he defers to a topographic map of the area produced by Joseph Falta in 1829.[37] This narrative strategy, whereby an omniscient bird's-eye perspective sets the scene from the very outset, serves to create a collective rather than mere individual sense of place. Contrary to the *Journalfassung*, in which Falta's map receives only passing mention at a later point in the text (see *HKG* 1,3:258), the *Buchfassung*—like all its counterparts in *Studien* and *Bunte Steine*—strives for "realist" (read: thing-oriented) objectivity over residual romantic subjectivity let alone sentimentality.[38]

---

37 See *Topographische Karte der in Böhmen budweiser Kreises liegenden Sr. Durchlaucht dem Fürsten zu Schwarzenberg Herzog zu Krummau gehörigen Herrschaft Krummau: Ausgefertigt und Lythographiert im Jahre 1829 von Joseph Falta* (Topographical Map of the Territory of Krumau, Located in the Budweis District of Bohemia and Belonging to His Highness the Prince of Schwarzenberg Duke of Krumau: Issued and Lithographed in the Year 1829 by Joseph Falta). A digitized and zoomable version, under a slightly different title, can be found at the Research Library of South Bohemia, https://lindat.mff.cuni.cz/services/catalog/view/uuid:3bf50cf3-00c9-11e5-b939-0800200c9a66 (accessed July 30, 2022).

38 Perhaps not surprisingly given its final position in *Studien VI, Der beschriebene Tännling* has been viewed as a precursor to Stifter's aloof and minimalistic "late style." See here Christian Begemann, *Die Welt der Zeichen: Stifter Lektüren* (Stuttgart: J. B. Metzler, 1995), 294. As Begemann himself notes, more

312 ♦ SEAN IRETON

The second paragraph, with its fact-based focus on a lone fir tree is an explicit example of this purgative practice. Here Stifter zooms in on what Falta's topographic map merely designates as "Wald beim beschriebenen Tännling," providing a detailed description of the titular tree, one that recalls the opening evocation of the equally titular granitic block in *Granit*. In both cases, Stifter devotes as much attention to the scrutinized object itself as to its respective appurtenances, for instance weathered sitting stones encircling the tree and sandstone slabs supporting the erratic boulder. But whereas he relies on a clearly autobiographical, indeed childhood-inflected, first-person perspective in the frame narrative of *Granit*, he adopts a disembodied third-person viewpoint in *Der beschriebene Tännling*. Like the granite rock, the fir tree is an otherwise rudimentary natural object that assumes an ever deeper symbolic function as the text unfolds. The various "Herzen, Kreuze[-], Namen und andern Zeichen" (*HKG* 1,6:382; hearts, crosses, names, and other signs,) that have been carved into its cortex and become encrusted over the years attest to the range of human activity and the duration of human inhabitancy that have transpired in its midst. Amorous relationships and (presumed) resulting kinships, mortality and religiosity, the presence and impermanence of the local inhabitants—these are all etched into a kind of bioregional register that transcends governmental and ecclesiastical bookkeeping. The fir tree thus operates as a *þing/ Ding/res* in the etymological sense of the word; that is, as a de facto site of communal affairs. Yet it also occupies an important more-than-human ecological niche. Despite the diminutive suffix that was conferred upon it long ago (*Tännling* implies that it is a "fir sapling"), it has since grown into a mature *Tanne*, here more descriptively: "ein riesenhaft großer und sehr alter Baum, der gewaltige Aeste, eine rauhe aufgeworfene Rinde, und mächtige in die Erde eingreifende Wurzeln hat" (a gigantic and very old tree, with enormous limbs, coarse bulging bark, and powerful roots that grip deep into the earth). It stands in the middle of the forest ("steht mitten in dem … Walde") surrounded by thousands of other firs, some of which are even taller and more massive than this exemplar singled out for testimonial incision by passersby. This fir forest, in turn, forms part of the greater woodlands that sweep across the distant crest which runs, by now not surprisingly, "zwischen Böhmen und Baiern" (between Bohemia and Bavaria). The inscribed fir, in sum, functions as a key piece of the bioregional puzzle that Stifter is gradually assembling in his eponymous tale, here not even two full pages into the text.

---

thorough studies of the text in this stylistic vein include: Marianne Ludwig, *Stifter als Realist: Untersuchung zur Gegenständlichkeit im "Beschriebenen Tännling"* (Basel: B. Schwabe, 1948); and Joseph Peter Stern, "Adalbert Stifters ontologischer Stil," in *Adalbert Stifter: Studien und Interpretationen: Gedenkschrift zum 100. Todestage*, ed. Lothar Stiehm (Heidelberg: Stiehm, 1968), 103–20.

On some further bioregional notes, Falta's topographic map conforms, in large part, to the "Fürstengarten" from the third and fourth *Mappe* drafts. Indeed, as the full cartographic title indicates, this southern Bohemian landscape was subsumed under the Duchy of Krumlov, which was one of several Central European land holdings owned by the House of Schwarzenberg. Thus, in both the later *Mappe* and here in *Der beschriebene Tännling*, Stifter carves out a utopian space of human-nature coexistence whose parameters are based on an historical aristocratic domain. (This paradox and Stifter's ambivalent relationship toward the Bohemian branch of the Schwarzenberg nobility will be addressed later.) In the process, he relies on a combination of maps and folkloric place names, both of which are considered hallmarks of bioregional writing, whether in its fictional, nonfictional, or creative-nonfictional modes. The importance of cartography for bioregionalism cannot be underestimated. Doug Aberley has, for instance, edited an innovative volume of essays that demonstrates "the use of mapping as one of many tools bioregionalists can use in reinhabiting place."[39] And one of the most hailed works of recent bioregional writing, Tim Robinson's *Connemara* trilogy (2006–11), celebrates maps and "placelore" or, as it is called in Irish Gaelic, "*dinnseanchas.*"[40] In broader geographical terms, this fascination with landscape and its linguistic articulation has been categorized as "topophilia," which can be defined as "the human being's affective ties with the material environment."[41] And here is where the personal-experiential component enters the greater literary-bioregional equation in Stifter's Bavarian-Bohemian oeuvre, which revels in physical geography and its human-bestowed terminology. For both cartography and placelore—the former an abstractive enterprise, the latter part of a collective-folkloric tradition—need to be grounded in individual experience, and nuanced accordingly, if they are to find a home in literature. Thus, while the "beschriebene Tännling" is, by all local-historical accounts, the name ascribed to an actual fir tree located near the former logging colony of Uhligstal north of Oberplan, Stifter imbues this once empirical and

39   Doug Aberley, "The Lure of Mapping: An Introduction," in *Boundaries of Home: Mapping for Local Empowerment*, ed. Doug Aberley, The New Catalyst Bioregional Series, vol. 6 (Gabriola Island, BC and Philadelphia, PA: New Society Publishers, 1993), 1–7; here 3.

40   See Christine Cusick, "Mapping Placelore: Tim Robinson's Ambulation and Articulation of Connemara as Bioregion," in *The Bioregional Imagination: Literature, Ecology, and Place*, ed. Tom Lynch, et al., 135–49 (Athens and London: University of Georgia Press, 2012), 136, 143.

41   Yi-Fu Tuan, *Topophilia: A Study of Environmental Perception, Attitudes, and Values* (New York: Columbia University Press, 1990) [Englewood Cliffs: Prentice-Hall, 1974], 93.

perhaps still traceable natural object with literary import and emblematic bioregional meaning.[42]

After he has established the initial parameters of what is slowly shaping up to be a bioregion, Stifter turns to a more anthropogenically modified tract of land, namely Oberplan and its neighboring hamlets. Here the narration abandons its initial cartographic vantage and immerses itself in the cultural landscape of a village-strewn valley that stretches along the meandering Moldau. This segment of the text is vintage Stifter, bursting with environmental ekphrasis. His early painting *Ansicht von Oberplan* (View of Oberplan, 1823) offers a visual extract of the more expansive and drawn-out narrative scene (see Figure 12.1). What eludes viewers of this detailed, if not highly mannered, painting is the greater environmental-historical context. After Stifter's opening paean to the boundless forests enveloping the region, readers soon learn that this zone has been subjected to near total deforestation, based on the principle: "je weniger Bäume überblieben, desto besser sei es" (*HKG* 1,5:382; the fewer trees left over, the better things are). Oberplan is, in other words, a *Rodungsplatz* or "cleared woodland." In *Witiko*, Stifter pays homage to "der obere Plan" ("the upper plain") and its medieval origins as precisely such a settled site carved out of the forest (see *HKG* 5,1:174–75). In *Der beschriebene Tännling*, which takes place during the latter half of the eighteenth century, the civilizing process is fast encroaching on this last wilderness holdout in Central Europe, both intensifying and amplifying its environmentally destructive practice of *Rodung*.[43] The flip side of this historical-locational setting is that pre-enlightenment customs still survive in such a remote recess, off the (literally) beaten track of "progress." Stifter's sustained evocation of Oberplan is based on superstitious-supernatural as well as religious-miraculous legends and traditions.[44]

---

42   In a letter to Heckenast from April 1, 1845, Stifter remarks that a tree by this name was to be found in the Bohemian Forest and local testimony from 2003 has confirmed the existence of its decayed remnants along with a weathered stone monument into which was chiseled: "Der beschriebene Tännling." See Adalbert Stifter, *Sämmtliche Werke*, ed. August Sauer, et al., vol. 17, 2nd ed. (Reichenberg: Kraus, 1929), 43; and Bernhard Dieckmann, *Verblendung, Volksglaube und Ethos: Eine Studie zu Adalbert Stifters Erzählung "Der beschriebene Tännling"* (Würzburg: Echter Verlag, 2014), 119–20.

43   For an historical account of this centuries-long process of *Rodung* on the Bavarian side of the divide, complete with maps, charts, photographs, and other visual aids, see Haversath, *Kleine Geschichte*, 42–92. For a discerning analysis of the literary tension between afforestation and deforestation in Stifter, see Christian Begemann, "Waldungen/Rodungen: Kulturation und Poetologie bei Adalbert Stifter," in *Stifters Mikrologien*, ed. Davide Giuriato and Sabine Schneider (Stuttgart: J. B. Metzler, 2019), 169–201.

44   For some background information on these local legends and their influence on the plot as well as the fairytale-like character of Hanna, see

Figure 12.1. Adalbert Stifter, *Ansicht von Oberplan* (View of Oberplan), circa 1823. Oil on canvas, 35 x 45 cm, Adalbert-Stifter-Geburtshaus, Oberplan/ Horní Planá. Public domain at Wikimedia: https://commons.wikimedia. org/wiki/File:Adalbert Stifter – Ansicht von Oberplan.jpg.

Folklore and the aforementioned placelore dominate the depiction of the village's landmarks, which include four main "Dinge[-]" or things: the bluffs known as "die Milchbäuerin," named after an ill-fated "milkmaid"; the "Brunnenhäuschen" or twin edifices built at the site of a wellspring in which a lifelike portrait of the Virgin Mary miraculously appeared; "das Gnadenkirchlein der schmerzhaften Mutter Gottes zum guten Wasser" (Church of Mercy Dedicated to the Dolorous Mother of God of the Good Water), which now houses this holy relic; and the curiously curtailed stone pathway that leads from the chapel to nowhere in particular (see *HKG* 1,5:383–89). Significantly, all these highlighted natural-cultural phenomena are located on the Kreuzberg, a knoll that rises directly above the town and bears a "blood-red" cross upon its summit

---

"Überblickskommentar," in *HKG* 1,9:398–99; Dieckmann, *Verblendung, Volksglaube und Ethos*, 97; and Günter Saße, "'Um gewisse Linien und Richtungen anzugeben': Zur symbolischen Ordnung in Stifters Erzählung *Der beschriebene Tännling*," *Zeitschrift für deutsche Philologie* 122 (2003): 509–25.

316 ♦ SEAN IRETON

from which a view of the valley's spatial-topographical coordinates is revealed. As various critics have argued, this environmental choreography typifies Stifterian *ordo*; everything, that is every *thing* (the word *Ding* occurs at key moments in this segment of the text), seems to occupy its proper if not prescribed place.[45] As I would further argue, such a systematic survey of the landscape and its inclusion of both physical and human spaces serve to conjure a coherent bioregional realm—or, in the alternative formulation of another scholar, "an intact biotope."[46] However, at this early point in the first chapterlike section of the *Buchfassung* (the *Journalfassung* has no such subdivided structure but is composed as one continuous narrative flow) the perspective remains restricted to the south, toward the Bavarian-Bohemian-Upper Austrian watershed and the distant Alps that are at times visible on the horizon. Not until the book-ended fourth part of the story does Stifter complement this southern purview with an analogous vista to the north, thereby creating a complete 360-degree panorama of southern Bohemia and beyond. But in the meantime, before things come, so to speak, full circle, he depicts two practices of environmental exploitation that reinforce the tale's reinhabitory subtext and further bolster its broader bioregional context.

In the most basic of terms, the middle two chapters deal with logging and hunting. Here, in a mixture of historical fact and situational fiction, Stifter details the processes of deforestation and species depredation that occurred in the woods surrounding Oberplan during the eighteenth and nineteenth centuries. In the former case, encamped woodcutters engage in an early form of clear-cutting, whereby trees are not selectively logged but indiscriminately felled and harvested, their remnant branches and stumps burned to ash. As a result, entire swaths of forest are denuded and left for dead by the loggers who then move on to new worksites and

---

45   See for instance Saße, "'Um gewisse Linien und Richtungen anzugeben'"; Jannetje Enklaar-Lagendijk, *Adalbert-Stifter: Landschaft und Raum* (Alphen aan den Rijn: Repro-Holland B. V., 1984), 165–200; and Stefan Gradmann, *Topographie/Text: Zur Funktion räumlicher Modellbildung in den Werken von Adalbert Stifter und Franz Kafka* (Frankfurt am Main: Hain, 1990), 21–37. The pathway remains, however, an oddity as it serves no apparent integrative function and its cobblestones have, moreover, sunken into the ground and shifted into "Unordnung" (disorder). See *HKG* 1,5:385.

46   Johann Lachinger, "Verschlüsselte Adelskritik: Stifters Erzählung *Der beschriebene Tännling*," in *Adalbert Stifter heute: Londoner Symposium 1983*, ed. Johann Lachinger, Alexander Stillmark, and Martin Swales (Linz: Schriftenreihe des Adalbert-Stifter-Instituts des Landes Oberösterreich; Publications of the Institute of Germanic Studies University of London, 1985), 101–20; here 105. Lachinger's more precise claim is that "das intakte Biotop" of the text lies in its totality of spatial representation, which embraces the realms of nature, religion, and society.

fresh stands of timber.[47] As Stifter soon makes clear, this devastation is but one phase in the "Leben[-]" (*HKG* 1,5:399; life) of a cleared woodland. Soon thereafter come regrowth and renewal, first in the form of wild berries and wildflowers, then grasses and underbrush, followed by insects and lizards, until finally: "mancher Schaft schießt empor mit den jungen feucht-grünen Blättern; es wird ein neuer, rauher hochruthiger Anflug, der unter sich einen nassen sumpfigen Boden hat, und endlich nach Jahren ist wieder die Pracht des Waldes" (*HKG* 1,5:400; many a stalk shoots upward with its young, moist-green leaves; tangled thickets of long-stemmed plant life emerge, the soil underneath wet and boggy, and at last, years later, the splendor of the forest returns). Stifter's attention to detail in this entire chapter is more impressive than usual, especially his depiction of ecological processes and incorporation of local environmental history. The former has been hinted at and partially cited above but is far richer in the full text. As for the latter, he not only provides abundant literary testimony of the deforestation that pinnacled in the region during the early 1800s; he also sheds light on the life and labor of the woodcutters in their logging camps. Though this latter aspect is in some measure conveyed through the experiences of the main character Hanns, most of this section is narrated in a nonfictional mode, indeed from an all-knowing ecological-historical perspective.

The same holds true for the next chapter, which is one of the most peculiar episodes in Stifter's entire oeuvre. As mentioned earlier in my introduction, this quasi-historical chronicle of an extravagant hunting festival is full of his customary narrative scrupulousness; but it is also replete with a grotesque ruthlessness that oscillates between the tragic and the absurd. Granted, such mass hunts were frequently organized by the aristocracy in the Bohemian Forest, both in the form of "Nezjagen" and "Treibjagen" (*HKG* 1,5:405); that is, the entrapment of wild animals in a vast setup of nets and the so-called "battue" or the goading of game toward (usually stationary) hunters by "beaters."[48] But there is some-

---

47 According to an expert on Central European forestry, these logged swaths were between thirty-eight and seventy-six meters wide and extended from ridgelines all the way down to valleys, not unlike (here my analogy) modern-day ski slopes. See Erlbeck, "Die Waldwelt Oberplans."

48 For more on these historical hunting practices in the context of Stifter's tale, see Paul Praxl, "Über das 'eingestellte' Jagen im Böhmerwald: Zu Adalbert Stifters Erzählung *Der beschriebene Tännling*," *Nachrichtenblatt der Rheinischen Adalbert-Stifter-Gemeinschaft* 132 (2011): 3–75; and Helmut Schrötter, "Adalbert Stifter und die Jagd," *Forst und Holz* 55 (2000): 775–78. For the most sustained literary analysis of this episode, see Gunter H. Hertling, "Adalbert Stifters Jagdallegorie *Der beschriebene Tännling*: Schande durch Schändung." *VASILO* 29 (1980): 41–65; reprinted in *Bleibende Lebensinhalte: Essays zu Adalbert Stifter und Gottfried Keller* (Bern: Peter Lang, 2003), 109–45.

thing unsettling about the detached and depersonalized manner in which Stifter recounts the systematic slaughter of several species (for instance stags, deer, hares, badgers, foxes, martens, even a lynx, and possibly a bear)[49] while impassive nobles in powdered wigs and fanatic commoners in their Sunday best look on. Yet this is perhaps precisely the point: unlike the clear-cut forests in the previous chapter, which will eventually grow back and return to some semblance of their former grandeur, the massacred animal population seems ecologically doomed. Stifter, at any rate, offers no restorative solution to their demise. As for a potential interpretive solution, Johann Lachinger offers two plausible possibilities. On the one hand, he proposes that the "orgy of murder" instigated by the nobles before the naïve populace is an "esoteric" forewarning on Stifter's part that they should not abuse their power and jeopardize the political status quo that he otherwise supports. This may be one reason why he chose to set his story in the prerevolutionary period of exaggerated rococo pomp and circumstance, thereby avoiding any overt connections to the Schwarzenberg family whose circles he frequented during the early 1840s (not long before an impending revolution in German-speaking lands, which he may have presciently sensed). Lachinger further points to the contemporaneous essay "Zur Psychologie der Tiere" (On the Psychology of Animals, 1845) as evidence of Stifter's belief in human-animal kinship and thus as a potential intertextual commentary on the violent breach of what now goes by such names as species equality, biocentric egalitarianism, or just plain animal rights. To be sure, sustainable populations of several endemic species—though not yet bears—have been reintroduced in the present-day Czech-German national parks and their adjacent protected zones. But it would seem that this aristocratic-sponsored hunt and its ruinous ecological aftermath represent the nadir of what Stifter idealized in the "Fürstengarten," which he of course conceived as a utopian blueprint of his bioregional orbit.

As mentioned above, Stifter revisits the natural-cultural landmarks of Oberplan in the fourth and final chapter of *Der beschriebene Tännling*, concluding the orbit that he half-depicted toward the beginning of the text. But this time he does so through the perambulations of Hanns, whose well-laid path of vengeance against the nobleman Guido for having seduced and won over Hanna, takes him past the Milchbäuerin to the Brunnenhäuschen and Gnadenkirchlein, where he lingers and appears to seek some form

---

49  On the extinction of bears in the Bohemian Forest, see Fritsch, "Der Schwarzenberg-Schwemmkanal," 56. Compare the historical fact that the (allegedly) last bear in the Bohemian Forest was killed in 1856 during a battue in which forty-six hunters and seventy-five beaters took part. There is, however, evidence that another bear was later shot in 1864 by a poacher, but this unsanctioned act was hushed up by the Schwarzenberg landowners.

of absolution for his imminent act. Finally, the narrative picks up on the vista afforded from the Kreuzberg as presented in the first chapter, but here Hanns demonstrably turns his back on Oberplan and directs his gaze toward the forested north, where the inscribed fir-tree is located and the hobby-huntsman Guido will soon be stationed for the morning battue (see *HKG* 1,5:425). While Hanns's gesture can be interpreted in a variety of ways (he is, for example, psychologically leaving the values of civilization behind and opening himself up to a more primitive brand of justice, as underscored by the sharpened axe he bears), its function within the larger "Texttopographie" (text-topography)[50] seems clear: the bioregional compass of the tale is now complete. Stifter has given his readers an all-encompassing view, and more figurative overview, of the nature-culture symbiosis of his Bavarian-Bohemian bioregion, ranging from its environmental vicissitudes to its human complexities. Ecological destruction and restoration, folkloric nomenclature and folk customs, religious rituals and social tensions—this is a sample list of the principal components that inform Stifter's tale, many of which have been proposed as essential ingredients of bioregionalism by the likes of Thomas Berry and Robert L. Thayer, who have expanded on the original ideas of Berg, Dasmann, and Snyder, especially as pertains to the human-cultural realm.[51]

## Toward a Bioregional Poetics of Reinhabitation and Restoration

If, in the foregoing, I have neglected to discuss the intricacies of plot, character development, and other such traditional literary trappings, then this is because they are largely absent in *Der beschriebene Tännling*. This is not to say that Stifter utterly abandons effective narrative devices in the text. Compare for instance the well-deployed color motif, which connects the red-headed Hanns with his diverse natural-cultural surroundings and thereby reinforces his deeper bioregional embeddedness. Such examples

---

50  Gradmann, *Topographie/Text*, 35.

51  See for instance Thomas Berry, *The Dream of the Earth* (Berkeley, CA: Counterpoint, 2015), 163–70; and Robert L. Thayer Jr., *LifePlace: Bioregional Thought and Practice* (Berkeley: University of California Press, 2003), 59–89. Both emphasize the spiritual component of bioregionalism, which can offer a deeper personal-psychological connection to one's life-place. Thayer even describes the practice of modern-day "watershed rituals" in his own northern Californian bioregion (see 72–78). See also David Robertson, "Bioregionalism in Nature Writing," in *American Nature Writers*, vol. 2, ed. John Elder (New York: Scribner's, 1996), 1013–24. As Robertson categorically states from the very outset of his article: "A bioregional study of literature attempts, self-consciously and rigorously, to fuse three disciplines: literary criticism, ecology, and religious studies" (1013).

include the previously mentioned "blood-red" cross upon the Kreuzberg; the red-painted chapel built to accommodate the portrait of the Virgin Mary; the red-tinged swaths of felled timber locally called *Füchse* (foxes) after their ruddy coloration; and the scarlet strawberries that first signal sylvan regeneration. Nevertheless, for a work of nineteenth-century literature the text is noticeably stripped down as a work of fiction. As various critics have observed, the narrative is even more *handlungsarm* than the average Stifter tale and its characters seem equally impoverished in terms of agency. Isolde Schiffermüller, for instance, asserts that the actual plot consists of *das Gehen*; that is, in the constant movement through space by the ever-ambulating Hanns. On a linguistic level, this activity or literal-physical *Handlung* is underlined by the repeated use of *gehen* (usually in the simple past: *er ging*), which Schiffermüller posits as the most frequently used verb in the text after *sein*.[52] With respect to the characters, Stefan Gradmann regards them as existing only within the *pre*existing configuration of the landscape; they are "woven into" (*eingesponnen*) this spatial order and hence their mere passive presence in the action-devoid plot.[53] After all, the anticipated climax of the storyline, namely Hanns's enactment of vengeance against Guido beneath the inscribed fir tree, never materializes thanks to an epiphany in which the image of the Virgin Mary from the Church of Good Water appears in its transfigured upper branches and imparts a stern reminder about the religious-communal value system into which Hanns himself is inscribed. This patently Catholic version of deus ex machina thus leads to inaction on the part of the main character, at least with respect to his premeditated act of murder. But as Stifter then narrates through a cluster of "er ging" phrases, Hanns resumes his characteristic activity of perpetual perambulation, whereby he departs from the epiphanic site and, after aimless wandering through a patchwork of forested and deforested terrain, eventually returns to his logging camp. The more important upshot of this anticlimactic scene, however, has less to do with Hanns than with the carefully choreographed textual topography. Though the earlier scenario upon the Kreuzberg would seem to have created narrative closure in this respect, a crucial landmark went unmentioned in the supplemental 180-degree northern prospect of the region that Hanns contemplated on his circuitous route to the fir-tree. Now, in a kind of topographical loophole, the outlying fir is revisited in the text and depicted in even greater detail (see *HKG* 1,5:426–27) than on the opening pages. More importantly, through the ensuing vision it becomes narratively linked with the wellspring and the church, where the

---

52 Isolde Schiffermüller, "Adalbert Stifters deskriptive Prosa: Eine Modellanalyse der Novelle *Der beschriebene Tännling*," *Deutsche Vierteljahreschrift für Literaturgeschichte und Geisteswissenschaft* 67 (1993): 267–301; here 283, 293–94.

53 Gradmann, *Topographie/Text*, 28, 35–36.

original votive image was respectively discovered and later housed. Stifter thus triangulates critical sites that can be said to make up the natural, cultural, and ethical node of his bioregional network. The true protagonist of *Der beschriebene Tännling* would thus appear to be the variegated environment rather than the unvarying characters that happen to inhabit it. While this prioritization may seem a fatal formula for literary fiction as we presume to know it—Why not instead engage in nonfictional "nature writing" like Thoreau, Muir, and their many successors and lesser-known predecessors?—recent bioregional poetics would argue otherwise.

The renowned Italian ecocritic Serenella Iovino defines "narrative reinhabitation" as "a cultural-educational practice that consists of restoring the ecological imagination of place by working with place-based stories." The educational component of this approach is crucial, for a kind of environmental-ethical message is often imparted in such texts. Drawing on Paul Ricoeur's notion of an "ethic of narration," she further maintains that "narrative reinhabitation means to plan ways of learning to live-in-place using place-based stories as 'moral instructions.'"[54] An alternative but essentially synonymous term, "reinhabitory discourse," has been proposed by Bart Welling, according to whom the literary text functions as a "thoroughly *emplaced* phenomenon" whose "bioregional 'whereness'" is to be taken seriously by readers in their appreciation and, ultimately, interpretation of a given fictional or nonfictional work of literature. In deference to Gary Snyder's efforts to reinhabit a "zone of ecological recovery" in the western Sierra Nevada, Welling specifies what bioregional literature tends to represent in its own unique fashion, namely "relatively wild landscapes, the built environment, and the human cultures associated with the place."[55] Finally, with respect solely to fiction, Ruth Blair has probed the viability of the "bioregional novel" as genre. In novels of this sort, there is no such thing as mere "setting"; human characters are "stitched" into the physical environment and their lives are "a constant process of relationship and negotiation among phenomena." One should therefore read them with a keen eye for the narrated bioregion, not with a preconceived fixation on plot and other conventional literary devices. Granted, such a proposed generic delineation raises a number of literary-theoretical questions (and perhaps concerns), the most general of which can be formulated as follows: How to navigate, as reader/interpreter, the oftentimes

---

54 Serenella Iovino, "Restoring the Imagination of Place: Narrative Reinhabitation and the Po Valley," in *The Bioregional Imagination*, 100–17; here 106.

55 Bart Welling, "'This Is What Matters': Reinhabitory Discourse and the 'Poetics of Responsibility' in the Work of Janisse Ray," in *The Bioregional Imagination*, 118–31; here 120, 122.

blurred line between story and description, between the oblique mode of storytelling and the more *realia*-based discourse of nature writing.[56]

As I have attempted to intimate in more inductive than deductive fashion, many if not most of these reflections on literary-bioregional aesthetics inform Stifter's own placed-based fiction set in the Bavarian-Bohemian Forest. This is especially true of *Der beschriebene Tännling*, which narratively prioritizes place over people; thematizes environmental fragility and recovery; and more generally strives to offer the fullest picture possible of both "geographical terrain and a [human] terrain of consciousness," to quote Berg and Dasmann's original bioregional maxim. As for the "moral instructions" mentioned by Iovino, Stifter, ever the literary moralist if not inveterate pedagogue, reverses the fairytale-like trajectory of the storyline and takes sides with Hanns, who "blieb immer im Holzschlage" (*HKG* 1,5:431; continued to stay in the logging areas) and thus implicitly chooses to inhabit—if only future—"ecological recovery zones." Hanns, in the end, remains true to his bioregional background, even does good (Catholic) works within the religious-spiritual fabric of society, adopting the three children of his deceased sister and leading a life of penury. Hanna, in contrast, is lured away by aristocratic extravagance, briefly revisits her hometown with negative character consequences, and receives unminced moral condemnation at the very end of the tale. Stifter's message here is, at best, broadmindedly bioregional, at worst bleakly provincial. But such, perhaps, is the dualistic cutting edge of bioregionalism as both a socially progressive and environmentally restorationist movement. Though this duality poses a much larger literary-theoretical problem and invites further text-based avenues of inquiry, Lawrence Buell has perfectly summarized the issue as pertains to *Der beschriebene Tännling* and its bioregional relevance:

> Now, environmental writing does not literally repair the biosphere, does not literally do anything directly to the environment. But ... it tries to practice a conceptual restorationism in reorienting the partially denaturized reader not to a primordial nature, which we cannot recover either in fact or in fantasy, but to an artefactual version of environment designed to evoke place-sense. ...
>
> Environmental texts, then, practice restorationism by calling places into being, that is, not just by naming objects but by dramatizing in the process how they matter.[57]

56  Ruth Blair, "Figures of Life: Beverly Farmer's *The Seal Woman* as an Australian Bioregional Novel," in *The Bioregional Imagination*, 164–80; here 165–66, 175.

57  Lawrence Buell, *The Environmental Imagination: Thoreau, Nature Writing, and the Formation of American Culture* (Cambridge, MA: Harvard University Press, 1995), 267.

# Selected Bibliography

*Sean Ireton*

A S INDICATED IN the sectional title above, the following bibliography offers a mere *selection* of major works by and on Adalbert Stifter. It includes some, but by no means all, of the sources referenced in the chapters of this volume as well as standard scholarly studies that readers would be remiss to ignore. Emphasis is placed on Anglophone scholarship published over the last thirty years. Furthermore, every effort has been made to strike an equitable balance among his diverse published works and creative phases, ranging from the serialized stories that would eventually appear in the book editions of *Studien* and *Bunte Steine*; to his non-revised and especially later prose; to more overarching assessments of his (mainly fictional) output.

This selected bibliography is organized as follows:

Works by Adalbert Stifter
    Collected Works
    Uncollected Works
    Major Works in English

Secondary Works
    Biographical in Emphasis
    General Secondary Literature
    On Individual Works
        Tales (later) included in *Studien*
        Tales (later) included in *Bunte Steine*
        Other Works

Comprehensive Bibliographies

## Works by Adalbert Stifter

### Collected Works

*Gesammelte Werke in vierzehn Bänden.* Edited by Konrad Steffen. Fourteen volumes. Basel and Stuttgart: Birkhäuser, 1962–72.

324 ♦ SELECTED BIBLIOGRAPHY

*Sämmtliche Werke*. Edited by August Sauer, Franz Hüller, Kamill Eben, Gustav Wilhelm, et al. Nineteen volumes. Prague: Calve; Reichenberg: Kraus, 1901–1940; Graz: Stiasny, 1958–60.

*Sämtliche Erzählungen nach den Erstdrucken*. Edited by Wolgang Matz. Munich: Deutscher Taschenbuch Verlag, 2005.

*Sämtliche Werke in fünf Einzelbänden*. Edited by Fritz Krökel and Magda Gerken. Five volumes. Munich: Winkler, 1949–. Reprinted: 1979; Artemis & Winkler, 1997.

*Werke*. Seventeen volumes. Pest: Heckenast, 1869–70.

*Werke und Briefe: Historisch-Kritische Gesamtausgabe*. Edited by Alfred Doppler, Wolfgang Frühwald, and Hartmut Laufhütte. Ten volumes; forty part-volumes. Stuttgart and Berlin: Kohlhammer, 1978–.

1,1: *Studien, Journalfassungen*. First volume. Edited by Helmut Bergner and Ulrich Dittmann. 1978.

1,2: *Studien, Journalfassungen*. Second volume. Edited by Helmut Bergner and Ulrich Dittmann. 1979.

1,3: *Studien, Journalfassungen*. Third volume. Edited by Helmut Bergner and Ulrich Dittmann. 1980.

1,4: *Studien, Buchfassungen*. First volume. Edited by Helmut Bergner and Ulrich Dittmann. 1980.

1,5: *Studien, Buchfassungen*. Second volume. Edited by Helmut Bergner and Ulrich Dittmann. 1982.

1,6: *Studien, Buchfassungen*. Third volume. Edited by Helmut Bergner and Ulrich Dittmann. 1982.

1,9: *Studien, Kommentar*. Eited by Ulrich Dittmann, 1997.

2,1: *Bunte Steine, Journalfassungen*. Edited by Helmut Bergner. 1982.

2,2: *Bunte Steine, Buchfassungen*. Edited by Helmut Bergner. 1982.

2,3: *Bunte Steine, Apparat, Part 1*. Edited by Walter Hettche.1995.

2,4: *Bunte Steine, Apparat, Part 2*. Edited by Walter Hettche. 1995

3,1: *Erzählungen*. First volume. Edited by Johannes John and Sibylle von Steinsdorff. 2003.

3,2: *Erzählungen*. Second volume. Edited by Johannes John and Sibylle von Steinsdorff. 2003.

4,1: *Der Nachsommer: Eine Erzählung*. First volume. Edited by Wolfgang Frühwald and Walter Hettche. 1997.

4,2: *Der Nachsommer: Eine Erzählung*. Second volume. Edited by Wolfgang Frühwald and Walter Hettche. 1999.

4,3: *Der Nachsommer: Eine Erzählung*. Third volume. Edited by Wolfgang Frühwald. 2000.

4,4: *Der Nachsommer, Apparat, Part 1*. Edited by Walter Hettche. 2014.

4,5: *Der Nachsommer, Apparat, Part 2*. Edited by Walter Hettche. 2014.

5,1: *Witiko: Eine Erzählung*. First volume. Edited by Alfred Doppler and Wolfgang Wiesmüller. 1984.

5,2: *Witiko: Eine Erzählung*. Second volume. Edited by Alfred Doppler and Wolfgang Wiesmüller. 1985.

5,3: *Witiko: Eine Erzählung.* Third volume. Edited by Alfred Doppler and Wolfgang Wiesmüller. 1986.

5,4: *Witiko, Apparat/Kommentar, Part 1.* Edited by Alfred Doppler. 1998.

5,5: *Witiko, Apparat/Kommentar, Part 2.* Edited by Alfred Doppler. 2002.

6,1: *Die Mappe meines Urgroßvaters: Dritte Fassung, Lesetext.* Edited by Herwig Gottwald and Adolf Hartlinger. 1998.

6,2: *Die Mappe meines Urgroßvaters: Vierte Fassung, Lesetext.* Edited by Herwig Gottwald. 2005.

6,3: *Die Mappe meines Urgroßvaters: Dritte und vierte Fassung, Integraler Apparat.* Edited by Herwig Gottwald. 1999.

6,4: *Die Mappe meines Urgroßvaters, Kommentar.* Edited by Silvia Bengesser and Herwig Gottwald. 2017.

8,1: *Schriften zu Literatur und Theater.* Edited by Werner M. Bauer. 1997.

8,2: *Schriften zu Politik und Bildung.* Edited by Alfred Doppler. 2010.

8,3: *Schriften zu Politik und Bildung, Apparat/Kommentar.* Edited by Alfred Doppler. 2012.

8,4: *Schriften zur Bildenden Kunst.* Edited by Johannes John and Karl Möseneder. 2012.

8,5: *Schriften zur Bildenden Kunst, Apparat/Kommentar.* Edited by Karl Möseneder. 2014.

9,1: *Wien und die Wiener in Bildern aus dem Leben.* Edited by Johann Lachinger. 2015.

9,2: *Wien und die Wiener in Bildern aus dem Leben, Apparat/Kommentar.* Edited by Johann Lachinger. Forthcoming.

10,1: *Amtliche Schriften zu Schule und Universität, Part 1.* Edited by Alfred Doppler and Walter Seifert. 2007.

10,2: *Amtliche Schriften zu Schule und Universität, Part 2.* Edited by Alfred Doppler and Walter Seifert. 2008.

10,3: *Amtliche Schriften zu Schule und Universität, Part 3.* Edited by Alfred Doppler and Walter Seifert. 2010.

10,4: *Amtliche Schriften zu Schule und Universität, Apparat/Kommentar, Part 1.* Edited by Walter Seifert. 2016.

10,5: *Amtliche Schriften zu Schule und Universität, Apparat/Kommentar, Part 2.* Edited by Walter Seifert. 2018.

10,6: *Amtliche Schriften zu Schule und Universität, Apparat/Kommentar, Part 3.* Edited by Walter Seifert. 2019.

## Uncollected Works (as readily available in paperback)

*Bergkristall und andere Erzählungen.* Frankfurt am Main: Insel Taschenbuch, 2017.

*Bunte Steine: Erzählungen.* Edited by Helmut Bachmaier. Stuttgart: Reclam: 1994.

*Der Nachsommer.* Munich: Goldmann, 2005.

*Der Nachsommer.* Edited by Benedikt Jeßing. Stuttgart: Reclam: 2005.

*Der Nachsommer.* Munich: Deutscher Taschenbuch Verlag, 2017.

## 326 ♦ Selected Bibliography

*Studien*. Edited by Ulrich Dittmann. Stuttgart: Reclam, 2007.
(Almost all tales from *Bunte Steine* and *Studien* are also available in single
  Reclam paperback editions.)

### Works in English

*The Bachelors*. Translated by David Bryer. London: Pushkin Press, 2008.
*Brigitta, with Abdias, Limestone, and the Forest Path*. Translated by Helen
  Watanabe-O'Kelly. London: Angel Books; Chester Springs, PA: Dufour
  Editions, 1990. Reprinted as *Brigitta and Other Tales*. London: Penguin,
  1995.
*Granite*. Translated by Jeffrey L. Sammons. In *German Novellas of Realism*.
  Volume One. Edited by Jeffrey L. Sammons, 7–34. New York: Contin-
  uum, 1989. (The German Library, volume 37.)
*Indian Summer*. Translated by Wendell Frye. Fourth edition. New York:
  Peter Lang, 2009.
*Limestone*. Translated by David Luke. In *German Novellas of Realism*. Vol-
  ume One. Edited by Jeffrey L. Sammons, 35–87. New York: Contin-
  uum, 1989. (The German Library, volume 37.)
*Limestone and Other Stories*. Translated by David Luke. New York: Harcourt,
  Brace & World, 1968.
*Motley Stones*. Translated by Isabel Fargo Cole. New York: New York Review
  Books, 2021.
"Preface to Many-colored Stones." Translated by Jeffrey L. Sammons. In
  *German Novellas of Realism*. Volume One. Edited by Jeffrey L. Sam-
  mons, 2–6. New York: Continuum, 1989. (The German Library, volume
  37.)
*Rock Crystal*. Translated by Marianne Moore and Elizabeth Mayer. New
  York: New York Review Books, 2008.
*Tales from Old Vienna and Other Prose*. Translated by Alexander Stillmark.
  Riverside, CA: Ariadne Press, 2016.
*Witiko*. Translated by Wendell Frye. Second edition. New York: Peter Lang,
  2006.

### Correspondence

*Briefe*. Edited by Johannes Aprent. Three volumes. Pest: Heckenast, 1869.
Fischer, Kurt Gerhard, ed. *Adalbert Stifters Leben und Werk in Briefen und
  Dokumenten*. Frankfurt am Main: Insel, 1962.
*Sämmtliche Werke*. Edited by August Sauer, Franz Hüller, Kamill Eben, Gus-
  tav Wilhelm, et al. Volumes seventeen to twenty-four. Prague: Calve;
  Reichenberg: Kraus, 1901–1940.
*Werke und Briefe: Historisch-Kritische Gesamtausgabe*. Edited by Paul Keck-
  ein, Werner Michler, Karl Wagner, et al. Volumes 11,1–11,5. Stuttgart
  and Berlin: Kohlhammer, 2021–.

SELECTED BIBLIOGRAPHY ♦ 327

# Secondary Works

## Biographical in Emphasis

Aprent, Johannes. *Adalbert Stifter: Eine biografische Skizze.* [1869.] Nuremberg: Stifterbibliothek, 1955.

Becher, Peter. *Adalbert Stifter: Sehnsucht nach Harmonie, Eine Biografie.* Regensburg: Verlag Friedrich Pustet, 2005.

Enziger, Moriz. *Adalbert Stifters Studienjahre (1818–1830).* Innsbruck: Österreichische Verlagsanstalt, 1950.

Fischer, Kurt Gerhard. *Adalbert Stifter: Psychologische Beiträge zur Biographie.* Linz: Adalbert-Stifter-Institut, 1961.

Matz, Wolfgang. *Adalbert Stifter, oder Diese fürchterliche Wendung der Dinge: Biographie.* Göttingen: Wallstein: 2016.

Roedl, Urban. *Adalbert Stifter: Geschichte seines Lebens.* Bern: Francke, 1958.

———. *Adalbert Stifter, mit Selbstzeugnissen und Bilddokumenten.* Reinbek bei Hamburg: Rowohlt, 1965.

Schoenborn, Peter A. *Adalbert Stifter: Sein Leben und Werk.* Second edition. Tübingen and Basel: Francke, 1999.

## General Secondary Literature

Andrews, John S. "The Reception of Stifter in Nineteenth-Century Britain." *The Modern Language Review* 53, no. 4 (1958): 537–44.

Attanucci, Timothy. "The 'Gentle Law' of Large Numbers: Stifter's Urban Meteorology." *Monatshefte* 112, no. 1 (2020): 1–19.

———. *The Restorative Poetics of a Geological Age: Stifter, Viollet-le-Duc, and the Aesthetic Practices of Geohistoricism.* Berlin and Boston, MA: De Gruyter, 2020.

Becker, Sabina, and Katharina Grätz, eds. *Ordnung—Raum—Ritual: Adalbert Stifters artifizieller Realismus.* Heidelberg: Universitätsverlag Winter, 2007.

Begemann, Christian. "Ding und Fetisch: Überlegungen zu Stifters Dingen." In *Der Code der Leidenschaften: Fetischismus in den Künsten*, edited by Hartmut Böhme and Johannes Endres, 324–43. Munich: Wilhelm Fink, 2010.

———. "Metaphysik und Empirie: Konkurrierende Naturkonzepte im Werk Adalbert Stifters." In *Wissen in Literatur im 19. Jahrhundert*, edited by Lutz Danneberg and Friedrich Vollhardt, 92–126. Tübingen: Niemeyer, 2002.

———. *Die Welt der Zeichen: Stifter-Lektüren.* Stuttgart: J. B. Metzler, 1995.

Begemann, Christian, and Davide Giuriato, eds. *Stifter-Handbuch: Leben—Werk—Wirkung.* Stuttgart: J. B. Metzler, 2017.

Blackall, Eric A. *Adalbert Stifter: A Critical Study.* Cambridge: Cambridge University Press, 1948.

328 ◆ SELECTED BIBLIOGRAPHY

Byrd, Vance. "Reading Stifter in America." In *German Literature as a Transnational Field of Production, 1848–1919*, edited by Lynne Tatlock and Kurt Beals, 59–78. Rochester, NY: Camden House, 2023.

Gabriel, Hans. "'The Final Irrationality of Existence': The Language of Madness and the Madness of Language in Stifter's *Adbias* and *Bergkristall*." In *Crime and Madness in Modern Austria: Myth, Metaphor and Cultural Realities*, edited by Rebecca S. Thomas, 1–28. Newcastle upon Tyne: Cambridge Scholars Publishing; 2008.

Gamper, Michael, and Karl Wagner, eds. *Figuren der Übertragung: Adalbert Stifter und das Wissen seiner Zeit*. Zurich: Chronos, 2009.

Geulen, Eva. "Depicting Description: Lukács and Stifter," *The Germanic Review: Literature, Culture, Theory* 73, no. 3 (1998): 267–79.

———. *Worthörig wider Willen: Darstellungsproblematik und Sprachreflexion in der Prosa Adalbert Stifters*. Munich: iudicum, 1992.

Giuriato, Davide, and Sabine Schneider. *Stifters Mikrologien*. Stuttgart: J. B. Metzler, 2019.

Haines, Brigid. *Dialogue and Narrative Design in the Works of Adalbert Stifter*. London: Modern Humanities Research Association for the Institute of Germanic Studies, University of London, 1991.

Hoffmann, Agnes. "A Poetics of Scaling: Adalbert Stifter and the Measures of Nature around 1850." In *Before Photography: German Visual Culture in the Nineteenth Century*, edited by Kirsten Belgum, Vance Byrd, and John D. Benjamin, 267–92. Berlin and Boston, MA: De Gruyter, 2021.

Holmes, Tove. "An Archive of the Earth: Stifter's Geologus." *Seminar: A Journal of Germanic Studies* 54, no. 3 (2018): 281–307.

Horn, Eva. "Adalbert Stifters Klimatologie: Die Kultivierung der Luft und des Menschen." *Colloquia Germanica: Internationale Zeitschrift für Germanistik* 53, no. 4 (2021): 323–47.

Ireton, Sean. "Adalbert Stifter and the Gentle Anthropocene." In *Readings in the Anthropocene: The Environmental Humanities, German Studies, and Beyond*, edited by Sabine Wilke, 195–221. New York: Bloomsbury, 2017.

———. "Between Dirty and Disruptive Nature: Adalbert Stifter in the Context of Nineteenth-Century American Environmental Literature." *Colloquia Germanica: Internationale Zeitschrift für Germanistik* 44, no. 2 (2011): 149–71.

———. "Nature as Therapy: Case Studies from Austria (Adalbert Stifter) and North America (Doug Peacock)." *Pacific Coast Philology* 46, no. 2 (2011): 122–38.

Keleman, Pál. "The Epistemology of the Arbour: On the Intersection of Nature and Technology in Adalbert Stifter." In *Discourses of Space*, edited by Judit Pieldner and Zsuszanna Ajtony, 198–225. Newcastle Upon Tyne: Cambridge Scholars Publishing, 2013.

Kopf, James M. "Ecogods: Nature, Adalbert Stifter, and Heidegger." *Interdisciplinary Studies in Literature and Environment* 29, no. 3 (2022): 857–76.

Lachinger, Johann, Alexander Stillmark, and Martin Swales, eds. *Adalbert Stifter heute: Londoner Symposium 1983*. Linz: Schriftenreihe des Adalbert-Stifter-Instituts des Landes Oberösterreich; London: Publications of the English Goethe Society, 1985.

Macho, Thomas. "Stifters Dinge." *Merkur: Deutsche Zeitschrift für europäisches Denken* 59 (2005): 735–41.

Martyn, David. "The Picturesque as Art of the Average: Stifter's Statistical Poetics of Observation." *Monatshefte* 105, no. 3 (2013): 426–42.

Matz, Wolfgang. "Gewalt des Gewordenen: Adalbert Stifters Werk zwischen Idylle und Angst." *Deutsche Vierteljahresschrift für Literaturwissenschaft und Geistesgeschichte* 63 (1989): 715–50.

———. *Gewalt des Gewordenen: Zu Adalbert Stifter*. Graz: Literaturverlag Droschl, 2005.

Maurer, Kathrin. "Adalbert Stifter's Poetics of Clouds and Nineteenth-Century Meteorology." *Oxford German Studies* 45, no. 4 (2016): 421–33.

———. "Adalbert Stifter's Poetics of Collecting: Representing the Past against the Grand Narrative of Academic Historicism." *Modern Austrian Literature* 40, no. 1 (2007): 1–17.

Mayer, Matthias. *Adalbert Stifter: Erzählen als Erkennen*. Stuttgart: Reclam, 2001.

Naumann, Ursula. *Adalbert Stifter*. Stuttgart: J. B. Metzler, 1979.

Preisendanz, Wolfgang. "Die Erzählfunktion der Naturdarstellung bei Stifter." *Wirkendes Wort* 16, no. 6 (1966): 407–18.

Ragg-Kirkby, Helena. "'Eine immerwährende Umwandlung der Ansichten:' Narrators and Their Perspectives in the Works of Adalbert Stifter." *The Modern Language Review* 95, no. 1 (2000): 127–43.

———. "'Die Kinder liebten ihre Eltern nicht mehr und die Eltern die Kinder nicht': Adalbert Stifter and the Happy Family." *Oxford German Studies* 27, no. 1 (1998): 64–101.

———. "'Sie geht in ihren großen eigenen Gesetzen fort, die uns in tiefen Fernen liegen, […] und wir können nur stehen und bewundern': Adalbert Stifter and the Alienation of Man and Nature." *The German Quarterly* 72, no. 4 (1999): 349–61.

———. "'So ward die Wüste immer grösser': Zones of Otherness in the Stories of Adalbert Stifter." *Forum for Modern Language Studies* 35, no. 2 (1999): 207–22.

———. "'Warum nun dieses?': *Verblendung* and *Verschulden* in the Stories of Adalbert Stifter." *German Life and Letters* 55, no. 1 (2002): 24–40.

Reddick, John. "The Wild Beyond: Symbolic Journeyings in the Stories of Adalbert Stifter." *Oxford German Studies* 20 (1991): 104–24.

Resvick, Jessica. "Picturesque Mediations: Adalbert Stifter, Washington Irving, and the Transfiguration of the Mundane." *PMLA* 137, no. 5 (2022): 841–56.

Schiffermüller, Isolde. *Buchstäblichkeit und Bildlichkeit bei Adalbert Stifter: Dekonstruktive Lektüren*. Bozen: Edition Sturzflüge, 1996.

330 ◆ SELECTED BIBLIOGRAPHY

Selge, Martin. *Adalbert Stifter: Poesie aus dem Geist der Naturwissenschaft.* Stuttgart: W. Kohlhammer, 1976.

Sng, Zachary. "Not Forgotten: On Stifter and Peirce." *Modern Language Notes* 121, no. 3 (2006): 631–46.

Steffen, Konrad. *Adalbert Stifter: Deutungen.* Basel and Stuttgart: Birkhäuser, 1955.

Stern, Joseph Peter. "Adalbert Stifters ontologischer Stil." In *Adalbert Stifter: Studien und Interpretationen; Gedenkschrift zum 100. Todestage,* edited by Lothar Stiehm, 103–20. Heidelberg: Lothar Stiehm, 1968.

Stiehm, Lothar, ed. *Adalbert Stifter: Studien und Interpretationen; Gedenkschrift zum 100. Todestage.* Heidelberg: Lothar Stiehm, 1968.

Strowick, Elisabeth. "'Dumpfe Dauer': Langeweile und Atmosphärisches bei Fontane und Stifter." *The Germanic Review: Literature, Culture, Theory* 90, no. 3 (2015): 187–203.

———. "Poetological-Technical Operations: Representation of Motion in Adalbert Stifter." *Configurations* 18, no. 3 (2010): 273–89.

Swales, Martin, and Erika Swales. *Adalbert Stifter: A Critical Study.* Cambridge: Cambridge University Press, 1984.

Weissberg, Liliane. "Taking Steps: Writing Traces in Adalbert Stifter." In *Thematics Reconsidered (Essays in Honor of Horst Daemmrich),* edited by Frank Trommler, 253–74. Amsterdam: Brill, 1995.

Wilczek, Markus. "Jenseits der Reife: Zu Bildung und Nachhaltigkeit bei Stifter." *Monatshefte* 109, no. 3 (2017): 369–90.

## On Individual Works

### Tales (later) included in *Studien*

Block, Richard. "Stone Deaf: The Gentleness of Law in Stifter's *Brigitta*." *Monatshefte* 90, no. 1 (1998): 17–33.

Browning, Barton W. "Cooper's Influence on Stifter: Fact or Scholarly Myth?" *Modern Language Notes* 89, no. 5 (1974): 821–28.

Downing, Eric. "Adalbert Stifter and the Scope of Realism." *The Germanic Review: Literature, Culture, Theory* 74, no. 3 (1999): 229–41.

———. "Double Visions: Chiastic Mimesis and the Politics of Realism in Stifter's 'The Mountain Forest' ('Der Hochwald')." In *Double Exposures: Repetition and Realism in Nineteenth-Century German Fiction,* 41–90. Stanford, CA: Stanford University Press, 2000.

Frost, Sabine. "Autobiographisches Schreiben als Vergletscherung des Ich: Adalbert Stifter's *Die Mappe meines Urgroßvaters*." *Literatur für Leser* 39, no. 1 (2016): 43–59.

Gordon, Kevin A. "Historical Rupture and the Devastation of Memory in Adalbert Stifter's *Der Hagestolz*." *Journal of Austrian Studies* 45, nos. 3/4 (2012): 87–112.

Grell, Erik J. "Homoerotic Travel, Classical *Bildung*, and Liberal Allegory in Adalbert Stifter's *Brigitta* (1844–47)." *The German Quarterly* 88, no. 4 (2015): 514–35.

Helfer, Martha B. "Natural Ant-Semitism: Stifter's *Abdias*." *Deutsche Vierteljahresschrift für Literaturwissenschaft und Geistesgeschichte* 78, no. 2 (2004): 261–86.

Hertling, Gunter H. "Adalbert Stifters Jagdallegorie *Der beschriebene Tännling*: Schande durch Schändung." *VASILO* 29 (1980): 41–65. Reprinted in *Bleibende Lebensinhalte: Essays zu Adalbert Stifter und Gottfried Keller*, 109–45. Bern: Peter Lang, 2003.

Holub, Robert C. "Adalbert Stifter's *Brigitta*, or the Lesson of Realism." In *A Companion to German Realism, 1848–1900*, edited by Todd Kontje, 29–51. Rochester, NY: Camden House, 2002.

Ireton, Sean. "Walden in the Bohemian Forest: Adalbert Stifter's Transcendental Ecocentrism in *Der Hochwald*." *Modern Austrian Literature* 43, no. 3 (2010): 1–18.

Lauer, Gerhard. "Der Trost der Poesie: Stifters *Abdias*." *German Life and Letters* 68, no. 4 (2015): 569–83.

Mautz, Kurt. "Das antagonistische Naturbild in Stifters *Studien*." In: *Adalbert Stifter: Studien und Interpretationen; Gedenkschrift zum 100. Todestage*, edited by Lothar Stiehm, 23–55. Heidelberg: Stiehm, 1968.

Mettler, Heinrich. *Natur in Stifters frühen "Studien": Zu Stifters gegenständlichem Stil*. Zurich: Atlantis, 1968.

Metz, Joseph. "Austrian Inner Colonialism and the Visibility of Difference in Stifter's *Die Narrenburg*." *PMLA* 121, no. 5 (2006): 1475–92.

———. "The Jew as Sign in Stifter's *Abdias*." *The Germanic Review: Literature, Culture, Theory* 77, no. 3 (2002): 219–32.

Nagel, Barbara N. "Versioning Violence: On Gender, Genetic, and Jealously in Adalbert Stifter's *Die Mappe*." *Zeitschrift für deutsche Philologie* 139, no. 2 (2020): 287–307.

Phillips, Alexander. "Adalbert Stifter's Alternative Anthropocene: Reimagining Social Nature in *Brigitta* and *Abdias*." In *German Ecocriticism in the Anthropocene*, edited by Caroline Schaumann and Heather I. Sullivan, 65–85. New York: Palgrave Macmillan, 2017.

Reddick, John. "Mystification, Perspectivism and Symbolism in *Der Hochwald*." In *Adalbert Stifter heute: Londoner Symposium 1983*, edited by Johann Lachinger, Alexander Stillmark, and Martin Swales, 44–74. Linz: Schriftenreihe des Adalbert-Stifter-Instituts des Landes Oberösterreich; London: Publications of the English Goethe Society, 1985.

Resvick, Jessica. "The Author as Editor: The Aesthetics of Recension in Adalbert Stifter's *Die Mappe meines Urgroßvaters*." In *Market Strategies and German Literature in the Long Nineteenth Century*, edited by Vance Byrd and Ervin Malakaj, 163–66. Berlin and Boston, MA: De Gruyter, 2020.

Sauer, Pamela S. "Victor's Journey in Adalbert Stifter's Novella 'Der Hagestolz.'" *The South Carolina Modern Language Review* 9, no. 1 (2010): 62–79.

332 ♦ SEAN IRETON

Turner, David. "Time and the Almost: Tradition, Anachronism and Routine in Stifter's *Das alte Siegel.*" *German Life and Letters* 45, no. 2 (1992): 114–25.

## Tales (later) included in *Bunte Steine*

Alkire, Brian, and Stefanie Heine. "'So lange die Natur so bleibt'" The Alpine Abstract in Stifters 'Bergkristall.'" *Austrian Studies* 30 (2022): 31–46.

Densky, Doreen. "Pre-Positioning the Narrator: Circumspection, Speaking-For, and Foreknowledge in Adalbert Stifter's 'Granit.'" *Journal of Austrian Studies* 49, nos. 3/4 (2016): 17–42.

Domandl, Sepp. "Die philosophische Tradition von Adalbert Stifters 'Sanftem Gesetz.'" *VASILO* 21, nos. 3/4 (1972): 79–103.

Downing, Eric. "Common Ground: Conditions of Realism in Stifter's 'Vorrede.'" *Colloquia Germanica: Internationale Zeitschrift für Germanistik* 28, no. 1 (1995): 35–53.

———. "Real and Recurrent Problems: Stifter's Preface to 'Many-colored Stones' ('Bunte Steine')." In *Double Exposures: Repetition and Realism in Nineteenth-Century German Fiction*, 24–40. Stanford, CA: Stanford University Press, 2000.

———. "With Wandering Steps and Slow: *Schwellenkunst* in Adalbert Stifter's *Granit.*" *Deutsche Vierteljahresschrift für Literaturwissenschaft und Geistesgeschichte* 94, no. 1 (2020): 69–86.

Gabriel, Hans P. "Prescribing Reality: The Preface as a Device of Literary Realism in Auerbach, Keller, and Stifter." *Colloquia Germanica: Internationale Zeitschrift für Germanistik* 32, no. 4 (1999): 325–44.

Gray, Richard T. "The (Mis)Fortune of Commerce: Economic Transformation in Adalbert Stifter's *Bergkristall.*" In *Money Matters: Economics and the German Cultural Imagination, 1770–1850*, 314–45. Seattle: University of Washington Press, 2008.

Groves, Jason. "Erratische Blöcke: Stifters *Bunte Steine.*" In *Séma: Wendepunkte der Philologie*, edited by Joachim Harst and Kristina Mendicino, 255–269. Würzburg: Königshausen & Neumann, 2013.

Halse, Sven. "Strategies for Dealing with Nature in Adalbert Stifter's *Bunte Steine.*" *Orbis litterarum* 53 (1998): 117–28.

Hamilton, Andrew, B. "Stifter's *Granit* and the Art of Seeing." *Monatshefte* 109, no. 3 (2017): 391–403.

Hertling, G. H. "Adalbert Stifter's 'Forewords' to *Bunte Steine* in English: His Poetics, Aesthetics, and Weltanschauung." *Modern Austrian Literature* 32, no. 1 (1999): 1–21.

Howards, Alyssa Lonner. "Telling a Realist Folktale: Folklore and Cultural Preservation in Adalbert Stifter's 'Katzensilber,'" *Modern Austrian Literature* 43, no. 4 (2010): 1–21

Jeter, Joseph Carroll. *Adalbert Stifter's "Bunte Steine": An Analysis of Theme, Style, and Structure in Three Novellas.* New York: Peter Lang, 1996.

Latini, Micaela. "Angels and Monsters: On Stifter's *Turmalin*." In *Monstrous Anatomies: Literary and Scientific Imagination in Britain and Germany during the Long Nineteenth Century*, edited by Raul Calzoni and Greta Perletti, 81–94. Göttingen: Vandenhoeck & Ruprecht, 2015.

Mason, Eve. "Stifter's *Katzensilber* and the Fairy-Tale Mode." *The Modern Language Review* 77, no. 1 (1982): 114–29.

———. "Stifter's 'Turmalin': A Reconsideration." *The Modern Language Review* 72, no. 2 (1977): 348–58.

McDonald, Edward R. "The Family Legacy of Values as the Redemptive Rock of Ages in Stifter's *Granit*." *Modern Language Studies* 24, no. 2 (1994): 75–98.

Mottram, Robert E. "Stifter's Realism and the Avant-Garde: Affect and Materiality in 'Kalkstein.'" *Colloquia Germanica: Internationale Zeitschrift für Germanistik* 54, no. 2 (2002): 411–31.

Nitschke, Claudia. "Chaos und Form, Raum und Ethos in Stifters *Bunte Steine*." *German Life and Letters* 68, no. 4 (2015): 554–68.

Paulus, Dagmar. "Remembering Two Mad Women: Female Madness and Society in Adalbert Stifter's Turmalin and Wilhelm Raabe's *Im Siegeskranze*." *Germanistik in Ireland: Yearbook of the German Studies Association of Ireland* 12 (2017): 21–33.

Prutti, Brigitte. "Zwischen Ansteckung und Auslöschung: Zur Seuchenerzählung bei Stifter—*Die Pechbrenner* versus *Granit*." *Oxford German Studies* 37, no. 1 (2008): 49–73.

Schmidt, Hugo. "Eishöhle und Steinhäuschen: Zur Weihnachtssymbolik in Stifters 'Bergkristall.'" *Monatshefte* 56, no. 7 (1964): 321–35.

Smith, Duncan. "The Subjunctive of Anxiety in Adalbert Stifter's *Kalkstein*." *Jahrbuch für Internationale Germanistik* 42, no. 2 (2010): 93–104.

Stopp, Frederick. "Die Symbolik in Stifters 'Bunten Steinen.'" *Deutsche Vierteljahresschrift für Literaturwissenschaft und Geistesgeschichte* 28 (1954): 165–93.

Swales, Martin. "Homeliness and Otherness: Reflections on Stifter's *Bergkristall*." In *The German Bestseller in the Late Nineteenth Century*, edited by Charlotte Woodford and Benedict Schofield, 115–26. Rochester, NY: Camden House, 2012.

Wagner, Lori. "Schick, Schichten, Geschichte: Geological Theory in Stifter's *Bunte Steine*." *Jahrbuch des Adalbert Stifter-Instituts des Landes Oberösterreich* 2 (1995): 17–41.

Weitzman, Erica. "Despite Language: Adalbert Stifter's Revenge Fantasies." *Monatshefte* 111, no. 3 (2019): 362–79.


### Der Nachsommer

Belgum, Kirsten L. "High Historicism and Narrative Restoration: The Seamless Interior of Adalbert Stifter's *Nachsommer*." *The Germanic Review: Literature, Culture, Theory* 67, no. 1 (1992): 15–25.

Berman, Russell A. "The Authority of Address: Adalbert Stifter." In *The Rise of the German Novel: Crisis and Charisma*, 105–33. Cambridge, MA: Harvard University Press, 1986.

Borchmeyer, Dieter. "Stifters *Nachsommer*: Eine restaurative Utopie?" *Poetica* 12 (1980): 59–82.

Bulang, Tobias. "Die Rettung der Geschichte in Adalbert Stifters *Nachsommer*." *Poetica* 32 (2000): 373–405.

Finkelde, Dominik. "Tautologien der Ordnung: Zu einer Poetologie des Sammelns bei Adalbert Stifter." *The German Quarterly* 80, no. 1 (2007): 1–19.

Frederick, Samuel. "Overcoming Narration: Adalbert Stifter's *Indian Summer* as a Post-Narrative Novel." In *Narratives Unsettled: Digression in Robert Walser, Thomas Bernhard, and Adalbert Stifter*, 129–70. Evanston, IL: Northwestern University Pres, 2012.

Grill, Oliver. "Weather—Or Not? Meteorology and the Art of Prediction in Humboldt's *Kosmos* and Stifter's *Der Nachsommer*." *REAL: The Yearbook of Research in English and American Literature* 33 (2017): 101–19.

Glaser, Horst Albert. *Die Restauration des Schönen: Stifters "Nachsommer."* Stuttgart: J. B. Metzler, 1965.

Goodbody, Axel. "Gardening as an Ecological and Educational Project: Stifter's Anticipation of Anthropocene Thinking and Aesthetics in *Der Nachsommer*." *Austrian Studies* 30 (2022): 15–30.

Ireton, Sean. "Geology, Mountaineering, and Self-Formation in Adalbert Stifter's *Der Nachsommer*." In *Heights of Reflection: Mountains in the German Imagination from the Middle Ages to the Twenty-First Century*, edited by Sean Ireton and Caroline Schaumann, 193–209. Rochester, NY: Camden House, 2012.

McIsaac, Peter. "The Museal Path to *Bildung*: Collecting, Gender and Exchange in Stifter's *Der Nachsommer*." *German Life and Letters* 57, no. 3 (2004): 268–89.

Neuburger, Karin. "Sprache und Dingwelt: Politischer Realismus in Adalbert Stifters *Ein Gang durch die Katakomben* und *Der Nachsommer*." *Colloquia Germanica: Internationale Zeitschrift für Germanistik* 53, no. 4 (2021): 349–72.

Rosenbaum, Lars. "Allgegenwärtig und nirgends zu sehen? Die Bedeutung von Abfällen in Adalbert Stifters *Nachsommer*." *Zeitschrift für deutsche Philologie* 133 (2014): 197–218.

Schär, Kathrin. *Erdgeschichte(n) und Entwicklungsromane: Geologisches Wissen und Selbstkonstitution in der Poetlogie der frühen Moderne: Goethes "Wanderjahre" und Stifters "Nachsommer."* Bielefeld: transcript, 2021.

Schweiger, Franziska. "Networking Matters: Literary Representations of Reality in Stifter's *Nachsommer*." *Colloquia Germanica: Internationale Zeitschrift für Germanistik* 47, no. 3 (2014): 201–16.

Sjögren, Christine Oertel. *The Marble Statue as Idea: Collected Essays on Adalbert Stifter's "Der Nachsommer."* Chapel Hill: University of North Carolina Press, 1972.

Weitzman, Erica. "Against Nature: Adalbert Stifter." In *At the Limit of the Obscene: German Realism and the Disgrace of Matter*, 25–48. Evanston, IL: Northwestern University Press, 2021.

## Other Works

Bantli, Jann Duri, and Ansgar Mohnkern. "Ungeheuer: Zur Unlesbarkeit von Stifters *Aus dem bairischen Walde* heute." *Monatshefte* 114, no. 2 (2022): 200–19.

Bowen-Wefuan, Bethany. "Intersecting at the Real: Painting, Writing, and Human Community in Adalbert Stifter's *Nachkommenschaften* (1864)." *New German Review: A Journal of Germanic Studies* 27 (2016): 21–36.

Byrd, Vance. "The Politics of Commemoration in *Wien und die Wiener* (1841–44)." *Journal of Austrian Studies* 47, no. 1 (2014): 1–20.

Frederick, Samuel. "Moss (Stifter)." In *The Redemption of Things: Collecting and Dispersal in German Realism and Modernism*, 69–100. Ithaca, NY and London: Cornell University Press, 2021.

Garrard, Malcolm. "Medieval Take and Medieval Telling: History, *Das Nibelungenlied* and Stifter's *Witiko*." *German Life and Letters* 46, no. 3 (1993): 236–53.

Giuriato, Davide. "Kinder retten: Biopolitik in Stifter's Erzählung *Der Waldgänger*." *Internationales Archiv für Sozialgeschichte der deutschen Literatur* 40, no. 2 (2015): 441–58.

Grossmann Stone, Barbara S. *Adalbert Stifter and the Idyll: A Study of "Witiko."* New York: Peter Lang, 1989.

Sjögren, Christine Oertel. "The Frame of *Der Waldbrunnen* Reconsidered: A Note on Adalbert Stifter's Aesthetics." *Modern Austrian Literature* 19, no. 1 (1986): 9–25.

Strowick, Elisabeth. "'Nachkommenschaften': Stifter's Series." In *Truth in Serial Form: Serial Formats and the Form of the Series, 1850–1930*, edited by Malika Maskarinec, 83–113. Berlin: De Gruyter, 2023.

Ragg-Kirkby, Helena. *Adalbert Stifter's Late Prose: The Mania for Moderation*. Rochester, NY: Camden House, 2000.

# Comprehensive Bibliographies

Eisenmeier, Eduard. *Adalbert-Stifter Bibliographie*. Linz: Oberösterreichischer Landesverlag, 1964. (Schriftenreihe des Adalbert-Stifter-Instituts des Landes Oberösterreich, vol. 21); First continuation 1971 (Schriftenreihe des Adalbert-Stifter-Instituts des Landes Oberösterreich, vol. 26); Second continuation 1978 (Schriftenreihe des Adalbert-Stifter-Instituts des Landes Oberösterreich, vol. 31).

———. *Adalbert Stifter-Bibliographie*. Linz: Adalbert-Stifter-Instituts des Landes Oberösterreich, 1983. Third continuation. (Schriftenreihe des Adalbert-Stifter-Instituts des Landes Oberösterreich, vol. 34)

# Contributors

MATTHEW H. BIRKHOLD is Associate Professor of Germanic Languages and Literatures at The Ohio State University. He is the author, most recently, of *Chasing Icebergs* (Pegasus/Simon and Schuster, 2023). His research focuses on eighteenth- and nineteenth-century German literature, environmental humanities, and the intersections of law and culture.

VANCE BYRD is a Presidential Associate Professor of Germanic Languages and Literatures at the University of Pennsylvania, where he holds a secondary appointment in History of Art. His teaching and research focus on literature in German, visual culture, and print culture since the nineteenth century. His research has been supported by the Andrew W. Mellon Foundation, the National Humanities Center, and the Getty Research Institute.

SEAN FRANZEL is Professor of German at the University of Missouri. He has published widely on media discourses in the eighteenth and nineteenth centuries. He is the author of *Writing Time: Studies in Serial Literature, 1780-1850* (Cornell University Press, 2023) and *Connected by the Ear: The Media, Pedagogy, and Politics of the Romantic Lecture* (Northwestern University Press, 2013), the co-editor and co-translator of a 2018 volume of essays by the historian Reinhart Koselleck, and the co-editor, with Ilinca Iurascu and Petra McGillen, of *Taking Stock: Media Inventories in the German Nineteenth Century* (De Gruyter, 2024).

SAMUEL FREDERICK is Professor of German at the Pennsylvania State University and the author of three books: *The Last Laugh* (German Cinema Classics, Camden House, 2023); *The Redemption of Things: Collecting and Dispersal in German Realism and Modernism* (Cornell University Press, 2021); and *Narratives Unsettled: Digression in Robert Walser, Thomas Bernhard, and Adalbert Stifter* (Northwestern University Press, 2012). He has also co-edited the collections *Information: Keywords* (Columbia University Press, 2021) and *Robert Walser: A Companion* (Northwestern University Press, 2018). With Graham Foust he has translated four volumes of poetry by Ernst Meister (Wave Books).

338 ◆ Contributors

Jason Groves is Associate Professor of German Studies at the University of Washington. He is the author of *The Geological Unconscious: German Literature and the Mineral Imaginary* (Fordham University Press, 2020) and translator of Sonja Neef's *The Babylonian Planet: Culture and Encounter under Globalization* (Bloomsbury, 2021). His current book project looks at Holocaust remembrance in the Anthropocene.

Tove Holmes is Associate Professor of German Studies at McGill University. Her research areas include German literature and thought from the eighteenth century to the present, visual studies, history of science, literary theory, and environmental humanities. Her book, *Performing Images: Goethe, Stifter, Storm, and the Visual Potential of Literature* is appearing with McGill-Queen's University Press. Her current book project, which is funded by grants from the Fonds de Recherche du Québec and the Social Sciences and Humanities Research Council, examines the visual aesthetics of science communication in Alexander von Humboldt's travelogues.

Sean Ireton is Associate Professor of German at the University of Missouri. He is the author of *An Ontological Study of Death: From Hegel to Heidegger* (Duquesne University Press, 2007) and coeditor of *Heights of Reflection: Mountains in the German Imagination from the Middle Ages to the Twenty-First Century* (Camden House, 2012) as well as *Mountains and the German Mind: Translations from Gessner to Messner, 1541–2009* (Camden House, 2020). He has recently completed a book manuscript titled *German Literary and Philosophical Ecologies: Idealism, Realism, Fascism, Bioregionalism.*

Alexander Robert Phillips is Assistant Professor of English at Ashoka University in India. He is the author of *Ecology and German Realism: Poetics, Politics, and the Conquest of Nature* (forthcoming with Camden House), and his scholarship has appeared in venues such as *Interdisciplinary Studies in Literature and Environment, The German Quarterly*, and a variety of edited volumes. He has published on literature and ecology, nineteenth-century German mass media, and literary discourses on eating and consumption.

Jessica C. Resvick is Assistant Professor of German at Oberlin College. After receiving her Ph.D. in Germanic Studies from the University of Chicago, she was an Andrew W. Mellon Postdoctoral Fellow at Dartmouth College and Assistant Professor at Oklahoma State University. Her research centers on nineteenth- and twentieth-century literature, media, and material culture. Her publications on Stifter have appeared in

*PMLA* and the edited volume *Market Strategies and German Literature in the Long Nineteenth Century* (De Gruyter, 2020).

LARS ROSENBAUM studied German and history at the University of Bielefeld. He completed his doctorate with a dissertation titled *Die Verschmutzung der Literatur* (The Pollution of Literature, transcript, 2019), in which he analyzed the rise of 'dirty semantics' in cultural discourses of the 'long nineteenth century.' His research specialization includes the social history of literature and historical semantics, particularly as manifested in nineteenth-century Germanophone literature.

ZACHARY SNG is Professor of Comparative Literature and German Studies at Brown University, where he also currently serves as Senior Associate Dean of the Faculty. He is the author of two books: *The Rhetoric of Error from Locke to Kleist* (Stanford University Press, 2010) and *Middling Romanticism: Reading in the Gaps from Kant to Ashbery* (Fordham University Press, 2020). He is currently working on a project about 'bare'-ness and the poetics of subtraction.

ERICA WEITZMAN is Associate Professor in the Department of German and Affiliate Professor of Comparative Literary Studies at Northwestern University. She is the author of the monograph *Irony's Antics: Walser, Kafka, Roth, and the German Comic Tradition* (Northwestern University Press, 2015), the co-editor of the collected volume *Suspensionen: Über das Untote* (*Suspensions: On the Undead*, Fink, 2015), and has published numerous articles on topics in German and comparative literature, philosophy, and critical theory. Her most recent book, *At the Limit of the Obscene: German Realism and the Disgrace of Matter*, appeared with Northwestern University Press in 2021.

# Index

Adami, Heinrich, 88, 99; works by:
  *Alt- und Neu-Wien*, 67
Adorno, Theodor, 56–57, 266
Alexis, Willibald, 88; works by: *Wiener
  Bilder*, 67
Alps, 6, 19, 27, 28, 32, 47, 232, 237,
  249, 250–51, 253–54, 256, 259,
  269, 272, 282, 316
Anthropocene, 239, 246
antisemitism, 240–41
Aprent, Johannes, 80–81, 182
Arendt, Hannah, 138n, 250
assimilation (Jewish), 227, 238, 240–
  42, 246, 249
Atlas Mountains, 232
Augustine, works by: *Confessions*, 82
Austrian Empire, 4, 5, 127, 182, 228,
  254, 277–78

Bakhtin, Mikhail, 40, 57
Balzac, Honoré de, 60
Baumgartner, Andreas von, 22, 76,
  277; works by: *Die Naturlehre nach
  ihrem gegenständigen Zustande
  mit Rücksicht auf mathematische
  Begründing*, 277
Bavarian and/or Bohemian Forest,
  4–7, 33, 250, 294, 295, 296–97,
  302, 305–10, 317, 322
Beethoven, Ludwig van, 143–44;
  works by: *Pastoral Symphony*, 143
Benda, Georg (Jiří), 142
Benjamin, Walter, 175, 181
Berg, Peter, 298–300, 302–3, 305,
  319, 322
Berg, Peter and Raymond Dasmann,
  works by: "Reinhabiting
  California," 298–300, 302, 305,
  322
Biedermeier, 8, 51, 84, 127, 138, 149

*Bildung*, 39, 50, 52, 223, 249
*Bildungsroman*, 5, 29, 37–40, 57,
  146, 247, 250
bioregional aesethetics/poetics, 296,
  319, 321–22
bioregionalism, 294–322
Bohemia, 4, 7, 22, 26, 29, 86, 107,
  294, 295, 297, 305, 307, 312, 316
Böhm, Wilhelm, 88
Böhme, Gernot, works by:
  *Atmosphäre: Essays zur neuen
  Ästhetik*, 275
Braunthal, Braun von, 88
Brown, Bill, 17
*Buchfassungen* (also book versions),
  3n, 9, 11, 59, 68, 111, 148, 162,
  165, 170–72, 174, 311, 316; see
  also *Studienfassung*

Chráněná Krajinná Oblast Šumava
  (Šumava Protected Landscape
  Area), 310

Dachstein (glacier, massif, mountain),
  251, 257, 259, 265
Danube River, 9, 279, 294, 302, 306,
  309
Dasmann, Raymond, 298–303, 305,
  319,
Daumier, Honoré, 60
deforestation, 4, 301, 308, 314,
  316–17
Dickens, Charles, works by: *Oliver
  Twist*, 92
*Ding(e)* (also thing[s]), 2, 14–17,
  18–20, 45–46, 113, 122, 123,
  124–28, 132, 133, 138, 147, 153,
  155–57, 160, 195, 198, 211, 219,
  227, 273–74, 277, 279, 280–81,
  285–86, 289, 311, 312, 315–16

342 ◆ INDEX

Dodge, Jim, works by: "Living by Life: Some Bioregional Theory and Practice, 302–3, 306,
Dreisesselberg, (Three-Chair Mountain), 7

Eichendorff, Joseph von, works by: "Wünschelrute," 16
erosion, 72, 233, 234, 235, 245

Falta, Joseph, works by: *Topographische Karte der in Böhmen budweiser Kreises liegenden Sr. Durchlaucht dem Fürsten zu Schwarzenberg Herzog zu Krummau gehörigen Herrschaft Krummau*, 311–13
Flaubert, Gustave, works by: "Un cœur simple," 173, 177; *Madame Bovary*, 42
Fontane, Theodor, 66
Forst-Lehranstalt Mariabrunn, 8
Franz II (Austrian emperor), 6
Franziszeische Landesaufnahme survey, 254, 256, 261, 266, 272
Friedberg (Frymburk), 7, 294
Friedrich, Caspar David, works by: *Der Wanderer über dem Nebelmeer*, 278–79
Friepes, Franz (maternal grandfather), 5
Friepes, Magdalena (mother), 1

*Gartenlaube, Die*, 59–60, 66, 84
*Gartenlaube für Österreich, Die*, 60, 81
Gauss, Carl Friedrich, 167–68
*Gegenwart, Die*, 166, 260
Glassbrenner, Adolph, 88; works by: *Bilder und Träume aus Wien*, 67
Goebbels, Heiner, works by: *Stifters Dinge*, 273
Goethe, Johann Wolfgang, 6, 10, 11, 17n, 21, 24n, 52, 57, 58; works by: "Auf dem See," 148–49; "Granit I," 166n; *Die Leiden des jungen Werther* 10; *Ur-Faust*, 59; *Wilhelm Meisters Lehrjahre*, 40, 146
Gräffner, Franz, works by: *Kleine Wiener Memoiren*, 67

Grass, Günter, works by: *Die Blechtrommel*: 2–3
Greipl, Franziska, 7–8, 294
Groos, Karl, works by: *Die Spiele der Menschen, Die Spiele der Tiere*, 194–99

Habsburg (Empire, monarchy, etc.), 6, 88, 89, 96, 102, 105, 254, 272
Hall, Placidus, 5
Haller, Albrecht von, works by: "Die Alpen," 253, 256
Hallstatt, 258
Hallstätter Glacier (also Karls-Eisfeld), 257, 258, 259
Hebbel, Friedrich, 21, 41–42, 64, 137, 167, 183
Heckenast, Gustav, 38, 92, 165, 170
Hegel, Georg Friedrich Wilhelm, 43
Hegesippus, 177
Heidegger, Martin, 17, 176
Henle, Jacob, 279
Herder, Johann Gottfried, 21
Hobbes, Thomas, works by: *Leviathan*, 102
Hoffmann, E.T.A., 10
Humboldt, Alexander von, 49–50, 167–68, 285, 288, 290

*Jahrbuch des Oesterreichischen Alpenvereins*, 256
Jean Paul (Friedrich Richter), 10, 62, 144, 148
Jewish Question, 238–40, 243, 248–49
*Journalfassungen* (also journal versions) 3n, 9, 11, 25, 59, 80, 231, 240, 241, 283, 285, 302, 311, 316
Joseph II (Austrian emperor), 6
Josephinische Landesaufnahme survey, 254, 255, 261, 266, 272

Kafka, Franz, 187
Kant, Immanuel, 6, 21, 280, 282–83, 286; works by: *Kritik der Urteilskraft*, 187–88
Kepler, Johannes, 6

Kirchschlag, 278–79, 294
Koch, Matthias
Kreil, Karl, 22
Kremsmünster (monastery and
    secondary school), 4–6, 277
Kuh, Emil, 257, 271
*Künstlerroman*, 144

Latour, Bruno, 16
Lessing, Gotthold Ephraim, works by:
    *Laokoon*, 41, 43
Linz, 8, 12–13, 23, 29, 278–79, 294,
    296, 297, 306
Lukács, Georg, works by: "Erzählen
    oder Beschreiben?" 42–43, 47,
    64, 121; *Die Theorie des Romans*,
    39–40, 56–57

Mahlknecht, Carl, 68, 92
Mann, Thomas, works by: *Die
    Entstehung des Doktor Faustus:
    Roman eines Romans*, 2, 139; *Der
    Zauberberg*, 13
March revolts (also 1848 revolutions/
    uprisings, *Märzrevolution*), 12, 23,
    150, 182
Matz, Wolfgang, 9–10, 24, 27, 123–
    25, 127
melodrama, 137–61
Menzel, Adolph, 66, 88
meteorology, 76, 276–77, 288
Metternich, Prince Klemens von, 8
Metternich, Richard von, 182
Mohaupt, Amalia/Amalie (wife), 8
Mohaupt, Juliane (niece/foster child),
    8–9
Moldau/Vltava River, 302, 306, 309,
    311, 314
*Morgenblatt für gebildete Stände*,
    59–60
Mozart, Wolfgang Amadeus, 143
Mühlkreis (also Mühlviertel), 294,
    295, 307, 310
Musil, Robert, works by: *Der Mann
    ohne Eigenschaften*, 277

Národní Park Šumava (Šumava
    National Park), 309–10

narrative reinhabitation, 296, 310,
    391
Nationalpark Bayerischer Wald
    (Bavarian Forest National Park),
    305, 309, 310

Oberplan (also Horní Planá), 4–5, 7,
    13, 294, 306, 308, 310–11, 313–
    16, 318–19
*Ordnung* (also order, *ordo*), 1, 2,
    6, 12, 14, 23–25, 27–28, 32,
    33, 112–13, 115, 123–26, 133;
    200–201, 203–11, 214, 216–17,
    219–20, 223–24, 234, 244, 274,
    287, 288, 291, 316, 320
Orpheus and Eurydice, 169–70, 178
*Österreichische Blätter für Literatur
    und Kunst*, 271
Österreichischer Alpenverein, 257
*Österreichischer Novellenalmanach für
    1843*, 229
Ottoman Empire, 97

pedagogy, 182–84, 186, 190–94, 197,
    199
Pezzl, Johann, 88
Poe, Edgar Allan, works by: "The Man
    of the Crowd," 100–101
Pietznigg, Franz, 88
Plöckensteinsee (Lake Plöckenstein), 7
Prague, 8
Pranghofer, Albert (godfather), 4

race, 231–32, 238, 241, 248
realism, 10, 16–17, 30, 39, 68, 140,
    158–59, 161, 174, 202, 224, 228,
    229, 235, 276
realist (aesthetic[s], poetics, practice,
    etc.), 51, 86, 91, 102, 109, 122,
    133, 161, 224, 229, 235, 248,
    251, 270, 277, 280, 289, 290,
    293, 311
Reiberstorffer, Friedrich, works by:
    "Der Zettelausträger," 100
reinhabitation, 298–302, 319 (see also
    narrative reinhabitation)
*Rheinisches Tagebuch auf das Jahr
    1846*, 311

344 ◆ INDEX

Richter, Eduard, works by:
"Beobachtungen an den Gletschern der Ostalpen," 256
romanticism, 10, 11, 16, 159
Rousseau, Jean-Jaques, works by:
*Pygmalion*, 141

*sanft, Sanftheit* (also gentle, gentleness), 2, 4, 14, 17–20, 24, 25, 28, 31, 166, 178
*sanftmütig, Sanftmut* (also placid, placidity), 2, 18, 31, 163, 179
*sanfte Gesetz, das* (also the gentle law) 5, 17, 18, 20, 22–26, 31, 32, 139–40; 168, 173, 183–84, 187–88, 235, 241, 246, 289–91
Schaubach, Adolph, works by: *Die deutschen Alpen: Ein Handbuch für Reisende*, 259
Schiller, Friedrich, 6, 21; works by: *Die Räuber* 10
Schröckinger-Neudenberg, Julius von, works by: *Reisegefährte durch Ober-Oesterreichs Gebirgsland*, 259
Schubert, Franz, 143
Schwarzenberg (House of), 309, 313, 318
Schwarzenberg floating canal, 302
Sebald, W.G., 173
Simony, Friedrich, 230, 251, 257–62, 267, 269, 271, 272; works by: "Drei Dezembertage auf dem Dachsteingebirge," 257–59; "Zwei Septembernächte auf der Hohen Dachsteinspitze," 257
smog, 279–80
Snyder, Gary, 298, 300–303, 306, 319, 321; works by: "Coming into the Watershed," 302; *The Practice of the Wild*, 303; "Reinhabitation," 301–2
Stelzhamer, Franz, 65–67
Stifter, Adalbert, works of fiction:
*Abdias*, 32, 227–49, 306; *Der alte Hofmeister*, 37, 44–45; *Das alte Siegel*, 250, 259; *Aus dem bairischen Walde*, 13, 110, 174, 282, 297, 306; *Bergkristall*, 23, 32, 166–67, 174, 230, 250–52,

257–72; *Bergmilch*, 23; *Der beschriebene Tännling*, 4, 296–97, 302, 306, 308, 310–22; *Brigitta*, 27, 33; 18, 27, 28, 242, 275; *Bunte Steine*, 3n, 9, 10, 13–15, 20–24, 28–29, 31–32, 38, 61–62, 84, 138, 161, 166–67, 173–74, 181–99, 227, 229, 233, 235, 243, 245, 247, 249, 260, 270, 274, 287, 289–91, 293, 311; *Der Condor*, 9; 33, 67, 74, 274, 276, 282–86; *Feldblumen*, 10, 30, 137–61; *Der fromme Spruch*, 30, 110–12, 119–20, 124–25, 128, 131–32; *Granit*, 3, 14, 23, 32, 182, 191–95, 270, 306, 308, 311, 312; *Der Hagestolz*, 9, 17, 233; *Das Haidedorf*, 297, 306, 311; "Der heilige Abend," 166, 260, 263, 265, 271; *Der Hochwald*, 4;12, 26, 306, 307, 308; *Julius*, 9; *Kalkstein*, 23, 32, 33, 182, 188–89, 195, 242, 278, 291; *Kazensilber*, 9, 23, 33, 182, 190–92, 242, 245, 247, 291, 306, 308; *Der Kuß von Sentze*, 30, 110–12, 121, 124, 131, 306; *Die Mappe meines Urgroßvaters*, 1, 4, 11, 18, 30–31, 78, 80–81, 111, 162–80, 280–82, 306, 308–9; *Nachkommenschaften*, 75, 80, 110, 144; *Der Nachsommer*, 5, 6, 12, 13, 14, 18, 19; 22, 23–24n, 25, 27, 28, 29, 31, 32, 37–39, 41, 43–54, 57, 100, 118, 120, 123, 124, 137, 144, 200–224, 229, 230, 243, 247–49, 250, 257, 259, 267–72, 287–89; *Die Narrenburg*, 163, 231; "Die Pechbrenner," 3, 306, 311; *Studien*, 3, 9, 10, 14, 19, 29, 31, 61–62, 78, 162, 229, 297, 311; *Turmalin*, 23, 198–99, 270, 291–92; *Der Waldbrunnen*, 9, 110, 306; *Der Waldgänger*, 9, 294–96, 306, 308; *Witiko*, 12, 13, 19, 30, 111–18, 121–22, 124–28, 131, 306, 307, 314; *Zwei Schwestern*, 19, 27, 28; *Zwei Witwen*, 110

Stifter, Adalbert, other works
(anthologies, essays, edited
volumes): *Lesebuch zur Förderung
humaner Bildung in Realschulen
und in anderen zu weiterer Bildung
vorbereitenden Mittelschulen*, 62,
182; "Die Sonnenfinsternis am 8.
Juli, 1842," 33, 285–87; *Vermischte
Schriften*, 29, 79–84; esp. "Der
Sylvesterabend," 81–84; *Wien und
die Wiener*, 7, 29, 30, 60–61, 63–65,
68–79, 86–109 (individual essays:
"Aussicht und Betrachtungen von
der Spitze des Stephansthurmes,"
63, 69–74, 79, 83, 102–3, 105;
"Die Charwoche in Wien," 105,
107–9; "Ein Gang durch die
Katakomben," 105–7, 227, 244–45,
247; "Leben und Haushalt dreier
Wienerstudenten," 96–97; "Wiener
Salonscenen," 86, 101;"Wiener
Wetter," 74–79, 286); "Winterbriefe
aus Kirchschlag," 278–80, 287
Stifter, Adalbert, paintings: *Ansicht
von Oberplan*, 314–15, *Die
Bewegung I/II*, 54–56; *Blick auf
Wiener Vorstadthäuser* 54–55;
*Westungarische Landschaft*, 52–54;
*Wolkenstudie*, 53
Stifter, Anton (brother), 10
Stifter, Augustin (parental
grandfather), 5
Stifter, Johann (father), 1, 5, 7
Stifter, Josefine (niece/foster child), 9
Stifter, Ursula, (paternal grandmother),
5
*Studienfassung*, 162, 165, 170–72,
174, 240, 285–87
sublime (concept), 22, 279–80, 282–
83, 285–87

Thompson, Michael, works by:
*Rubbish Theory*: 200–201, 204–5,
213, 218, 219, 221
Tieck, Ludwig, 10
time (concept), 40, 41, 48, 52, 56,
57, 63, 64, 65, 78, 79, 82–85,
113, 122, 126, 128, 132

Trollope, Francis (Milton), 88,
99; works by: *Vienna and the
Austrians*, 67

Upper Austria, 6, 12, 23, 31, 182,
206, 250, 259, 294, 295, 307,
308, 310, 316

Vienna, 1,7, 8, 12, 23, 29, 31, 60, 65,
67, 69, 72, 77, 78, 86–109, 144,
146, 182, 198, 200, 249, 277,
282, 292, 294, 297, 302, 306
Virchow, Rudolf, 279

Wagner, Moritz, 230
Wagner, Sylvester, works by: "Female
Ragpicker," 95–95, 99–100, "Der
Greißler," 103, "Die Kohlbauern,"
103
Walcher, Joseph, 253
waste (concept), 200–208, 210–19,
221–24
watershed (also *Wasserscheide*), 294–
96, 298–304, 306–09, 316
weather, 23, 33, 45, 74–79, 85, 243,
259, 276–77, 281, 287–89, 311
*Wien und die Wiener*, texts by
other contributors: "Die
Lumpensammlerin" (Female
Ragpicker), 95–95, 99–100; "Der
Greißler," 103; "Die Kohlbauern,"
103; "Der Ladendiener des
Modehändlers," 97–98;"Der
Musik-Enthusiast," 98–99;
"Der Pfeifentod," 97; "Das
Stubenmädchen," 96; "Wiener
Salonleben," 78, 83; "Der
Zettelausträger," 100
*Wiener Bote*, 182
*Wiener Zeitschrift für Kunst, Literatur,
Theater und Mode*, 9, 59–60, 162,
257, 285
Wittinghausen (Castle), 7
Wolf, Caspar, 253–54

*Zeitschrift des Deutschen und
Österreichischen Alpenvereins*, 256
*Zeitung für die elegante Welt*, 59

Printed in the United States
by Baker & Taylor Publisher Services